The New Development Economics

The New Development Economics

After the Washington Consensus

Edited by
JOMO K.S.
BEN FINE

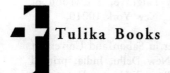

Tulika Books

Zed Books
London and New York

First published in India in 2006 by
Tulika Books
35 A/1 (third floor), Shahpur Jat, New Delhi 110 049, India

First published outside South Asia in 2006 by
Zed Books
7 Cynthia Street, London N1 9JF, UK, and Room 400, 175 Fifth
Avenue, New York, NY 10010, USA. www.zedbooks.demon.co.uk

© Jomo K.S. and Ben Fine, 2006

The rights of Jomo K.S. and Ben Fine to be identified as the editors of
this work has been asserted by them in accordance with the Copyright,
Designs and Patents Act, 1988.

ISBN (Tulika Books edition): 81-85229-96-1

ISBN (Zed Books edition): 1 84277 642 8 hb   1 84277 643 6 pb

A catalogue record for this book is available from the British Library.
US CIP data is available from the Library of Congress.

Distributed in the USA exclusively by Palgrave, a division of
St. Martin's Press, LLC, 175 Fifth Avenue, New York 10010.

Cover designed by Ram Rahman; typeset in Sabon and Univers at
Tulika Print Communication Services, New Delhi, India; printed
and bound at Chaman Enterprises, 1603 Pataudi House, Daryaganj,
New Delhi 110 002.

Contents

Preface

Development economics emerged as a distinct branch of economics after World War II, especially from the 1950s (Bardhan 1993; Hirschman 1981). Its antecedents are to be found in earlier schools of economics, for much of economic thinking over the centuries has been concerned with accelerating economic growth and transformation (Chang 2002). The emergence of development economics as a distinct field was encouraged by widespread recognition of the different economic and other conditions that prevailed in what has come to be referred to as the third world, or the South, or the developing world. Much of East Asia, then South Asia and later Southeast Asia, as well as Africa and the Caribbean, gained independence from colonial powers in the two decades after the end of World War II. The post-war ascendance of the United States of America at the expense of war-torn Europe, especially the United Kingdom, and the beginning of its Cold War with the Soviet-led 'communist bloc' provided the political motivation and intellectual space for the emergence and particular content of what is now termed old, or classical, development economics.

The experience of the Great Depression, the continuing reverberations and apparent relevance of the Keynesian revolution, and the preoccupation of pre-war Central European economists with 'catching up' and 'late industrialization' inspired and encouraged heterodox economic thinking that was distinct from the increasingly dominant mainstream, marginalist or neoclassical economics. It ranged much more widely in every respect than the limits imposed by the dominant debate in the United States between Paul Samuelson's neoclassical synthesis (US neo-Keynesianism) and free market conservatism led by Milton Friedman's 'monetarism'. Most importantly, the rationale for development economics derived from the very different economic conditions believed to prevail in Asia, Africa and Latin America. These included the generally larger significance of agriculture and primary commodity production, and the correspondingly modest role of manufacturing as well as different types of labour markets. Later, the understanding of economic development was extended beyond the conventional focus on generating economic growth (and employment) in different conditions, to include considerations of equity or distribution.

The 1980s saw a dramatic reversal in the fortunes of mainstream development economics, and an equally dramatic shift in its content and approach. With the ascendance of the Washington Consensus, there was growing official support from the Reagan and Thatcher governments for the 'counter-revolution' against development economics (Toye 1993). Often ignoring the earlier rich debates within development economics, the counter-revolution insisted on the universal relevance of its presumed notion of economic rationality, and, hence, of laws of supply and demand based on the optimizing behaviour of individuals. The apparent failure of Keynesianism after the post-war Golden Age, with the emergence of 'stagflation' (higher unemployment and inflation), contributed to greater antipathy towards state intervention generally, including towards a developmental role for government. The earlier sympathy of West European social democracy for developmental aspirations also eroded and changed in the new political conditions created by Blair's 'third way' and its continental parallels. The transitions from Soviet-led state socialism in the 1990s served to strengthen this trend.

Following the oil price hike of 1973–74 and the economic slowdown in the west, rapidly rising interest rates precipitated fiscal and sovereign debt crises in Latin America and elsewhere. Most of these heavily indebted governments had little choice but to seek emergency and other credit facilities from the Bretton Woods institutions (BWIs). This initiated a new phase of conditionality-based lending, with the International Monetary Fund (IMF) focusing on short-term macroeconomic stabilization (that is, deflationary) programmes and the World Bank on medium-term structural adjustment (that is, liberalization). (For example, see World Bank 1981. For critical assessments of the consequences of these programmes, see Cornia, Jolly and Stewart, eds 1987; Mosley, Harrigan and Toye 1991; SAPRIN 2004.) The McNamara–Chenery era of the World Bank – of 'growth with redistribution' (Chenery et al. 1974), 'meeting basic needs' and development finance – was set aside by Anne Krueger's (1974) efforts to roll back the state, ostensibly to eliminate rent-seeking and other governmental failures. Such policy perspectives had their intellectual counterpart in seeking to 'rubbish' a caricatured development economics, not least by appointing ideologue Deepak Lal (1983) as head of research at the World Bank (Kapur, Lewis and Webb 1997a, Kapur, Lewis and Webb, eds 1997b). More importantly, the Reagan and Thatcher administrations led western efforts to undermine the United Nations system by withdrawing from membership of those agencies they failed to 'reform' to their own advantage, while strengthening the role, profile and authority of the Bank, including its research resources and capacity. Meanwhile, recruitment to the BWIs from graduate economics departments in the United States became a matter of course as these departments increasingly treated development economics as 'ersatz', in favour of open macroeconomics, international trade and the esoterica of rational expectations. Soon, especially within the United States of America, other social sciences, led by sociology and political science, began to mimic the new fads in economics – for example, rational choice, sociometrics and other applied statistics.

These academic developments profoundly transformed the nature of development economics, and this volume seeks to identify and critically assess how academic trends since the 1980s have given rise to new approaches in the study of economic development, especially through the mainstream redefinition of development economics itself. The crude and simplistic prognostications of neoliberal market fundamentalism have enjoyed an influential but short shelf-life of a couple of decades or so. Few, however, would now openly attach themselves to the original versions and policies of the Washington Consensus (for example, see Bhagwati 1998; Feldstein 1998). And, on a higher analytical plane, commitment to the virtues of the market has made way for a more nuanced comprehension of how the market does or does not work, and of the complementary role of non-market factors. In its own technical fashion, development economics has restored some multidisciplinarity, although it is limited relative to the interdisciplinary political economy of the pre-Washington Consensus.

It was enough, however, for senior vice president and chief economist Joseph Stiglitz (2001a, 2001b), while still at the World Bank, in 1998, to announce a post-Washington Consensus, ostensibly based on a new development economics (Stiglitz 1986; also see Krugman 1999). At that time, besides opposing the unduly severe deflationary policies of the IMF, he had only sought to supplement John Williamson's (1990) original list of ten neoliberal policies with better financial regulation, competition policy, more attention to technology transfer, environmental sustainability, reduced income and asset inequality, and democratization. After being forced to resign from the Bank by the US Treasury Secretary, Laurence Summers (Wade 2001), Stiglitz's (2002) opposition to the BWIs' Washington Consensus became more explicit and total. In this sense, then, his announcement of a post-Washington Consensus was premature and, as Williamson (1990) has made clear, the Washington Consensus itself has evolved significantly over time (see Wade 1996). Hence, Stiglitz's 1998 version of the post-Washington Consensus is better characterized as a modified or updated version of the Washington Consensus rather than as its abandonment – just as subsequent generations of structural adjustment programmes (SAPs) eventually departed in substance from the early programmes.

In so far as several chapters in this volume criticize the post-Washington Consensus, they are at their strongest in referring to the post-Krueger modifications to the Washington Consensus, especially those associated with the Wolfensohn–Stiglitz leadership of the World Bank. At most, it has seen a modest retreat from Krueger's extremist neoliberal fundamentalism, although even the IMF has been forced to concede that the empirical case for its advocacy of financial liberalization has collapsed (for example, see Kaminsky and Schmukler 2003; Kose, Prasad and Terrones 2003; Prasad *et al.* 2003). While acknowledging that Stiglitz's critique of the BWIs has since gone much farther (also see Peet 2003; Pincus and Winters, eds 2002; Wade 2002), most of the contributors here still doubt that his alternative ('imperfect competition') micro-foundations approach provides an adequate critique of, let alone an alternative approach to, development studies or even development economics. Such an assessment is explored across the range of topics covered. There remain many omissions in the volume: for example, women, gender and the family; civil society (other than social capital); popular governance; environment; decentralization (also see Chang 2003; Fine, Lapavitsas and Pincus, eds 2001). These and other important subjects will, hopefully, soon belong to a more comprehensive critique of new development studies.

References

Bardhan, Pranab (1993), 'Economics of Development and the Development of Economics', *Journal of Economic Perspectives*, 7 (2): 129–42.

Bhagwati, Jagdish (1998), 'The Capital Myth: The Difference between Trade in Widgets and Dollars', *Foreign Affairs*, 77 (3): 7–12.

Chang, Ha-Joon (2002), *Kicking Away the Ladder: Development Strategy in Historical Perspective* (London: Anthem Press).

——, ed., (2003), *Rethinking Development Economics* (London: Anthem Press).

Chenery, Hollis, Montek Ahluwalia, Clive Bell, John Duloy and Richard Jolly (1974), *Redistribution with Growth* (London: Oxford University Press).

Cornia, G.A., Richard Jolly and Frances Stewart, eds (1987), *Adjustment with a Human Face: Protecting the Vulnerable and Promoting Growth* (Oxford: Clarendon Press).

Feldstein, Martin (1998), 'Refocussing the IMF', *Foreign Affairs*, 77 (2).

Fine, Ben, Costas Lapavitsas and Jonathan Pincus, eds (2001), *Development Policy in the Twenty-first Century: Beyond the Post-Washington Consensus* (London: Routledge).

Hirschman, Albert (1981), 'The Rise and Decline of Development Economics', in Albert Hirschman, *Essays in Trespassing* (Cambridge: Cambridge University Press).

Kaminsky, Graciela and Sergio Schmukler (2003), 'Short-Run Pain, Long-Run Gain: The Effects of Financial Liberalization', IMF Working Paper 03/34, International Monetary Fund, Washington DC.

Kapur, Devesh, John Lewis and Richard Webb (1997a), *The World Bank: Its First Half-Century, Volume I: History* (Washington DC: Brookings Institution).

——, eds (1997b), *The World Bank: Its First Half-Century, Volume II: Perspectives* (Washington DC: Brookings Institution).

Kose, M. Ayhan, Eswar S. Prasad and Marco E. Terrones (2003), 'Volatility and Co-movement in a Globalized World Economy: An Empirical Exploration', IMF Working Paper 246, International Monetary Fund, Washington DC, December.

Krueger, Anne (1974), 'The Political Economy of a Rent-seeking Society', *American Economic Review*, 64 (4): 291–303.

Krugman, Paul (1999), 'The Fall and Rise of Development Economics', http://web.mit.edu/krugman/www/dishpan.html.

Lal, Deepak (1983), *The Poverty of 'Development Economics'* (London: Institute of Economic Affairs).

Mosley, Paul, Jane Harrigan and John Toye (1991), *Aid and Power: The World Bank and Policy-based Lending* (London: Routledge).

Peet, Richard (2003), *Unholy Trinity: The IMF, World Bank and WTO* (London: Zed Books).

Pincus, Jonathan and Jeffrey Winters, eds (2002), *Reinventing the World Bank* (Ithaca: Cornell University Press).

Prasad, Eswar, Kenneth Rogoff, Shang-Jin Wei and M. Ayhan Kose (2003), 'The Effects of Financial Globalization on Developing Countries: Some Empirical Evidence', International Monetary Fund, www.imf.org/research.

SAPRIN (2004), 'Structural Adjustment: The Saprin Report', *The Policy Roots of Economic Crisis, Poverty and Inequality* (London: Zed Books).

Stiglitz, Joseph (1986), 'The New Development Economics', *World Development* 14 (2): 257–65.

—— (2001a), 'More Instruments and Broader Goals: Moving towards the Post-Washington Consensus' (Wider Annual Lecture, Helsinki, 7 January 1998), in Ha-Joon Chang, ed., *Joseph Stiglitz and the World Bank: The Rebel Within* (London: Anthem Press).

—— (2001b), 'Towards a New Paradigm for Development: Strategies, Policies and Processes' (Prebisch Lecture, Geneva, UNCTAD, October 1998), in Ha-Joon Chang, ed., *Joseph Stiglitz and the World Bank: The Rebel Within* (London: Anthem Press).

—— (2001c), 'An Agenda for the New Development Economics', paper at UNRISD meeting on 'The Need to Rethink Development Economics', Cape Town, September, http://www.unrisd.org/engindex/research/rethink.htm.

—— (2002), *Globalization and its Discontents* (New York: Norton).

Toye, John (1993), *Dilemmas of Development*, second edition (Oxford: Blackwell); first edition, 1986.

Wade, Robert (1996), 'Japan, the World Bank, and the Art of Paradigm Maintenance: The East Asian Miracle in Political Perspective', *New Left Review*, 217: 3–37.

—— (2001), 'Showdown at the World Bank', *New Left Review*, 7: 124–37.

—— (2002), 'US Hegemony and the World Bank: The Fight over People and Ideas', *Review of International Political Economy*, 9 (2), Summer.

Williamson, John (1990), 'What Washington Means by Policy Reform', in John Williamson, ed., *Latin American Adjustment: How Much Has Happened?* (Washington DC: Institute for International Economics).

—— (2000), 'What Should the World Bank Think about the Washington Consensus', *The World Bank Research Observer*, 15 (2): 251–64.

World Bank (1981), *Accelerated Development in Sub-Saharan Africa: An Agenda for Action* (Washington DC: World Bank).

Acknowledgements

Each of the chapters in this book draws upon existing work and continuing research programmes. While all the pieces are newly written, there is overlap with earlier contributions to a greater or lesser extent and, where appropriate, these are referenced in the text. We are grateful to SEPHIS for the opportunity to bring together these individual contributions in a single volume.

Introduction

The Economics of Development and

the Development of Economics

Ben Fine

Mainstream economics as we know it today was established in broad brush as long ago as the marginalist revolution of the 1870s. It has displayed itself to be a truly remarkable, or should that be unremarkable, academic discipline. Certainly, by comparison with other subjects, its record of achievement is underwhelming. While the physical sciences have explored the nature of the universe from the Big Bang to the tiniest elements, the history of life from dinosaurs and before to DNA, other social sciences have revealed much about the human psyche, the nature of social structures, processes and agencies, and their history.

How does economics compare? Does it have an equivalent to a landing on the moon, nuclear science, penicillin, the welfare state or commitment to the values of democracy and human rights? Even as we are able to search for water and signs of life on Mars, we seem unable to design our economies in such a way that water is readily available to all here on earth. Instead of resolving such practical matters of life and death, at the heart of twentieth-century mainstream economics, in method as well as in achievement, stands general equilibrium theory: under what conditions does a perfectly competitive economy guarantee an equilibrium that is efficient in some limited sense? Even one of the leading practitioners of general equilibrium, Frank Hahn, was forced to conclude as follows in looking back over one hundred years of the United Kingdom's Royal Economic Society, and forward to the next one hundred years:

> My point has not been that twentieth-century theory sheds no light, nor indeed that its methods will not continue to provide some illumination. But it is my prediction that the latter will increasingly be found to be too faint in the search for answers to questions which have quite naturally arisen from twentieth-century theoretical developments. (Hahn 1991: 50)

Put more bluntly, Hahn is simply saying that economic theory has posed questions that it has not been able to resolve – hardly surprising, given its preoccupation with the weakest conditions that guarantee the existence of general equilibrium. And, having offered some solution to this purely *theoretical* problem, it is equally unsurprising that economics should have difficulty in dealing with *empirical* problems, the ones occupying those worlds that depart from the ideal-ized assumptions of models, and inhabit economies as we live and experience them. While the world undoubtedly moves in mysterious ways, the connection between the esoteric theory of economics and the making of the world's econo-mies as they are, rather than as they cannot be (perfect competition, full employ-ment, no market imperfections, etc.), is, to say the least, elusive. Interestingly, Hahn looks to history, biology and sociology to bring economics down to earth, possibly the most explicit acknowledgement of the discipline's failure.

At times, of course, economics has engaged with the pressing problems that are posed by the inescapable departure in reality from the virtual world of general equilibrium. Keynesianism readily springs to mind, not least because of its emphasis on the idea that markets, certainly in aggregate, do not work per-fectly and can generate persistent levels of unemployment. Yet, ten years after Hahn's downbeat assessment of the achievements of economics and of its pros-pects if not complemented by other disciplines, Robert Lucas (2000) was also offered, at the turn of the millennium, the opportunity to look forward to the future of economics. Lucas is best known as a Nobel Laureate for having launched the new classical economics in the 1970s, an explicit rejection of Keynesianism in favour of the free market (on which, see below). He treats the history and distribution of the world's economic growth as little more than a random walk to a starting line for industrialization, after which free flow of technology between those in the race increases the gap with those that are not. But no need to worry; all countries will eventually cross the starting line and more or less catch up with the others over the coming century (see the chapter on 'New Growth Theory: More Problem than Solution' in this volume).

Lucas is a leading representative of the new generation of Nobel Laure-ates in economics whose qualifications for prominence rest on making assump-tions that depart as far as possible from realism. Such was the explicit methodological stance of his Nobel predecessor, Milton Friedman (1953). It is worth exploring further the relationship between economics and 'realism', and to suggest a regularity, if not a law, concerning them: that the worse economic performance is and the more obviously pressing economic problems are, the less, not more, realistic does economics become. At the birth of the discipline as we know it today, not least through Alfred Marshall's *Principles of Economics*, preoccupation settled on supply and demand, utility maximization, partial equili-brium, consumer surplus, and so on. Yet, this was the period, as nineteenth turned to twentieth century, that witnessed Britain's economic eclipse, when the United States of America and Germany caught up with and overtook it, leading to inter-imperialist wars. Trade unions and social democratic parties were in the process of formation. Economic and financial crises of greater or lesser duration were endemic. Only by taking history out of economics (and, to a large extent, leav-ing political economy out of economic history) was it possible for economics to establish itself as the science of the market, ultimately to become the science of choice (see the chapter on 'Pioneers of Economic History' in this volume). In the midst of massive unemployment in the 1930s, Lionel Robbins could infamously define economics as the allocation of scarce resources between competing ends.

Admittedly, in reaction to the Great Depression of the 1930s and to Say's Law of markets, Keynes narrowed the yawning gap between economics and reality. Keynesianism and the post-war boom prospered together. And much more besides. Mainstream economics equally displayed a degree of modesty and tolerance, both within itself as a discipline and externally towards other disciplines. Alternative schools of thought survived, even prospered, alongside the orthodoxy – post-Keynesianism, institutionalism, even Marxist political economy. And mainstream economists respected their limitations, recognizing that they took preferences, endowments and technology as fixed, whereas others did not and had much to contribute in understanding them from within the perspectives of other disciplines.

To a large extent, this enabled development economics to be captured by different scholars and traditions than those to be found within the mainstream, with the classics of development (including Nobel Laureates Myrdal and Lewis, for example) different in style and scope to fellow Laureates such as Hicks, Samuelson and Solow. By the same token, other, especially more applied, fields incorporated an empirical and policy content distinct from the preoccupations of Keynesian macroeconomics and general equilibrium microeconomics.

While the cosiness of this division of labour and approaches can be exaggerated, especially in view of the challenges from the new economic history, human capital theory and public choice theory, there can be no doubt that it was rudely shattered by the collapse of the post-war boom, and the emergence of neoliberalism and monetarism. Remarkably, this most forcible evidence of market failure ultimately led mainstream economics, through the new classical economics, to posit that markets clear instantaneously (that is, work perfectly), and that agents form rational expectations (essentially, form and work with models of the economy as good as those of economists themselves). We were also introduced to the so-called representative agent, as if the economy could be reduced to the behaviour of a single individual seeking to coordinate his or her acts of supply and demand through the market. The only reason why this economy did not remain in a state of blissful equilibrium was because of its being subject to random shocks, leading to misinformation to its representative agent. As there is very little that can be done about random shocks, and if markets and representative agent otherwise work perfectly, the dramatic conclusion drawn is that state economic intervention at the macroeconomic level is essentially rendered ineffective by the countervailing reaction of our optimizing agent. At most, the impact of state economic intervention is to introduce uncertainty and inefficient microeconomic market distortions.

It is precisely at this time that the new development economics emerges and, with the Washington Consensus, sets a developmental agenda of state versus market, while falling over heavily on the side of the market (see the chapters on 'The New Development Economics' and 'From Washington to Post-

Washington Consensus: Illusions of Development' in this volume). Much broader developments were also taking place within economics and in its relationship to the other social sciences. Lack of consideration of, and respect for, economic realities was extended to alternative schools and history of economic thought, to historical experience, to methodology and to the other social sciences. The latest model is the thing, complemented by econometric investigation through ever-more powerful computing and data-sets. With the exception of the East Asian newly industrializing countries (NICs), astonishingly interpreted against the most blatant evidence as market-conforming, the last thirty years have witnessed lost decades not only as far as development is concerned, but also for development economics itself.

Fortunately, not all was lost; the old traditions have survived and some new ones have emerged. And, over the last decade, there has been an increasing reaction against the extremes of neoliberalism and its intellectual apologists. In this respect, yet another Nobel Laureate, Joseph Stiglitz, stands out for his analytical emphasis upon the significance of the market and institutional failures, and for his principled opposition to the Washington Consensus. His own post-Washington Consensus and what has been termed (in the chapter on 'The New Development Economics' in this volume) the *newer* development economics, to which it belongs, explicitly acknowledge that institutions, history and the social more generally matter. Further, it is accepted that much can be learnt in these respects from the old classics of development economics (although those who sustained these during the period of neoliberalism are often roughly pushed aside).

Nonetheless, the newer development economics does not restore the old. In many respects, it displays continuities with the new development economics, rather than breaking with it. Although, to some extent, through its own prism of market imperfections, it returns to and retrieves the classics and the more statist approach to development that preceded the Washington Consensus, it also embraces and extends the scope of mainstream economics in understanding the nature of development. Fundamentally, the newer development economics continues to proceed on the basis of optimizing, if imperfectly informed, individuals, located within axiomatic models without social and historical content and context (as sharply revealed by the chapter on 'New Growth Theory: More Problem than Solution' in this volume). As such, it is essentially incapable of satisfactorily incorporating, at the outset, the social and historical structures, processes and agencies that comprise the key determinants and characteristics of development, and that constituted the concern of classical development economics and its predecessors in classical political economy. This not only circumscribes the extent to which the insights of earlier traditions and the other social sciences can be incorporated, but also limits the extent to which the current intellectual, ideological and policy prognoses of the World Bank and the International Monetary Fund (IMF) can be assessed and challenged, although they are subject to critique from a market imperfection perspective.

There are, then, a number of tensions in the newer development economics that endow it with a shifting and uncertain content and significance, according to the context in which it is deployed. As Byres shows (see the chapter on 'Agriculture and Development: Towards a Critique of the "Neoclassical Neopopulism"' in this volume), it can be used to rationalize radical neopopulist land redistribution. More generally, it undoubtedly departs from the Washington Consensus and neoliberalism, but it also favours reliance upon markets, seeking to make them work well through market or non-market (institutional) reform. Its method can allow for incorporation of the social and the historical, but only on the limited basis of the path-dependent outcome of individual optimizing. Its understanding of development itself shifts from one of reliance upon the market to one of correcting market and non-market imperfections.

But this remains far removed from what might be termed the pre-Washington Consensus of the McNamara era with its emphasis on structural change (summarized as modernization) and socio-economic processes, most notably that of industrialization. Symbolically the amorphous character of the post-Washington Consensus is reflected in that its most prominent exponent, Joseph Stiglitz, deploys it most effectively as a critique of the World Bank and the IMF. Yet, these institutions can adopt 'Stiglitz-speak' not only to rationalize unchanged policy as far as the nostrums of the Washington Consensus and its conditionalities are concerned, but also to extend the market-based approach from the market to the non-market arena (for the building of good governance, social capital and so on). Further, in the intellectual arena, the appropriation of the language and ideas of the old classical development economics, and of various schools of radical political economy, from dependency theory and Marxism through structuralism, is striking. As Goodacre shows (see the chapter on 'Development and Geography: Current Debates in Historical Perspective' in this volume) in the case of the new economic geography, the new development economics purports to provide a mathematical model of core–periphery development. In the clearest possible terms, leading theorists of international financial institutions claim complete compatibility between the methodological individualism of neoclassical economics and the structuralism of more radical approaches. Agénor and Montiel insist that development economics requires the same analytical principle of the rational optimizing individual, but that this principle can now not only reproduce but even advance the cause of structuralism: 'Many of the areas in which "orthodox" thinking has provided much insight [has] . . . ironically, even strengthened new structuralist arguments' (Agénor and Montiel 1996: 3). It is crucial to recognize that such structuralist arguments (and development economics and studies, more generally) are being appropriated and reinterpreted within a mainstream neoclassical microeconomic framework.

Against this background, this volume seeks to assess the new and the newer development economics critically, as a means to rescue, restore and advance alternative perspectives. It does so while recognizing that there are complex relationships among scholarship, rhetoric and policy in practice, especially within the World Bank and the IMF themselves. Consider, for example, the recent turn of these institutions to poverty. This has been extremely prominent within the development literature over a longer period, not least through the work of Amartya Sen. His intellectual trajectory has traversed social choice theory, inequality, entitlements, capabilities and freedom. In conjunction with the associated literature, poverty has been recognized to be complex and diverse. How should it be defined in relative or absolute terms? How should it be measured – by income or by consumption? What are its determinants and incidence by (un)employment, gender, race, ethnicity, age, region, rural/urban divide, and within and between household types? What about the definition and understanding of poverty by the poor themselves? And how reliable and representative are data, even if these other issues can be satisfactorily resolved?

Despite these well-established and detailed difficulties in addressing poverty, they seem to evaporate in the prognoses of the international financial institutions. Poverty itself is taken as more or less unproblematic, and is examined against individual policy issues taken in isolation from one another. In the case of IMF financial programming, for example, the assumption is made of a single, fully employed labour market, effectively precluding consideration of the causes and incidence of poverty other than as a byproduct of relative price movements (see the chapter on 'Financial Programming and the International Monetary Fund' in this volume). For the very different case of the impact of trade policy, regressions of poverty on simple (and questionable) measures of openness are deemed sufficient to crack the complex and diverse conduits between the two (as the chapter titled 'Kicking Away the Logic: Free Trade is Neither the Question Nor the Answer for Development' in this volume shows). Much the same oversimplifications are to be found in other areas of policy for which the benefits of trade openness and the free market, more generally, are declared. This is so in considering the (developmental) state's economic interventions, the purported benefits of privatization and the ways in which technological advance can accrue (as the chapters titled 'The Developmental State and the Political Economy of Development', 'Privatization Theory and Practice: A Critical Analysis of Policy Evolution in the Development Context', and 'The Analysis of Technology and Development: A Critical Review' show). In each case, scant regard is paid to the theoretical and empirical evidence to the contrary or, indeed, to pinpointing the range of factors that have to be considered.

Thus, in abstract formal terms, the international financial institutions have a predilection for taking complex issues X and Y, and, by combining them, imagining that the complexities can be set aside and the issue settled by running a simple econometric model (more often a single equation) relating the two. In a way, this is usefully summarized in the notion that, for the international financial institutions, one model fits all. Inevitably, where X is a policy variable and Y is poverty or, otherwise, a goal to be achieved, X consistently conforms to the dictates of Washington Consensus stabilization and structural adjustment, and, more recently, to the rhetoric of poverty alleviation, good governance, country ownership and so on.

Consider, for example, the conclusion to a study by a World Bank economist that includes the impact of social capital, a marker of the newer development economics (see the chapter on 'Social Capital' in this volume), on objective Y, to be revealed in a moment. To target Y, Bonnel (2000: 849) will require three sets of measures:

(i) sound macroeconomic policies,
(ii) structural policy reforms, and
(iii) modifying further the system of incentives faced by individuals.

This can only come as a surprise to the soft-boiled, but even the most cynical will surely be surprised to learn that Y is, in this case, 'reversing the spread of the HIV/AIDS epidemics and mitigating its impact'! The complexities of the epidemic, and the corresponding policy options, are reduced to a regression in which the policy stance of the Washington Consensus offers appropriate treatment. The major difference with other areas of policy is merely that lack of plausibility and connection to the issue at hand is not immediate.

Is this all a recipe for despair? For, the general law, if such it is, of growing divide between economic fortune and economics realism, is complemented within the international financial institutions by rigid policy-making and rhetorical acrobatics. Further, the weight of their influence over policy, thinking and other donors as sources of resources has been deliberately built upon the leverage gained from the limited funding that they themselves provide (see the chapter entitled 'From Washington to Post-Washington Consensus: Illusions of Development' in this volume). As a putative knowledge bank, advice is freely dispensed, but very few dissenting deposits are made, let alone withdrawn. Yet, none of this is fixed in stone. It is necessary to be both realistic and active in targeting debate around development, to oppose and expose entrenched orthodoxies and to propose alternatives. It is in this spirit that this book is offered as a selective engagement across the battleground of development economics.

References

Agénor, Pierre-Richard and Peter J. Montiel (1996), *Development Macroeconomics* (Princeton: Princeton University Press).

Bonnel, René (2000), 'HIV/AIDS and Economic Growth: A Global Perspective', *South African Journal of Economics*, 68 (5): 820–55.

Friedman, Milton (1953), 'The Methodology of Positive Economics', in Milton Friedman, *Essays in Positive Economics* (Chicago: Chicago University Press).

Hahn, Frank (1991), 'The Next Hundred Years', *Economic Journal*, 101 (404): 47–50.

Lucas, Robert (2000), 'Some Macroeconomics for the 21st Century', *Journal of Economic Perspectives*, 14 (1): 159–68.

Contributors

KATE BAYLISS is an independent researcher specializing in privatization and its effects in developing countries. Until recently, she was a Research Fellow at the Public Services International Research Unit at the University of Greenwich, UK, analysing international developments in the privatization of water and energy. Her recent publications include 'Utility Privatization in Sub-Saharan Africa: A Case Study of Water' (*Journal of Modern African Studies*, 2003) and 'Privatization and Poverty: The Distributional Impact of Utility Privatization' (*Annals of Public and Cooperative Economics*, 2002).

TERENCE J. BYRES is Emeritus Professor of Political Economy in the University of London. His books include *Capitalism from Above and Capitalism from Below: An Essay in Comparative Political Economy* (Macmillan, 1996), and he has edited *The Indian Economy: Major Debates since Independence* (Oxford University Press, 1998), *The State, Development Planning and Liberalization in India* (Oxford University Press, 1998), and *Redistributive Land Reform Today* (forthcoming, already having appeared as a special issue of the *Journal of Agrarian Change*, Vol. 4, Nos. 1 and 2, January and April, 2004).

SONALI DERANIYAGALA is a Lecturer in Economics at the School of Oriental and African Studies, University of London, with recent publications in the areas of industrial performance, industrial policy, trade theory and trade policy in developing countries.

BEN FINE is Professor of Economics at the School of Oriental and African Studies, University of London. His recent books include *Social Capital versus Social Theory: Political Economy and Social Science at the Turn of the Millennium* (Routledge, 2001), *Development Policy in the Twenty-First Century: Beyond the Post-Washington Consensus*, edited with C. Lapavitsas and J. Pincus (Routledge, 2001), *The World of Consumption: The Material and Cultural Revisited* (Routledge, 2002), and *Marx's Capital*, with A. Saad-Filho, fourth edition (Pluto, 2004). In preparation is a two-volume book on the shifting relations between history and economics (with D. Milonakis) as part of broader research on economics imperialism.

HUGH GOODACRE was a Curator in the Asia, Pacific and Africa Department of the British Library from 1972 to 1996. He has since written a Ph.D. thesis on William Petty, and currently teaches economics at City University, London. He is preparing for further publications on the colonialist roots of economics.

JOHN HARRISS is Professor of Development Studies at the London School of Economics. His recent publications are *Reinventing India: Economic Liberalization, Hindu Nationalism and Popular Democracy*, with Stuart Corbridge (Polity, 2000), *Depoliticizing Development: The World Bank and Social Capital* (LeftWord, 2001 and Anthem Press, 2002), and *Politicizing Democracy: Local Politics and Democratization in Developing Countries*, edited with Kristian Stokke and Olle Tornquist (Palgrave, 2004).

JOMO K.S. was Professor in the Applied Economics Department, University of Malaya, Kuala Lumpur, and Senior Visiting Research Fellow at the Asia Research Institute, National University of Singapore, before joining the United Nations. He is Founder Chair of IDEAs, International Development Economics Associates (www.networkideas.org). His most recent books include *Tigers in Trouble* (Zed Books, 1998), *Rents, Rent-Seeking and Economic Development: Theory and Evidence in Asia*, edited with Mushtaq H. Khan (Cambridge University Press, 2000), *Globalization versus Development: Heterodox Perspectives*, edited with Shyamala Nagaraj (Palgrave, 2001), *M Way: Mahathir's Economic Policy Legacy* (INSAN, 2003), and *Globalization and its Discontents Revisited*, edited with Khoo Khay Jin (Tulika Books, 2003).

MUSHTAQ HUSAIN KHAN is Senior Lecturer in Economics at the School of Oriental and African Studies, University of London. His recent books include *Rents, Rent-Seeking and Economic Development: Theory and Evidence in Asia*, edited with Jomo K.S. (Cambridge University Press, 2000) and *State Formation in Palestine: Viability and Governance during a Social Transformation*, edited with George Giacaman and Inge Amundsen (Routledge, 2004).

DIMITRIS MILONAKIS is Assistant Professor in the Department of Economics, University of Crete. He has published on various aspects of political economy in journals like the *Cambridge Journal of Economics, Journal of Peasant Studies, Science and Society* and *Capital and Class*, and is co-editor of the book *Marx Revisited* (in Greek). He is currently preparing two books (with Ben Fine) on economic theory and history (Routledge, 2005).

PAULINE ROSE is Lecturer in International Education, University of Sussex, Institute of Education, Brighton, Sussex, UK.

ELISA VAN WAEYENBERGE is a Ph.D. student at the School of Oriental and African Studies, University of London. She is working on the latest efforts at 'reinvention' of the World Bank, with a particular interest in the newly propagated aid paradigm and its associated emphasis on the Bank's 'knowledge' advantage.

The New Development Economics

Ben Fine

This chapter is concerned with what is known as the new development economics. It is, however, now sufficiently old that it has already spawned and includes what might be dubbed the newer development economics, which is probably better known as the post-Washington Consensus and is closely associated with its initiator, Joseph Stiglitz, previously chief economist at the World Bank.[1] The supposedly 'old' development economics that the new takes as its point of departure has rarely been identified by the new other than by what it is not. In a sense, the slate of development economics was wiped clean in order to start afresh from different analytical principles and intellectual traditions. So the old development economics was not so much superseded as set aside. But it can be presumed to have included the 'classics' in the study of development. However, the shortsightedness of the new approach is such that, even when it recognizes the old, it rarely does so by tracing the lineage of how we understand development back beyond World War II.

Despite their considerable differences, and hence equally considerable richness and diversity, what the old approaches do share in common are two fundamental features. First is the idea that development involves profound historical, economic and social change that must be studied as such through a methodology that reflects systemic change. Second, not surprisingly, is the recognition of interdisciplinarity, of combining development economics with what is now known as development studies. So well established is the new development economics these days that to appeal to an alternative development economics with these features is to court the charge of being some sort of antiquated leftie. It is also subject to being accused of lacking rigour and science. For, as Amariglio and Ruccio observe of the new mainstream orthodoxy within economics: 'Academic economists tend to privilege the form of reasoning associated with economic science – the "economic way of thinking" . . . the formal methods that serve to guarantee scientific rigor' (Amariglio and Ruccio 1999: 23).[2] Such is worth bearing in mind as this chapter reviews the rise of the new development economics, and its change of both subject matter and the methods by which it is examined.

The next section begins with a prominent example of the old development economics. This sets the scene for charting the rise of the new development economics, especially in the form of the Washington Consensus. The latter's extreme form of neoliberalism has inevitably prompted a reaction whose content is examined in a subsequent section through the prism of Kuhn's ideas of paradigm and scientific revolution. But the *status quo ex ante* has not been restored. It can even be argued that the newer development economics, in the form of the post-Washington Consensus, looks much more like the Washington Consensus than the old development economics that the Washington Consensus sought to displace. This is especially so within the World Bank, from where the post-Washington Consensus, if not the new development economics, first emerged.

The attempt by Stiglitz to deploy the newer development economics to shift the thinking *and* policies of the Washington institutions gave rise to his abrupt, enforced departure from an internal position of influence. It is a moot point whether he has had any lasting influence in promoting his views within the World Bank. It is apparent, though, that the post-Washington Consensus can be used to support both radical and conservative posturing (if not as extreme as neoliberalism). That it can do so suggests that it needs to be critically assessed in light of both its relationship to the old (rather than new) development economics and the dangers of its offering an all-embracing framework for addressing the economics of development at the expense of other approaches. These themes recur throughout the chapter, and the concluding remarks briefly look to the future in light of how the idea of globalization has potentially reopened the way in which we understand and examine development.

Rise and Fall of the Washington Consensus?

It is worth recalling that one of the most prominent old-style development economists was an economic historian of impeccable 'ideological credentials' and healthy respect for economic theory. I refer to W.W. Rostow. His aim was to provide a model for development drawn from historical experience, and to offer an alternative to the Soviet system during the Cold War. He did so in a book, first published in 1960, that went through three editions and sold 300,000 copies. It was entitled *The Stages of Economic Growth: A Non-Communist Manifesto*. Not surprisingly, he displayed considerable antipathy to Marxism, and his reasons for doing so are revealing, despite offering a flawed representation of Marx and the classics: 'The first and most fundamental difference between the two analyses lies in the view taken of human motivation. Marx's system is, like classical economics, a set of more or less sophisticated logical deductions from the notion of profit maximization.' For himself, by contrast:

> In the stages-of-growth sequence man is viewed as a more complex unit. He seeks, not merely economic advantage, but also power, leisure, adventure, continuity of experience and security; he is concerned with his family, the familiar values of his regional and national culture, and a bit of fun down at the local. . . . In short, net human behaviour is seen not as an act of maximization, but as an act of balancing alternative and often conflicting human objectives in

the face of the range of choices men perceive to be open to them. (Rostow 1990: 149)

And, in his own way, Rostow exposes what he considers to be the limitations of a purely economic analysis as far as the historian of development is concerned: 'The theorist has generally been uneasy if not awkward if forced to work outside Marshallian short-period assumptions; the historian – like the human beings he writes about – cannot avoid working in a world of changing tastes and institutions, changing population, technology, and capacity' (Rostow 1957: 514). Ironically, Rostow's critique of economic determinism in the form of profit maximization, and his appeal for a more rounded treatment of individuals and the context in which they are situated, are more appropriate for the new development economics as it first emerged. Essentially, this sought to draw increasingly upon mainstream neoclassical economics, setting aside both non-economic factors and non-individualistic accounts of development.

As such, it could make very little analytical purchase on the problems of development. There seemed to be no way of explaining why some countries should be developed and others not, especially, as recognized by Rostow, if the major factors in development are taken as exogenous, from tastes through to technology. The real boost to the new development economics, for it to recognizably emerge, could only come by extending the scope of the subject matter of economics itself. It needed to incorporate those exogenous factors that had previously been taken for granted in an economics primarily directed towards understanding efficient allocation of resources in *developed* economies.

This did not prove too difficult from a logical point of view. For, it was only by convention, laid down with the emergence of economics as a separate discipline alongside the other social sciences at the end of the nineteenth century, that its scope was confined to the market, to the laws of supply and demand. The analytical principle of pursuit of self-interest or of utility maximization, for which profit maximization is just a part, is not necessarily confined to economic matters alone. There is no reason why it should not be applied to a whole range of pursuits. In economics itself, the extension of what one of its leading practitioners, Gary Becker, was to call the 'economic approach', was soon underway. Its most prominent and early successes proved to be human capital theory and public choice theory. For one, the process of attaining skills (especially education) and being rewarded for them was viewed as equivalent to a market mechanism with corresponding costs and benefits. For the other, politics was simply the pursuit of economic self-interest in an 'as if' marketplace for votes.

Further, the extension of the economic approach, which Becker (1996) himself saw as incorporating all human behaviour, also materialized in Rostow's own discipline of economic history with a vengeance. The new economic history or cliometrics, as it is now known, emerged, notoriously treating slavery, for example, as a matter of costs and benefits in the calculating minds of slave owners who needed to decide whether to shift to a wage system or not.

Significantly, and not surprisingly, many historians were no more prepared to accept economic reductionism than Rostow. With the meteoric rise of cliometrics in economics departments in the United States, where economic history tended to be located, the discipline of history was split between economic and social history, with separate journals and professional organizations (see Lamoreaux 1998 for an account).

This is not to say that all neoclassical economists accepted that economics should be confined to examining the market as well as supply and demand. There were those who sought to extend the application of 'economic rationality' to non-economic areas. But even they tended to accept that there were limits to the application of economic rationality, especially in its 'as if' perfect market form, as if crime or the family was simply a matter of calculated costs and benefits. In retrospect, it is natural to dwell upon how the use of economic rationality was extended at this time – to human capital and public choice, for example – rather than to dwell upon acknowledged limits to doing so that have become forgotten with the passage of time.

But, for many of those seeking to extend the boundaries of the subject matter of economics, there was a clear recognition of interdisciplinary boundaries, and this was shared by economists who respected them. As one of the leading exponents of public choice theory put it: 'The purpose of this article is not to extol the virtue of economic analysis but rather to reflect on its limitations' (McKenzie 1979: 145). And he elaborated in a footnote: 'It may seem especially unusual for me to examine the limitation of economic analysis since I have, in much of my writing in the last few years [through public choice theory], attempted to see how far the boundaries of economics can be stretched.'

Old development economics continued to receive some protection from what has come to be known as 'economics imperialism', as a result of the continuing influence of those such as Rostow, who, while accepting the economic approach, considered that it needed to be complemented by insights from other disciplines. Further, World Bank policy in the 1970s, under the influence of Robert McNamara as president, very much viewed development in terms of modernization, as emulation of the path taken by the now-developed economies. Keynesianism and welfarism provided policy support for substantial state intervention. And development, as both process and goal, was identified with industrialization and urbanization, for example, as preconditions for substantial rises in per capita incomes.

In short, prior to the emergence of neoliberalism in the 1980s, development was understood primarily in terms of modernization, with three stylized (and heavily over-generalized) elements (Toye 1993). First, developing economies are primarily agricultural; second, they need to undertake a transition to become developed (like the United States); third, that transition follows the one previously taken by the now-developed economies. Moreover, the influence of Keynesianism in particular (together with a major and increasing economic role of the state in modernized and modernizing economies) suggested that the state should be significant as an economic agent as part of and in achieving modernization.[3] As Toye put it:

> The original theory of socioeconomic development that accompanied the post-1945 decolonization of Asia and Africa rested on the idea of modern society as the goal of development. Modern society supposedly had typical social patterns of demography, urbanization and literacy; typical economic patterns of production and consumption, investment, trade and government finance; and typical psychological attributes of rationality, ascriptive identity and achievement motivation. The process of development consisted, on this theory, of moving from traditional society, which was taken as the polar opposite of the modern type, through a series of stages of development – derived essentially from the history of Europe, North America and Japan – to modernity, that is, approximately the United States of the 1950s. (Toye 1993: 30–31)

But this was to change, and dramatically, with the rise of neoliberalism. As Toye (ibid.) has shown, the crisis of Keynesianism in the developed world, prompted by the collapse of the post-war boom and the stagflation of the 1970s, had the effect of discrediting state intervention in general (and not just for short-run macroeconomic demand management). The neoliberal shift against state economic intervention of any sort was then carried over to development, shooting rapidly to prominence those, such as Peter Bauer and Deepak Lal, who had previously been seen as right-wing mavericks. With little or no sound foundation within mainstream economics itself, free market, supply-side economics – the economics of leaving production to the unregulated price system – came to the fore, to conform to and support an anti-statist politics and ideology. More specifically, the emergence of the Washington Consensus in the 1980s was pioneered by Anne Krueger as the World Bank's chief economist.

The old development economics was swept aside with a number of unsurprising effects. First, the economic approach was to be extended to non-economic applications. At the forefront was the notion of rent-seeking as a pursuit of self-interest other than in the domain of the market. Not only, it was argued, does successful rent-seeking distort the perfectly working market, it also wastes resources in pursuit of gain, whether successful or not, in competition with others playing the same game. The implication is that the role of the state should be minimized, not only because it is a direct source of inefficiency, but also because its potential activity encourages wasteful use of resources to gain essentially corrupt advantage, whether from within or from without.

Second, the Washington Consensus marked a far from subtle, although often overlooked, shift in how development is understood. Whether through the prism of modernization and emulation or the emphasis on major socio-economic transformation, the old development economics displayed a clear, and remarkably common, understanding that development involved a transition from one sort of economy and society to another. In the case of the Washington Consensus, apart from the goal of increasing per capita income, productivity and so on, the nature of development has been more or less excised. In its place has been put a set of mechanisms or, more exactly, one mechanism for achieving development, that is, reliance on the market through a minimal state. By the same token, low levels of per capita income and high proportions of primary production apart, there seems to be little way of distinguishing developing from developed countries. Paradoxically, developing countries tend to have lower proportions of state expenditure than developed ones.

Third, development economics, as such, no longer warrants the claim to be a separate discipline or field within economics. Exactly the same universal theoretical principles apply to developing as to developed countries. At most, differences in history as well as social and economic structure mark the exogenous factors within which *homo economicus* goes about maximizing utility. For Agénor and Montiel, for example:

> We do not believe that economic agents in developing countries behave differently from those in industrial economies, in ways that are inconsistent with the rational optimizing principle of neoclassical microeconomics; rather, we believe that they behave similarly to their industrial counterparts, but operate in a different environment. Our perspective is that the standard analytical tools of modern macroeconomics are indeed of as much relevance to developing countries as they are to industrial countries, but that different models are needed to analyse familiar issues. (Agénor and Montiel 1996: 11–12)

As a result, any sufficiently trained economist is able to have a go at development economics, the only requirement being to build a mathematical model that can be tested against the evidence by deploying increasingly sophisticated techniques, data-sets and computing power.

In practice, many neoliberal development economists did not live up to these requirements (see the chapter on 'Financial Programming' for macroeconomics, for example). Yet, it is important to emphasize that at this time mainstream economics was, to put it kindly, going through a particularly esoteric phase in terms of its 'realism' (see Fine 1998: Chapter 2, for an overview). The dominant macroeconomic theory shooting to prominence was a sort of hypermonetarism. The so-called new classical economics was based on the idea that all markets work perfectly and instantaneously, that all agents predict the future as well as possible, and that all government intervention is futile as it is nullified by agents' anticipation of its necessarily negative effects.

More generally, Blaug, for example, reported from John Hey – previously managing editor of the United Kingdom's leading academic publication, *Economic Journal* – that the discipline had been taken over by a 'journal game' (Blaug 1998a: 12). Contributions were based on use of irrelevant material, the stylized facts observed by an author, and designed to demonstrate cleverness rather than address crucial economic problems. Blaug offered his own opinion: 'I am very pessimistic about whether we can actually pull out of this. I think we have created a locomotive. This is the sociology of the economics profession. We have created a monster that is very difficult to stop' (Blaug 1998b: 45). Blaug also reported from a survey of elite graduate economics students that there is a complete lack of interest in the real world, as opposed to honing their skills in the latest econometrics and mathematical economics (Blaug 1998a: 11).

Thus, the pioneers of the new development economics, or the counter-revolutionaries against the old, as Toye dubs them, depended more on *laissez-faire* dogma and political opportunism than occupation of the frontiers of mainstream economics. At most, they could claim to be signalling a return to idealized classical propositions and universal economic laws emphasizing the benefits of free market forces. But their success in attracting establishment support, especially in Washington DC, undermined the corresponding position of the old development economics. This opened the way for more technically advanced economists to flood the development field. Such was the economics being released upon development in the 1980s with the Washington Consensus, through the World Bank and the IMF, as ideological and material back-up. It inspired considerable reaction and resistance, not least for its lack of realism across a number of aspects. The historical experience of the role of the state in success-fully industrializing countries was evident, especially in East Asia in recent times. The economic reductionism and failure to comprehend development and devel-oping countries more broadly entailed a neglect of adjustment with a human face. And, with the passage of time, vigorous if flawed defence to the contrary, the policies inspired by the Washington Consensus were failing to deliver discrete improvements in economic performance, let alone the broader and more de-manding goal of development. In the mid-1990s, both the IMF and the World Bank were in the doldrums, suffering a severe crisis of legitimacy across theo-retical, ideological and policy aspects.

The Post-Washington Consensus: New Wine in New Bottles?

Temporary relief was, however, close at hand from within the discipline of economics itself. It had begun to react against the extremes to which 'the eco-nomic approach' had pushed itself. Akerlof, who was to inspire a new approach, commented on Becker in terms of his having learnt how to spell 'ba-nana' but not knowing where to stop (Akerlof 1990: 73). This seems to have had some resonance with the earlier objections of McKenzie against over-extending the application of economic rationality. But this is misleading in so far as the new approach has sought to emphasize the role of market imperfections as the basis for a new economic theory.

While recognition of market imperfections had long been well estab-lished, the new twist to be added by Akerlof was in emphasizing the absence of perfect information between contracting parties in the marketplace. His classic example is the market for 'lemons', slang in the United States for second-hand cars of dubious quality (Akerlof 1970). Because sellers know more about the commodity than buyers, the latter fear they will be duped, driving down the price they are prepared to pay. This, in turn, drives down the quality of the cars on offer at the lower price, leading to a downward spiral of price and quality.

Such considerations explain why markets might not work perfectly despite epitomizing individuals and no exogenous impediments to movements in prices. The theory suggests that there are three possible outcomes: markets clear but are Pareto-inefficient (there are buyers and sellers who would like to exchange at some other price); markets do not clear (those on the short side of the market do not have an incentive to change price in their favour because this will change the average quality of what is brought to the market); there is no market at all (undermined by the presence of what is known as moral hazard or adverse selection[4]).

So the market for lemons is rich in providing explanations for market imperfections, rather than assuming them to be exogenous. But it has another, possibly more compelling, implication – the capacity to explain non-economic behaviour. Buyers and sellers might build up trust relations over time, rather than always buying cheapest and selling dearest, for example; it might become customary to follow conventions as a means of overcoming differences in information; and institutions, either cooperative between agents or imposed by the state, might serve as a remedy (a guarantee scheme, for example).

The result is striking in four respects. First, in contrast to the economic approach, institutions, customs, as well as economic and social structures are taken seriously, rather than presumed to be equivalent to an 'as if' market situation. Second, the analysis is extended, as before, to non-economic factors, but in ways that are liable to be more palatable both to non-economists and opponents of neoliberalism. Third, in contrast to the banana-like economic approach, the market imperfection approach is better able to claim some hold on the realities of contemporary capitalism. Fourth, despite all this, the theory continues to rest on the assumption of *homo economicus*, only one whose rationality is bounded both by imperfect information and historically evolved non-market factors.

Such properties are reflected in the proliferation of 'new' fields of economics over the past decade – the new institutional economics, the new economic sociology, the new political economy, the new growth theory, the new labour economics, the new economic geography, the new financial economics, the new development economics and so on. In this vein, Stiglitz felt able to claim that a new approach to economics has been established, drawing on market imperfections to explain non-market factors and outcomes. It diverges from the old mainstream, enhances the understanding of how markets work and is applicable across a wide range of subject matter:

> During the past fifteen years, a new paradigm, sometimes referred to as the information-theoretic approach to economics . . . has developed. . . . This paradigm has already provided us with insights into development economics and macroeconomics. It has provided us with a new welfare economics, a new theory of the firm, and a new understanding of the role and functioning of financial markets. (Stiglitz 1994: 5)

So, as is apparent, a more nuanced theory than the economic approach, but one that continues to claim universal applicability, necessarily encompassing development economics. To a large extent, the process is symbolized by the transition from the Washington to the post-Washington Consensus, and through the weight of Stiglitz's influence and contributions. In launching the post-Washington Consensus as newly appointed chief economist at the World Bank, he soon referred 'to providing the foundations of an alternative paradigm, especially one relevant to the least developing country. It is based on a broad conception of development.' Further, 'I shall explain why not only the Washington Consensus, but earlier development paradigms failed: they viewed development too narrowly' (Stiglitz 2001a: 57–58).[5]

These are extremely clear, if excessively grand, claims. Nor is it clear, through frequent appeal to the notion of paradigm, whether the resonance with Kuhn's notion of scientific revolution is intended, or simply incidental and unconscious. Either way, it is worth considering the new self-styled paradigm from a Kuhnian perspective. It is now forty years since Thomas Kuhn laid out his theory of scientific revolution. He was initially concerned to explain how the physical sciences changed, drawing a distinction between normal, smoothly evolving science within a given paradigm, and revolutionary science that blazes a shorter, if not short, sharp shift between paradigms. As a result, Kuhn's language, especially the notion of paradigm, for example, has become commonplace, even as substantive knowledge and understanding of his contribution, and criticism of it, have declined. In the field of science, his approach has been superseded by postmodernism's notion of the social construction of scientific knowledge.

Further, in the scholarly literature, more than enough time has passed for his approach to have become fully traversed, if not forgotten, territory for understanding the sources and nature of intellectual change. For those economists who participated, even if merely as an audience, in the Kuhnian revolution, it ought, in retrospect, to stand out as a remarkably rare period of self-examination of a discipline that is notoriously unaware of, and uninterested in, its own history and methodological underpinnings (de Vroey 1975). While primarily concerned with the history of science, Kuhnian notions were readily transposed to the social sciences without economics standing on the sidelines as an exception, as has been so for other intellectual fashions, such as postmodernism, in the more recent period.[6]

But what exactly is the Kuhnian approach to scientific revolution?[7] Central is the notion of paradigm, with science proceeding through discontinuous breaks between them rather than through a continuous evolution. As the highly cited Masterman (1970) has observed, although Kuhn's notion of paradigm has been attached to as many as twenty-one different interpretations, these can be boiled down to three – first as exemplar, second as world vision, third as a community of professionals. Irrespective of the validity of the Kuhnian framework for addressing intellectual change or the sociology of knowledge, examining each of these core elements of a paradigm is useful in shedding light on current developments within and around (development) economics.

For paradigm as exemplar, the distinctive character of the new phase of economics imperialism, represented by the information-theoretic economic approach, is clearly delineated. Masterman understood a 'construct paradigm' as an 'artefact', and 'only with an artefact can you solve puzzles' (Masterman 1970: 70). With the creation and solving of problems within a paradigm as normal science, it is not difficult to identify the artefact involved in the newer development economics. It is the notion of asymmetric information, and the consequences this has for market and non-market outcomes. Indeed, the founding artefact is an exemplary exemplar – Akerlof's market for 'lemons'.

Following Akerlof, information-theoretic economics has proceeded by accumulating different types of informational asymmetries and applying them across an equally diverse range of markets. Although with the physical sciences in mind, Masterman astonishingly and unwittingly anticipated recent developments within economics, as economists have searched out applications for asymmetric information: 'A normal-scientific puzzle always has a solution which is guaranteed by the paradigm, but which it takes ingenuity and resourcefulness to find' (ibid.). Further, as Chase observed, a paradigm fills out new analytical terrain:

> The acceptance of a new exemplary paradigm by a community of scientists will often require a redefinition of the corresponding science . . . some old problems may be relegated to another science or declared entirely 'unscientific', while others that were previously nonexistent or trivial may . . . become the very archetypes of scientific achievement. (Chase 1983: 816)

In the case of economics imperialism, a wider definition of economic science is involved since it is not simply a matter of explaining market imperfections, but also of incorporating non-market responses to them, thereby establishing a presence within the other social sciences. Masterman suggests that a paradigm is established by taking an exemplar, A, and finding other applications for it, B, by analogy, whereby B becomes A-like. This is precisely what has been characteristic of the newer development economics – economic and social analyses have been reduced, respectively, to market imperfections and non-market responses to them. From lemons, or the market for second-hand cars, the entire terrain of economic and social theory is opened up!

Interestingly, Masterman (1970) considered that the exemplar attached to a paradigm is more important than its world view, and this seems to be borne out by the 'disciplinary matrix' attached to information-theoretic economics. How does the new information-theoretic economics differ from what went before? It takes as its point of departure the model of perfectly competitive equilibrium. In its place is posited an imperfectly competitive world with imperfect markets and imperfect information, leading both to inefficiencies and to non-market responses to them (whether these correct market imperfections or not).

In other words, the world vision of the new approach is its micro-foundations, its exemplars combined together and writ large. This is borne out in an apparently unwitting deployment of the new Kuhnian paradigm as exemplar and vision by Stiglitz: 'There is no single, overarching model to replace the competitive equilibrium model: the world is too complex. But there are a set of tools and perspectives (such as those that derive from models of imperfect information and incomplete markets) that can be used' (Stiglitz 2001c: 5). More specifically, in the case of development economics, Stiglitz and Hoff (1999) argued that:

> In leaving out history, institutions, and distributional considerations, neoclassical economics was leaving out the heart of development economics. Modern economic theory argues that the fundamentals (resources, technology, and preferences) are not the only . . . determinants of economic outcomes . . . even without government failures, market failures are pervasive, especially in less developed countries.[8]

Further, with casual reference to the black plague, as an illustrative accident of history (like AIDS today?), and multiple equilibria, an explanation was provided for the fundamental problem of why 'developed and less developed countries are on different production functions': 'We emphasize that accidents of history matter . . . partly because of pervasive complementarities among agents . . . and partly because even a set of dysfunctional institutions and behaviors in the past can constitute a Nash equilibrium from which an economy need not be inevitably dislodged.'

Apart from specifying exactly what is meant by a 'broader vision' of development (Stiglitz 2001b: 58), this appears to be an ideal illustration of how Kuhn (1970) understood paradigms as being generated by, and transformed into, an evolving disciplinary matrix. There are 'symbolic generalizations', of which production functions and Nash equilibria are archetypal. The 'metaphysical content' of 'modern economic theory' is one source of 'failures' – market, government or otherwise – as opposed to the ideal, perfectly competitive world of 'neoclassical economics'. 'Values' within a paradigm are of two types – those concerning predictions and puzzle formulation, and those attached to overall consistency, simplicity and plausibility. For the new approach, there is a common reliance, as with the old, both upon econometrics and upon a method of optimizing individuals, but the puzzles are about how the market (understandably) works imperfectly, rather than how it diverges from perfection because of externally imposed constraints (especially through the state).

The third broad category of meaning of paradigm identified by Masterman (1970) is the sociological, as opposed to the metaphysical (world view) or the construct (exemplar). This refers to the community of scientists and their common practices that, in retrospect, Kuhn (1970) confessed he would have preferred to have taken as his analytical and expositional starting point. Now, such a community can be understood in a narrow or wide sense. It varies from a set of like-minded individuals to include their influence and position in society more generally. As far as the academic discipline of economics is concerned, paradoxically, although the new approach appropriately presents itself as less dogmatic than the model of perfect competition that it has sought to replace, it has prospered in an intellectual climate in which the discipline has itself become even more intolerant of alternatives.

So, while the newer development economics of Stiglitz and others, such as Krugman, who emphasize market imperfections, tends to consolidate the pre-existing reaction against the neoliberalism of the counter-revolutionaries that assaulted the old development economics, it has itself held an ambiguous position with respect to the old development economics. It is acceptable only if rein-terpreted through the prism of the new approach – development as the emergence and correction of market and non-market imperfections. Radical political economy has been considerably weakened, and, even where it has not, the modelling and statistical techniques of the orthodoxy are increasingly imperative as a condition of entry to the profession, to the exclusion of almost all else, ostensibly for lack of rigour and science.[9]

Particularly striking in this respect is the degree of 'Americanization' of economics. This is not simply the excessive and irrelevant use of mathematics, statistics, methodological individualism of a special type, and obsessive preoccu-pation with equilibrium and efficiency. It is marked by the excessive command of journals, textbooks, appointments, doctoral training, even Nobel Prizes, by a limited range of institutions and individuals. Significantly, while the number of doctoral students in economics is increasing in the United States, the number of British origin is in decline, revealing the export and adoption of its economics at the top of the profession throughout the world.

But perhaps the most rhetorically persuasive and satisfying evidence of the Americanization of economics is provided by the leading proponent of the new paradigm. For Stiglitz, 'the question is, how can we *institutionally* facilitate the replacement of the old [neoliberal, competitive equilibrium] paradigm with the new perspectives?' (Stiglitz 2001c: 6). The answer is through networking and PhD programmes, to be sponsored by foundations. However, tenured jobs are hard to find as these depend upon publications and 'many journals are not as open to alternative perspectives as they should be' (ibid.). So, new journals will also be necessary. Yet, this is the view of a Nobel Laureate, a former chief economist to the President of the United States and to the World Bank. His contri-bution, ten years ago, on the (negative) prospects for socialism (Stiglitz 1994) contained over one hundred citations to his own work, predominantly published in the major journals. Thus, while Stiglitz is correct to point to the strength of neoliberal thinking and the stranglehold of (American) orthodoxy on the eco-nomics profession, it is not a monopoly, either at his expense or of the (equally American) approach, that he would seek to foist upon the understanding of eco-nomic development.

To some extent, then, while Stiglitz presents himself as against neoclas-sical orthodoxy,[10] his approach incorporates considerable continuities with it, especially in its methodology, other than assuming perfect competition. On a more mundane level, to what extent has the new information-theoretic approach to economics and to development been associated with a shift from the orthodoxy in 'habit-governed, puzzle-solving activity'? On the face of it, very little has changed. Mainstream economics has remained firmly committed to methodological individualism of a special type – utility maximization, to equilibrium as an organizing concept, and to considerations of efficiency. In addition, the technical apparatus and barrage of associated techniques have, at most, become a little more sophisticated and extensive, with the fundamentals – in terms of production and utility functions – being instantly recognizable, albeit supplemented by the incidence and sources of (market and government) failure.

Thus there can be little doubt, as Garnett (1999) observed, that mainstream economics as a profession continually and dogmatically reasserts its scientific status and superiority relative to other forms of economic discourse, thereby creating boundaries for definition of the profession, entry conditions, and associated benefits in employment, prestige, financial support and intellectual independence. But why, as a discipline, should it seek to extend its supposedly superior form of science to other disciplines, and to development in particular, over and above its enhanced capacity to do so in light of the new information-theoretic economics?

It is possible to posit a certain maturing in the current dynamics of the discipline and its disciples. First, the conditions of entry to the intellectual vanguard of the profession are extremely technically demanding. As the degree of mathematical and statistical sophistication has been ratcheted up, so existing professionals who do not conform have found themselves marginalized to a greater or lesser extent. On the other hand, the newly trained academic economists have been highly tuned into the new techniques and are growing in numbers. There is now no shortage of 'American-trained' economists searching out careers.

Second, in a world of publish or perish, in which a doctorate is not enough, the new recruits need outlets for their abilities, satisfied, to some extent, by the emergence of new journals. But a crucial intellectual factor is involved here: the analytical and technical *principles* underlying the new information-theoretic approach are demanding, but, once commanded, are limited in scope and economic application. It is simply one market imperfection after another. Whether by virtue of intellectual boredom of those who are already well established – one more market, one more twist on a technique – or the search for new avenues by those who have yet to establish themselves, the other social sciences provide a virgin terrain on which to play out those skills that would otherwise exhibit rapidly declining marginal productivity! In effect, neoliberalism is the death of economics because, if the market works perfectly, there is no need to study it. By contrast, the market-imperfect, information-theoretic approach keeps the discipline alive, but only at the expense of intensifying technical virtuosity, relying upon ever-more esoteric models and, most important in reserves of potential, by their extension to non-market applications.

Third, academia in general increasingly depends upon external research funding. Compared to their colleagues in business, accounting, marketing and finance, academic economists are generally unsuited to serving the needs of the private sector. Where they are able to oblige, the rewards they can command by being there heavily outweigh those of remaining within academia. On the other hand, economists have also been less than willing and attractive participants in more publicly-minded research, not least because of being unworldly. As Balakrishnan and Grown revealed in their study of foundation support for economic research:

> When the Ford Foundation funded multidisciplinary graduate programs in social science and health, for example, it found it impossible to convince economists to join the effort. Similarly, when the MacArthur Foundation sponsored a competition for multidisciplinary research on the human dimensions of global environmental change, economists were generally absent from the teams of investigators. (Balakrishnan and Grown 1999: 135)

However, in deploring this absence of economics, Balakrishnan and Grown were heartened by 'recent developments in economics and philanthropy [that] provide new openings to re-examine and renegotiate this relationship' (ibid.: 124–25). They referred specifically to 'lively interest in the economics of information and incentive problems due to asymmetric information in settings as varied as the provision of public services, labour markets, credit markets, insurance markets, and Third World agriculture'. Thus, intellectual, professional and personal imperatives have been conducive to the spread of information-theoretic economics imperialism, consolidating a paradigm of market imperfections extended to non-market outcomes, despite internally unexamined analytical weaknesses from the perspectives of other social sciences. In short, the newer development economics allows for intellectual complacency, (competition for) jobs, publications and research grants!

Lastly, bringing these other factors together – in cementing a core community of development economists – is the World Bank. Previously, throughout the 1980s and into the 1990s, it occupied a hegemonic position in setting the developmental agenda of market versus state. It did so through its own research and research commissioned by others, and through its more general rhetoric in support of structural adjustment and stabilization. While the World Bank and the IMF set the terms of debate through the Washington Consensus, and leaned exclusively to one side, they could not prevent the emergence of the increasingly influential stances of its opponents. Key in this respect have been the ideas of adjustment with a human face, and the significant historical and prospective role of developmental states.

The position of the post-Washington Consensus, while more temperate in its attitude towards the virtues of the market, is otherwise more disturbing. For, it not only seeks to set the analytical agenda as being confined to uncovering and addressing the incidence and consequences of market and non-market imperfections, it also claims that this exhausts the problem of development. Hence the previously quoted claims by Stiglitz for a broader approach to development than earlier, and the idea that the new information-theoretic approach breaks with, rather than promotes, mainstream neoclassical economics.

In this and other respects, a considerable rewriting of the history of development economics is underway, with two disturbing elements. On the one hand, development – as a process as well as a field of study – is reduced to market and non-market imperfections. On the other hand, it is as if the critique of the Washington Consensus only began with the post-Washington Consensus, and with the World Bank's *East Asian Miracle* (1993) perceived as a watershed.[11] Subsequently, all earlier contributions to, and problems within, development tend to be filtered through the information-theoretic or market imperfection approach, as the post-war classics are rediscovered, brushed down and reinterpreted as no longer anomalous through the prism of the new paradigm.[12]

Whither Development Economics?

But, in this account, there are two anomalies. The first is the undue focus on Stiglitz, as if he alone was responsible for these changes. The second, in part explaining the first, is his prominence as economist, Nobel Prize winner and chief economist at the World Bank, from which position he was sacked.[13] This tells us something more about the recent shifts in development economics and how it has been, and not been, appropriated by the Washington institutions. For, at the level of scholarship and general rhetoric, the post-Washington Consensus helped to extract the Washington Consensus from its crisis of legitimacy by offering a more state- and poverty-friendly approach. Further, in principle, it could do so without necessarily departing significantly from the policies of stabilization and adjustment that have been adopted by the Washington Consensus over most of the previous two decades. After all, the post-Washington Consensus merely supports state intervention in identifiable circumstances of market imperfections, for which the cure is demonstrably preferable to the disease. If you really believe in the Washington Consensus, the post-Washington Consensus can allow you to retain a preference for the market and the discretion to intervene for pragmatic or other purposes – and over a wider range of economic and social policy.

In this respect, the post-Washington Consensus is a paler, micro, contingent version of the welfarism/modernization/Keynesianism of the McNamara era, with which it is more usefully and unfavourably (and less often) contrasted than with the Washington Consensus. Its vision of development and how to achieve it is considerably weaker, and confronts less conducive circumstances. Indeed, like the Washington Consensus, the post-Washington Consensus is extremely weak on the nature of development itself, once again substituting means (correct market and institutional imperfections) for processes and outcomes.

To his credit, Stiglitz took his intellectual position to its logical conclusion, heavily criticizing the IMF from within the World Bank for its policies in general (and for privatization in Russia and austere macroeconomic policy in

South Korea). After his departure from the Bank, his criticisms have intensified. There are good reasons, then, for welcoming the post-Washington Consensus, as it supports the turn away from neoliberalism. But, on the other hand, the Washington Consensus was never primarily about withdrawal of the state in practice but of rationalizing discretionary intervention under the veil of being pro-market. There is justifiable concern that the post-Washington Consensus provides a rationale, where one did not exist before, for that intervention and for more besides, in terms of correcting both market and non-market imperfections (Hildyard 1998).

In short, while it is important not to over-generalize on the motives for, and impact of, its policies, the World Bank does appeal to the post-Washington Consensus for rhetorical purposes to signify a more poverty-oriented and state-friendly stance, while policy displays stronger continuities with the Washington Consensus despite equally rhetorical appeals to good governance, country ownership of adjustment programmes, etc. Nor is it possible to exaggerate the influence of the World Bank in development economics. With a research budget in the region of $25 million, Ranis observed of the Bank that: 'Its dissemination efforts, especially in the third world, are prodigious and overwhelming. At the same time, the Bank has paid relatively little attention to the output of other national and international organizations. . . . Indeed even much relevant output by academia is largely ignored' (Ranis 1997: 75).[14]

Such a luxury, or is it disdain, follows from the sheer weight of research, backed up with the power to lend:

> In analyzing the Bank's influence on development economics it must be recognized that the Bank's size gives it a unique position. The Bank employs around 800 professional economists. . . . These resources dwarf those of any university department or research institution working on development economics. There are more than 3,000 additional professionals in the Bank. The size of the Bank's lending program (of the order of $15 billion to $20 billion a year) allows it to exert considerable influence on the thinking and policies of borrowing countries. The weight of the number of development economists, the research budget, and the leverage from lending means that the Bank's potential influence is profound, and that the Bank cannot be seen as just one of a number of fairly equal actors in the world of development economics. (Stern and Ferreira 1997: 524)

Ranis revealed that this role is reactive, rather than proactive, to developmental initiatives:

> The Bank has shown a tendency not to innovate but to take over quickly the leadership on any given theme. . . . More current examples include the environment, women in development, military expenditures and governance. Subjects accepted as topical from either a functional or political point of view are quickly incorporated into Bank language . . . become part of the Bank's research

and analysis agenda, and sometimes even of its stated lending criteria. (Ranis 1997: 74)

There is, however, at least one possible exception to – or is it stunning evidence of Ranis' rule – the lead taken by the World Bank in promoting the neoliberal Washington Consensus from 1980. As Kapur, Lewis and Webb (1997a: 22) reported, the departure of McNamara as president of the World Bank was followed by that of old-style developmentalist, Hollis Chenery, as chief economist. He was succeeded by Anne Krueger, who, 'in turn, replaces large fractions of the Bank's central economics establishment until she had a highly compatible staff'. In contrast to this creation of a community of scholars, the putative shift to the post-Washington Consensus has been marked by the dismissal of its leading proponent! This sharply illustrates that there are connections between the World Bank's rhetoric, scholarship and policies. By stretching those connections a little too far, Stiglitz's goal of a post-Washington Consensus could only be pursued outside of the Washington institutions themselves.

As already mentioned, this places the newer development economics in an ambiguous position. While critical of neoliberalism and the Washington Consensus, it is readily incorporated and neutralized by the Washington institutions, even if more in rhetorical principle than in policy practice. Such is evident from the use made of the new trade theory, the new growth theory and of social capital (see the chapter on 'Social Capital' in this volume). While each of these is rich in dependence upon market imperfections, they have been readily turned towards pro-market and minimalist state perspectives. To a large extent, this is possible (as is the opposite were a McNamara era to be in place) because the post-Washington Consensus and new(er) development economics, more generally, precisely because of their roots in mainstream economics, lag far behind the political economy associated with the attempt to understand problems of development through the idea of globalization. While this concept has its own weaknesses (Fine 2004), it does reflect a genuine attempt to understand the nature of contemporary capitalism as an economic system, to acknowledge the role of the state in that system, and to address issues of power and conflict in the process of development. In some respects, this is to return to the concerns of the old development economics in a way that can only be welcomed.

Notes

1 For critical accounts of the shift from the Washington to the post-Washington Consensus, see Fine (2001), Standing (2000), and Pincus and Winters, eds (2002). For a useful collection of Stiglitz's, see Chang, ed. (2001).

2 That this is a false image of what economists actually do, has long been recognized. See Blaug (1980), McCloskey (1986) and Lawson (1997), for example.

3 Here, the views of Simon Kuznets, Nobel Prize winner as leading empiricist in the study of economic history and development, are instructive. As Huff, Dewit and Oughton commented: 'Modern economic growth, Kuznets (1971: 346) points out, requires a modern nation-state to serve as a clearing house for institutional innovations and to possess the ability to act as "an agency for resolution of conflicts among

group interests; and as a major entrepreneur for the socially required infrastructure"'. (Huff, Dewit and Oughton 2001: 719).

[4] Moral hazard involves not being able to monitor contracts, as in false insurance claims, while adverse selection refers to attraction of lower quality at a lower price.

[5] Hence, when awarded the Nobel Prize with Akerlof and Spence for information-theoretic economics, Stiglitz was specifically cited for 'being one of the founders of modern development economics' (Nobel 2001: 10).

[6] For Kuhn applied across the social sciences, see Gutting, ed. (1980). Khalil (1987) reviews the application of Kuhn to economics, but also see Argyrous (1992, 1994) in debate with Dow (1994).

[7] For a fuller account in the context of development, see Fine (2002).

[8] The approach was previously aired in Stiglitz (1989). Note that, at the same time, a survey of the new development economics by Stiglitz's subsequent successor as chief economist at the World Bank devoted a single paragraph to the issues that he recognized he had omitted. As these included natural resources and the environment, gender, Marxist analysis, transnational corporations, and human capital formation through education, the priorities of his subsequent research agenda, to which the absences are carried over, not surprisingly, were exceedingly narrow (Stern 1989: 672).

[9] On this, related issues and for what follows, see Coats, ed. (1996), Hodgson and Rothman (1999), Bernstein (1999), Siegfried and Stock (1999), Ehrenberg (1999), and Lee and Harley (1998), for example.

[10] Hardly surprising, in view of his earlier definition of it as 'the perfect competition, perfect market model in all of its representations' (Stiglitz 1991: 135). This piece, looking forward to another century of economics science, is also remarkable, in light of later prognostications, for its pessimism over development economics, the 'one important area in which I am less sanguine about the future success of our profession' (ibid.: 140).

[11] This publication represented the last contorted attempt to explain development as a consequence of non-replicable, market-conforming state interventions against all the theoretical and empirical evidence. See Wade (1996).

[12] The most stunning illustration is provided by Paul Krugman. His 'The Fall and Rise of Development Economics' (http://www/wws/edu/~pkrugman/dishpan.html) offers a reconstruction of the lost development economics of the 1940s and 1950s in general, and of Albert Hirschman in particular, but opens by confessing that 'My acquaintance with Hirschman's works is very limited'!

[13] For an account, see Wade (2001).

[14] See also de Vries (1996: 238), who reported that the World Bank distributes one million books and papers, has a catalogue list of five hundred titles, and a scale of publishing equivalent to a sales volume of between $10 and $30 million. For a more wide-ranging account, see Fine (2001).

References

Agénor, Pierre-Richard and Peter J. Montiel (1996), *Development Macroeconomics* (Princeton: Princeton University Press).

Akerlof, George A. (1970), 'The Market for "Lemons": Quality Uncertainty and the Market Mechanism', *Quarterly Journal of Economics*, 84 (3): 488–500.

—— (1990), 'George A. Akerlof', in Richard Swedberg, ed., *Economics and Sociology, Redefining Their Boundaries: Conversations with Economists and Sociologists* (Princeton: Princeton University Press).

Amariglio, Jack L. and David F. Ruccio (1998), 'Postmodernism, Marxism, and the Critique of Modern Economic Thought', in David L. Prychitko, ed., *Why Economists Disagree: An Introduction to the Alternative Schools of Thought* (Albany: SUNY Press).

Argyrous, George (1992), 'Kuhn's Paradigms and Neoclassical Economics', *Economics and Philosophy*, 8 (2): 231–48.

—— (1994), 'Kuhn's Paradigms and Neoclassical Economics: Reply to Dow', *Economics and Philosophy*, 10 (1): 123–26.

Balakrishnan, Radhika and Caren Grown (1999), 'Foundations and Economic Knowledge', in Robert Garnett, ed., *What Do Economists Know? New Economics of Knowledge* (London: Routledge).

Becker, Gary S. (1996), *Accounting for Tastes* (Cambridge, Massachusetts: Harvard University Press).

Bernstein, Michael A. (1999), 'Economic Knowledge, Professional Authority, and the State: The Case of American Economics during and after World War II', in Robert Garnett, ed., *What Do Economists Know? New Economics of Knowledge* (London: Routledge).

Blaug, Mark (1980), *The Methodology of Economics: Or How Economists Explain* (Cambridge: Cambridge University Press).

—— (1998a), 'Disturbing Currents in Modern Economics', *Challenge*, 41 (3): 11–34.

—— (1998b), 'The Problems with Formalism: Interview with Mark Blaug', *Challenge*, 41 (3), 35–45.

Chang, Ha-Joon, ed. (2001), *Joseph Stiglitz and the World Bank: The Rebel Within* (London: Anthem Press).

Chase, Richard (1983), 'The Kuhnian Paradigm Thesis as a Dialectical Process and its Application to Economics', *Rivista Internazionale di Scienze Economiche e Commerciali*, 30 (9): 809–28.

Coats, A.W., ed. (1996), 'The post-1945 Internationalization of Economics', *History of Political Economy*, 28 (Supplement) (Durham, NC: Duke University Press).

de Vries, Barend (1996), 'The World Bank as an International Player in Economic Analysis', *History of Political Economy*, 28 (Supplement): 225–44.

de Vroey, Michel (1975), 'The Transition from Classical to Neoclassical Economics: A Scientific Revolution', *Journal of Economic Issues*, 9 (3): 415–39.

Dow, Sheila (1994), 'Kuhn's Paradigms and Neoclassical Economics', *Economics and Philosophy*, 10 (1): 119–22.

Ehrenberg, Ronald (1999), 'The Changing Distributions of New Ph.D. Economists and their Employment: Implications for the Future', *Journal of Economic Perspectives*, 13 (3): 135–38.

Fine, Ben (1998), *Labour Market Theory: A Constructive Reassessment* (London: Routledge).

—— (2001), *Social Capital versus Social Theory: Political Economy and Social Science at the Turn of the Millennium* (London: Routledge).

—— (2002), 'Economics Imperialism and the New Development Economics as Kuhnian Paradigm Shift', *World Development*, 30 (12): 2057–70.

—— (2004), 'Examining the Idea of Globalization and Development Critically: What Role for Political Economy?', *New Political Economy*, 9 (2): 213–31.

Garnett, Robert (1999), 'Economics of Knowledge: Old and New', in Robert Garnett, ed., *What Do Economists Know? New Economics of Knowledge* (London: Routledge).

Gutting, Gary, ed. (1980), *Paradigms and Revolutions: Applications and Appraisals of Thomas Kuhn's Philosophy of Science* (Notre Dame: Notre Dame University Press).

Hildyard, Nicholas (1998), *The World Bank and the State: A Recipe for Change?* (London: Bretton Woods Project).

Hodgson, Geoffrey and Harry Rothman (1999), 'The Editors and Authors of Economics Journals: A Case of Institutional Oligopoly?', *Economic Journal*, 109 (453): F165–86.

Huff, W.G., G. Dewit and C. Oughton (2001), 'Credibility and Reputation Building in the Developmental State: A Model with East Asian Applications', *World Development*, 29 (4): 711–24.

Kapur, Devesh, John Lewis and Richard Webb (1997a), *The World Bank: Its First Half-Century, Volume I: History* (Washington DC: Brookings Institution).

——, eds (1997b), *The World Bank: Its First Half-Century, Volume II: Perspectives* (Washington DC: Brookings Institution).

Khalil, Elias L. (1987), 'Kuhn, Lakatos, and the History of Economic Thought', *International Journal of Social Economics*, 14 (3): 118–31.

Kuhn, Thomas (1970), *The Structure of Scientific Revolutions*, second edition with postscript (Chicago: Chicago University Press); first edition, 1962.

Kuznets, Simon (1971), *Economic Growth of Nations: Total Output and Production Structure* (Cambridge: Harvard University Press).

Lamoreaux, Naomi R. (1998), 'Economic History and the Cliometric Revolution', in Anthony Molho and Gordon Wood, eds, *Imagined Histories: American Historians Interpret the Past* (Princeton: Princeton University Press).

Lawson, Tony (1997), *Economics and Reality* (London: Routledge).

Lee, Frederic S. and Sandra Harley (1998), 'Peer Review, the Research Assessment Exercise and the Demise of Non-Mainstream Economics', *Capital and Class*, 66: 23–51.

Masterman, Margaret (1970), 'The Nature of a Paradigm', in Imre Lakatos and Alan Musgrave, eds, *Criticism and the Growth of Knowledge* (Cambridge: Cambridge University Press).

McCloskey, Donald (1986), *The Rhetoric of Economics* (Brighton: Wheatsheaf).

McKenzie, Richard (1979), 'The Non-Rational Domain and the Limits of Economic Analysis', *Southern Economic Journal*, 46 (1): 145–57.

Nobel (2001), 'Markets with Asymmetric Information, Advanced Information', www.nobel.se/economics/laureates/2001/public.html.

Pincus, Jonathan and Jeffrey A. Winters, eds (2002), *Reinventing the World Bank* (Ithaca: Cornell University Press).

Ranis, Gustav (1997), 'The World Bank Near the Turn of the Century', in Roy Culpeper, Albert Berry and Frances Stewart, eds, *Global Development Fifty Years after Bretton Woods* (London: Macmillan).

Rostow, Walt W. (1957), 'The Interrelation of Theory and Economic History', *Journal of Economic History*, 17 (4): 509–23.

——— (1990), *The Stages of Economic Growth: A Non-Communist Manifesto*, third revised edition (Cambridge: Cambridge University Press); first edition, 1960.

Siegfried, John and Wendy A. Stock (1999), 'The Labor Market for New Ph.D. Economists', *Journal of Economic Perspectives*, 13 (3): 115–34.

Standing, Guy (2000), 'Brave New Worlds?: A Critique of Stiglitz's World Bank Rethink', *Development and Change*, 31 (4): 737–63.

Stern, Nicholas (1989), 'The Economics of Development: A Survey', *Economic Journal*, 99 (3).

Stern, Nicholas and Francisco Ferreira (1997), 'The World Bank as "Intellectual Actor"', in Devesh Kapur, John Lewis and Richard Webb, eds, *The World Bank: Its First Half-Century, Volume II: Perspectives* (Washington DC: Brookings Institution).

Stiglitz, Joseph E. (1989), 'Markets, Market Failures and Development', *American Economic Review*, 79 (2): 197–202.

——— (1991), 'Another Century of Economic Science', *Economic Journal*, 101 (1): 134–41.

——— (1994), *Whither Socialism?* (Cambridge: MIT Press).

——— (2001a), 'More Instruments and Broader Goals: Moving towards the Post-Washington Consensus', (Wider Annual Lecture, Helsinki, 7 January 1998), in Ha-Joon Chang, ed., *Joseph Stiglitz and the World Bank: The Rebel Within* (London: Anthem Press).

——— (2001b), 'Towards a New Paradigm for Development: Strategies, Policies and Processes', (Prebisch Lecture, UNCTAD, Geneva, 1998), in Ha-Joon Chang, ed., *Joseph Stiglitz and the World Bank: The Rebel Within* (London: Anthem Press).

——— (2001c), 'An Agenda for the New Development Economics', paper at UNRISD meeting on 'The Need to Rethink Development Economics', Cape Town, September, http://www.unrisd.org/engindex/research/rethink.htm.

Stiglitz, Joseph E. and Karla Hoff (1999), 'Modern Economic Theory and Development', Symposium on Future of Development Economics in Perspective, Dubrovnik, 13–14 May.

Toye, John (1993), *Dilemmas of Development*, second edition (Oxford: Blackwell).

Wade, Robert (1996), 'Japan, the World Bank, and the Art of Paradigm Maintenance: *The East Asian Miracle* in Political Perspective', *New Left Review*, 217, May–June: 3–37.

——— (2001), 'Showdown at the World Bank', *New Left Review*, 7: 124–37.

World Bank (1993), *The East Asian Miracle: Economic Growth and Public Policy* (New York: Oxford University Press).

From Washington to Post-Washington Consensus

Illusions of Development

Elisa Van Waeyenberge

Ever since the McNamara presidency, the World Bank has aspired to a leadership role in both the intellectual and policy realms of economic development. Its capacity to do so has varied with the broader environment in which it operates. The 1980s saw a conjunction of events that promoted such a role for the Bank and, by the early 1990s, it attained leadership in an 'aid regime' structured around its identified priorities.

The Bank has since attempted to confront mounting criticism by expanding the reach of its agenda, in the course affecting the broader development agenda. As such, its discourse has moved from an initial focus on stabilization and structural adjustment under the Washington Consensus to promotion of participatory approaches, incorporation of environmental concerns and attention to 'governance', institutional reform, etc. This trend culminated in the Comprehensive Development Framework proposed by its president in the late 1990s, and the concomitant call for a post-Washington Consensus by its senior vice president and chief economist. Development was once again allowed to become a 'broader' process, evoking echoes of the developmental mandate associated with the McNamara era of the past.

This chapter attempts to review the ideas and practices of aid over the last three decades. This is done with a focus on the World Bank as a lead player in both respects, and with a focus on 'economic' issues. It addresses the analytical frameworks drawn upon, compares successive positions and hints at the dynamics affecting agenda change. Significantly, the reasons for changes in aid policy have been multifaceted, relating to factors such as the performance of aid, the particular political, economic and financial environment of aid, the leadership ambitions of key figures in the aid establishment, inter-institutional politics, etc. Ideas regarding development intersect with these variables in different ways at different times.

The main purpose of the chapter is to assess the adequacy, for an understanding of development, of the various frameworks that have been put forward by the World Bank. Predominantly, it seeks to situate the agenda that was implied by the Washington Consensus, and to assess the extent to which the current agenda articulated by the Bank offers substantially new and different insights. Where the Washington Consensus was admittedly characterized by an excessive macro-bias towards stabilization and a restricted micro-agenda of price incentives, the current agenda seeks to 'broaden' the understanding of development. Closer inspection of the latter, however, reveals its intrinsic limitations and weaknesses. The rupture between the Washington and post-Washington Consensuses appears rather circumscribed, with the latter framework perpetuating the incapacity to accommodate the actual economic and social realities of development. Between the Washington and post-Washington Consensuses, illusions of development persist.

The first section of the chapter documents how the approach to development at the World Bank was considerably downscaled in the 1980s, with a neoclassical resurgence superseding the more comprehensive development imperatives of the McNamara Bank. A subsequent section illustrates how, at the policy level, 'monoeconomics' translated into the Washington Consensus, for which policy-based lending provided an opportune conduit. The chapter proceeds to show how, in the wake of poor performance of its programmes and growing criticism, the Bank expanded the reach of its agenda. Poverty was reintegrated into its discourse and implementation was focused upon, with poor economic performance invariably attributed to inadequacies in the latter. Furthermore, it documents how 'fundamental' precepts were safely guarded when the Japanese aid authority sponsored a study of the East Asian miracle in an attempt to move the frontiers of economic orthodoxy at the Bank. Finally, the analysis turns to the emergence of the post-Washington Consensus at the Bank. The innovations in economic theory that provided the backdrop against which the post-Washington Consensus emerged are briefly touched upon, followed by an appraisal of the extent to which it might offer a basis upon which the World Bank can reassert its developmental mandate. Micro-foundations as well as the political–economic realities of aid, however, appear as strongly impairing the prospects for more constructive engagements with development.

From 'Poverty' to 'Structural Adjustment'

During the first two decades of the aid phenomenon (the 1950s and 1960s), its primary goal was to increase the aggregate growth rate of its recipients. Benefits from growth were supposed to trickle down: all members of society, including the poor, would benefit from employment creation and increased production of goods and services. No explicit attention was given to more direct poverty alleviation. Poverty reduction was to be the unspoken but expected and indirect consequence of economic growth. In this vein, development cooperation was primarily concerned with lending for infrastructure (communications, power, transport), which accounted for over 60 per cent of the Bank's portfolio in that period.[1]

By the late 1960s, however, the apparent failure of trickle-down mechanisms spawned increasing concern regarding poverty. The United Nations' General Assembly approved a strategy for the Second Development Decade, which shifted emphasis from GNP growth to combining economic growth with greater satisfaction of 'basic human needs' (United Nations 1973). At the same time, a new president, Robert McNamara, arrived at the World Bank, who perceived it to be his mission to recast the Bank as a leading 'development agency' and to bring poverty to the forefront of the development agenda. During McNamara's term, the Bank saw a nearly fourfold increase in its lending in real terms (Lateef 1995), a redefinition of the nature of development cooperation with a strong emphasis on poverty (McNamara 1981b), and a strengthening of its research functions (Mason and Asher 1973), with a shift towards an economy-wide view and a broadening perspective on what constituted development 'beyond the simple limits of economic growth' (McNamara 1981a). These changes significantly affected the stature and position of the World Bank in development, even if its ensuing dominance mainly unfolded in the subsequent decade.

In his speech at the 1973 Nairobi Annual Meeting of the Bank, McNamara outlined his vision for poverty reduction. Rural development took central place, and lending for smallholder agriculture was to become the chief instrument for poverty alleviation (McNamara 1981b). *Redistribution with Growth* provided the intellectual backbone to the Bank's approach to poverty. It characterized the poor as: first, predominantly rural, and engaged in agriculture and allied rural occupations; second, primarily self-employed; third, lacking capital as measured by ownership of productive assets (for example, land) (Chenery *et al.* 1974: xiv–xv). The key objectives of a poverty reduction strategy included: first, to encourage the use of more labour-intensive processes and products; second, to remove discriminations against small producers; third, to shift public investment and credit in favour of small producers. These were complemented by proposals for redistribution of income through the fiscal system or through direct allocation of consumer goods, and of assets through land reform.

Hence, the World Bank's original poverty reduction strategy mainly focused on increasing the productivity (and, as such, the output and income) of those it perceived to be poor. This implied improving the access to credit, extension assistance, production inputs, etc., complemented by an expansion of public services such as education, health, water supply and public transportation, with specific attention to access by the poor. Later, in the late 1970s, the Bank's agenda broadened to incorporate the notion of 'basic needs'. This agenda, however, was operationalized only to a limited extent. Pure 'welfare spending' without obvious 'productive' outcomes was still frowned upon, and an understanding of basic education or primary health as productive investment was to take hold of the World Bank only subsequently (see Kapur, Lewis and Webb 1997a, Kapur, Lewis and Webb, eds 1997b).[2]

By the end of the 1970s, the proportion of 'poverty lending' in the Bank's total lending had risen to almost 30 per cent (from 5 per cent at the beginning of the decade), while the share of lending for infrastructure had fallen to around 30 per cent (World Bank 1980). Within the 'poverty lending' portfolio, small farmer projects accounted for about 55 per cent, water supply and sewerage for 25 per cent, and other urban poverty loans for 10 per cent. What were subsequently referred to as human resource investments – including primary schooling, health, nutrition and population – accounted for 7 per cent (Kapur, Lewis and Webb 1997a: 310).

The McNamara era at the World Bank was also characterized by a novel stance, which was emphatically disowned by the Bank with the Berg Report (World Bank 1981) regarding the linkage between markets and private ownership (Kapur, Lewis and Webb 1997a). According to McNamara, market incentives did not depend on ownership structures, and so a whole spectrum of mixed types of ownership and control was sanctioned through Bank lending. Traditionally, however, it had been common wisdom at the Bank that a satisfactory market had to be mainly occupied by private firms. Along with market structuring and flexibility, private ownership had always been critical. In this vein, the Bank had aimed to finance public sector industries only in the case of 'natural' monopolies (ibid.). Yet, by the late 1970s, government-owned development finance companies and state-owned industrial enterprises constituted important beneficiaries of Bank lending (World Bank 1980: 6). For McNamara, the state played a key role in development.

The turn of the decade saw a set of events that were to affect the development scene dramatically: a second oil shock provoked another oil price hike, interest rates followed suit (the Volcker shock), and right-wing administrations came to power in the major OECD (Organization for Economic Cooperation and Development) countries. The last implied political hostility to aid, and the former two resulted in a dramatic increase in the financial needs of developing countries. Furthermore, inside the Bank, concern mounted with regard to the limited influence of project lending over policy.

In 1980, the World Bank launched its lending for 'structural adjustment'. Under this programme, a loan would 'promote dialogue' with the borrowing country about development policy and policy reform; would provide finance over a period of several years in direct support of specific policy reforms; and would not be linked to a specific investment programme (non-project) (Mosley, Harrigan and Toye 1991). Where the Bank's finance was originally tied to a particular investment project, it was now obtained for 'untied' balance of payments support. This, however, came at the cost of a conditionality severely impairing the borrower's capacity to set its own development agenda.[3] Furthermore, in the context of the debt crisis (of 1982), the instrument proved to be most useful in allowing money to be moved swiftly (Pereira 1995; Gwin 1997).

Policy lending easily lent itself to ideological affiliation with the right-wing leadership of core shareholders in the Bank (mainly the United States), tempering the initial hostility towards development cooperation as its substantive content was coloured in with a new 'aid discourse' (Gibbon 1993). The latter was articulated in its clearest form for the first time in the Berg Report (World Bank 1981), and the tendency consolidated with the appointment of Anne Krueger as vice president for research at the Bank, replacing Hollis Chenery. The Berg Report presented the stagnant and deteriorating economic conditions in Africa as a product of 'distortions' due to inappropriate government policy interventions. The most damaging of these had been 'over-protection' of industry (with a pro-industry bias in price, tax and exchange rate regimes) and 'over-extension' of the state as a development agency (ibid.: 4). Such a state of affairs had resulted from the 'power of entrenched local interests', mainly urban consumers and producers, employees of industrial parastatals, civil servants, and others (ibid.: 7), a coalition of interests reflecting an 'urban bias' (Lipton 1977). The principal effect had been a secular decline in export performance, particularly agricultural exports.

The Berg Report recommended, first, that agricultural producers' prices be restored to market levels accompanied by a complementary exchange rate adjustment; second, that crop marketing and input supply be opened up to the private sector (involving abolition of export crop parastatals, as well as removal of subsidies and price controls); and third, that agricultural extension and research services be restructured.[4] Thus, the report basically argued for 'restoration' of the 'superior' allocative role of the price system and 're-establishment' of the incentives deriving from private ownership, the quintessential agenda of subsequent structural adjustment. This indicated the rise of 'monoeconomics' in development, as applicable across time and space, with which development economics ceased to exist as a sub-discipline (Hirschman 1981). 'Economic rationality' characterized agents in the less as well as more developed countries, and the universality of neoclassical economics with the postulates of rationality and principles of maximization came to have general applicability (Meier 1999).

As clearly articulated by Krueger (in the first issue of the *World Bank Research Observer*): 'Once it is recognized that individuals respond to incentives, and that "market failure" is the result of inappropriate incentives rather than of non-responsiveness, the separateness of development economics as a field largely disappears' (Krueger 1986: 62). In a similar vein, Williamson (1990: 19) had remarked, in a closing note to his famous statement on the Washington Consensus (see below), how the latter implied a dismissal of the development literature 'as a diversion from the harsh realities of the dismal science', with none of the ideas spawned by the development literature – such as the big push, balanced or unbalanced growth, surplus labour, the two-gap model – playing any role in it.

So, the beginning of the 1980s saw a disappearance of poverty from the aid agenda, a new preoccupation with macroeconomic imbalances, a narrowing of the understanding of development (economics) and a dramatic increase in the imposition of conditionalities. Significantly, aid became increasingly structured around the ideas and practices of the World Bank and its Bretton Woods twin, the International Monetary Fund (IMF) (see Gibbon 1993; Killick and Hewitt 1996; Ferreira and Stern 1997).

Policy-based Lending and the Washington Consensus

By the mid-1980s, the ideas about economic management underlying the structural adjustment and stabilization programmes advocated by the Bretton Woods institutions had become readily accepted orthodoxy in the official donor community. The conditions set by the World Bank and the IMF aimed at economic policy reform with the purpose of eliminating all obstacles to a 'perfect market' as the presumed optimal path to growth. What came to be referred to as the 'Washington Consensus' (Williamson 1990) proposed (or rather imposed) stabilization of the economy through control of money supply, and enhancement of growth through a set of supply-side measures aimed at boosting private sector activity.

More specifically, it gave recommendations regarding ten policy instruments. First, budget deficits, which cause inflation and capital flight, needed to be kept under strict control ('fiscal discipline'). Second, government subsidies needed to be curtailed and government expenditures redirected towards education, health, infrastructure ('public expenditure redirection'). Third, the tax base needed to be broadened and marginal tax rates cut ('tax reform'). Fourth, interest rates were to be market-determined ('interest rate liberalization'). Fifth, exchange rates were to be 'competitive', stimulating exports ('exchange rate management'). Sixth, tariffs were to replace quotas, and reduced as fast as possible ('trade liberalization'). Seventh, foreign direct investment was to be encouraged by dismantling barriers to entry ('liberalization of FDI'). Eighth, state-owned enterprises were to be privatized ('privatization'). Ninth, the economy needed to be deregulated, that is, regulations that impede the entry of new firms or restrict competition were to be abolished ('deregulation'). And tenth, property rights had to be established and enforced ('secure property rights').

While the World Bank was originally involved in structural adjustment programmes (SAPs), acting on the supply side of an economy, the IMF concentrated on the demand side through its stabilization programmes. This initial division of labour implied different working areas for both institutions: the IMF would concentrate on money supply, budget deficits and the exchange rate; the World Bank would concentrate on liberalization of the economy (internally and externally) in order to eliminate distortions to the market mechanism ('getting prices right'), and to allow for the savings and foreign exchange constraint on investment to be overcome, hence allowing growth to materialize.

By the end of the 1980s, however, the World Bank increasingly incorporated performance conditions with regard to inflation and balance of payments in its adjustment programmes. Specific programme instruments were assigned new objectives: fiscal policy's main concern was to reduce inflation, that of the real exchange rate to improve the current account, and that of monetary policy to set right the external balance in terms of foreign exchange reserves (World Bank 1992: 2). Such respecification of the roles of fiscal and monetary policies showed greater emphasis on demand management (stabilization) than on economic growth. The World Bank and the IMF had evolved from 'fraternal' to 'identical' twins (Mosley, Subasat and Weeks 1995). Analytically, Khan and Montiel (1989) attempted to 'marry' the IMF stabilization (Polak) model and the World Bank's growth framework (revised minimum standard model) to produce a framework of 'growth-oriented adjustment'.[5]

Policy-based lending grew significantly during the 1980s.[6] The Bank's 'structural adjustment lending' (SAL) was supplemented with 'sectoral adjustment lending' (SECAL, 1982), aiming to reform policy with a sectoral focus and allowing for policy-based lending to expand more rapidly (Mosley, Harrigan and Toye 1991: 52). The IMF initiated its 'structural adjustment facility' (SAF) in 1986, followed by the 'enhanced structural adjustment facility' (ESAF) a year later. By the end of the 1980s, programme or adjustment lending constituted some 20 per cent of all bilateral aid flows (17 per cent, excluding debt reorganization) (White 1996), while, for the Bank, adjustment lending made up 26 per cent of its portfolio in 1989 (Kapur, Lewis and Webb 1997a: 520). In the mid-1990s, programme aid still constituted over 20 per cent of all aid flows (Mosley 1999).

During 1980–90, the World Bank's conditionalities were distributed across various sectors approximately as follows: trade 15 per cent, industry 7 per cent, energy 5 per cent, agriculture 18 per cent, social sector 1 per cent, financial sector 8 per cent, public institutions and regulation 8 per cent, public enterprise reform 13 per cent, fiscal 17 per cent, monetary 1 per cent, exchange rate 2 per cent, wages 1 per cent. These averages mask strong growth in the relative shares of public enterprise reform, public institutions/regulation and the financial sector, while conditionalities bearing on trade, industry, energy and agriculture relatively declined (Kapur, Lewis and Webb 1997a: 521).

Policy-based lending prompted a large literature (see Wood 1997). The critical literature aimed to expose the limited understanding of development (and/or stabilization) encapsulated in the World Bank/IMF-advocated approaches, and served to document its pernicious implications. A sketchy account follows, of some of the main issues.[7]

The Washington Consensus relies on the theory of perfectly working markets. In the Arrow–Debreu framework of general equilibrium (GE) theory, the competitive market yields welfare-maximizing (Pareto-efficient) outcomes in the absence of externalities, public goods and natural monopolies, when there is a complete set of markets, and for given preferences, initial endowments and technology (first welfare theorem). Further, every Pareto-efficient allocation can be attained through the market (second welfare theorem), implying a distributionally neutral market mechanism. Within this framework, government activity is limited to lump-sum redistributions and correction of a well-defined set of market failures. Government should allow prices to be 'right' (reflecting scarcity and preferences) and individual economic agents to allocate resources efficiently in response to these signals. In the context of growth, the emphasis is on capital shortage as the main constraint.[8]

Within the remit of mainstream economic theory, a set of issues can be raised revealing the limitations of the above for an understanding of developing economies.[9] First is the general inadequacy of GE theory for an analysis of developing economies characterized by missing markets and imperfect information (Stiglitz 1986, 1989; see further below). Second are the implications of the theory of the second best in the context of manifold 'distortions' (Mosley 1991; Falvey and Dong Kim 1992). Third are the limited (static) efficiency gains to result from 'perfectly working markets' (Lall 1995). Fourth is the inadequate understanding of constraints on growth implied in a Harrod–Domar framework (capital as sole constraint) (Weeks 1992; Pack 1993) and no accommodation for structural change (fixed capital–output ratio).

Fundamentally, the highly abstract assumptions upon which the policy prescriptions of the Bretton Woods institutions were based are incapable of accommodating country-specific features (Stein 1992). Furthermore, there are inconsistencies between the tools used for stabilization and structural adjustment, with significantly damaging implications for investment levels (ibid.; Stewart 1994; Bird 1997). Finally, the theory of perfectly working markets was supplemented with a set of strongly biased normative presumptions regarding the public sector (Streeten 1993). Essentially, in the 'new political economy', governments consist of self-serving bureaucrats who pursue their own interests at the expense of the common good.[10] Furthermore, public sector investment 'crowds out' private activity.[11]

Critical observations along these lines mainly implied a re-emphasis on the need for state intervention for successful development. While, in this manner, rejoining a large literature that had demonstrated the successful and pervasive role of the state in promoting economic development, such a predisposition tended to perpetuate an underlying analytical dichotomy of market versus state, to the detriment of an investigation of the political-economic dynamics steering both state and market outcomes (Fine and Rustomjee 1996). An analysis along the latter lines would imply particular attention to socio-economic structures and processes, how these change in the wake of structural adjustment, and the concomitant implications for accumulation and economic development (see Gibbon 1996; Bangura 1994; Olukoshi 1996; Chachage 1993; Sachihonye 1993; Wuyts 1994). With the difficulty of singling out the implications of 'reform' from those of the aid flows that reduce stringent balance of payments constraints (Helleiner 1992, Doriye, White and Wuyts 1992),[12] the evidence on structural adjustment and stabilization has been mainly negative, or ambiguous at most (see Mosley and Weeks 1993; Stein 1992; Pack 1993; Cornia, Jolly and Stewart, eds 1987; Gibbon, Havnevik and Hermele 1993; White 1996c; Adam 1995; Elbadawi 1992; Mosley, Subasat and Weeks 1995; Bleaney and Fielding 1995; de Valk 1994; Bourguignon, de Melo and Morrisson 1991; Lall 1995; Bennell 1995; Cornia and Stewart 1990).

From 'Structural Adjustment' to 'Institutions' and 'Poverty': The Washington Consensus Expands

By the late 1980s, one decade into structural adjustment, the World Bank itself could not avoid admitting the poor economic performance of a number of countries that had engaged in World Bank/IMF-inspired reform programmes (World Bank 1989).[13] Moreover, the performance of the Bank portfolio had declined, with the percentage of evaluated operations with satisfactory outcomes falling from 85 at the beginning of the decade to 69 at its end (Kapur, Lewis and Webb 1997a: 42). However, rather than questioning the general presumptions regarding market efficiency contained in its programmes, or reflecting upon the somewhat restricted nature of the presumed 'growth' benefits associated with free market interaction, it proposed to extend conditionality to 'areas responsible for the adoption of good policies'. 'The fundamental weakness in these programmes [SAPs]', it was argued, 'is the lack of local capacity, both private and public, in their design and execution' (World Bank 1989: 62). Logically, 'good' policy not only needed to be made (or accepted), but also needed to be implemented. The advocates of adjustment and stabilization programmes shifted the analysis towards mechanisms of implementation. This was supported by a growing literature on the 'political economy' of reform in developing countries (Haggard and Webb 1993; Johnson and Wasty 1993; Krueger 1993; Sahn, ed. 1994).[14]

Hence, the macroeconomic reforms advocated by the international financial institutions became conceived of as 'technical', with their implementation requiring 'governance' reforms (Frischtak 1994; Gordon 1996; Leighton 1996). The traditional (economic) reform agenda of the 1980s, exemplified in the conditionalities attached to the structural adjustment/stabilization programmes, was extended to incorporate issues of a traditionally more political nature. These encompassed public sector management, accountability and transparency of the public sector, the legal framework, corruption, military expenditure, etc. (World Bank 1994b). In addition, recipient governments were urged to adopt a more participatory approach to setting and implementing their development priorities (World Bank 1994c).[15] Further, 'effective change' could no longer be imposed from outside. The donor–recipient relationship was cast in a new light. New, 'more consultative' approaches (with an emphasis on 'ownership') were promoted. Implementation of aid programmes now involved 'partnerships' with recipient governments as well as non-governmental organizations ('civil society').

The World Bank's report on adjustment in Sub-Saharan Africa (World Bank 1989: 45) had equally conceded that growth did not necessarily reduce poverty. Admittedly, a preoccupation with adjustment had diverted attention from social issues. The challenge now was 'to make up for lost time' (ibid.). The 1990 *World Development Report* on poverty purportedly put it back on the agenda. A three-pronged strategy was elaborated. The opportunities of the poor to use their most abundant asset, labour, had to be increased (primarily through agriculture-driven growth); the quality of their labour had to be enhanced (through improved targeting of social services), augmenting their capacity to take advantage of increased opportunities; and, secondarily, there was a need for social safety nets or targeted transfer programmes (for residual poverty groups who could not benefit immediately from the first two measures) (World Bank 1990: 3).

Implementation of the strategy was to be guided by the general principles that, first, the volume of lending should be linked to a country's effort to reduce poverty; and, second, the composition of lending should support efforts to reduce poverty (World Bank 1991: 20).[16] Furthermore, the renewed preoccupation with poverty aimed to incorporate the 'multidimensional' or 'institutional' aspects of the phenomenon (Salmen 1990). This implied a set of different propositions regarding 'adequate' role of government. While, with the focus on poverty of the 1970s, the government had been assigned the central responsibility for the implementation of poverty-reducing programmes, now a 'pluralistic' approach was advocated. A whole range of organizations (private contractors, NGOs, community groups) was to be drawn upon for implementation of social programmes in 'partnership' with public agencies (Psacharopoulos and Nguyen 1997). The conception of social policy as professional and/or hierarchical provision of social services was replaced by the idea of provision by commercial and public interest bodies, with the state playing a regulatory, purchasing and residual provider role (McKintosh 1995).

These various additions to a set of core precepts attested to the Bank's capacity to manage new issues successfully while glossing over unchanged underlying realities (Gibbon 1993). The Bank had comfortably confronted various criticisms by opportunistically expanding its social agenda, safeguarding the underlying economic agenda. The latter was strongly confirmed with the 1991 *World Development Report: The Challenge of Development*. As observed by Gibbon:

> The organization had recognized that its best chance of survival was expansion and subsequently worked to a game plan which involved launching bids for expert status with regard to current issues, manufacturing a consensus around its interpretation of them, blaming others for its own earlier mistakes in the area, proposing market solutions with mitigatory or compensatory elements, using plans for mitigation/compensation as a basis for attracting new funding, and using the outcome to promote cross-conditionality and through it strengthen its own hegemony. (ibid.: 60)

The author added: '[W]hile the World Bank has been the gainer in this process, the issues themselves have suffered theoretical and practical trivialization.' In practice, the expansion of the agenda gave birth to successive generations of SAPs, pegging 'social concerns' (expenditure reviews, social safety nets, compensatory programmes) and 'participatory measures' ('transparency', 'ownership', role of 'social partners') on to the core policies of stabilization, liberalization and privatization (see van der Geest and van der Hoeven 1999).

When Japan, the Bank's second most important shareholder, attempted to challenge its (core) economic orthodoxy, the institute once again displayed its faculty for 'paradigm maintenance' (Wade 1996). In what a Japanese aid official was to describe as the intellectual awakening of a sleeping partner at the Bank (Goto 1998), the Overseas Economic Cooperation Fund (OECF) – the main Japanese aid agency – began to question the Bank's stance on structural adjustment (Overseas Economic Cooperation Fund 1991). The issues raised touched upon: first, sustainability of growth in the context of structural adjustment and the possible need for additional investment promotion measures; second, the possible need for protection of certain industries in order for some viable export industry to develop (instead of the Bretton Woods institutions' blanket liberalization policies); third, doubts regarding the (exclusive) reliance on market mechanisms for the mobilization of development finance (accompanied by a proposal for subsidized lending under certain circumstances); and fourth, the conditions under which privatization was being carried out (ibid.).

Subsequently, Japan commissioned the World Bank to undertake a study of the East Asian development experience. The consequent report, *East Asian Miracle: Economic Growth and Public Policy*, explored 'the contribution of fundamental and interventionist policies to East Asia's remarkable growth' (World Bank 1993: 26). The report argued that East Asia's economic success had been largely achieved by 'getting the basics right'. A stable macroeconomic environment had provided the 'essential framework for private investment', policies had raised financial savings levels, successful education policies had been pursued (building human capital), and a bias against the agricultural sector had been avoided. Further, price distortions had been kept within reasonable bounds, the economies had been opened to foreign ideas and technology (ibid.: 5), and the 'necessary' levels of flexibility had been maintained in labour markets (ibid.: 19).

The report continued, however, that these 'fundamentals' did not tell the entire story. In most of these economies, 'the government intervened . . . to foster development, and in some cases the development of specific industries'. Assessing whether these interventions were successful or not in contributing to growth then became the 'most difficult question' the report tried to answer (ibid.: 24). It drew the conclusion that 'in a few economies, mainly in Northeast Asia, in some instances, government interventions resulted in higher and more equal growth than otherwise would have occurred'. However, the 'prerequisites for success' had been so rigorous that policy-makers seeking to follow similar paths in other developing economies would meet with failure. This touched upon issues of external environment (the particulars of the trading regime) and institutional capabilities of the particular governments (high-quality bureaucracies).

The final conclusion, then, unsurprisingly, was that 'although the sheer diversity of these policies precludes drawing any simple lessons', 'pragmatic adherence' to the fundamentals (the market-oriented aspects of East Asia's experience) could be recommended with few reservations (ibid.: 26). Thus, in the same report, the World Bank managed, first, to admit a theoretical case for

industrial policy; second, to refute its empirical importance for industrial performance in East Asia; and third, to offer practical objections on why the policy was
not transferable to other countries (Chang 1999).[17]

However, even if, to the consternation of its initiators, the *East Asian
Miracle* report endorsed a continuing 'market-friendly' approach in a neoclassical framework, to a certain extent, it facilitated 'a shift from the simple dichotomy of government or market towards the seeking of a cooperative relationship
between the two – government as well as market' (Goto 1998: 59). Next, the
Bank was to find a way to move beyond structural adjustment and the East Asian
miracle, that is, to move on from neoclassical economics, a question 'at the
frontier of development economics' (Goto 1997: 7). Stiglitz was to take up the
challenge, one that became compelling with the scant fruits of international financial institutions-led transitions in the Eastern European countries (see Florio 2002)
and the outbreak of a series of international financial crises (Mexico in 1994,
East Asia in 1997–98, Russia in 1998, Brazil in 1999).

The Post-Washington Consensus

In his 1998 WIDER lecture, Stiglitz strongly argued for a reconsidera-
tion of the Washington Consensus, which, for him, had advocated the use of 'a
small set of instruments (including macroeconomic stability, liberalized trade,
and privatization)' to achieve 'a relatively narrow goal (economic growth)' (Stiglitz
1998a: 13). Furthermore, while the Washington Consensus may not have been
sufficient for development, certain successful performers 'paid little heed to it'. A
narrow focus on economic issues no longer sufficed – development, now involving 'transformation of society', implied issues of sustainability, equity and democracy (ibid.). In its core area (the economic realm), the Washington Consensus
had been 'at best incomplete and at worst misguided' (ibid.: 3). A focus on inflation, for Stiglitz, had led to macroeconomic policies that were not the most
conducive to long-term growth, and had detracted attention from other sources
of macroeconomic instability such as weak financial sectors.

More generally, the focus on trade liberalization, deregulation and
privatization had been to the detriment of important other conditions ('ingredients') for stability and long-term development. These comprised: robust financial
systems which necessitate a strong legal framework as well as regulatory and
oversight institutions, regulation for the privatized industries, competition policy,
investments in human capital, technology policies, etc. In all these areas, government was to complement the market (see below). Furthermore, the new
approach sought 'broader' goals. Development was no longer a 'mere interplay
of economic variables' but a 'holistic' process, a transformation of society (Stiglitz
1998b). Most of the previous development strategies had only focused on 'pieces
of that transformation', often 'failing miserably' (ibid.: 5). Their most important
failure had been a narrow focus on economics, conceiving development as a
'technical problem requiring technical solutions' (ibid.: 6). The Comprehensive
Development Framework, put forward by the World Bank president, endorsed

the 'holistic broad-based approach to development'. Constraints on development were now 'structural' and 'social', not remediable solely through economic stabilization and/or structural adjustment (World Bank 1999).

The new agenda thus tried, at least in principle, to move beyond the reductionist conception of the development process characterized by a macro-economic bias towards stabilization, a microeconomic bias towards price incentives and a focus on physical capital as the predominant constraint on growth. It further sought to project a different view of state–society interactions. Following the 1997 *World Development Report*, development became an 'inter-sectoral cooperation process'. Such posturing was stronger on rhetoric than substance, and conveniently failed to extend its vision of past development thinking and policy to the *pre*-Washington (McNamara) Consensus. Nonetheless, the projected antagonism between state and society/market had given way to a notion of 'partnership': the private and the public sector had become intimately 'entwined' (Stiglitz 1998a).

The persistence of market failure and missing markets was increasingly recognized. Such failures, however, no longer implied 'old-style' government intervention where the state 'supplanted' the market. Now, 'modern' ways were to be deployed. Furthermore, with different sources and degrees of market failure (and states with varying levels of 'capability'), the implications for the role of the state could differ significantly across countries (World Bank 1997: 26). The issue then became a quest for a particular institutional set-up (a 'partnership' between state and society – private profit and non-profit sectors) that maximizes 'benefits to society'. Crucially, the state is to make sure that market failures are overcome without imposing 'unnecessary' costs on society. As a result, when its 'capability' is low, the state is to rely, as much as possible, on the relative strengths of the private sector, the community, the family and the individual ('citizen') (Stiglitz 1998b).

This redefinition of the World Bank's approach also attempted to recast its (perceived) relationship with the IMF. While the era of structural adjustment had entailed important overlaps in activities undertaken by the two, this re-styling of the World Bank's agenda implied an explicit differentiation of its activities and, hence (again), a separate role for the two institutions. As averred by the World Bank president, Wolfensohn, at the 1998 Annual Meeting of the Bretton Woods institutions: 'In rewriting the 1989 Concordat which governed the relationship between the Bank and the Fund, the institutions have . . . reasserted the conventional demarcation between the Fund's predominantly short-term macro-economic focus and the Bank's longer-term structural focus'.[18] However, when the new agenda provided a platform for opposition to the cherished policies of the Washington Consensus, the fragility of the new 'consensus' swiftly surfaced (see below).

The new agenda reflected a set of propositions that had become increasingly popular in development economics. These drew on a collection of mainstream innovations, rejecting an implicit framework of general equilibrium and exogenous growth. More particularly, assumptions regarding market structure (imperfect competition), attributes of the economic agent (imperfect information and/or bounded rationality), production characteristics (increasing returns to scale) and/or presence of complete set of markets were challenged with a set of theoretical innovations, each of which had important implications for the workings of the price system. Meanwhile, growth theory had moved from an 'exogenous' description to new conceptualizations of growth, endogenizing the technology variable and/or incorporating increasing returns (see Fine 2003, and chapter entitled 'New Growth Theory: More Problem than Solution' in this volume). Further, either through these theoretical innovations or through extension of the old (orthodox) on to new analytical terrain, traditionally non-economic issues came to be increasingly addressed within the discipline (see Fine 1997, 2002).

In sum, two trends were at work: on the one hand, a restatement of mainstream economic theory, which incorporated economic features recognized as increasingly important in the 'real' world (economies of scale, imperfect information, missing markets, etc.); on the other, through both this type of innovation and 'Becker-type endeavours' (Fine 1997), the economic analysis moved to address features beyond the 'economic' (institutions, family, social networks, etc.). These innovations purportedly accommodated the context of development. As asserted by Bardhan: 'In particular, as economic theory has turned more towards the study of information-based market failures, coordination failures, multiple roles of prices and the general idea of the potential complexity of market interactions, it has *inevitably* turned to questions that have long exercised development economics' (Bardhan 1993: 139; emphasis added).

Moreover, with this endeavour, it was claimed that the 'old debates' of development economics, with their particular emphasis on economies of scale, were being revisited (see Murphy, Shleifer and Vishny 1989; Coricelli, de Matteo and Hahn, eds 1998; Krugman 1999; Ros 2000) but with recently acquired 'scientific legitimacy'. As Krugman put it:

> Good ideas were left to gather dust in the economics attic for more than a generation; great minds retreated to the intellectual periphery. . . . The truth is, I fear, that there is not much that can be done about the kind of intellectual waste that took place during the fall and rise of development economics. A temporary evolution of ignorance may be the price of *progress*, an inevitable part of what happens when we try to make sense of the world's complexity. (Krugman 1999; emphasis added)

Finally, these theoretical 'advances' took place in the context of the end of the Cold War, which apparently implied the 'liberation' of thinking about development issues: 'Although the end of the cold war did not produce a windfall of resources for development cooperation, it has liberated thinking about development issues from the constraints of competing ideologies and world views. A greater convergence of views between industrialized and developing countries about issues is evident' (Organization for Economic Cooperation and Development 1995: 3). If there had not been a convergence of income, at least there seemed to be 'convergence' of ideas, with those derived from the erstwhile socialist bloc disturbing thinking much as the state had been seen as distorting policy.

Hence, after a temporary retreat of development from economics during the reign of the Washington Consensus, a 'resurgence' of 'development economics' seemed to be taking place. This new framework purportedly incorporated issues whose neglect had rendered the preceding analysis incomplete, and claimed to revisit important matters touched upon in earlier debates on, and approaches to, development (in the 1950s). Furthermore, the new approach allegedly anchored the economic analysis of development in its broader 'social reality'.

Also, while the Washington Consensus was built on a theoretical body of 'perfect markets' with a concomitant need for a retreat of the state, these mainstream innovations introduced a notion of 'imperfect markets' that required some intervention. They further drew attention to non-market (non-state) ways of coordinating economic/'social' activity arising out of optimizing behaviour. As such, the economy became conceived of beyond the market. The 'modern' theory of market failure, however, asserted that government interventions 'may not actually improve matters' (Stiglitz 1996: 156), and a set of specific ideas was put forward regarding the form intervention should take. The issue was no longer whether the state should or should not be involved but, rather, how it should. New ways of coordinating economic activity were explored, beyond the propositions of traditional welfare economics. Essentially, these were built around a set of incentive mechanisms (beyond the price system) that structure interaction between economic agents beyond the market (in collective action, 'civil society' organizations, etc.).

The Post-Washington Consensus: Comprehensive Development?

It remains then, to assess what the meaning of the post-Washington Consensus has been, and can be, for both the aid policy of the World Bank and the understanding of development. Consider the former issue first. A closer look at current Bank practice reveals a macroeconomic stance in which the Washington Consensus is 'alive and kicking'. Proposals to allocate aid flows 'selectively' (World Bank 1998a) have accompanied the Bank's newly asserted identity as a 'Knowledge Bank' (World Bank 1998b). Building on assertions of aid and conditionality ineffectiveness, it has been argued that aid only contributes to development when 'good' policies and institutions already prevail. Thereupon, a two-pronged approach to aid allocation has been proposed: channel lending ('aid flows') to countries with 'appropriate' policy/institutional environments, and use non-lending services ('aid ideas') to support the emergence of sound policies and good governance in countries lacking these initial parameters (see Gilbert, Powell and Vines 1999; Squire 2000; Gunning 2000; Collier 2000). As clearly stated in its policy document on aid:

> In sum, there is no value in providing large amounts of money to a country with poor policies, even if it technically commits to the conditions of a reform program. . . . In countries with poor policies donor should concentrate on activities that might support reform in the long run – overseas scholarships, dissemination of ideas about policy reform and development, and stimulation of debate in civil society. . . . The role of international institutions should be to disseminate information that might influence public dialogue about policy reform. (World Bank 1998a: 58–59)

Cleverly, low (and not 'large') levels of aid relative to need and potential impact become excused and justified as the spearheads of more appropriate policies and policy-making. The less we provide, the more we must advise! And poor policies are inevitably attached to recipient governments rather than to the international financial institutions themselves.

These propositions have been institutionalized in the use of Country Policy and Institutional Assessments (CPIAs) as allocative tools for aid flows (Collier and Dollar 2002), and (in) a whole set of 'knowledge' initiatives aimed at 'sharing' the Bank's 'expertise' on development (see World Bank 2003). Apart from being based on a dramatically biased reading of both aid and conditionality experiences (see Hansen and Tarp 2000; Lensink and White 2000; McGillivray and Morrissey 2000), the selectivity proposition is, furthermore, strongly anchored in Washington Consensus-style macroeconomic policies, with the CPIAs built around the core indicators of budget surplus, low inflation and trade openness (see Burnside and Dollar 2000). The imperatives of 'sound' policy that steered the Washington Consensus have obviously not lost their grip over aid practice (see Williamson 2000). If anything, their leverage has been enhanced with selective aid allocations. As noted by Fine: 'Whatever the academic significance of the post-Washington Consensus, its policy implications are to be subordinated to those attached to whatever is perceived to be sound, or, more exactly, globally free finance and reliance upon "fundamentals"' (Fine 2001a: 19; see also Peet 2003). Yet, the incompatibility of these 'fundamentals' with development imperatives remains (see Chang 2002).[19]

The latter 'contradiction' might have contributed to the resignations from the Bank of both Joseph Stiglitz and Ravi Kanbur (director of the 2000 *World Development Report* on poverty) (see Fine 2001a; Wade 2002). Stiglitz's resignation followed his critical comments on the IMF's handling of financial crises in East and Southeast Asia, in particular its high interest rate policy and policy conditionalities. Kanbur seems to have left over disagreements on the implications of trade liberalization, financial liberalization and privatization ('globalization') for the poor (Kanbur 2001). Soon after these officials left the Bank, Anne Krueger was appointed senior deputy managing director of the IMF, its sister institution.

As for the micro-part of the post-Washington Consensus, Bank practice seems to have been more permeated by it, particularly by its attention to non-market issues and micro-determinants. The 2000 *World Development Report* on poverty, to some extent, exemplified its approach,[20] and World Bank poverty projects have attempted to incorporate micro-determinants and 'non-economic' factors. The question remains as to whether the post-Washington Consensus provides us with useful insights into the processes of development, particularly given its alleged capacity to accommodate both the 'economic' and the 'non-economic', and to theorize 'beyond the market'. Unfortunately, the verdict on that front is also rather disappointing. The restatement of an analysis of development proposed by Stiglitz and others essentially proceeds on the same principles of optimization and rationality as its predecessor, setting it apart mainly by changes in the assumptions regarding the attributes of the economic agents and the environments in which they optimize. As such, 'softening' of the assumptions strengthens social theory on the basis of methodological individualism, with its well-known limitations for addressing either the 'economic' or the 'social', first taking the social out to reintroduce and 'reconstruct' it afterwards.[21] Hence, the extension of the analysis into the traditionally non-economic has been at the expense of substantive content and analytical power.[22]

Finally, in the context of its propositions regarding the role of the state, it is true that, compared to the 'rolling back of the state' – a precept of the Washington Consensus – some progress seems to have been made with the post-Washington Consensus, with its stronger recognition of the importance of the state for a sound working of the economy. The role of the latter, however, essentially remains confined to the creation of a conducive environment for the private sector to fulfil its 'dynamic' role in development. The government is there essentially to improve the institutional environment in which private agents steer their interaction in socially desirable directions (now beyond the market and in response to incentives other than just prices). The abiding legacy of the new political economy, with its normative presumptions regarding the public sector, implies a persistent (underlying) bias against direct management of economic resources by the state: the market (or now the non-market non-state) remains superior. Even in comparison with the pre-Washington Consensus, McNamara era, the post-Washington Consensus appears as a 'regression' (Fine 2001:15), contrasting with the former's tolerance (and support) for state-controlled development enterprises.[23]

A Final Note

Official aid has fallen persistently since the mid-1990s, both in absolute terms and as a percentage of donors' income (World Bank 2003). Meanwhile, the World Bank has successfully promoted its selective aid allocation process where 'bad' states receive less (or no) money; the deflationary bias that has characterized policy lending since the early 1980s persists; and private sector development (PSD) has become the Bank's most important activity, accounting for 30 per cent of total World Bank (Group) lending (and guarantee) activity. As observed by Miller-Adams (1999), the PSD agenda has been pursued by the World Bank with a vigour characterizing no other agenda since the 1980s, and PSD operations have doubled in low-income countries over the last twenty years. The PSD strategy has been a vehicle for the promotion of a role for the private (and often, foreign) sector in areas ranging from infrastructure to basic service provisioning.[24] Whatever the changes in Bank rhetoric, the underlying imperatives, even if shifting, remain pervasive (see also Fine and Stoneman 1996).

Notes

[1] The remaining 40 per cent was distributed among productive sectors, with only a very small share of less than 5 per cent allocated to the social sectors (education, population, nutrition, water supply, urbanization) (Kapur, Lewis and Webb 1997a, Kapur, Lewis and Webb, eds 1997b).

[2] See van de Laar (1980) on how the poverty emphasis at the Bank affected the aid agenda of other multilateral and bilateral donors during the 1970s.

[3] Policy-based lending, of course, was not new, arising out of the constitution of the International Monetary Fund (IMF). The advent, as such, of 'structural adjustment lending' (SAL) at the Bank implied issues of overlap, which the institutions attempted to deal with through increased cooperation and collaboration. See Mosley, Harrigan and Toye (1991) for lurking issues of consistency, and also Ahluwalia (1999). See Polak (1997) for an elaborate account of the changing relationship between the IMF and the World Bank.

[4] See Sender and Smith (1984), Lele (1989), and Gibbon, Havnevik and Hermele (1993) for comprehensive critiques of the Berg Report.

[5] See Fine and Hailu (2002) for the limits of this 'marriage'.

[6] Apart from this important increase in policy-based lending, the aid phenomenon additionally witnessed strong growth of two other novel trends: aid disbursed through NGOs and aid targeted directly at the private sector. These trends, however, fitted easily with the anti-state bias prevailing in the neoliberal aid paradigm (see Nelson 1995 for the former, and Miller-Adams 1999 for the latter).

[7] See van der Geest (1994) for a comprehensive overview.

[8] See Tarp (1993) for a comprehensive review of the analytical issues bearing on structural adjustment and stabilization.

[9] For a comprehensive critique of neoclassical general equilibrium theory, see Weeks (1989).

[10] See Chang (1996) for a comprehensive overview of the various theories that constitute the new political economy. See Chang and Singh (1992) for a reappraisal of public enterprise performance in developing countries.

[11] See Greene and Villanueva (1991) for evidence of 'crowding in'.

[12] See Mosley, Harrigan and Toye (1991) on issues regarding measurement of the impacts of reform packages.

[13] See Mosley and Weeks (1993) for a critical reading of World Bank reports on structural adjustment in Africa in the 1980s.

[14] See Gibbon, Bangura and Ofstad, eds (1992) for counter-arguments.

[15] For a critical analysis of the governance agenda, see Robinson, ed. (1995). See Cooke and Kothari, eds (1999) on participation.

[16] For critical comments, see Shaffer (1996), Toye and Jackson (1996), White (1996b), Emmerij (1995) and Rich (2002).

[17] For other critical dissection of the report, see Amsden (1994) and Singh (1998).

[18] The 1989 Bank–Fund Concordat was established after the Argentina incident in 1988, when the Bank had decided to go ahead with adjustment lending even though negotiations with the IMF for an extended fund facility had collapsed. Rather than eliminating the overlap between the World Bank and the IMF, however, the Concordat implicitly accepted it, and focused on improving the coordination between the IMF and the Bank (see Ahluwalia 1999).

[19] See also Weisbrot *et al.* (2000) in response to Dollar and Kraay (2000); Bird (1997) on the importance of the *financing* role of the international financial institutions for investment and growth; Bird (1999) on how 'sound' macroeconomics does not even guarantee private capital inflows.

[20] See Sender (2002) for comments on the report.

[21] See Fine (2002) for a comprehensive critique.

[22] See Fine (2001b) for an elaborate critique.

[23] For an engaging compilation of alternative propositions on various aspects of growth and development, see Chang, ed. (2003).

[24] See CNES (2001), and Bayliss and Hall (2001), for critical analyses of the World Bank's PSD strategy.

References

Adam, Christopher (1995), 'Adjustment in Africa: Reforms, Results and the Road Ahead', review article, *World Economy*, 18 (5): 729–35.

Ahluwalia, Montek (1999), 'The IMF and the World Bank in the New Financial Architecture', *International Monetary and Financial Issues for the 1990s, Volume 11* (Geneva: UNCTAD).

Arestis, Philip and Malcolm Sawyer, eds (1998), *The Political Economy of Economic Policies* (New York: St Martin's Press).

Amsden, Alice (1994), 'The World Bank's East Asian Miracle: Economic Growth and Public Policy', *World Development*, 22 (4), Special Section.

Bangura, Yusuf (1994), 'Economic Restructuring, Coping Strategies and Social Change: Implications for Institutional Development in Africa', UNRISD Discussion Paper 52, UNRISD, Geneva.

Bardhan, Pranab (1993), 'Economics of Development and the Development of Economics', *Journal of Economic Perspectives*, 7 (2), Spring: 129–42.

Bayliss, Kate and David Hall (2001), 'A PSIRU Response to the World Bank's "Private Sector Development Strategy: Issues and Options"', Public Services International Research Unit, University of Greenwich.

Bennell, Paul (1995), 'British Manufacturing Investment in Sub-Saharan Africa: Corporate Responses during Structural Adjustment', *The Journal of Development Studies*, 32 (2): 195–217.

Bird, Graham (1995), *IMF Lending to Developing Countries: Issues and Evidence* (London: Routledge).

—— (1997), 'External Financing and Balance of Payments Adjustment in Developing Countries: Getting a Better Policy Mix', *World Development*, 25 (9): 1409–20.

—— (1999), 'How Important is Sound Domestic Macroeconomics in Attracting Capital Inflows to Developing Countries?', *Journal of International Development*, 11: 1–26.

Bleaney, Michael and David Fielding (1995), 'Investment, Trade Liberalization and Structural Adjustment', *Journal of Development Studies*, 32 (2): 175–94.

Bourguignon, Francois, Jaime de Melo and Christian Morrisson (1991), 'Poverty and Income Distribution during Adjustment: Issues and Evidence from the OECD Project', *World Development*, 19 (11): 1485–508.

Burnside, Craig and David Dollar (2000), 'Aid, Policies and Growth', *American Economic Review*, 90 (4) (September): 847–68.

Chachage, C.S.L. (1993), 'Forms of Accumulation, Agriculture and Structural Adjustment in Tanzania', in Peter Gibbon, ed., *Social Change and Economic Reform in Africa* (Uppsala: Nordiska Afrikainstitutet), 215–43.

Chang, Ha-Joon (1996), *The Political Economy of Industrial Policy* (London: Macmillan).

—— (1999), 'Industrial Policy and East Asia: The Miracle, the Crisis and the Future', paper presented at the World Bank workshop on 'Re-thinking East Asian Miracle', San Francisco, February.

—— (2002), *Kicking Away the Ladder: Development Strategy in Historical Perspective* (London: Anthem Press).

Chang, Ha-Joon, ed. (2003), *Rethinking Development Economics* (London: Anthem Press).

Chang, Ha-Joon and Ajit Singh (1992), 'Public Enterprises in Developing Countries and Economic Efficiency', UNCTAD Discussion Paper 48, August.

Chenery, Hollis, Montek Ahluwalia, Clive Bell, John Duloy and Richard Jolly (1974), *Redistribution with Growth* (London: Oxford University Press).

CNES (2001), 'Growing Dangers of Service Apartheid: How the World Bank Group's Private Sector Development Strategy Threatens Infrastructure and Basic Service Provision', *News and Notices*, 2 (5), Winter.

Collier, Paul (2000), 'Conditionality, Dependence and Coordination: Three Current Debates in Aid Policy', in Christopher Gilbert and David Vines, eds, *The World Bank: Structure and Policies* (Cambridge: Cambridge University Press): 299–324.

Collier, Paul and David Dollar (2002), 'Aid Allocation and Poverty Reduction', *European Economic Review*, September: 46 (8): 1475–500.

Cooke, Bill and Uma Kothari, eds (1999), *Participation, the New Tyranny* (London: Zed Books).

Cornia, Giovanni A., Richard Jolly and Frances Stewart, eds (1987), *Adjustment with a Human Face: Protecting the Vulnerable and Promoting Growth* (Oxford: Clarendon Press).

Cornia, Giovanni A. and Frances Stewart (1990), 'The Fiscal System, Adjustment and the Poor', Innocenti Occasional Paper 11, UNICEF, Geneva.

Cornia, Giovanni A. and Gerald K. Helleiner, eds (1994), *From Adjustment to Development in Africa* (London: Macmillan).

Coricelli, Fabrizzo, Massimo di Matteo and Frank Hahn, eds (1998), *New Theories in Growth and Development* (Basingstoke: Macmillan).

Culpeper, Roy, Albert Berry and Frances Stewart, eds (1997), *Global Development Fifty Years after Bretton Woods* (London: Macmillan).

de Valk, Peter (1994), 'A Review of Research Literature on Industry in Sub-Saharan Africa under Structural Adjustment', in Rolf van der Hoeven and Fred van der Kraaij, eds, *Structural Adjustment and Beyond in Sub-Saharan Africa* (London: James Currey): 227–39.

Dollar, David (1999), 'The Comprehensive Development Report and Recent Development Research', Development Research Group, World Bank, Washington DC.

Dollar, David and Aart Kraay (2000), 'Growth is Good for the Poor', Policy Research Working Paper 2587, World Bank, Washington DC.

Doriye, Joshua, Howard White and Marc Wuyts (1992), 'Imports, Investment and Aid in Tanzania', in Karel Jansen and Rob Vos, eds, *External Finance and Adjustment: Failure and Success in the Developing World* (Basingstoke: Macmillan): 234–59.

Elbadawi, Ibrahim (1992), 'World Bank Adjustment Lending and Economic Performance in Sub-Saharan Africa in the 1980s: A Comparison of Early Adjusters, Late Adjusters and Non-Adjusters', Policy Research Working Paper 1001, World Bank, Washington DC.

Emmerij, Louis (1995), 'A Critical Review of the World Bank Approach to Social Sector Lending and Poverty Alleviation', *International Monetary and Financial Issues for the 1990s*, Vol. 5 (Geneva: UNCTAD).

Falvey, Rod and Cha Dong Kim (1992), 'Timing and Sequencing Issues in Trade Liberalization', *Economic Journal*, 102, July: 908–24.

Ferreira, Francisco and Nicholas Stern (1997), 'The World Bank as "Intellectual Actor"', in Devesh Kapur, John Lewis and Richard Webb, eds, *The World Bank: Its First Half-Century, Volume II: Perspectives* (Washington DC: Brookings Institution): 523–609.

Ferreira, Francisco and Louise Keely (2000), 'The World Bank and Structural Adjustment: Lessons from the 1980s', in Christopher Gilbert and David Vines, eds, *The World Bank: Structure and Policies* (Cambridge: Cambridge University Press): 159–95.

Fine, Ben (1997), 'The New Revolution in Economics', *Capital and Class*, 61, Spring: 143–48.

—— (2001a), 'Neither the Washington nor the post-Washington consensus: An Introduction', in Ben Fine, Costas Lapavitsas and Jonathan Pincus, eds, *Development Policy in the Twenty-first Century: Beyond the Post-Washington Consensus* (London: Routledge): 1–27.

—— (2001b), *Social Capital versus Social Theory: Political Economy and Social Science at the Turn of the Millennium* (London: Routledge).

—— (2002), 'Economics Imperialism and the New Development Economics as Kuhnian Paradigm Shift?', *World Development*, 30 (12), December: 2057–70.

—— (2003), 'New Growth Theory', in Ha-Joon Chang, ed., *Rethinking Development Economics* (London: Anthem Press): 201–18.

Fine, Ben and Zavareh Rustomjee (1996), *The Political Economy of South Africa* (London: Hurst and Company).

Fine, Ben and Colin Stoneman (1996), 'Introduction: State and Development', *Journal of Southern African Studies*, 22 (1), March: 5–26.

Fine, Ben, Costas Lapavitsas and Jonathan Pincus, eds (2001), *Development Policy in the Twenty-first Century: Beyond the Post-Washington Consensus* (London: Routledge).

Fine, Ben and Degol Hailu (2002), 'Convergence and Consensus: The Political Economy of Stabilization, Poverty and Growth', Centre for Development and Policy Research, Discussion Paper 22, School of Oriental and African Studies, University of London.

Florio, Massimo (2002), 'Economists, Privatization in Russia and the Waning of the "Washington Consensus"', *Review of International Political Economy*, 9 (2), Summer: 374–415.

Frischtak, Leila (1994), 'Governance, Capacity and Economic Reform in Developing Countries', Technical Paper 254, World Bank, Washington DC.

Gibbon, Peter (1993), 'The World Bank and the New Politics of Aid', *European Journal of Development Research*, 5 (1): 35–62.

—— (1996), 'Structural Adjustment and Structural Change in SSA: Some Provisional Conclusions', *Development and Change*, 27 (4), October: 751–84.

Gibbon, Peter, ed. (1993), *Social Change and Economic Reform in Africa* (Uppsala: Nordiska Afrikainstitutet).

Gibbon, Peter, Yusuf Bangura and Arve Ofstad, eds (1992), *Authoritarianism, Democracy and Adjustment: The Politics of Economic Reform in Africa* (Uppsala: Nordiska Afrikainstitutet).

Gibbon, Peter, Kjell Havnevik and Kenneth Hermele (1993), *A Blighted Harvest: The World Bank and African Agriculture in the 1980s* (London: James Currey).

Gibbon, Peter and Adebayo Olukoshi (1996), 'Structural Adjustment and Socio-Economic Change in Sub-Saharan Africa: Some Conceptual, Methodological and Research Issues', Research Report 102 (Uppsala: Nordiska Afrikainstitutet).

Gilbert, Christopher, Andrew Powell and David Vines (1999), 'Positioning the World Bank', *Economic Journal*, 109, November: 598–633.

Gilbert, Christopher and David Vines, eds (2000), *The World Bank: Structure and Policies*, (Cambridge: Cambridge University Press).

Gordon, David (1996), 'Sustaining Economic Reform under Political Liberalization in Africa: Issues and Implications', *World Development*, 24 (9): 1527–37.

Goto, Kazumi (1997), 'Some Thoughts on Development and Aid: Japan's Strategic Response', *OECF Journal of Development Assistance*, 3 (1): 1–18.

—— (1998), 'Concluding Remarks', Special Feature: A New Vision of Development Cooperation for the Twenty-first Century, *OECF Journal of Development Assistance*, 3 (2), March: 57–61.

Greene, Joshua and Delano Villanueva (1991), 'Private Investment in Developing Countries: An Empirical Analysis', *IMF Staff Papers* 38 (1): 33–53.

Gunning, Jan (2000), 'Rethinking Aid', paper presented at 12th Annual Bank Conference on Development Economics, World Bank, Washington DC, 18–20 April.

Gwin, Catherine (1997), 'US Relations with the World Bank, 1945–1992', in Devesh Kapur, John Lewis and Richard Webb, eds, *The World Bank: Its First Half-Century, Volume II: Perspectives* (Washington DC: Brookings Institution).

Haggard, Stephan and Steven B. Webb (1993), 'What Do We Know about the Political Economy of Economic Policy Reform', *The World Bank Research Observer*, 8 (2), July: 143–68.

Hansen, Henrik and Finn Tarp (2000), 'Aid Effectiveness Disputed', *Journal of International Development*, 12: 375–98.

Helleiner, Gerald (1992), 'The IMF, the World Bank and Africa's Adjustment and External Debt Problems: An Unofficial View', *World Development*, 20 (6): 779–92.

Hirschman, Albert (1981), 'The Rise and Decline of Development Economics', in Albert Hirschman, *Essays in Trespassing* (Cambridge: Cambridge University Press): 1–24.

Jansen, Karel and Rob Vos, eds (1995), *External Finance and Adjustment: Failure and Success in the Developing World* (Basingstoke: Macmillan).

Johnson, John and Sulaiman Wasty (1993), 'Borrower Ownership of Adjustment Programmes and the Political Economy of Reform', World Bank Discussion Paper 199, World Bank, Washington DC.

Kanbur, Ravi (2001), 'Economic Policy, Distribution and Poverty: The Nature of Disagreements', *World Development*, 29 (6), June: 1083–94.

Kapur, Devesh, John Lewis and Richard Webb (1997a), *The World Bank: Its First Half-Century, Volume I: History* (Washington DC: Brookings Institution).

——, eds (1997b), *The World Bank: Its First Half-Century, Volume II: Perspectives* (Washington DC: Brookings Institution).

Khan, Mohsin S. and Peter J. Montiel (1989), 'Growth-Oriented Adjustment Programs: A Conceptual Framework', *IMF Staff Papers* 36 (2): 279–306.

Killick, Tony (1998), 'Responding to the Aid Crisis', *International Monetary and Financial Issues for the 1990s*, Vol. 9 (Geneva: UNCTAD).

Killick, Tony and Adrian Hewitt (1996), 'Bilateral Aid Conditionality and Policy Leverage', in Olav Stokke, ed., *Foreign Aid towards the Year 2000: Experiences and Challenges*, (London: Frank Cass): 130–67.

Krueger, Anne (1986), 'Aid in the Development Process', *World Bank Research Observer*, 1 (1).

—— (1993), *Political Economy of Policy Reform in Developing Countries* (Cambridge, Massachusetts and London: MIT Press).

Krugman, Paul (1999), 'The Fall and Rise of Development Economics', http://web.mit.edu/krugman/www/dishpan.html.

Lall, Sanjaya (1995), 'Structural Adjustment and African Industry', *World Development*, 23 (12): 2019–31.

Lateef, Sarwar (1995), 'The First Half-Century: An Overview', in Sarwar Lateef, ed., *The Evolving Role of the World Bank* (Washington DC: World Bank).

Lele, Uma (1989), 'Agricultural Growth, Domestic Policies, the External Environment and Assistance to Africa: Lessons of a Quarter Century', MAIDA Discussion Paper 1, World Bank, Washington DC.

Leighton, Carolyn (1996), 'Strategies for Achieving Health Financing Reform in Africa', *World Development*, 24 (9), September: 1511–26.

Lensink, Robert and Howard White (2000), 'Aid Allocation, Poverty Reduction and the *Assessing Aid* Report', *Journal of International Development*, 12: 399–412.

Lipton, Michael (1977), *Why Poor People Stay Poor: A Study of Urban Bias in World Development* (London: Temple Smith).

Mason, Edward S. and Robert S. Asher (1973), *The World Bank Since Bretton Woods* (Washington DC: Brookings Institution).

McGillivray, Mark and Oliver Morrissey (2000), 'Aid Fungibility in *Assessing Aid*: Red Herring or True Concern?', *Journal of International Development*, 12: 413–28.

McKintosh, Maureen (1995), 'Competition and Contracting in Selective Social Provisioning', *European Journal of Development Research*, 17 (1), June: 26–52.

McNamara, Robert (1981a), Address to the Board of Governors, Copenhagen, Denmark, 21 September 1970, in Robert McNamara, *The McNamara Years at the World Bank* (Baltimore: Johns Hopkins University Press): 96–109.

—— (1981b), Address to the Board of Governors, Nairobi, Kenya, 24 September 1973, in Robert McNamara, *The McNamara Years at the World Bank* (Baltimore: Johns Hopkins University Press): 208–31.

Meier, Gerald (1999), 'The Old Generation of Development Economists and the New', paper presented at the World Bank symposium on the Future of Development Economics in Perspective, Dubrovnik, 13–14 May.

Miller-Adams, Michelle (1999), *The World Bank: New Agendas in a Changing World* (New York: Routledge).

Mosley, Paul (1991), 'Structural Adjustment: A General Overview, 1980–89', in V.N.

Balasubramanyam and Sanjaya Lall, eds, *Current Issues in Development Economics* (London: Macmillan): 223–42.

—— (1999), 'Recent Changes in Aid Technology: Is the White Paper an Adequate Response?', *Public Administration and Development*, 19 (1): 19–29.

Mosley, Paul, Jane Harrigan and John Toye (1991), *Aid and Power: The World Bank and Policy-based Lending* (London: Routledge).

Mosley, Paul and John Weeks (1993), 'Has Recovery Begun? Africa's Adjustment in the 1980s Revisited', *World Development*, 21 (10): 1583–606.

Mosley, Paul, Turan Subasat and John Weeks (1995), 'Assessing Adjustment in Africa', *World Development*, 23 (9): 1459–73.

Murphy, Kevin, Andrei Shleifer and Robert Vishny (1989), 'Industrialization and the Big Push', *Journal of Political Economy*, 97 (5): 1003–26.

Nelson, Joan (1996), 'Promoting Policy Reforms: The Twilight of Conditionality?', *World Development*, 24 (9): 1551–59.

—— (1995), *The World Bank and Non-Governmental Organizations: The Limits of Apolitical Development* (Houndmills: Macmillan).

Organization for Economic Cooperation and Development (OECD) (1995), *Participatory Development and Good Governance* (Paris: OECD/DAC).

Olukoshi, Adebayo (1996), 'Extending the Frontiers of Structural Adjustment Research in Africa: Some Notes on the Objectives of Phase II of the NAI Research Programme', in Peter Gibbon and Adebayo Olukoshi, eds, 'Structural Adjustment and Socio-Economic Change in Sub-Saharan Africa: Some Conceptual, Methodological and Research Issues', Research Report (Uppsala: Nordiska Afrikainstitutet).

Pack, Howard (1993), 'Productivity and Industrial Development in Sub-Saharan Africa', *World Development*, 21 (1): 1–16.

Peet, Richard (2003), *Unholy Trinity: The IMF, World Bank and WTO* (London: Zed Books).

Pereira, Luis (1995), 'Development Economics and the World Bank's Identity Crisis', *Review of International Political Economy*, 2 (2): 211–47.

Pincus, Jonathan and Jeffrey Winters, eds (2002), *Reinventing the World Bank* (Ithaca: Cornell University Press).

Polak, Jacques (1997), 'The World Bank and the IMF: A Changing Relationship', in Devesh Kapur, John Lewis and Richard Webb, eds, *The World Bank: Its First Half-Century, Volume II: Perspectives* (Washington DC: Brookings Institution): 473–521.

Psacharopoulos, George and Nguyen Xuan (1997), 'The Role of Government and the Private Sector in Fighting Poverty', Technical Paper 346, World Bank, Washington DC.

Ranis, Gustav (1997), 'The World Bank near the Turn of the Century', in Roy Culpeper, Albert Berry and Frances Stewart, eds, *Global Development Fifty Years after Bretton Woods* (London: Macmillan): 72–89.

Rich, Bruce (2002), 'The World Bank under James Wolfensohn', in Jonathan Pincus and Jeffrey Winters, eds, *Reinventing the World Bank* (Ithaca: Cornell University Press): 26–53.

Riddell, Roger (1987), *Foreign Aid Reconsidered* (London: James Currey).

Robinson, Mark, ed. (1995), *Towards Democratic Governance*, IDS Bulletin, 26 (2), April.

Ros, Jaime (2000), *Development Theory and the Economics of Growth* (Ann Arbor: Michigan University Press).

Sachihonye, Lloyd (1993), 'Structural Adjustment, State and Organized Labour in Zimbabwe', in Peter Gibbon, ed., *Social Change and Economic Reform in Africa* (Uppsala: Nordiska Afrikainstitutet).

Sahn, David, ed. (1994), *Adjusting to Policy Failure in African Economies* (London: Cornell University Press).

Shaffer, Paul (1996), 'Beneath the Poverty Debate: Some Issues', *IDS Bulletin*, 27 (1): 23–65.

Salmen, Lawrence (1990), 'Institutional Dimensions of Poverty', Policy, Research and External Affairs Working Paper 44, World Bank, Washington DC.

Sender, John and Sheila Smith (1984), 'What's Right with the Berg Report and What's Left of its Critics?', Discussion Paper 192, Institute of Development Studies, Brighton.

Sender, John (2002), 'Reassessing the Role of the World Bank in Sub-Saharan Africa', in Jonathan Pincus and Jeffrey Winters, eds, *Reinventing the World Bank* (Ithaca: Cornell University Press) 185–202.

Singh, Ajit (1998), 'Competitive Markets and Economic Development: A Commentary on World Bank Analyses', in Philip Arestis and Malcolm Sawyer, eds, *The Political Economy of Economic Policies* (New York: St Martin's Press).

Squire, Lyn (2000), 'Why the World Bank Should be Involved in Development Research', in Christopher Gilbert and David Vines, eds, *The World Bank: Structure and Policies* (Cambridge: Cambridge University Press): 108–31.

Stein, Howard (1992), 'Deindustrialization, Adjustment, the World Bank and the IMF in Africa', *World Development*, 20 (1): 83–95.

Stern, Nicholas (1989), 'The Economics of Development: A Survey', *Economic Journal*, 99, September: 597–685.

Stewart, Frances (1994), 'Are Short-Term Policies Consistent with Long-Term Development Needs in Africa?', in Giovanni A. Cornia and Gerald K. Helleiner, eds, *From Adjustment to Development in Africa* (London: Macmillan): 98–136.

Stiglitz, Joseph (1986), 'The New Development Economics', *World Development*, 14 (2): 257–65.

—— (1989), 'Markets, Market Failures and Development', *American Economic Review*, 79 (2): 197–202.

—— (1996), 'Some Lessons from the East–Asian Miracle', *World Bank Research Observer*, 11 (2): 151–77.

—— (1998a), 'More Instruments and Broader Goals: Moving towards the post-Washington Consensus', Wider Annual Lecture, Helsinki, 7 January.

—— (1998b), 'Towards a New Paradigm for Development: Strategies, Policies and Processes', Prebisch Lecture, Geneva, UNCTAD, October.

—— (1998c), 'Redefining the Role of the State – *What* should it do? *How* should it do it? And *how* should these decisions be made?', paper presented at the Tenth Anniversary of MITI Research Institute, Tokyo, March.

Stokke, Olav, ed. (1996), *Foreign Aid Towards the Year 2000: Experiences and Challenges* (London: Frank Cass).

Streeten, Paul (1987), 'Structural Adjustment: A Survey of the Issues and Options', *World Development*, 15 (12): 1469–82.

—— (1993), 'Markets and States: Against Minimalism', *World Development*, 21 (8): 1281–98.

Tarp, Finn (1993), *Stabilization and Structural Adjustment: Macroeconomic Frameworks for Analyzing the Crisis in SSA* (London: Routledge).

Toye, John and Carl Jackson (1996), 'Public Expenditure Policy and Poverty Reduction: Has the World Bank got it Right?', *IDS Bulletin*, 27 (1): 56–66.

United Nations (1973), *Implementation of the International Development Strategy* (New York: United Nations).

van de Laar, Aart (1980), *The World Bank and the Poor* (London: Nijhoff).

van der Geest, Willem (1994), 'A Review of the Research Literature on the Impact of Structural Adjustment in Sub-Saharan Africa', in Rolf van der Hoeven and Fred van der Kraaij, eds (1994), *Structural Adjustment and Beyond in Sub-Saharan Africa* (London: James Currey): 197–226.

van der Geest, Willem and Rolf van der Hoeven (1999), *Adjustment, Employment and Missing Institutions in Africa: The Experience of Eastern and Southern Africa* (Oxford: James Currey).

van der Hoeven, Rolf and Fred van der Kraaij, eds (1994), *Structural Adjustment and Beyond in Sub-Saharan Africa* (London: James Currey).

Wade, Robert (1996), 'Japan, the World Bank, and the Art of Paradigm Maintenance: The East Asian Miracle in Political Perspective', *New Left Review*, 217, May–June: 3–37.

—— (1997), 'Greening the Bank: The Struggle over the Environment 1970–1995', in Devesh Kapur, John Lewis and Richard Webb, eds, *The World Bank: Its First Half-Century, Volume II: Perspectives* (Washington DC: Brookings Institution).

—— (2002), 'US Hegemony and the World Bank: The Fight over People and Ideas', *Review of International Political Economy*, 9 (2), Summer.

Weeks, John (1989), *A Critique of Neoclassical Macroeconomics* (London: Macmillan).

—— (1992), *Development Strategy and the Economy of Sierra Leone* (New York: St Martin's Press).

Weisbrot, Mark, Dean Baker, Robert Naiman and Gila Neta (2000), 'Growth May Be Good for the Poor – But Are IMF and World Bank Policies Good for Growth?', CEPR Briefing Paper, Center for Economic Policy Research, Washington DC, August.

White, Howard (1996a), 'Evaluating Programme Aid: Introduction and Synthesis', *IDS Bulletin*, 27 (4): 1–13.

—— (1996b), 'How Much Aid is Used for Poverty Reduction', *IDS Bulletin*, 27 (1): 83–99.

—— (1996c), 'Review Article: Adjustment in Africa', *Development and Change*, 27 (4): 785–815.

Williamson, John (1990), 'What Washington Means by Policy Reform', in John Williamson, ed., *Latin American Adjustment: How Much Has Happened?* (Washington DC: Institute for International Economics).

—— (2000), 'What Should the World Bank Think about the Washington Consensus', *The World Bank Research Observer*, 15 (2), August: 251–64.

Wood, Angela (1997), *Structural Adjustment Programmes: A Bibliography* (London: Bretton Woods Project).

World Bank (1980), *The World Bank and the World's Poorest* (Washington DC: World Bank).

—— (1981), *Accelerated Development in Sub-Saharan Africa: An Agenda for Action* (Washington DC: World Bank).

—— (1989), *Sub-Saharan Africa: From Crisis to Sustainable Growth* (Washington DC: World Bank).

—— (1990), *World Development Report 1990: Poverty* (New York: Oxford University Press, for World Bank).

—— (1991), 'Assistance Strategies to Reduce Poverty', World Bank Policy Paper (Washington DC: World Bank).

—— (1992), *World Bank Structural and Sectoral Adjustment Operations: The Second OED Overview* (Washington DC: World Bank).

—— (1993), *East Asian Miracle: Economic Growth and Public Policy* (Washington DC: World Bank).

—— (1994a), *Adjustment in Africa: Reforms, Results and the Road Ahead* (Washington DC: World Bank).

—— (1994b), *Governance: the World Bank's Experience* (Washington DC: World Bank).

—— (1994c), *The World Bank and Participation* (Washington DC: World Bank).

—— (1997), *World Development Report 1997: The State in a Changing World* (New York: Oxford University Press, for World Bank).

—— (1998a), *Assessing Aid: What Works, What Doesn't, and Why*, World Bank Policy Research Report (New York: Oxford University Press, for World Bank).

—— (1998b), *World Development Report 1998–1999: Knowledge for Development* (New York: Oxford University Press, for World Bank).

——— (1999), A Proposal for a Comprehensive Development Framework, http://siteresources.worldbank.org/CDF/Resources/cdf.pdf.

—— (2003), *Global Development Finance 2003* (Washington DC: World Bank).

—— (2003), *Sharing Knowledge, Innovations and Remaining Challenges* (Washington DC: Operations Evaluation Department, World Bank).

Wuyts, Marc (1994), 'Accumulation, Industrialization and the Peasantry: A Reinterpretation of the Tanzanian Experience', *Journal of Peasant Studies*, 21 (2), January: 159–93.

Kicking Away the Logic

Free Trade is Neither the Question
Nor the Answer for Development

Sonali Deraniyagala and Ben Fine

Since the 1980s, neoliberal belief in free trade has come to be the ortho-doxy in international economics. This orthodoxy has been translated into policy advice, particularly for developing countries, for which trade liberalization has become a major policy objective. Over the past decade or so, there have been several theoretical and empirical challenges to this belief in the efficiency and equity of free trade. However, while the orthodoxy in trade policy has undergone some revisions since the late 1990s, the conviction that free trade promotes growth and prosperity remains steadfast. In particular, Prasch (1996) finds that support for free trade among academic economists in the United States is, astonishingly, as high as 97 per cent. This has allowed Anne Krueger (1997), a leading propo-nent of the Washington Consensus from the World Bank in the 1980s and from the International Monetary Fund (IMF) in the new millennium, to declare that a case for anything other than free trade marks the esoteric mischief-making of abstract economic theory far removed from economic realities. Such are the terms in which the ideologues of *laissez faire* contrast their virtual world (Carrier and Miller, eds 1998) with that of their critics. The latter merely seek to acknow-ledge the realities of imperfect competition, static and dynamic economies of scale, intra-affiliate trade by multinational corporations and, hence, doubts about the unambiguous virtues of free trade, especially in light of the historical experi-ence of the successfully industrialized countries.

A later section of this chapter takes up these issues in the context of 'effective protection rate', the key concept used to analyse, measure and reform trade policy. The concept is shown to be fundamentally flawed because of its dependence on the unrealistic assumptions of perfect competition, full employ-ment, etc. When we measure and seek to reduce the effective protection rate, we are including all the effects of imperfect competition, etc., but proceeding as if they did not exist. The effective protection rate offers no guide to policy.

Such insights are supported by the earlier, more general discussion of trade theory, empirics and policy. The next section examines the theoretical and empirical cases for free trade as a stimulus to development. The cases are found to be riddled with flaws, and it is shown that the claim that free trade is good for development is unproven. The same applies to the more recent view that poverty alleviation is enhanced by trade liberalization. Like other issues that have come on to the developmental agenda, free trade (as with other neoliberal *mantras*) offers a universal panacea.

The third section takes up developments within the new trade theory, which is itself becoming a not-so-new orthodoxy. The main conclusion to be derived from the new trade theory is that sector-specific conditions are paramount in determining the impact of trade policy, particularly the nature and incidence of market imperfections. Less recognized, but equally important, is trade policy's interaction with other elements of industrial policy – those dealing with skills, technology, spin-off linkages, competition, access to finance, etc. – favouring infant industry and import-substituting stances.

Two inescapable conclusions emerge from our review. First, general propositions concerning trade policy are misplaced. Attention must be devoted to country- and sector-specific conditions. Second, trade policy cannot be satisfactorily broached independently of other elements of policy. In effect, reducing tariffs by rote is a form of economic lobotomy – slash and see what happens. As a corollary to these propositions, some light is shed on the commitment to free trade. If forced, inappropriately, to pitch policy at the general and isolated level of trade reform by itself, there is an instinctive reaction to rely on the market in an intellectual environment of neoliberalism. To proceed otherwise would require our two conclusions to be confronted – the need to situate trade in relation to other policy, and in the context of specific countries and sectors. In other words, closing the door on trade policy is the first and foremost defence against more comprehensive, effective, and targeted trade and industrial policy that has proven indispensable in earlier paths to development.

Trade and Development: The Conventional Wisdom

The orthodox approach to international trade is based on the proposition that free trade promotes economic growth and global prosperity. The neoliberal resurgence in international economics since the early 1980s gave almost axiomatic status to the virtues of free trade, a view that is now the conventional wisdom. Belief in free trade was an essential part of the 'Washington Consensus' propagated by the neoliberal resurgence. This orthodox position on international trade and trade policy consists of several propositions on the benefits of free trade: optimizing global resource allocation; maximizing consumer welfare; increasing productivity growth and promoting economic growth. In contrast, government intervention in trade policy is generally presented as distortionary, reducing welfare and growth. Thus, countries with liberal trade regimes supposedly grow faster than countries with 'closed' regimes, while trade liberalization, by lowering tariffs and non-tariff barriers, should be the focus of trade policy.

Neoliberal trade policy in the 1980s supposedly responded to the economic collapse of developing countries which, until then, had followed protectionist import substitution policies. Orthodox trade economists blamed poor performance on interventionist trade policy. This interpretation was influenced by important empirical studies of trade protection that highlighted the magnitude of static inefficiencies in import substitution regimes (Balassa 1988; Little, Scitovsky and Scott 1970). As noted by Rodrik (2001), however, there are several problems with this. Many developing countries experienced satisfactory rates of economic growth under protection until around the mid-1970s, with some Sub-Saharan African countries being among the fastest growing developing countries. Productivity growth in some import substitution regimes, especially in Latin America, was also robust. While developing countries did experience serious economic downturns after the mid-1970s, this is better explained by external shocks (in particular, the 1973 oil price hike) and the inability to adjust macroeconomic policy to cope with these shocks. To attribute the growth collapse of the late 1970s to trade policy alone, therefore, involves confusing macroeconomic or other failures with trade policy failure.

Although the Washington Consensus has undergone some revisions since the late 1990s, faith in the efficacy of free trade still remains largely unquestioned (Deraniyagala 2001). The prevailing neoliberal view on trade policy – also referred to as the 'standard enlightened view' (Rodrik 2001) – augments earlier propositions with a newer set of trade policy reforms. Trade policy reform is no longer confined to tariff reduction, but also includes extensive institutional, legal and political reform. This approach is clearly reflected in the objectives of the international organization that coordinates global trade policy, the World Trade Organization (WTO). The WTO seeks to bring about international harmonization of institutional, regulatory and legal standards through a variety of agreements and standards. Trade policy, therefore, now extends to issues previously considered to be beyond the realm of international trade, such as domestic investment, intellectual property and legal reform. The central and defining feature of the revised orthodox view, however, remains the belief that free trade and global integration are the best ways to promote growth and development, and to reduce poverty.

The orthodox case for openness in trade policy emphasizes positive effects on growth, productivity and poverty. Below, we examine the theoretical and empirical bases of these propositions.

Trade and Growth
Several theoretical arguments are used to support the predictions that openness boosts economic growth and that more open economies grow faster than closed ones. Free trade is seen as leading to both static and dynamic gains, with the latter more significant than the former. Static, 'once-and-for-all' gains from trade arise as resources shift from inefficient to efficient sectors following the dismantling of trade restrictions. It is acknowledged, however, that the magnitude of these static gains is small (Bhagwati and Srinivasan 1975). The growth-enhancing effects of openness, therefore, essentially arise from the dynamic gains. A variety of arguments relating to the dynamic gains from free trade are evident

in the literature. Many of them, however, hinge on arbitrary assumptions and have been shown to be theoretically fragile (Rodrik 1995; Deraniyagala and Fine 2001; Lall and Latsch 1999). We examine a few of these arguments below.

Static welfare gains from trade have been increased by incorporating political economy issues, in particular, rent-seeking. It is argued that the resource costs of trade interventions are multiplied several-fold by rent-seeking (Krueger 1974). Freer trade regimes are seen to boost economic growth by reducing rents and increasing resources available for growth. The issue of whether trade liberalization inevitably limits rent-seeking, however, has received little analysis. While some estimates show the magnitude of rent-seeking costs under protection to be large (Gallagher 1991), their accuracy has been questioned (Ocampo and Taylor 1998).

Increasing returns to scale are frequently cited as an important source of dynamic gains from trade liberalization. The creation of a neutral trade regime is purported to encourage exporting and participation in world markets, allowing firms to produce higher output levels and to benefit from scale economies. This, in turn, boosts overall economic growth rates. This argument, however, is based on the assumption that liberalization will necessarily expand activities subject to increasing returns (Rodrik 1995). If scale economies are concentrated in protected sectors that decline after liberalization, dynamic gains from trade will not materialize (Deraniyagala and Fine 2001).

Many theoretical arguments relating to openness and growth are, therefore, contingent on specific assumptions and conditions, indicating that the positive causal link between openness and growth may be the exception rather than the norm. Partly for this reason, much of the debate on openness and growth has been largely empirical. Such country-level research on liberalization and growth consists of cross-section 'before and after' studies (Greenaway, Morgan and Wright 1997), 'with and without' studies (Mosley, Harrigan and Toye 1991; World Bank 1990), and country-specific time-series analysis (Papageorgiou, Michaeley and Choksi, eds 1991; Greenaway and Sapsford 1994; Onafowora, Owoye and Nyatepe–Coo 1996). In general, many of these studies suggest that the effects of liberalization on growth are ambiguous and complex; while some groups of countries show an improvement in growth (as well as other indicators such as investment), others show a marked deterioration. Recent attempts to provide a more consistent analysis, using panel data and alternative measures of liberalization, suggest a J curve-type effect of liberalization on per capita GDP growth (Greenaway, Morgan and Wright 1998). Here, again, the alternative models provide very different estimates of the long-run effects on growth (with the payoff ranging from 2 per cent to 46 per cent!), indicating the limitations of capturing complicated growth effects using cross-country, single equation growth regressions.

In the 1990s, the orthodox position on trade liberalization claimed strong support from a few highly influential cross-country econometric studies that estimated the effects of trade policy and economic growth (Dollar and Kraay 2000). These studies claimed to show a significant positive causal link between trade openness and economic growth. However, problems with econometrics and data have resulted in some damning critiques (Rodriguez and Rodrik 2001). At best, much of this empirical literature seeking to investigate the effects of shifts in trade policy (towards liberalization) develops a model from which a reduced form is estimated. At worst, simple regressions are run on some index of economic performance against some index of openness, although the best and worst often coincide in practice. Therefore, much of the cross-country work is plagued by measurement problems, with many measures of trade openness reflecting trade volume rather than trade policy orientation. The direction of causality is also difficult to establish, given the strong likelihood of faster growth leading to increased trade. It is also difficult to isolate the effects of trade policy on growth, given the numerous other potential influences.

Contrary to the claims of the neoliberal camp, therefore, empirical support for the argument that free trade boosts economic growth remains inconclusive. The orthodox belief in the growth-enhancing potential of free trade, however, remains undiminished. As Winters, McCulloch and McKay (2002: 10) note in their comprehensive review of empirical research on trade and growth, 'the attraction of simple generalizations has seduced much of the profession into taking their results seriously'.

Trade and Productivity

The case for free trade has also focused on identifying the specific channels by which trade affects long-term economic growth. A central focus is on productivity growth. It is claimed that trade liberalization will lead to faster productivity growth, particularly in manufacturing, but also in agriculture. Given that the static gains from liberalization are acknowledged to be negligible, productivity growth is seen as the key mechanism by which liberalization boosts growth. A closer examination of these claims, however, shows them to be theoretically and empirically inconclusive.

Long-term productivity gains are seen to ensue from the correction of the anti-competition bias of protection that discourages cost-cutting technological change. In much of the orthodox literature, however, the precise mechanisms by which trade liberalization promotes technological change and productivity are never spelt out, largely because orthodox theory is silent on the issue of the more proximate causes and sources of technological change and productivity increase. While static resource allocations gains occur within standard trade models such as the canonical Heckscher–Ohlin model, these static gains are simply assumed to translate into long-term productivity growth (Lall and Latsch 1999), and no theoretical tools are used to model this process. Some proponents of liberalization argue that increased levels of competition are sufficient to promote productivity-enhancing technological change across all sectors (Balassa

1988). Such simplistic propositions ignore alternative models which indicate that innovative activity is sometimes promoted by oligopolistic market structures (Deraniyagala and Fine 2001).

A substantial body of empirical literature has investigated the effects of trade policy and openness on total factor productivity (TFP) and efficiency at the industry and firm level. Evidence from these studies, however, is inconclusive. Some early empirical exercises found a negative (but weak) correlation between import substitution and productivity growth (Nishimizu and Robinson 1984). Others showed TFP growth rates to be high in highly protected industrial sectors (Waverman and Murphy 1992), while continuing and accelerating TFP growth rates in periods of both high and low protection have also been reported. High levels of import penetration have also been found to be associated with low rates of productivity growth (Nishimizu and Page 1991). Given the varying country coverage of these studies, the different industrial sectors included, and the varying definitions of liberalization and openness used, attempting to provide a rigorous net balance of the evidence would serve little purpose. Some key weaknesses of these industry-level studies, however, must be noted. None of them discriminates between the effects of trade policy and macro-policy choices and it is, therefore, difficult to attribute causality to trade policy itself. Many of them also fail to control adequately for other influences on productivity growth. In particular, the failure to control for industry effects is especially problematic.

The firm-level literature circumvents the need to control for industry effects, but still fails to establish a direct causal link between trade liberalization and improved economic performance. Some studies find support for the conjecture that efficiency levels are the highest among industries experiencing the largest declines in protection (Tybout, de Melo and Corbo 1991). Other studies have found exporting firms to be more efficient than their domestically oriented counterparts (Haddad 1993; Aw and Batra 1998), and have attributed this result to the positive learning effects that accrue from contact with foreign buyers.

There are three major weaknesses with this firm-level literature. Firstly, most studies examine one-time changes in the *level* of efficiency and, hence, their findings are consistent with the claim that trade liberalization generates static gains. They do not, however, provide conclusive evidence relating to dynamic, long-term improvements in firm-level efficiency. Secondly, they fail to establish the causal links between trade policy, export orientation and efficiency. For instance, the literature on exporting generally does not ask whether the direction of causality runs from exporting to efficiency or vice versa. Finally, much of this research fails to shed light on the various channels through which trade liberalization might affect productivity and efficiency in changing populations of heterogeneous firms (in innovating or not, small or large, public or private, exporting or importing, etc.).

The dynamic gains from liberalization are supposed to accrue largely from technology upgradation but few empirical studies have directly examined the technological response to liberalization at the firm level. One group of studies has examined the relationship between technology imports and domestic technological effort. Both Basant (1993) and Fikkert (1993) found that domestic R&D and foreign technology were substitutes in the case of India. Braga and Wilmore (1991) and Katrak (1997) examined whether improved access to imports increased the extent of 'absorptive' R&D (that is, undertaken not to generate new technologies but to enable firms to keep abreast of existing new technologies) at the firm level. They reported a positive but weak association between measures of technology imports and absorptive R&D. For most developing countries, however, informal technological efforts are more relevant than formal R&D, but the links between trade policy and such informal technological activity have rarely been explicitly examined. Some exceptions (Deraniyagala and Semboja 1999; Latsch and Robinson 1999) have examined the technological response to liberalization in Sub-Saharan African countries, finding very little evidence of widespread technology upgrading following import liberalization, with most firms hesitant or unable to invest in new technologies in the face of very intense import competition.

Trade liberalization is also said to bring productivity growth to the agricultural sector. Agriculture is seen as disadvantaged by protection of the import substitution urban sector. Agricultural prices are depressed as the inter-sectoral terms of trade are distorted in favour of the urban sector. Trade policy reform is seen as correcting this and providing improved incentives for agriculture (Winters 2000). Agricultural prices are expected to rise at the border following trade liberalization, with agricultural productivity and output also increasing. Output growth is supposedly influenced by improved access to new technologies following trade policy reform.

Again, many of these arguments do not stand up to empirical scrutiny. Empirical studies indicate that higher agricultural prices may not always have a positive effect on productivity and output growth (Weeks 1997). Farmers may not be responsive to price changes. This is especially true when commercialization of the agricultural sector is limited. Even when agriculture is commercialized, whether or not farmers change technology and raise output in response to higher prices will partly depend on what happens to input prices. If input prices rise more than output prices, positive output effects will not be forthcoming.

In general terms, then, there is little in the existing empirical research on trade liberalization to suggest that trade policy itself is an important and unambiguous determinant of productivity increase, either in manufacturing or in agriculture. This does not, however, seem to diminish claims about the positive effects of openness on productivity. Many orthodox analysts simply proceed by *assuming* the existence of a positive causal link. For instance, Edwards (1993: 3) assumes that 'more open economies are more efficient in absorbing exogenously generated innovations', while Thomas and Nash (1991: 9) claim that there 'is an empirically established correlation between outward orientation and growth of total factor productivity in an industry'.

Trade and Poverty Reduction

Since the 1990s, the orthodox approach to trade has strongly emphasized the claim that greater openness fosters poverty reduction. Trade and poverty are linked through economic growth, and faster economic growth following
trade liberalization is thought to be poverty-reducing. Although growth could be
inegalitarian, higher levels of income from higher growth, in turn the consequence of greater openness, are believed to offset any worsening in (relative)
income distribution (Winters, McCulloch and McKay 2002; Bruno, Squire and
Ravallion 1995). Again, however, the orthodox research on trade and poverty
has been marked by theoretical inconsistencies and empirical flaws, as was also
evident in much of the neoliberal literature on international trade.

Some mechanisms by which openness translates into poverty reduction
have been identified. Creating a neutral trade regime is supposed to increase
labour-intensive production in many developing countries, thus increasing the
demand for labour and unskilled employment. This, together with potential
upward pressure on unskilled wages, could lead to a reduction in the incidence of
poverty. Whether this leads to a fall in poverty would, however, depend on whether
incomes for unskilled workers rise above the poverty line. Further, there is the
possibility that the most intensively used labour in export sectors may be relatively skilled by developing country standards. If the relatively skilled are under-
represented among the poor (as is likely to be the case), a fall in poverty is
unlikely.

Agricultural growth following trade liberalization is also seen by orthodox trade economists as poverty-reducing as it is expected to translate into a
lower incidence of rural poverty. However, as noted earlier, the expected agricultural supply response to improved price incentives may not be forthcoming. Furthermore, even if a small group of farmers responds to price rises by expanding
output, poor farmers may be left out of this process (if they are engaged in
subsistence farming with little disposable surplus) and the positive effect on rural
poverty will be small. Trade policy reform is also predicted to induce a switch
from subsistence agriculture to cash crops, bringing increased incomes for the
poor (Winters 2000). There could, however, be other effects that counteract this.
If cash crop prices are subject to fluctuations, farmers may not be willing to bear
increased risk and the output of cash crops may not increase. The effects of
liberalization on poverty will also depend on whether the rural poor are largely
net sellers or buyers of agricultural produce, especially food. If the majority of
the poor are net buyers of food, a rise in food prices could lead to increased
poverty.

Trade openness is also argued to reduce poverty via its effects on corruption and rent-seeking (Krueger 1998). The neoliberal assumption that rent-
seeking falls after trade liberalization leads to the claim that resources for poverty reduction will be greater following reform. Apart from the problems with
the assumption of a fall in rent-seeking, it is important to note that the resource
and revenue implications of trade policy reform are more complex than this.

Openness can sometimes constrain poverty reduction efforts if it constrains the ability of governments to increase revenue by taxing mobile factors such as capital (Rodrik 2000). Trade liberalization can also affect poverty indirectly via its impact on trade taxes. In the very early stages of liberalization, revenue collected from trade taxes may, in fact, rise as a country moves from quantitative restrictions to fairly high-level tariffs. Subsequently, however, revenue will fall with the average level of tariffs. This fall in revenues is seen as constraining government expenditure on poverty reduction. As Winters (2000) points out, however, this link is not immutable but must certainly be borne in mind when analysing the effects of openness on poverty.

Since the early 1990s, cross-country econometric work has been highly influential in propagating positive links between trade, growth and poverty reduction. Some studies (for example, Dollar and Kraay 2000; White and Anderson 2001; Lundeberg and Squire 2001) are particularly noteworthy in their conclusion that 'globalizers' perform better in terms of growth and poverty reduction than 'non-globalizers'. Again, however, the limitations of this research have been noted by many analysts (Rodrik 2000). The econometric estimations are highly sensitive to the inclusion/exclusion of specific countries, while the data on poverty are subject to large measurement errors. There is also likely to be a problem with causality, with poverty reduction promoting growth rather than vice versa. This leads Rodrik (ibid.: 5) to conclude that the 'authors' statements regarding the benefits of trade liberalization on poverty have to be seen as statements based on faith rather than evidence'.

The conceptual and empirical literature on trade and poverty has become vast. One conclusion to emerge from an evaluation of this literature is that the effect of liberalization on poverty is likely to be complex. It will depend on a host of factors – including the profile of the poor in a country, the structure of production and consumption, the effects of other reforms, and so on. It is difficult, therefore, to conclude that trade liberalization and openness unambiguously result in a reduction of poverty.

New Trade Theory and the Implications for Trade Policy

Within trade theory, the conclusion that free trade is optimal is derived from the Heckscher–Ohlin model, which, under highly restrictive assumptions, shows that optimal resource allocation can be achieved by the liberalization of all trade restrictions. Over the past two decades, however, these conclusions and assumptions have been questioned by a huge body of 'new trade theories', which address the complexities of international trade, and show that deviations from free trade can often enhance growth and welfare (Krugman 1984; Eaton and Grossman 1986; Grossman and Helpman 1991). As will emerge from much of the discussion that follows, the recent trade literature has, within the confines of an evolving neoclassical theory of market imperfections, made great attempts to address at least some of the realities of trade. Despite this, its conclusions have been largely over-ruled by the forward march of support for trade liberalization.

New trade theory is now entering middle age, having been established in the 1980s (Ethier 1982; Krugman 1984, 1986; Brander and Spencer 1985; Eaton and Grossman 1986; Grossman and Horn 1988; Grossman and Helpman 1991). Essentially, even if in a more sophisticated way and with a fuller range of factors, the corresponding debate over trade policy simply revisits 'infant industry' arguments, while complementing previous discussion with 'political economy' factors. To some extent, it is simply old wine in new bottles, but it also incorporates and complements several innovations within neoclassical economics, which we now consider in turn.

Scale Economies and Imperfect Competition

The increasing returns to scale used to justify protection have been complemented by a range of other market imperfections. These include informational asymmetries and imperfections that inform so much of recent innovation within mainstream microeconomics, which is itself usually seamlessly transformed into understandings of the workings of the economy as a whole.

Inevitably, corresponding models involve consideration of strategic behaviour by all agents, firms as well as governments, so that the new trade theory, secondly, also draws upon the new industrial economics. This can involve game theory, inter-temporal optimization and issues of time consistency or credibility, especially for government policy (the possibility of its changing policy commitments after the private sector has committed itself to investment on the basis of policy promises, anticipation of which deters that investment). Ohyama and Jones (1995), for example, consider optimal technology choice over time. With adjustment costs, their model allows for one country to deliberately fall behind another so that, with adjustment costs, leaping ahead in the future becomes less expensive. It becomes possible to explain both falling behind, catch-up and leapfrogging. Thus, Durkin (1997) shows that pursuit of comparative advantage can itself lead to inefficiency in producing technological progress. In models involving strategic behaviour, results differ, depending upon stylized assumptions about the sorts of competition (and oligopolistic behaviour) and economic factors considered, the policy instruments that governments are allowed to deploy, and the sequencing of decision-making. Bhattacharjea (1995) finds that both strategic industrial policy (on entry/exit) and tariffs are necessary under imperfect competition at home and abroad, and endogenous market structure. Fuerst and Kim (1997) take account of heterogeneity in costs functions with trade policy, affecting the distribution of production across (more or less efficient) firms within countries as well as across countries.

As is evident, more or less any model of oligopoly and market imperfections can be projected on to the trade arena. These models are highly diverse, given the underlying factors and assumptions over which they range. But what they all tend to share in common is the result that strategic trade policy is justified and, in addition, that it should be complemented by other forms of policy (or should take a variety of forms). Such a conclusion should not come as a surprise.

For, it is presumably only by accident that free trade will be optimal in the presence of market imperfections, and, further, the more the imperfections, the more the instruments we need to deal with them. Given the diversity of the models, it also follows that interventions will need to be selective and country/sector-specific, depending upon the type and strength of market imperfections involved.

The relevance of these models to developing countries has been debated (Lucas 1988; Bardhan 1995; Ruttan 1998). While some strategic models with oligopolistic players dominating world markets may be of limited relevance to low-income developing countries (Stewart 1991), arguments for intervention based on scale economies and imperfect competition are widespread in developing countries, rendering these theories especially relevant for them (Helleiner 1992). Empirical evidence indicates that imperfect competition is indeed rampant (Lee 1992), although the evidence on scale economies is much more limited.

Of course, the standard neoliberal response to these models is to claim that government has neither the knowledge nor the ability to be selective in its policy interventions. It is argued that policy interventions will result in directly unproductive subsidy-seeking behaviour by private firms and that the informational requirements for such interventions may be huge, especially in developing countries. Statements such as 'the history of developing countries is littered with proof of misguided and excessive government interventions' are made with little consideration of whether selective interventions have been successful in any country, and of the conditions for such success.

The supposedly large informational requirements are one reason why the analytical thrust of trade theory in justifying interventionist trade policy has been rejected, even by those at the forefront of the theory. Yet, the literature is itself well-suited to handle such issues since it has drawn upon the economics of imperfect and asymmetric information. If governments are less well-informed (and less able) than the private sector, does it follow they should do nothing? The answer is resoundingly in the negative, and should not come as a surprise. For, the implication is that we should leave the generals and the military industrial complex to make defence policy, since they know more about waging war and the true costs and capabilities of weapons!

Clearly, as in any principal agent problem, there is a trade-off between (lesser) knowledge and (others') motives. Brainard and Martimort (1997: 56) address the issue directly, and their conclusion is striking: 'Attainment of the informationally constrained social optimum requires a complicated menu of contracts combining per-unit subsidies and lump-sum transfers.' Even more remarkable is the conclusion reached by Creane (1998), to the effect that policy-makers may be better off and justified in using trade policy, the *less* information they have. It is not, however, necessary to engage in trade theory to see why this conclusion arises in the context of imperfect competition. For a monopolist who wishes to exercise product discrimination, customers (including countries contemplating trade policy) must have the knowledge to discriminate products (as is recognized in practice by advertising, irrespective of whether or not 'genuine' differences are involved). Without this, monopolists may be forced to rely upon a more Pareto-efficient but less profitable strategy, and be unable to exploit product discrimination. Nor is this some esoteric point in the context of development where, both for welfare and growth, economies are better served by supply to a cheap mass market than to a more profitable elite.

Resonance with New Growth Theory

Apart from strategic behaviour and market imperfections, the new trade theory draws upon or, more exactly, contributes to, or is integrated with the new growth theory, which is also essentially based upon market imperfections (see the chapter on 'New Growth Theory'). Despite the link between endogenous growth theory and market imperfections, and the presumption that the growth rate could be improved by government policy to induce a higher savings rate and/or to incorporate externalities, much of the literature has favoured trade liberalization.

In their classic work, Grossman and Helpman (1991) showed how international trade opens channels that facilitate the transmission of technological information, promotes competition and entrepreneurial effort, and increases the size of the market in which innovative firms operate. In their model, however, countries can gain as well as lose from trade. Countries with developed technology sectors and high levels of human capital may gain relative to countries with large supplies of unskilled labour (ibid.: 237–38).

Drawing on these insights, one group of models mainly emphasized the role of capital goods imports in promoting economic growth, with trade liberalization having generally positive effects (Coe, Helpman and Hoffmaister 1995; Lee 1995; Pissarides 1997). These models were based on technology spill-overs, where these spill-overs are generally proportional to imports. Imported capital goods embody information about new technologies, and developing country producers exposed to this information are seen as more likely to innovate. In some models, innovation is directed at imitation, while in others, R&D activities are directed towards learning how to use and absorb imported technology. Romer (1992) described these processes as 'using ideas' (as opposed to 'producing ideas'), while Pack (1992), following Gerschenkron (1962), saw them essentially as a free dividend for being a late-comer. Many of these models implied that developing countries will devote increased amounts of resources to R&D following trade liberalization.

These models made an important contribution by focusing attention on the non-convexities involved in the process of diffusion and adoption of new goods and technologies in a developing country. Many of them, however, suffered from an inaccurate conceptualization of technology. Most of the models were based on an assumption of 'blueprint technology' – that is, technology can be perfectly codified and easily transferred. Their positive conclusions about trade liberalization and 'learning from trading' can be reversed when the definition of technology is changed and refined. Keller (1996) argued that the all-inclusive notion of technology (information, hardware and capabilities) used in most models is misleading, and, instead, differentiated between technology embodied in capital goods and capabilities (or 'absorptive capacity'). Using a Rivera–Batiz and Romer (1991)-type endogenous growth model, he showed that the productivity and growth effects of increased access to foreign capital goods will be shortlived unless absorptive capacity increases at a more rapid rate than during the period prior to trade reform. In the long run, the rate of growth of output is forced down to the rate of human capital growth. Similarly, van de Klundert and Smulders (1996) allow for technology spill-overs between North and South, but the latter's low level of high-tech production limits learning by doing. In the light of recent evidence that increased openness leads to less invest-ment in human capital at the secondary and tertiary levels (Wood and Ridao–Cano 1999), all this implies that the gains for developing countries from access to technology imports can be limited.

Models dealing with convergence also provided few robust conclusions, with convergence or divergence depending upon how openly competitive inter-national trade is. Lau and Wan (1994) argued that trade is necessary but not sufficient for poorer countries to converge. Middle-income countries will be able to accrue the benefits of catch-up since the costs of doing so declines with growth, whereas the poorest countries will experience a widening income gap.

In general, while models linking trade and growth provided few unambi-guous results, one robust conclusion to emerge was that the more asymmetric the trading countries, the more likely growth effects are to be asymmetric. This raises the real possibility that developing countries may lose out from trade as their innovative sectors are crowded out due to intense competition, or because low levels of capabilities prevent them from realizing the benefits of technology spill-overs. In these models, the gains from trade are largest for countries at similar levels of development.

Political Economy Arguments

The marriage between new trade and growth theories serves to render each more complex. In addition, they also tend to share a particularly under-developed notion of what constitutes a nation. Indeed, in conformity with long-standing traditions in trade theory, the nation is simply a special individual, usually with both benevolent goals (social welfare) and special powers (policy). A simple step is taken to progress beyond such simplicity once account is taken of internal influences upon government policy, thereby incorporating an additional factor in new trade theory, that of political economy in general and rent-seeking in particular.

Rodrik and Fouroutan (1998), for example, debated whether trade liber-alization has stalled in Africa because of a combination of distributional and informational problems (who anticipates consequences, and who gains or loses from trade reform, including proposed compensation for adjustment to employ-ers and/or employees). Fung (1995) examined the redistribution between capital and labour as rents are shifted and shared with change in trade policy in the presence of oligopoly. In a model of electoral competition, Riezman and Wilson (1997) found that limits on the number of donors and the amounts of donations by interest groups can lead to inefficiency in the making of trade policy.

Most important, though, in the political economy of trade policy have been rent-seeking arguments. It is as if all of the arguments in favour of anything other than free trade can be set aside. For, to act upon their prescriptions is to solicit unproductive rent-seeking in pursuit of self-serving trade policy. Here, however, there is a major problem. If there are underlying economic and political interests in favour of trade policy, why would they allow trade liberalization to proceed? And, if they have no choice, might they not engage in even more costly forms of pursuing their advantage?

Selective Intervention in Practice

While the theoretical justification for interventionist trade policy provided by new trade theories has been rejected, both by the orthodox camp and by some theorists at the forefront of the new trade theories, empirically based research indicates that selective interventions in trade and industrial policies have been essential ingredients for rapid growth in a range of countries. The role of protection in early industrialization in western Europe has been well documented (see Chang 2003 for a recent review). In addition, detailed empirical studies of the East Asian newly industrializing countries (NICs) have documented the role of strategic trade interventions in promoting manufacturing growth, technology upgrading as well as industrial deepening (Wade 1990; Lall 2003). These studies showed selective trade and industrial policies to have been instrumental in achieving international competitiveness. The policies involved identifying new areas of competitiveness, providing trade protection for these sectors, and creating the relevant endowments and skills needed for dynamism in domestic and export markets. Trade policies in these countries did not follow the principle of comparative advantage but deliberately sought to create new areas of competitiveness. One of the best known examples, of course, is the case of Pohang Steel, which the Korean government created and nurtured under infant industry protection. While this was strongly opposed by orthodox economists and policymakers (such as the World Bank) at the time, on the grounds that Korea had no comparative advantage in steel, Pohang is now the world's most efficient steelmaker (Lall 2003), and has spawned a range of spin-off activities, from car- and ship-building to microelectronics.

Taking Issue with Effective Protection

As indicated in the discussion so far, free trade has become an article of faith among academic economists in general, and for neoliberal policy-making in particular, *despite* the theoretical and empirical evidence to the contrary that has been casually dismissed as mischief-making. In practice, the policy counterpart of such free trade principles has been tariff reform (inevitably reduction).

The need for, and measurement of, changes in the *system* of protection have been attached to what has been known as the effective protection rate (EPR). The nominal tariff on an *output* does not indicate the extent to which it is protected or cushioned against competition, because there may also be tariffs on *inputs* that increase costs or production. Without going into details, the EPR takes this into account sector by sector. On this basis, as Greenaway and Milner (2003: 444) reported, 'the initial work on effective protection stimulated a literature which quite simply exploded'. However, they also found 'that the concept has had such an influence and been estimated so extensively is, for some, surprising on the grounds that it is "fatally flawed"' (ibid.: 441). It is our purpose here to expose these flaws of EPR measures and to assess their deadly significance.

The problems in using measures of EPRs are three-fold. First, is there a sound theoretical basis for measuring EPRs, especially in the context of policy-making? Second, how well can EPRs be calculated in practice? Third, are the anticipated (beneficial) effects of shifting (lowering) EPRs liable to materialize? The following discussion deals with these issues in turn, although they do over-lap and inform one another.

The theoretical assumptions on which EPRs are measured have long been recognized to be highly restrictive. In particular, changes in the tariff struc-ture will bring about shifts in economic activity, as is intended. Levels and pro-portions of inputs and outputs will change with shifts in tariff structure across the whole economy. In other words, the same EPR levels for two different sectors can be associated with entirely different potential for change across the economy, depending upon demand and supply elasticities of response to tariff reform. In a general equilibrium context, this gives rise to what is known as the substitution problem. For example, in a three-sector general equilibrium model with substi-tutability in production, introduction of the third, non-traded sector to comple-ment the import and export sectors suffices to undermine conventional measures of EPRs.

The substitution problem arises out of the comparative statics of measur-ing EPRs. It is essentially an equilibrium measure and is undermined by general equilibrium considerations in moving from one equilibrium to another in res-ponse to change in tariff structure. A distinct problem but one also related to changing conditions of production, if not comparative statics, is that concerning productivity increase and its relationship to trade. As recognized in new growth and trade theories, productivity can be affected by the level of and openness to trade. Two opposite effects can be discerned as archetypal, the empirical inci-dence of which cannot be determined by theoretical speculation. Reserving domes-tic markets for domestic producers or promoting exports can induce productivity increase on the basis of dynamic economies of scale and scope. To the contrary, trade liberalization can also induce productivity increase through the greater availability and cheapness of imported inputs.[1] It would not appear to make sense to discuss trade reform and EPRs separate from, and prior to, supply-side measures, and other factors and effects associated with productivity increase. In short, the comparative statics method for calculation of EPRs simply sets aside both exogenous and endogenous sources of supply-side change, even though these ought to be the object of policy of which trade policy is an interactive aspect.

A further theoretical reservation concerning the measurement of EPRs is the assumption of perfect competition upon which it is based. For such an assumption, the patterns of trade observed throughout the world would be anomalous since economies would specialize in their well-defined sectors of comparative advantage. Trade of the same commodities in both directions simply could not occur between countries. Yet, it is endemic, especially within the developed world. Accordingly, even in an orthodox approach, trade theory must be modified to account for the impact of market imperfections, without which observed trade patterns are impossible. An immediate implication, however, is that EPRs, calculated as if the world and domestic economies were perfectly competitive, are unacceptable.

There are, then, overwhelming conceptual and theoretical issues even in defining levels of EPRs. These are compounded by, and reflected in, practical and empirical difficulties. This is not just a matter of more and better data being available, but the rarefied assumptions needed to *define* EPRs mean that data, however good, cannot correspond to the concept being measured. Very careful account, for example, needs to be taken of the role played by the capital stock and investment. As is recognized in the literature, EPRs should be worked out net of depreciation allowances, and distinctions must be drawn between X-inefficiency in the use of capital (underutilization and ineffective use of capacity) and the cost of capital (usually interpreted as the interest rate).[2] High interest rates, an old or dated capital stock and substantial excess capacity, are all liable to result in unduly high measures of EPRs, as these factors would all reduce competitiveness. But we live in a world removed from perfect competition where there is excess capacity and a rhythm of economic, rather than physical, depreciation.

In addition, indirectly related to the treatment of capital is the variation in the riskiness of investment across sectors. A higher tariff on inputs, for example, implies more capital will be advanced until a return accrues with sales. This distorts the impact of tariffs across otherwise equivalent sectors through making riskier investments less attractive. An entirely different practical issue in measuring EPRs is the use of world prices as a reference point. These can be inappropriate in the case of heavy internal transport charges, for example, with the impact of this non-tradeable being crucial, as are other internal factors besides tariffs, such as domestic taxes and subsidies, that might affect the wedge between domestic and world prices.

Not surprisingly, then, EPRs measure all the divergencies of the economy from a perfectly competitive partial equilibrium.[3] But put aside the conceptual and practical problems of accurately defining and measuring EPRs. How well do they serve as a guide to policy by suggesting outcomes that ought to be pursued for their beneficial effects or complemented by other policies to moderate their ill-effects? Implicit in the earlier discussion, and what ought to be made explicit in the policy debate, is that such policy analysis is crucially dependent upon the use of counter-factuals – what would happen in the absence of tariff changes, what would happen with them? Hence the impact of tariff reform is deduced. Now, all the points already made greatly undermine the counter-factual basis upon which EPRs are calculated. What they show is that the economy does not work in the way suggested by the restrictive assumptions made.

By the same token, the inferred comparative static impacts are unacceptable even if the calculated EPRs are well-defined and empirically accurate in some sense – an impossible eventuality, since exactly the same conditions that distort the calculation of EPRs also suggest that they should *not* be used as a simple, *exclusive* or *independent* object of policy. For example, much trade is internal to multinational enterprises, involving movement of products between affiliates engaging in transfer pricing. Such considerations imply that there is a role for tariffs, which depend, in part, upon how competitive the domestic markets within which multinationals operate are (Itagaki 1983). Similarly, irrespective of the presence of multinationals, imperfect competition may be endemic with variations in the quality of output and intra-industry trade (making EPRs difficult to measure because of the need to disentangle the gap between world and domestic prices according to the role of quality, oligopoly, tariffs, etc.).

A slightly different way of illustrating these and other points is by reference to the formula for the EPR itself. As a *ratio* of value added at domestic prices to that at world prices, it is necessarily *scale-independent*. It makes no difference how large or small is the absolute level of economic activity concerned. This could be large-scale steel or small-scale clothing. The very simplicity of the formula demonstrates that it has no direct concern for dynamic and static economies of scale and scope, excess capacity, capital–labour intensity, market structure, presence of multinationals, skill requirements of the labour force and management, developments in world markets, product differentiation and quality, commercial risk, age structure of capital stock, etc. Quite apart from failing to incorporate these factors in its definition, the EPR is inappropriately measured by exclusion of these and other factors, such as the differential impact of non-tradeables, and the substitution between capital and labour in production in response to changing input prices. In this light, it is inconceivable how EPRs can be justifiably used as the basis for industrial policy-making, of which trade policy is an integral part. Doubts must be equally strong over its usefulness for measuring macroeconomic impacts on employment, inflation and growth, as it is used as an independent variable in regressions.

In short, it is erroneous to presume that shifts in effective rates of protection act in a relatively uniform, linear fashion within economic sectors, simply serving to shift output marginally in unambiguous directions in response to the induced raising or lowering of prices. This takes no account of the competitive structure of industries and the role of strategic behaviour (by both domestic and foreign firms), for which differential pricing in export and domestic markets can be crucial in the presence of economies of scale and scope, and market imperfections. At best, the models underlying the calculation and use of EPRs offer very poor guides to anything other than a summary of extrapolated, but questionable, marginal changes in the economy, which are unable to pick up critical collapses in sectors that result from shifting disadvantage in protection, and/or strategic withdrawal or entry by dominant domestic and importing foreign firms, respectively.

Concluding Remarks

A number of conclusions follow from this discussion. First, free or freer trade is heavily favoured by the economics profession. Second, the thrust of theoretical and empirical literature is far from supportive of such postures. Third, the use of measures of effective protection is totally fallacious, and grounded in a virtual economy that departs significantly from the realities of both developing and developed countries. Finally, to the extent that the neoliberal consensus has promoted trade liberalization, it has done a double disservice, both by undermining interventionist trade policy and by its integration with other policy areas.

The implementation of trade liberalization policies and their effects are highly contingent on historical and political factors specific to individual countries. The experience of trade liberalization in developing countries over the past two decades shows that a uniform set of trade policies can have divergent effects on key indicators such as growth and poverty. The promotion of trade liberalization by the neoliberal consensus has done little to deepen our understanding of country-specific historical and political economy factors that make the outcome of any trade policy complex and hard to predict.

There are two important respects, then, in which Krueger's dismissal of new trade theory, unless it supports her conclusions, is apposite. Firstly, with the incorporation of market imperfections, the models become flexible enough, so that sufficiently sophisticated theory can support any conclusion, regardless of the facts. Secondly, then, it is time to get real – to ensure that trade theory and policy conform to, rather than diverge from, the factors that determine trade performance and its consequences. It is here that the old and, to a large if lesser extent, the new trade theory are deficient. For, the most important reality they overlook is that every industrialization, from Britain to the East Asian NICs, has depended upon protection to a greater or lesser extent. There may now be more than one model of trade but the myth that only one free trade policy fits all is at odds with historical experience. It must be rejected for a more rounded, grounded, targeted and effective policy perspective focused on selective protection in conjunction with other factors and policies.

Notes

[1] See Venables (1996: 179): 'It may be the case that trade liberalization triggers a dramatic expansion of output and possibly also a reduction in imports. This arises as import liberalization lowers costs in downstream industries, expanding their output, and triggering a "big push" of industrialization.'

[2] See Ettori (1992) for a full discussion with application to India.

[3] A stunning illustration of the lack of realism involved in calculating EPRs is provided by the World Bank's (1995) study for Mozambique. It provides a table of EPRs for eighteen products, the simple average for which is +47 per cent. In addition, however, it provides corresponding calculations for what these rates have the potential to be in view of large-scale non-payment of duties by importers, that is, smuggling. In this light, the average EPR becomes –131 per cent!

References

Aw, B.-Y. and Geeta Batra (1998), 'Technological Capability and Firm Efficiency in Taiwan', *World Bank Economic Review*, 12 (1): 59–79.

Balassa, Bela (1988), 'Interests of Developing Countries in the Uruguay Round', *World Economy*, 11 (1): 39–54.

Bardhan, Pranab (1995), 'The Contribution of Endogenous Growth Theory to the Analysis of Development Problems: An Assessment', in Jere Behrman and T.N. Srinivisan, eds, *Handbook of Development Economics*, Vol. 3B (Oxford: Elsevier).

Basant, Rakesh (1993), 'R&D, Foreign Technology Purchase and Technology Spillovers on Indian Industrial Productivity', Processed, United Nations University Institute for New Technologies, Maastricht.

Bhagwati, Jagdish and T.N. Srinivasan (1975), *Foreign Trade Regimes and Economic Development: India* (New York: Columbia University Press).

Bhattacharjea, Aditya (1995), 'Strategic Tariffs and Endogenous Market Structures: Trade and Industrial Policies under Imperfect Competition', *Journal of Development Economics*, 47 (2): 287–312.

Braga, Helson and Larry Wilmore (1991), 'Technological Imports and Technological Effort: An Analysis of their Determinants in Brazilian Firms', *Journal of Industrial Economics*, 39 (4): 421–32.

Brainard, S. Lael and David Martimort (1997), 'Strategic Trade Policy with Incompletely Informed Policymakers', *Journal of International Economics*, 42 (1–2): 33–66.

Brander, James and Barbara Spencer (1985), 'Export Subsidies and Market Share Rivalry', *Journal of International Economics*, 18 (1–2): 83–100.

Bruno, Michael, Lyn Squire and Martin Ravallion (1995), 'Equity and Growth in Developing Countries', in Vito Tanzi and Ke-young Chu, eds, *Income Distribution and High Quality Growth* (Cambridge, Massachusetts: MIT Press).

Carrier, James and Danny Miller, eds, (1998), *Virtualism: The New Political Economy* (London: Berg).

Chang, Ha-Joon (2003), 'Kicking Away the Ladder: Development Strategy in Historical Perspective', *Oxford Development Studies*, 31 (1): 21–31.

Coe, David, Elhanan Helpman and Alexander Hoffmaister (1995), 'North-South R&D Spillovers', CEPR Discussion Paper 1133, Centre for Economic Policy Research, London.

Creane, Anthony (1998), 'Ignorance Is Bliss as Trade Policy', *Review of International Economics*, 6 (4): 616–24.

Deraniyagala, Sonali (2001), 'From Washington to Post-Washington: Does it Matter for Industrial Policy?', in Ben Fine, Costas Lapavitsas and Jonathan Pincus, eds, *Development Policy in the Twenty First Century* (London: Routledge).

Deraniyagala, Sonali and Ben Fine (2001), 'New Trade Theory versus Old Trade Policy: A Continuing Enigma', *Cambridge Journal of Economics*, 25 (6): 809–25.

Deraniyagala, Sonali and Haji Semboja (1999), 'Technology Upgrading and Trade Liberalization in Tanzania', in Sanjaya Lall, ed., *The Technological Response to Import Liberalization in Sub-Saharan Africa* (Basingstoke: Macmillan).

Dollar, David and Aart Kraay (2000), 'Growth is Good for the Poor', The World Bank Development Research Group Working Paper 2507, Washington DC.

Durkin, John (1997), 'Perfect Competition and Endogenous Comparative Advantage', *Review of International Economics*, 5 (3): 401–11.

Eaton, Jonathan and Gene Grossman (1986), 'Optimal Trade and Industrial Policy under Oligopoly', *Quarterly Journal of Economics*, 101 (2): 383–406.

Edwards, Sebastian (1993), 'Openness, Trade Liberalization and Growth in Developing Countries', *Journal of Economic Literature*, 31 (3): 1358–93.

Ethier, Wilfred (1982), 'National and International Returns to Scale in the Modern Theory of International Trade', *American Economic Review*, 72 (3): 389–405.

Ettori, Francois (1992), 'Measure and Interpretation of Effective Protection in the Presence of High Capital Costs: Evidence from India', Policy Research Paper 873, World Bank.

Fikkert, Brian (1993), 'Complementary Technology Imports and Domestic R&D', Processed, Princeton University.

Fuerst, Timothy and Kyoo Kim (1997), 'Two Part Trade Policy under Imperfect Competition', *Review of International Economics*, 5 (1): 63–71.

Fung, K.C. (1995), 'Rent Shifting and Rent Sharing: A Re-examination of the Strategic Industrial Policy Problem', *Canadian Journal of Economics*, 28 (2): 450–62.

Gallagher, Mark (1991), *Rent Seeking and Economic Growth in Africa* (Boulder: Westview Press).

Gerschenkron, Alexander (1962), *Economic Backwardness in Historical Perspective* (Cambridge, Massachusetts: Harvard University Press).

Greenaway, David and Chris Milner (1987), 'Effective Protection and Intra-Industry Trade – Some Positive and Normative Issues', *Journal of Economic Issues*, 14 (5): 38–53.

—— (2003), 'Effective Protection, Policy Appraisal and Trade Policy Reform', *World Economy*, 26 (4): 441–56.

Greenaway, David and David Sapsford (1994), 'What Does Liberalization Do for Exports and Growth?', *Weltwirtschaftliches Archiv*, 130 (1): 152–74.

Greenaway, David, William Morgan and Pat Wright (1997), 'Trade Liberalization and Growth in Developing Countries: Some New Evidence', *World Development*, 25 (11): 1885–92.

—— (1998), 'Trade Reform, Adjustment and Growth: What Does the Evidence Tell Us?', *Economic Journal*, 108 (3): 1547–64.

Grossman, Gene and Elhanan Helpman (1991), *Innovation and Growth in the Global Economy* (Cambridge, Massachusetts: MIT Press).

Grossman, Gene and Henrik Horn (1988), 'Infant Industry Protection Reconsidered: The Case of International Barriers to Entry', *Quarterly Journal of Economics*, 103 (4): 767–87.

Haddad, Mona (1993), 'How Trade Liberalization Affected Productivity in Morocco', World Bank Policy Research Working Paper 1096, Washington DC.

Helleiner, Gerald (1992), 'Introduction', in Gerald Helleiner, ed., *Trade Policy, Industrialization and Development* (Oxford: Clarendon Press).

Itagaki, Takao (1983), 'Multinational Firms and the Theory of Effective Protection', *Oxford Economic Papers*, 35 (3): 447–62.

Katrak, Homi (1997), 'Developing Countries' Imports of Technology, In-House Technological Capabilities and Efforts: An Analysis of the Indian Experience', *Journal of Development Economics*, 53 (1): 67–83.

Keller, Wolfgang (1996), 'Absorptive Capacity: On the Creation and Acquisition of Technology in Development', *Journal of Development Economics*, 49 (1): 199–228.

Krueger, Anne (1974), 'The Political Economy of a Rent-seeking Society', *American Economic Review*, 64 (4): 291–303.

—— (1997), 'Trade Policy and Economic Development: How We Learn', *American Economic Review*, 87 (1): 1–22.

—— (1998), 'Why Trade Liberalization Is Good for Growth', *Economic Journal*, 108 (3): 1513–32.

Krugman, Paul (1984), ' Import Protection as Export promotion', in Henryk Kierzkowski, ed., *Monopolistic Competition and International Trade* (Oxford: Oxford University Press).

—— (1986), *Strategic Trade Policy and the New International Economics* (Cambridge, Massachusetts: MIT Press).

Lal, Deepak and Sarath Rajapathirana (1987), 'Foreign Trade Regimes and Growth in Developing Countries', *World Bank Research Observer*, 2: 189–217.

Lall, Sanjaya (2003), 'Symposium on Infant Industries', *Oxford Development Studies*, 31 (1): 3–20.

Lall, Sanjaya and Wolfram Latsch (1999), ' Import Liberalization and Industrial Performance: Theory and Evidence', in Sanjaya Lall, ed., *The Technological Response to Import Liberalization in Sub-Saharan Africa* (London: Macmillan).

Latsch, Wolfram and Peter Robinson (1999), 'Technology Upgrading in Post-Liberalization Zimbabwe', in Sanjaya Lall, ed., *The Technological Response to Import Liberalization in Sub-Saharan Africa* (London: Macmillan).

Lau, Max and Henry Wan (1994), 'On the Mechanism of Catching Up', *European Economic Review*, 38 (3–4): 952–63.

Lee, Jong-Wha (1995), 'Capital Goods Imports and Long-Run Growth', *Journal of Development Economics*, 48 (1): 91–110.

Lee, Norman (1992), 'Market Structure and Trade in Developing Countries', in Gerry Helleiner, ed., *Trade Policy, Industrialization and Development* (Clarendon Press: Oxford).

Little, Ian, Tibor Scitovsky and Maurice Scott (1970), *Industry and Trade in Some Developing Countries* (Oxford: Oxford University Press).

Lucas, Robert (1988), 'On the Mechanics of Economic Development', *Journal of Monetary Economics*, 22: 3–42.

Lundeberg, Mattias and Lyn Squire (2001), 'The Simultaneous Evolution of Growth and Inequality', processed, Development Research Group, World Bank, Washington DC.

Mosley, Paul, Jane Harrigan and John Toye (1991), *Aid and Power: The World Bank and Policy-Based Lending* (London: Routledge).

Nishimizu, Mieko and John Page (1991), 'Trade Policy, Market Orientation and Productivity in Industry', in Jaime de Melo and André Sapir, eds, *Trade Theory and Economic Reform* (Oxford: Basil Blackwell).

Nishimizu, Mieko and Sherman Robinson (1984), 'Trade Policy and Productivity in Semi Industrialized Countries', *Journal of Development Economics*, 16 (1): 117–206.

Ocampo, Jose A. and Lance Taylor (1998), 'Trade Liberalization in Developing Countries; Modest Benefits, but Problems with Productivity Growth, Macro Prices and Income Distribution', *Economic Journal*, 108 (3): 1523–46.

Ohyama, Michihiro and Ronald Jones (1995), 'Technology Choice, Overtaking and Comparative Advantage', *Review of International Economics*, 3 (2): 224–34.

Onafowora, Olugbenga, Oluwole Owoye and Akorlie Nyatepe-Coo (1996), 'Trade Policy, Export Performance and Economic Growth: Evidence from Sub-Saharan Africa', *Journal of International Trade and Economic Development*, 5 (3): 341–60.

Pack, Howard (1993), 'Technology Gaps between Industrial and Developing Countries', Proceedings of the World Bank Annual Conference on Development Economics 1992, Supplement to *World Bank Economic Review* and *World Bank Research Observer*: 283–302.

Papageorgiou, Demetris, Michael Michaely and Armeane Choksi, eds, (1991), *Liberalizing Foreign Trade* (Oxford: Basil Blackwell).

Pissarides, Christopher (1997), 'Learning by Trading and Returns to Human Capital in Developing Countries', *World Bank Economic Review*, 11 (1): 17–21.

Prasch, Robert (1996), 'Reassessing the Theory of Comparative Advantage', *Review of Political Economy*, 8 (1): 37–55.

Riezman, Raymond and John Wilson (1997), 'Political Reform and Trade Policy', *Journal of International Economics*, 42 (1–2): 67–90.

Rivera-Batiz, Luis and Paul Romer (1991), 'International Trade with Endogenous Technological Change', *European Economic Review*, 35 (4): 971–1001.

Rodriguez, Francisco and Dani Rodrik (2001), 'Trade Policy and Economic Growth; A Skeptic's Guide to Cross National Evidence', in Ben Bernanke and Kenneth Rogoff, eds, *NBER Macroeconomics Annual* (Cambridge: MIT Press).

Rodrik, Dani (1995), 'Trade and Industrial Policy Reform', in Jere Behrman and T.N. Srinivasan, eds, *Handbook of Development Economics*, Vol. IIIB (North-Holland).

—— (2000), 'Comments on Trade, Growth and Poverty', http://Rodrik%20on%20Dollar-Kraay.pdf.

—— (2001), 'The Global Governance of Trade as if Development Really Matters', http://ksghome.harvard.edu/~drodrik.academic.ksg/UNDPtrade.pdf.

Rodrik, Dani and Faezeh Fouroutan (1998), 'Why Is Trade Reform So Difficult in Africa?', *Journal of African Economies*, 7, Supplement: 10–36.

Romer, Paul (1992), 'Two Strategies for Economic Development: Using Ideas and Producing Ideas', Supplement to *World Bank Economic Review*: 63–91.

Ruttan, Vernon (1998), 'The New Growth Theory and Development Economics: A Survey', *Journal of Development Studies*, 35 (2): 1–26.

Stewart, Frances (1991), 'A Note on Strategic Trade Theory and the South', *Journal of International Development*, 3 (5): 467–84.

Thomas, Vinod and John Nash (1991), 'Reform of Trade Policy: Recent Evidence from Theory and Practice', *World Bank Research Observer*, 6: 219–40.

Tybout, James, Jamie de Melo and Vittorio Corbo (1991), 'The Effects of Trade Reforms on Scale and Technical Efficiency: New Evidence from Chile', *Journal of International Economics*, 31 (3–4): 231–50.

van de Klundert, Theo and Sjak Smulders (1996), 'North-South Knowledge Spill-Overs and Competition: Convergence versus Divergence', *Journal of Development Economics*, 50 (2): 213–32.

Venables, Anthony (1996), 'Trade Policy, Cumulative Causation, and Industrial Development', *Journal of Development Economics*, 49 (1): 179–97.

Wade, Robert (1990), *Governing the Market: Economic Theory and the Role of Government in East Asian Industrialization* (Princeton: Princeton University Press).

Waverman, Leonard and Steven Murphy (1992), 'Total Factor Productivity in Automobile Production in Argentina, Mexico, Korea and Canada', in Gerald Helleiner, ed., *Trade Policy, Industrialization and Development* (Oxford: Clarendon Press).

Weeks, John (1997), 'Central America's Free Trade Flop: Why Liberalization Failed to Boost Agricultural Performance', unpublished FAO Report, Rome.

White, Howard and Ed Anderson (2001), 'Growth versus Distribution: Does the Pattern of Growth Matter?', *Development Policy Review*, 19 (3): 267–89.

Winters, Alan (2000), 'Trade Liberalization and Poverty', Discussion Paper 7, Poverty Research Unit, University of Sussex, Falmer, Brighton.

Winters, Alan, Neil McCulloch and Andrew McKay (2002), ' Trade Liberalization and Poverty; the Empirical Evidence', CREDIT Research Paper 02/22, University of Nottingham: Nottingham.

Wood, Adrian and Cristóbal Ridao-Cano (1999), 'Skill, Trade and International Inequality', *Oxford Economic Papers*, 51 (1): 89–119.

World Bank (1990), 'Report on Adjustment Lending II: Policies for the Recovery of Growth', Document R90099 (Washington DC: World Bank).

—— (1995), 'Mozambique: Impediments to Industrial Sector Recovery', Macro-Industry and Finance Division, Southern African Department, Report 13752–MOZ.

New Growth Theory

More Problem than Solution

Ben Fine

Growth in the History of Economic Thought[1]

Growth theory has a prominent, if shifting position in the history of economic thought. For classical political economy, beginning with Adam Smith in the late eighteenth century and lasting for a hundred years or more, preoccupation with growth was central. Smith himself is famous for opening the *Wealth of Nations* with an account of the division of labour as a source of productivity increase, making reference to the manufacture of pins. For him, the wealth of nations depended upon the productivity to be gained from a growing division of labour. But this was itself liable to be constrained by the extent of markets. Large-scale pin manufacture depended upon mass markets. For this reason, it was important to Smith that feudal barriers to the expansion of commerce should be overcome. This is an important perspective in which to set his commitment to the invisible hand, that is all too commonly perceived to be more about the efficiency of free markets in light of modern theories of equilibrium.

Nonetheless, Smith believed that growth could not be sustained indefinitely because the growing division of labour would ultimately exhaust the market, leading to over-investment and declining profitability. The result would be what was known to classical political economy as a stationary state. Smith's argument, while usefully raising the issue of how technical change and productivity increase is accommodated by the market, is incorrect because it extrapolates, from a single sector to the economy as a whole, what is known as a fallacy of composition. There is no reason why all markets should not expand together indefinitely.

With Ricardo and his contemporaries, writing some fifty years later, a different reason was given for the common belief that a stationary state was the inevitable fate for capitalism. Rather than arguing that growing productivity across all sectors would exhaust growth, they argued that declining productivity in one particular sector would be responsible. That sector was agriculture. To accommodate the nutritional needs of a growing population, it was believed that ever-less productive land would need to be brought into cultivation ultimately, once again, reducing profitability as the cost of provisioning wages grew, and undermining the capacity for further growth.

Marx's political economy took a different view. He argued that accumulation was unavoidable under capitalism. For it was a consequence of the competition between capitalists in pursuit of profitability through productivity increases. Larger capitals had better chances of success and survival. For Marx, there were neither market nor natural absolute barriers to growth under capitalism, but the growing economy would intensify stresses and strains that could not be accommodated by the market mechanism alone. As a result, economic growth would be punctuated by crises of greater or lesser severity and frequency. These, once resolved, would furnish the basis for a renewal of growth, unless capitalism was itself overthrown by socialist revolution.

With the emergence of the marginalist revolution in economic thought in the 1870s, and despite a major depression soon afterwards across the capitalist world, the last decades of the nineteenth century were marked by a lack of interest in growth theory. The newly emerging discipline of economics – it had previously been political economy – focused instead on problems of efficiency through the market mechanism. This was to remain the case for fifty years until the end of the Great Depression, when Harrod raised the question of whether equilibrium growth was possible and, if so, whether it was stable. He was doubtful of positive answers in both cases.

But, by the mid-1950s, what is now known as old growth theory came to the fore, explaining growth in terms of flexible combinations of capital and labour in the production process – growth in factor inputs – and unexamined growth in productivity. Old growth theory will be examined in greater detail later. For the moment, it suffices to report that it faded from prominence towards the end of the post-war boom, its swansong being prompted by the oil crises of the early 1970s. Growth could be sustained, even with a scarce resource such as oil, as long as productivity in its use rose or substitutes for it were invented sufficiently fast. It was more than a decade before growth theory once again occupied a leading position in economics. What distinguished it from what came before?

Pinpointing New Growth Theory

Crafts (1996: 30), one of Britain's leading economic historians, reports from just a decade ago: 'In a speech in the autumn of 1994, the Shadow Chancellor, Gordon Brown, referred to "post-neoclassical endogenous growth theory". The press seized upon this phrase and lampooned Mr Brown.' This anecdote says much about the press' reaction, both to what is taken to be esoteric economic theory and a pretentious appeal to it by a prospective First Treasury Minister with an otherwise dour reputation. At that time, endogenous or new growth theory was less than a decade old, its emergence generally being credited to what are now deemed to be the classic articles of Romer (1986) and Lucas (1988). Over the last twenty years, new growth theory (NGT) has enjoyed a meteoric rise in the academic world, spawning thousands of published articles, numerous books, a secure place in core graduate teaching of economics, and a favoured topic for student dissertations and essays.

For these reasons alone, it is worthy of close critical attention – whether it warrants lampooning or not is a different matter. NGT addresses at least three compelling, and closely inter-related, questions. These are:

1. What are the sources of productivity increase?

2. Do, and if so why, some economies persist in growing faster than others? Or do laggard economies tend to catch up with leaders, the so-called convergence hypothesis?

3. What is the impact of socio-economic variables such as institutions and culture on economic growth, as opposed to the simple accumulation of factor inputs such as capital, and more or less skilled labour?

These are big questions, and they are far from new. But, remarkably, they have tended to be absent from the forefront of mainstream, neoclassical economic theory. When previously they have been addressed within the discipline of economics, it has usually been on the margins, as part of applied economics, political economy, or in economic histories of technologies or particular countries. As if to make up for its neglect in the past, mainstream economics has swung to the opposite extreme, purporting to examine the three questions listed above within a general framework, as opposed to the piecemeal efforts of applied economists, economic historians and development economists. It has also warranted the claim of being post-neoclassical.

In presenting NGT, it would be natural to begin by comparing it to old growth theory, or exogenous growth theory, as it is known, in contrast to endogenous or new growth theory,[2] which will be taken up later. But for purposes of exposition, it is more instructive (and less demanding on those unfamiliar with the old), to examine how new growth theory has turned out, not least in its empirical work. This has revolved around statistical investigation of the second question listed above. Do economies converge upon one another (in per capita income)? If so, those with a lower starting level of income would be expected to grow faster than those with a higher level. This suggests a simple statistical test of what is known as the hypothesis of *absolute* convergence. Run a regression on the following equation:

$$g = c - a_0 y_0$$

where g is growth rate, y_0 is initial level of income, and c and a_0 are parameters to be estimated. The expectation (for convergence) is that a_0 is positive, so that those with lower starting incomes grow faster and those with higher initial incomes grow more slowly.

While appealing in its simplicity, there are very serious problems with this statistical exercise that are worth highlighting, before engaging with the more sophisticated statistical work around NGT. First, it is not necessarily the case that convergence is being tested.[3] Suppose, for example, just for the sake of argument, that growth rates are randomly distributed across countries – each country has a growth rate that depends upon the throw of dice (which can also have negative numbers on them) from one period to the next. Those countries that have grown rapidly in the past, by chance, it must be emphasized, will have higher incomes and, by the law of averages, their growth rates will tend to be lower in the future, simply because they have been lucky enough to hit the jackpot in the past. Of course, exactly the opposite is true for those countries that have been unlucky in the past. On average, they will be luckier in the future. As a result, under these assumptions, there is an inbuilt automatic inverse relationship between past and future economic performance, even though, it should be emphasized, that performance is purely random. In other words, to the extent that the world is random, there is a bias towards supporting the hypothesis of absolute convergence.

Second, putting this aside, there is a more complex issue of whether like is being compared with like. An economy recovering from recession, for example, will tend to grow faster than another about to enter a recession. How do we know that we are comparing economies fairly over the phases of growth and cycles? It is not a simple matter of separating out peaks and troughs in growth performance, and only comparing peaks with peaks or troughs with troughs. This is to doctor the results, for the regression is supposed to explain differences in performance, and one economy's apparent trough might represent lower long-term growth as opposed to a temporary blip.

The problem can be illustrated in a different way by introducing the distinction between the short run and the long run, and the idea of steady state balanced growth (SSBG). For the latter, a term first put forward in the context of old growth theory, the economy is essentially in a growing equilibrium. A constant growth rate applies to all variables – capital, labour, savings and investment – and to output itself augmented by productivity. The economy from one period to the next looks just like an enlarged snapshot of what went before. The significance of SSBG will be examined later but, for the moment, the issue of peaks and troughs can be interpreted in terms of whether economies are adjusting along or towards their SSBG paths.

In other words, are we comparing the SSBG path of one country, as opposed to another (presumably, the ultimate determinant of convergence or otherwise), or the adjustment to such paths? If, as seems most likely in empirical work, it is the latter, then, there are serious problems, as illustrated by the diagrams. In Figure 1, it seems as if the two growth paths are converging without doubt. But what if, as illustrated in Figure 2, this is a perverse adjustment to SSBGs that are far from converging?[4]

The third problem with the simple regression of growth against initial level of per capita income is that it tends to presume that growth rates are independent of one another – they only depend on one's own initial level of income. But the world economy is full of interdependencies, which means that the growth rate of one country will depend not only on its own characteristics, but also on those of other countries. As the saying goes, when the US sneezes, the whole world catches a cold. But some have worse symptoms than others (and the same is true of feedback effects). As with the adjustment to SSBG paths, the

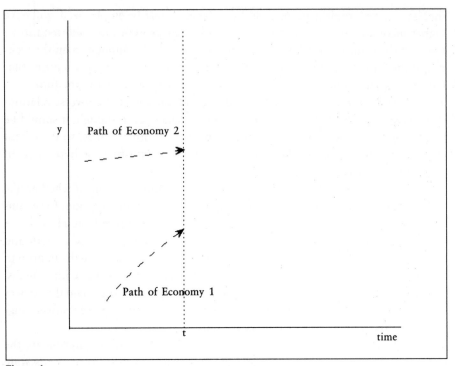

Figure 1

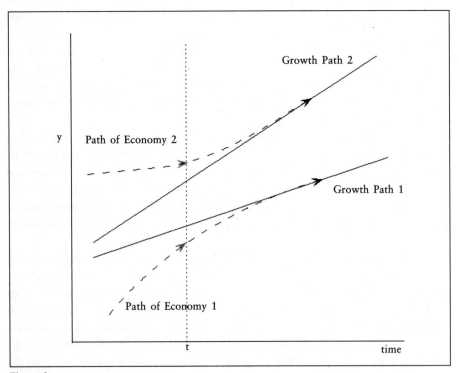

Figure 2

regression may be picking up short-run interactive effects, rather than a process of convergence.

Fourth, the equation as such does not explicitly lay out a full model and test it against any alternatives. As already seen, there might be random explanations for an inverse relationship. More generally, for any model from which the estimated equation is derived (as a reduced form), there are other empirical implications that ought to be tested as well – at least, in principle, as far as data allow. This is a way of interpreting the second problem: how does the equation relate to growth along SSBG, as opposed to adjustment to it? More substantive and wide-ranging, the process of growth will incorporate all sorts of other relations, such as those with savings and investment, and the distribution of income between wages and profits. Any model allowing for the reduced form is liable to have implications for these aspects as well. They ought to be used to test the model. Putting this another way, and more bluntly, even if the regression gives a good fit in some statistical sense, it would tell us very little about the causes of growth. This is partly because these are excluded from the regression itself; and partly because their own roles in the economy, in relation to other variables, have been set aside (how growth might affect such variables rather than vice versa – does the savings share tend to rise or fall with the growth rate, for example).

The first of these issues has been extensively examined in the NGT literature, under the rubric of testing for what is termed *conditional* convergence. The growth rates of two economies might differ not only because they differ in initial levels of per capita income, allowing for catch-up, but also because of differences in other variables that affect growth. Obvious candidates are levels of skills, however measured, but, in principle and in practice, a hundred variables or more could be reckoned to effect growth performance – from trade performance to levels of trust of one another, the judiciary and politicians. In this light, the equation for testing convergence is modified to introduce other independent variables, as many as a hundred, say, X_1, X_2, X_3 . . . X_{100}. Accordingly, the regression becomes:

$$g = c - a_0 y_0 + a_1 X_1 + a_2 X_2 + a_3 X_3 + \ldots + a_{100} X_{100}$$

These are known as Barro-type regressions.[5] As remarked, they have the effect of correcting for differences between countries in other variables when testing for convergence from higher or lower levels of initial per capita income. But they also incorporate another effect of much greater significance. Not only do they 'correct' the test by shifting from absolute to conditional convergence, they also test for the impact on growth of each variable X_i. The estimated parameters, a_i, inform us of the quantitative effect of each of the hundred variables or more on growth. In a nutshell, we are provided with a complete calculus for the causes of growth.

Unfortunately, apart from whatever is gained by adding more variables, Barro-type regressions suffer from exactly the same problems as the simpler test for absolute convergence. Indeed, they both intensify the earlier problems and add others of their own. Any model or theory underpinning the regression has faded into the distant background, at best. The result is remarkable. On the one hand, it is presumed that the quantitative impact of a hundred or more variables can be simply gauged for their impact on growth without regard to time, place and other specificities. On the other hand, the interaction among these variables is collapsed into a one-dimensional contribution to growth, while, in principle, ranging over all economic and non-economic variables as if they were independent of one another. Can we really expect to explain the levels of growth across all times and places by what is little more than a highly computerized process of graph-drawing and extrapolation?

The Barro-type regressions also add another statistical problem of their own: what is known as the stability of the regression. With a hundred or more variables that can be included or excluded, what happens if you add another variable or two, take some away, or do both? The answer is that not only, and not surprisingly, can the estimated effects of the variables change in magnitude – maybe trade liberalization was not so important after all – but also, the signs on the variables can change. What appears to indicate that a variable contributes to growth in one regression suggests that it does the opposite in another.

This conundrum is beautifully illustrated by the title of a paper by one of the leading practitioners in the field and Barro's co-author, Sala-i-Martin (1997), 'I Just Ran Four Million Regressions'. In order to get around the problem of the stability of the regression, he sets his computer to run that number of calculations automatically, including and excluding different sets of variables. The whole exercise is motivated by the idea that if a certain variable appears to affect growth significantly and in the same direction a sufficient number of times, then, it can be presumed to be reliable as a source of growth. In days gone by, such a procedure, albeit on the basis of considerably less computer power, would have been understood as 'data-fishing' and be considered illegitimate.

The classic example is the correlation, but not causation, between the rise of young women's miniskirts and the decline of the church. But the point can be made in more sophisticated fashion. Suppose, once again, for the sake of argument, that all variables – both growth and X_i – are randomly distributed. There is no relationship between any of them. By statistical chance, some will appear to be correlated (just like miniskirts and the church). Running four million regressions is one way of finding random correlations that are almost bound to exist. And if you ran the regressions in ten years' time, when the data have changed, the results might be entirely different.

In other words, the empirics of NGT are liable to teach us very little about the causes of growth (Kenny and Williams 2001). This is because of the failure to address the complex interactions among various variables in generating growth, and the different ways in which those variables interact with one another from one country to another, and from one time to another. In short, the empirical work is not well founded in theory. This is paradoxical, given its claim to derive from new or endogenous growth *theory*. So it is appropriate to look at the theory on its own merits, and see how it relates to the empirical work just described.

New Growth Theory for Old?

As already mentioned, new or endogenous growth theory takes the old or exogenous growth theory as its point of departure, and comparison between the two is instructive in highlighting how the new version is deemed to be an improvement on the old. Without going into great detail,[6] old growth theory is essentially a view of how the simple accumulation of resources leads to an expansion of output. The growth rate is, first and foremost, heavily constrained by the rate of growth of population, known as the natural rate of growth, and taken to be fixed, say, n. This is the rate at which the labour force can grow. On the other hand, capital stock grows at the rate s/v, where s is the savings rate and v is the capital–output rate (the inverse of how well capital resources are turned into output). This is known as the warranted rate of growth, say, g.

There is no immediate reason why g and n should be equal. If g is greater than n, there will be labour shortages for full utilization of available capital, and if n is greater than g, there will be high unemployment. The old neoclassical growth theory addressed this problem by presuming that capital and labour could be brought together in any combination. With a high savings rate (or low v), capital growth would not outstrip available labour because more capital-intensive techniques could be used, guaranteeing full employment of all resources at all times. Crucially, though, in such circumstances, the long-run growth rate still remains tied to n, taken as exogenous. At most, the high savings rate has the effect of increasing v (to bring s/v down to the level of n) and output per worker, but the growth rate remains the same.

Thus, old growth theory is unable – indeed, does not attempt – to explain productivity increase over time. At most, it can explain that one economy has a higher *level* of productivity than another (because of higher savings rate or lower rate of population growth). Productivity increase as a source of growth is taken as *exogenous*, falling like manna from heaven, to deploy a phrase used at the time, and explaining how the old growth theory got its name. As a result, in statistical work using the old growth theory, productivity increase is, at most, measured, rather than explained.

This is done through a technique known as growth accounting or measuring changes in total factor productivity. Consider an economy at two different points of time. Output, capital and labour will all have grown by a certain amount. Suppose output has grown by 6 per cent, capital by 4 per cent and labour by 2 per cent. Clearly, there has been some growth in productivity (2 per cent capital productivity, and 4 per cent labour productivity). Change in total factor productivity is measured by taking a weighted average of the two (using share of profit to weigh capital's contribution to growth, and share of wages for labour's). It is worth re-emphasizing that productivity increase is not being explained here; it is only being measured after deducting any contribution that has been made by capital and labour (or growth of inputs) from output growth. Explicitly, what is left over was called the residual or unexplained contribution to growth, and it was deemed to be the result of technological progress – how the economy better uses resources to turn inputs into outputs.

Despite these limited ambitions, there are a number of devastating problems with old growth theory worth highlighting. First, without going into details, it is based upon the assumption of perfect competition and full employment in all markets (possibly justified by the view that such assumptions hold in some nebulous long run). If resources are not fully employed at all times, then, changes in factor use will be measured as a change in productivity, even though technology may have remained unchanged. Similarly, if, for example, there are trade unions or monopolies, shifting the weights assigned to labour and capital, these will distort (upwards) the measured contributions made by these inputs. Paradoxically, a standard procedure is to measure shifting total factor productivity over time, and then to explain its patterns by the emergence of trade unions, or a long depression, for example. But such explanations violate the assumptions on which the calculations have been made in the first place!

Second, old growth theory is based on SSBG, previously described in terms of an economy growing at a constant rate and, otherwise, everything remaining in the same proportions. Casual acquaintance with the history of growth suggests how inappropriate this is. In particular, development is based upon major transformations in the proportions of activity in the economy – as agriculture, for example, gives way to industry, which, in turn, gives way to services in 'mature' economies. This is indicative of a broader point that, even if we reduce development to growth, the process is embedded in major socio-economic transformations that are omitted from consideration by the old growth theory – industrialization, urbanization, the creation of health, education and welfare systems, etc., all tied to the emergence of a modern state.

Third, empirical measures of the residual depend heavily on what inputs are included at what levels of disaggregation. As more inputs are incorporated – such as the skills of the workforce, for example – the unexplained part of the residual tends to be nibbled away. So the division between the explained and the unexplained contributions to growth depends on how far the explanation is taken.

But the most destructive weakness of the old growth theory in its neoclassical version derives from what is known as the Cambridge critique or controversy over capital theory.[7] This has many dimensions, and is open to a number of complementary interpretations. It is best summarized here as follows. The old neoclassical growth model treats the economy as if it has only one sector or one good that serves, for example, in this capacity for all consumption and investment purposes in all respects. The issue is whether such a model, with only one good, offers theoretical and empirical results that can stand as representative for models (and hence, economies) with more than one good. Not surprisingly, the answer is a simple negative.

Even on its own neoclassical terms, the one-sector model necessarily misrepresents the properties of more general models. In general, for example, any change in the more complicated model must be interpreted as if it is due to change within the one-sector model. If there is a shift in demand alone, that is, with no change in conditions of supply or total factor productivity, this can only be measured as a change in the latter. Suppose preferences shift towards consumption goods that are more capital-intensive in production. This will tend to increase the demand for capital goods and their price. In one-sector terms, this will have to be measured as an increase in the supply of capital itself (as there is, in the one-sector model, with no relative prices between goods, no way of distinguishing a change in the quantity of capital and a change in its price).

Such unavoidable problems in the empirical measurement of total factor productivity have equally devastating counterparts in the theoretical results of the one-sector model – the idea, for example, that there is necessarily an inverse relationship between the quantity of capital and the profit rate, or that the marginal product of capital from a production function can determine the rate of profit, and similarly for the marginal product of labour and wages. The simple conclusion is that the old growth theory is an unacceptable shambles.

Tellingly, such had been accepted, after considerable resistance, in the closely fought controversy itself. Literally, the conclusion drawn in the very last word in the debate at the time went to leading neoclassical economist and Nobel Prize winner, Paul Samuelson (1966: 582): 'If all this causes headaches for those nostalgic for the old time parables of neoclassical writing, we must remind ourselves that scholars are not born to live an easy existence. We must respect, and appraise, the facts of life.' Unfortunately, his advice has not been heeded, and the neoclassical parables drawn from the one-sector model have continued to be prominent in both theoretical and empirical work.

This is an apposite point at which to assess the extent to which NGT represents a theoretical advance over the old growth theory, and whether and in what sense it warrants Gordon Brown's nomenclature of 'post-neoclassical', as suggested in the earlier quotation. In terms of the consequences of the Cambridge critique of capital theory, it might just as well not exist, as far as NGT is concerned. The whole literature suffers a collective memory loss and proceeds, for example, as if production can still be based on a simple production function, with marginal products determining distribution, etc.[8] In this and, as will be seen, in other respects, NGT displays total continuity with its predecessor. The failure to formulate proper hypotheses with alternatives, to explore the full empirical implications of the model as a whole, and the fallacies of the empirical techniques employed are also carried over from old to new, even if with changed characteristics. In addition, both draw heavily upon SSBG as an organizing concept, although NGT does allow the possibility for multiple equilibria (the same model might have two or more equilibrium growth rates, the exact outcome depending on initial conditions or choices, over saving rates, for example).

In what sense, then, is NGT new? Its own claims to novelty rest upon a breach with the assumption that productivity increase is exogenous, and that the growth rate is otherwise tied to the rate of population growth. For the old growth theory, if there is mobility of capital and of technology, for example, then there would be a tendency for capital–labour ratios to be equalized across the world. This is because capital-deficient (rich) countries would have higher (lower) marginal products of capital, and stimulate inflows (outflows) in pursuit of higher profitability. Similarly, it would make sense to use best available technology with available resources, or, in more technical terms, the same production function should prevail across the world. All this leads to the conclusion of the absolute convergence of per capita income, an inevitable conclusion of the old growth theory (for factor and technology mobility). Such explains the focus in NGT empirical work on the convergence hypothesis.

Now, it might be argued that the assumption of free flows of capital and technology is unrealistic. At least implicit in the old growth theory is the idea that countries are integral in some sense, and form barriers to such free flows. NGT does not necessarily dispute the presence of such barriers but, equally, it does not take them to be exogenous. If capital and technology do not flow freely to equalize per capita incomes around the world, this should be studied as a matter of choice within economic theory itself. Why would optimizing agents persist in accumulating more capital in one place, rather than spreading it around, and why would not best-practice technology always be made widely available, even if at a price?

Answers to this question, arising out of the perceived weaknesses of the old growth theory in unambiguously predicting convergence, also open up examination of the sources of productivity increase (whether equalized or not). Underpinning old growth theory are two crucial assumptions: perfectly working markets and constant returns to scale. In order to endogenize growth and productivity, NGT breaches both of these assumptions.

It assumes increasing returns to scale. The implications of doing so are immediate and dramatic. With increasing returns, the level of productivity depends upon the absolute size of the economy, and there is an incentive to concentrate production in one place (although this may have to be balanced against the costs of monopoly, transport and other costs to consumers, and so on). Further, whichever economy has an initial advantage, for whatever reason, in 'industrialization' will tend to maintain and even widen that advantage. Put in slightly different terms, if an economy has a higher savings rate, it will tend to attract higher productivity increases as it accrues economies of scale. Not surprisingly, NGT tends to argue that, left to the market, the savings rate will be too low relative to some social optimum.

Interestingly, the explanation for endogenous productivity increase in the previous paragraph, based on given increasing returns to scale, is limited for examining technical change. To use the vernacular, it does allow for shifts along the production function (increasing returns) but does not explain shifts (upwards) in the production function. This is where the bulk of the NGT literature lies, as it seeks to explain and endogenize increasing returns to scale through the presence of market imperfections (of which increasing returns is an example in and of itself, since competitive price-taking cannot lead to equilibrium, given 'natural' monopoly).

Broadly, this is done in three different, if often overlapping, ways. The first is to posit a theory of the production of productivity increase. This can be direct, with a production function itself for technical change, with choices being made over the level of R&D expenditure or other social and economic infrastructure that contribute, directly or indirectly, to productivity performance. Here, there can be a trade-off between use of current resources (at the expense of consumption) and higher productivity in the future. Whatever is achieved in productivity increase may not be generalized because of market imperfections such as a patent system or the non-marketability of new technology. By the same token, productivity increase can arise from resources devoted to raising the skills (human capital, training, etc.) of the workforce. Such direct methods of raising productivity (through allocation of resources to that end) are complemented by indirect methods derived automatically from economic activity itself, the most prominent example being learning-by-doing or on-the-job training.

The second way of generating productivity increase in NGT is by appeal to externalities (that lead to increasing returns to scale). A most favoured example is that of the industrial district and its generation of spill-over effects. One firm's activity may create advantages for others that do not accrue to itself (and vice versa). Consequently, there is a tendency to underinvest; but, the more investment there is, the faster is the growth of productivity. Of course, any positive externality can be interpreted in this way.

Third, NGT can rely upon some sort of structural (mis)match to explain differences in growth performance. Suppose there are two different paths that an economy can take – low and high roads. For the low road, workers do not bother to train themselves because no skilled jobs are available, and firms do not invest in new technology because there are no skilled workers available to use it. The opposite holds for the high road, in which workers commit to training and firms are innovative. For economic theory, it is an interesting modelling exercise to determine whether the economy goes for the high or the low road, and what might make it switch from one to the other.

This account offers an overall perspective on how NGT proceeds analytically. In a nutshell, some forms of market imperfections lead directly or indirectly to increasing returns to scale, and thus allow for differences in productivity and, hence, growth rates. More detailed and critical scrutiny of the literature offers the following insights.

First, the literature has grown explosively. The reason is that there is such a wealth of market imperfections on which to draw and to project on to productivity increases. Learning-by-doing, for example, can be disaggregated into learning by adopting, adapting, importing and exporting. Without exaggeration, it is appropriate to see the literature as drawing upon the idea of technical change in two different ways. One is purely speculative, invented. Let us suppose that education is created through a production function and the corresponding skills are used similarly. The other, less prominent, is to draw parasitically upon earlier literature, and strip it out of its broader vision and context, for which reliance upon Schumpeter is an example (for his waves of creative destruction).

In either case, the complex and diverse ways in which technological change and productivity increase are generated, and how scholars of (the history of) technology have highlighted this, are studiously ignored.[9] The same is true of the approaches of classical political economy and Marxism. Adam Smith, for example, opens the *Wealth of Nations* with a discussion of the division of labour and its impact on productivity increase (not least through the famous pin factory).[10] And Marx's mature political economy is heavily concentrated on the sources and implications of productivity increase.[11]

Second, whether in terms of its analytical origins or in terms of the model as theory itself, NGT is profoundly microeconomic in content. Individuals optimize and/or the economy is treated as if made up of representative individuals. In this respect, it is worth citing Lucas (1987: 108) to the effect that 'the term "macroeconomic" will simply disappear from use and the modifier "micro" will be superfluous'. This is not simply, however, a matter of commitment or otherwise to methodological individualism – the idea that there is no such thing as society or holistic or systemic analysis other than through aggregating over individuals.

Even accepting its individualism, the NGT literature is remarkable in going from one contribution to another for each to draw upon a single microeconomic idea. Lucas (1988), for example, draws on produced human capital as a source of productivity increase, projecting it on to the performance of the economy as a whole. Perversely, when we aggregate thousands of individual contributions in this vein, the result is at least hundreds of different microeconomic effects on macroeconomic performance. These will have different interactions and impacts by sector, country and other circumstances. How can we study each micro-factor in isolation as if it were macro? The answer is that we cannot, but, as already seen above, an entirely unacceptable resolution is found by banging out questionable Barro-type regressions.

Third, such conundrums shed light on the mathematics and modelling of NGT. Given that the literature as a whole is made up of any number of microeconomic factors generating productivity increases, it would make sense to combine as many of these as possible into a single model. The problem is that the mathematics becomes intractable once more than one or two factors are introduced. Despite this, NGT models are able to generate more or less any sort of dynamic behaviour required – across both multiple equilibria and complex dynamics. Choose any stylized facts about patterns of growth, and a competent mathematical economist can model them.

Even so, the models tend to be subject to restrictive requirements in order to be able to generate SSBG as the focal point for the dynamics, and without which they tend to lead to infinite output in finite time or the decline of endogenous productivity increases to marginal proportions. Solow (1992), the initiating author of old growth theory, shows, for example, that Lucas' (1988) model of endogenous growth through skilled labour depends upon the arbitrary and apparently unwitting assumption of constant returns to scale in producing skills and increasing returns in using them! In this light of – dependence on SSBG, intractability of the model when including relevant variables, sensitivity of the model to its assumptions – it is hardly surprising that the empirical work should have such loose and questionable connections to the theory.

At this point, it is worth commenting, in passing, that proponents of the old growth theory tend to be disparaging about the pretensions of the new. This is not simply, as the new might have it, a defence of old ideas for the sake of it. In his summary of prospects for macroeconomics in the twenty-first century, Solow (2000: 153, 154) comments that new growth theory 'appears to be dwindling to a modest flow of normal science. This is not a bad thing. . . . It is hard to see where growth theory is going.' Indeed, 'endogenous growth theory is no longer expected to be the key that unlocks the secret of the universe. . . . Does endogenous growth theory have anything to tell us about [growth in the US over the next few decades]'?

In contrast, as if to prove Solow's case of barely concealed contempt for the gap between the ambition and achievement of the new growth theory, in the same issue of the journal, on the same topic of twenty-first-century macro, Lucas (2000) offers a model of the history of industrialization across the world in which national economies *randomly* enter a growth and catch-up process. The model did not work (that is, fit the data) until modified to allow rate of entry to growth to increase over time. Lucas recognizes that the model

> is mechanical, without much in the way of explicit economics. It lacks an explicit description of preferences, technology, and market arrangements. . . . It entirely omits factors, like capital flows and the demographic transition, that continue to play essential roles in the diffusion of the industrial revolution: why it began in England, why it began in the eighteenth century, why it spread first to other European economies, or why it diffused so slowly for so long.

And, without any sense of irony, he adds: 'But for all these deficiencies, it is undeniably an *economic* model: No one but a theoretical economist would have written it down' (ibid.: 166).

Further, it leads Lucas to predict that the inequality of the past industrial revolutions will be overcome as others industrialize over the coming century. This is all because people across time and space behave much the same, and differ only in the resources at their disposal – and these will tend to be equalized with the mobility of capital to its highest rate of return. No wonder, Solow, schooled in an intellectual environment of greater respect for Lucas' omitted factors and lesser expectations of *economic* models, is little short of scathing in his assessment of new growth theory.

Fourth, in view of the properties of NGT, in what sense does it warrant the claim to advance and novelty over the old? Note that neither market imperfections nor increasing returns to scale are new to neoclassical economics. And, in this sense, NGT cannot legitimately claim to be post-neoclassical. However, the traditional neoclassical treatment of market imperfections (externalities and increasing returns) is through partial equilibrium, and, as such, goes back to Alfred Marshall more than a century earlier. His treatment gave rise to the idea of lost consumer surplus as a result of the inefficiencies associated with market imperfections.

Essentially, NGT departs from this in two significant ways. On the one hand, it elevates the microeconomics of market imperfections to the economy as a whole. On the other hand, it translates static shifts in consumer surplus (what are termed once and for all 'dead-weight' gains or losses) into permanent differences in growth rates. As it were, the consumer surplus associated with market imperfections is allowed to accrue over time. Nor is the treatment of productivity increase through a variety of mechanisms new to NGT. Arrow (1962), for example, is the classic source for learning-by-doing. He drew his theory from the empirical example of the construction of wooden aircraft frames, with labour time declining with output. It is hardly surprising that this and other studies of productivity increase in the past should have hesitated before positing their insights as a general theory of growth for economies as a whole.

Significantly, older neoclassical economists steeped in old growth theory have limited sympathy for NGT. One reason is that the presence of market imperfections and increasing returns to scale effectively undermines any remaining rationale for a one-sector model. The mainstream preoccupation with general equilibrium theory coincided with the emergence of the old growth theory. It seemed to justify the idea, as with Keynesian macroeconomics, that some simultaneous equilibrium of markets, with corresponding prices ironed out of supply and demand, lay behind the simpler one-sector model of growth. For Arrow (2000: 173), though:

> The steady history of competitive equilibrium theory and the contrasting history of increasing returns theory are themselves conditions on the coherence of one theory and the lack of it in the other. . . . Increasing returns arguments have been applied fruitfully . . . but one has to start again each time. In particular, what should be the core of any economic theory, a theory of value, is still not yet well defined.

Thus, paradoxically, in seeking to explain why capitalist economies experience differences in rates of growth and productivity, NGT effectively assumes away the presence of markets by failing to provide, or being able to fall back upon, a theory of value.

Another reason for antipathy to NGT from within traditional mainstream neoclassical economics derives from the extent to which NGT simplistically incorporates non-economic variables into the explanation for growth. This is transparent in the case of the Barro-type regressions or, indeed, for the role of 'human capital' through the education and skill system. But traditional neo-classical economics also displays reservations over the extent to which rational choice can be extended beyond the market sphere, as if each and every variable and outcome is explicable in terms of agents optimizing over given preferences. But this is to engage with the very different intellectual climates in which old and new growth theory emerged. Addressing these sheds different light on the relationship between the two than suggested by the idea of the new as the improved version of the old.

New Theory for New Times

Old growth theory dates from 1956, in the middle of the Cold War, when developing countries were first beginning to experience independence. A key text of the time, linking economics to history and history to development, was Rostow's *Stages of Economic Growth*.[12] It sought to draw out stylized stages of development from the experience of the industrialized countries in order to provide lessons for the developing world in ways that would offer alternatives to the Soviet-type system. In this respect, old growth theory had very limited aims. It showed what could and could not be achieved through the simple accumulation of resources. Indeed, Solow's (1957) original calculation of the residual contribution to growth put it as high as 87.5 per cent. Consequently, the drive to the stage of mass production and consumption could not rely exclusively on high rates of savings and investment. For Rostow, it also depended upon the release of entrepreneurial spirit from the confines of both authoritarian communism, as well as Rostow's pre-capitalist custom and culture.

Consequently, his 'non-communist manifesto' sought to persuade developing countries to follow the lead taken by the western world. This had to be interpreted and understood in terms of Keynesianism, welfarism and modernization in the first decades of the post-war period. It involved considerable intervention by the state, to provide socio-economic infrastructure and also the policies necessary for successful industrialization. Such were the perspectives informing the McNamara era at the World Bank. They were, however, complemented by a particular understanding of the relationship between economics and the other social sciences. Questions concerning custom and culture were perceived to lie outside of economics as a discipline, alongside more focused attention on entrepreneurship and technological change. In short, old growth theory displayed an acute awareness of its limits and limitations. At most, it represented a theory of resource accumulation as a core process around which other, unexplained processes revolved.

In the 1980s, however, when NGT first appeared, the appeal of the Soviet system was in decline, and neoliberalism had emerged as the ideological response to the end of the post-war boom and as the driving force behind development policy in what came to be known as the Washington Consensus. Not surprisingly, the Washington Consensus had no point of contact with NGT since the latter suggested that market forces do not work well in the presence of market imperfections and increasing returns to scale. But, by the mid-1990s, the appeal and legitimacy of the Washington Consensus had begun to fade and it ultimately gave way to the post-Washington Consensus launched by Joseph Stiglitz.[13] In principle and rhetoric, the corresponding new development economics emphasizes the heavy incidence of market imperfections and how they give rise to both economic *and* non-economic outcomes in the form of institutions, for example. Further, the new development economics pioneered by Stiglitz and arising out of market imperfections is itself part and parcel of a much broader expansion of the approach. It incorporates the new economic sociology, the new institutional economics, the new political economy, the new economic geography and so on.[14]

In this respect, it is hardly surprising that NGT should so readily discard the traditional respect for the boundaries of the economic approach and incorporate socio-economic variables into its analysis. It does so with little or no regard for the insights of other disciplines except to provide lists of variables to incorporate within Barro-type regressions. The result is to allow for a redefinition of developing countries and development. First, the modernization of the McNamara era is displaced by the neoliberalism of the Washington Consensus. The latter, it should be noted, rests on an appeal to a mechanism – the market – without specifying what it brings as development, especially in terms of the traditional concerns of modernization.

By the same token, the more rounded post-Washington Consensus appeals to development as the correction of market and institutional failings, with limited acknowledgement of what development is in terms of the major transformations associated with industrialization, urbanization and so on. In the case of NGT, this limited understanding of the complexity and diversity of development – a one regression fits all – has its counterpart in the vanity of almost perfect economic and social engineering. For, what the regression tells us is the way in which growth will respond to each and every (policy) variable. From telephone lines per thousand population to the impact of a black market in foreign exchange, the policy-maker is empowered with a calculus of cause and effect that can only be envied in a world so riddled with poverty.[15]

Notes

[1] See Fine (1982) for a fuller account of classical political economy in these terms, and Fine and Saad–Filho (2003) for Marx's political economy.

[2] See Fine (2003a) and Fine (2000) for a more extensive, if earlier, critical review of the literature. See Aghion and Howitt (1998) for an excellent overview *from an orthodox perspective*.

[3] What follows refers to a long-established statistical fallacy, known as Galton's regression to the mean.

[4] On all of this, see especially Quah (1995, 1996a, 1996b).

5 See Barro and Sala-i-Martin (1995).

6 For an excellent outline of the old growth theory, see Sen, ed. (1970), especially his introduction. Solow (1956, 1957) are the classic contributions.

7 The name derives from the debate that took place primarily between Cambridge, England (the critics) and MIT, Cambridge, USA (the orthodoxy). For reviews of the debate, see Harcourt (1976) and Fine (1980: Chapters 5, 6).

8 See Hodgson (1997) and Fine (2003b).

9 NGT makes practically no reference, for example, to the national system of innovation approach or to evolutionary approaches. See Nelson (1997), for example.

10 See Kurz (1997).

11 See Fine and Saad–Filho (2003).

12 See the chapter titled 'The New Development Economics' in this volume for a broader discussion of what follows.

13 For a useful collection of Stiglitz's articles elaborating the post-Washington Consensus, see Chang, ed. (2001), and Fine, Lapavitsas and Pincus, eds (2001) for critical assessments.

14 For an assessment in these terms, see Fine (2002).

15 The example is taken from the first and, for some time, the only theoretical paper purporting to support PRSPs (Devarajan *et al.* 2000). For a critique, see the chapter on 'Financial Programming and the IMF' in this volume.

References

Aghion, Phillipe and Peter Howitt (1998), *Endogenous Growth Theory* (Cambridge, Massachusetts: MIT Press).

Arrow, Kenneth (1962), 'The Economic Implications of Learning by Doing', *Review of Economic Studies*, 28 (1): 155–73.

—— (2000), 'Increasing Returns: Historiographic Issues and Path Dependence', *European Journal of History of Economic Thought*, 7 (2): 171–80.

Barro, Robert J. and Xavier Sala-i-Martin (1995), *Economic Growth* (New York: McGraw-Hill).

Chang, Ha-Joon, ed. (2001), *Joseph Stiglitz and the World Bank: The Rebel Within* (London: Anthem Press).

Crafts, Nick (1996), 'Post-Neoclassical Endogenous Growth Theory – What are its Policy Implications?', *Oxford Review of Economic Policy*, 12 (2): 30–47.

Devarajan, Shantayanan, William Easterly, Hippolyte Fofack, Delfin S. Go, Alejandro Izquierdo, Christian Petersen, Lodovico Pizzati, Christopher Scott and Luis Serven (2000), 'A Macroeconomic Framework for Poverty Reduction Strategy Papers', World Bank, Washington DC; http://www.worldbank.org/research/growth/pdfiles/devarajan%20etal.pdf, subsequently with an application to Zambia, 2002, http://www.worldbank.org/files/12937_TK_Paper_Chap_13_Devarajan_Go.pdf.

Fine, Ben (1980), *Economic Theory and Ideology* (London: Edward Arnold).

—— (1982), *Theories of the Capitalist Economy* (London: Edward Arnold).

—— (2000), 'Endogenous Growth Theory: A Critical Assessment', *Cambridge Journal of Economics*, 24 (2): 245–65.

—— (2002), 'Economics Imperialism and the New Development Economics as Kuhnian Paradigm Shift', *World Development*, 30 (12): 2057–70.

—— (2003a), 'New Growth Theory', in Ha-Joon Chang, ed., *Rethinking Development Economics* (London: Anthem Press).

—— (2003b), 'Capital Theory', in John E. King, ed., *The Elgar Companion to Post-Keynesian Economics* (Cheltenham: Edward Elgar).

Fine, Ben and Alfredo Saad–Filho (2003), *Marx's 'Capital'*, fourth edition (London: Pluto).

Fine, Ben, Costas Lapavitsas and Jonathan Pincus, eds (2001), *Development Policy in the Twenty-First Century: Beyond the Post-Washington Consensus* (London: Routledge).

Harcourt, Geoffrey (1976), 'The Cambridge Controversies: Old Ways and New Horizons – or Dead End', *Oxford Economic Papers*, 28 (1): 25–65.

Hodgson, Geoffrey (1997), 'The Fate of the Cambridge Capital Controversy', in Philip Arestis,

Gabriel Palma and Malcolm Sawyer, eds, *Capital Controversy, Post-Keynesian Economics and the History of Economics: Essays in Honour of Geoff Harcourt, Volume I* (London: Routledge).

Lucas, Robert (1987), *Models of Business Cycles* (Oxford: Blackwell).

—— (1988), 'On the Mechanics of Economic Development', *Journal of Monetary Economics*, 22 (1): 3–42.

—— (2000), 'Some Macroeconomics for the Twenty-First Century', *Journal of Economic Perspectives*, 14 (1): 159–68.

Kenny, Charles and David Williams (2001), 'What Do We Know about Economic Growth? Or, Why Don't We Know Very Much?', *World Development*, 29 (1): 1–22.

Kurz, Heinz D. (1997), 'What Could the "New" Growth Theory Teach Smith or Ricardo?', *Economic Issues*, 2 (2): 1–20.

McKenzie, Richard (1979), 'The Non-Rational Domain and the Limits of Economic Analysis', *Southern Economic Journal*, 46 (1): 145–57.

Nelson, Richard (1997), 'How New is New Growth Theory?', *Challenge*, September/October: 29–58.

Quah, Danny (1995), 'Galton's Fallacy and Tests of the Convergence Hypothesis', in Torben M. Andersen and Karl O. Moene, eds, *Endogenous Growth* (Oxford: Blackwell); reproduced from *Scandinavian Journal of Economics*, 95 (4), 1993.

—— (1996a), 'Twin Peaks: Growth and Convergence in Models of Distribution Dynamics', *Economic Journal*, 106 (437): 1045–55.

—— (1996b), 'Empirics for Economic Growth and Convergence', *European Economic Review*, 40 (6): 1353–75.

Romer, Paul M. (1986), 'Increasing Returns and Long-Run Growth', *Journal of Political Economy*, 94 (5): 1002–37.

Rostow, Walt W. (1960), *The Stages of Economic Growth: A Non-Communist Manifesto* (Cambridge: Cambridge University Press); third revised edition, 1990.

Sala-i-Martin, Xavier (1997), 'I Just Ran Four Million Regressions', processed, Colombia University; revised to appear as, 'I Just Ran Two Million Regressions', *American Economic Review*, 87 (2): 178–83.

Samuelson, Paul (1966), 'A Summing Up', *Quarterly Journal of Economics*, 80 (4): 568–83.

Sen, Amartya, ed. (1970), *Growth Economics* (Harmondsworth: Penguin).

Solow, Robert (1956), 'A Contribution to the Theory of Economic Growth', *Quarterly Journal of Economics*, 70 (1): 65–94.

—— (1957), 'Technical Change and the Aggregate Production Function', *Review of Economics and Statistics*, 39 (3): 312–20.

—— (1992), *Siena Lectures on Endogenous Growth Theory* (Siena: University of Siena).

—— (2000), 'Toward a Macroeconomics of the Medium Run', *Journal of Economic Perspectives*, 14 (1): 151–58.

Financial Programming and the IMF[1]

Ben Fine

This chapter is concerned with the financial programming (FP), or macro-economics, of the International Monetary Fund (IMF). FP, in principle, is associated with preferential loans to member countries of the IMF that need support to adjust to severe balance of payments problems. In practice, FP has gone far beyond this. First, it has been much more than a temporary set of measures in response to acute crises. Rather, the so-called conditionalities have been attached to loans over relatively long periods of time. Second, they have also been extended to cover far more policy variables than those usually associated with a short-term response to a balance of payments crisis.

Of course, this could be rationalized on the grounds that FP is required not only to make short-term adjustments, but also to guard against recreating the causes of balance of payments problems in the future. This is, in a sense, to acknowledge that short-run adjustment needs to be set in the context of the longer term, which, for developing countries, means promoting development itself. It is also to raise the issue of the relationship between the IMF and the World Bank, with the latter presumed to be more concerned with longer-term issues (and, as a mirror image, its concern that short-term crises should not undermine its project and other finance). At times, there have been tensions between the two organizations over who makes what sorts of loans and with what conditionalities. More often than not, these tensions have been resolved with a division of responsibilities and/or conformity of approach, most notably in the Washington Consensus and, equally, its successor in the form of poverty reduction strategy papers (PRSPs).[2]

These concerns raise other issues worth highlighting. One is how development itself is conceived within the framework of FP. This is something on which some emphasis will be placed in what follows. If FP is designed to stabilize or adjust the economy, it is reasonable to ask to what end the economy is being guided. Further, it is important to distinguish the scholarship (or analytical) content of FP from its rhetorical or ideological role, and these, in turn, from policies in practice. Thus, for example, the IMF has been closely associated variously with monetarism, neoliberalism, Reaganism and Thatcherism. And for good reason.

A mean and lean state has been promoted, together with the dictum that markets work well and the state works badly. But in some respects, as will be shown, the analytical framework of FP is not monetarist. Indeed, and in addition, this is necessary in order for policy to incorporate a degree of discretion. And, in practice, policy has been highly discretionary and increasingly interventionist as adjusting economies are given more and more instructions on more and more issues, notwithstanding recent concessions to bolster the fiction of 'national ownership' instead of policy conditionalities.

The focus here will be on the shifting analytical framework underpinning FP. How does the IMF justify what it does theoretically? This is not necessarily identical with its rhetoric or its policies in practice. Indeed, I would argue that the relationship between these three aspects is complex, and varies across time, place and policy area itself. Sometimes they conform to one another, and sometimes they do not. To what extent, for example, does the recent apparent increase in concern with poverty reflect a change in approach, ideology and policy? And, to introduce another factor, how is this affected by external pressures, political, ideological or otherwise?[3] The discussion that follows only bears on these issues in passing.

The chapter is organized as follows. In the following sections, it critically evaluates four 'main events' in the evolution of the theory informing FP. This might be thought to be unduly selective, both for its limited coverage and for its failure to address diversity of opinion and debate, and how they have been resolved. But there is no alternative. For, as is observed after thirty years of FP, in a paper intended to elaborate 'theoretical aspects of the design of fund-supported adjustment programs' (IMF 1987: 1), the approach 'is based largely on oral tradition. There is surprisingly little readily accessible written material on its theoretical underpinnings, in particular, on the interaction among policy measures in achieving the ultimate objectives. . . . Since the early 1970s, however, the conception and the structure of adjustment programs have gradually evolved and expanded.'

Unfortunately, the oral tradition continues to prosper and, correspondingly, accessible material remains notable for its absence, whether this be an omission in translation of the oral tradition to the written word or not. As will be seen, this outcome is not surprising, given the quality of what has made the transition. It is for the reader to judge whether this does – or does not – reflect little or lots waiting in the pipeline. But the concluding remarks suggest that the low rate of transfer between the two is most likely due to the absence of substance than a blockage in the passage to wider access through writing and reading.

The Polak Model

Analytical justification for, and exposition of, FP derives from the classic paper of Jean-Jacques Polak, head of research at the IMF from 1958 until 1979 (Polak 1957). First of all, it is interesting to recall the justification for his framework, one that he clearly considered to be inadequate in some sense.[4] A focus on financial variables was motivated by the belief that these were the source of the only reliable data and, equally, the main lever of policy through control of domestic credit creation (or money supply). This is, however, a weak rationale, as can be shown by appeal to a medical analogy. We might only have a thermometer for diagnosing illness and aspirin for treating temperature, but this hardly renders them most appropriate for all illnesses!

As mentioned, FP is associated with the taint of monetarism because of its neoliberalism. But matters are not so simple. It is worth elaborating monetarism's approach to the balance of payments in its simplest version in order to reveal how FP differs from it, at least in principle. Monetarism in an international context is known as the monetary approach to the balance of payments (MABP), and is dependent upon a much older tradition known as the species-flow mechanism. Essentially, if an economy has a balance of trade deficit, then, it will have to pay for it through release of its currency reserves. This will reduce the domestic money supply and the domestic price level. Imports will become more expensive and exports cheaper. This is presumed to correct the balance of trade deficit and the net outcome will have been to reduce the level of domestic reserves of money.

There are two fundamental properties of this account. One is the assumption of full employment so that the deficit economy, for example, shifts effortlessly and instantly into producing more export goods and import substitutes. The other is that prices immediately adjust to international levels, so that the law of one price holds across the world (subject to transport costs, etc.). In other words, markets are deemed to work perfectly and instantaneously in determining the level and composition of output. There are also some simplifying assumptions, such as absence of any capital flows, other than those that are out of official reserves, to correct for balance of trade.

Now, FP is not as extreme as the MABP, although as late as 1977, the IMF (1977) seemed to indicate otherwise in terms of how it described itself. This divergence from the MABP follows because FP offers a theory of nominal national income (output times price) that can vary. For it to do so, either prices must change and, therefore, not be fixed, as required by the MABP's law of one price, or real output must change, violating the assumption of always being at full employment. Essentially, FP makes one minor adjustment to the species-flow mechanism of the MABP. This is to allow for imports only to be paid for after a lag of one period. As a result, an increase in domestic credit will allow nominal income to increase without an immediate and compensating outflow of reserves.

A key issue for FP becomes how that extra nominal income turns out in practice. It can come in the form of either increased real output or increased prices. No answer is given within the model itself. Instead, presumably through a visiting team, a separate assessment is made of capacity potential and whether it will be brought into play by increased demand. Here, a degree of discretion is available. The more pessimistic the assessment, the stronger is the advice to conform to potential output and to restrict sources of demand, or to face inflation and loss of currency reserves.

Polak provides a very simple model in the first version of FP. Its details need not detain us, but it is important to recognize the properties of any such model. First, what are its equilibrium properties? Second is the stability of equilibrium. In other words, does the model have a point of rest and does the economy tend to converge upon it? Significantly, somewhat illogically, the proponents have been more concerned with the second than the first point. In particular, where will the economy move to in the next period or two? The motivation for being so short-sighted is that conditions will have changed in a couple of years, and the IMF team will have returned in order to make another discretionary judgement about potential output.

Analytically, however, this is not the correct way to proceed. Before we examine the movement of the economy, we need to know what it is moving around or towards, as this represents the core of the economy – what the IMF and others like to term the fundamentals. In the case of the original Polak model, the answer is very simple. The equilibrium turns out to be equal to A/m, where A is the ability to pay for imports (through exports, domestic credit creation and foreign aid, for example) and m is the propensity to spend on imports out of domestic income. This looks very like a simple Keynesian multiplier, with A as autonomous expenditure and m the propensity to save. It does have similarities. But the underlying logic is slightly different. All the model tells us is that the economy is bound to conform to its given capacity to pay for its import bill. For example, if m is one-quarter, then, equilibrium requires that nominal income does not exceed four times capacity to pay for imports. For m equal to one-third, the 'multiplier' is three times.

Two telling points can be made at this stage. First, if the economy or, more exactly, the model of the economy is stable, as would be wanted, it is tied to an equilibrium. This means the model cannot tell us anything about growth, let alone more wide-ranging aspects of development. Essentially, it precludes consideration of development. Implicitly, it is presumed that adjusting the economy around a given short-term equilibrium is the best way to promote change from that equilibrium. But the model has no way of investigating or incorporating that change from equilibrium to growth.

Second, to some extent putting the same point in a different way, all the interesting issues concerned with development are set aside in the model – capacity to pay for imports, import propensity, capacity for growth and so on. Development policy should not be geared towards tying an economy to its equilibrium but should seek to change the so-called 'fundamentals', as this is the process of development itself. Further, austere macroeconomic policy cannot be presumed, as has been heavily emphasized by critics of neoliberalism in general and of FP in particular, to be neutral with respect to longer-term outcomes. Depressed investment and output in the short run, for example, as a consequence of deflationary policies to correct balance of payments, will reduce growth and development. In short, FP based on the initial Polak model sets aside considerations of growth and development altogether, and has no basis on which to claim justification for such a procedure in terms of the beneficial knock-on effects of the short run for the long run. This issue is simply not addressed.

Keynesianism as Development?

The next major development in FP's use of macroeconomic theory was offered by Polak in collaboration with Argy in 1971. Details of the model are confined to the Appendix. Here, a more informal account will be given of its key properties. First, as is apparent, it is much more complicated from a technical point of view. There are far more equations and also more economics. The Polak model relied almost exclusively on national income identities, as do its successors, but the latter are complemented by many more behavioural equations. Essentially, the only economics in the Polak model is the assumption of lagged payment for imports with the associated propensity to import given by m. Casual inspection of the equations in the Appendix reveals it has many more behavioural equations and corresponding parameters. There are investment, consumption, demand for money and foreign capital flow functions.

This reflects a key property of all models – that they are disaggregated, to a greater or lesser extent, to accommodate a particular view of how the economy is constructed out of its constituent markets. Otherwise, this does not offer anything different by way of economic theory as such. This depends upon the behavioural equations themselves. As was recognized by Polak and Argy themselves, the model they are putting forward is simply what came to be known as the neoclassical synthesis or, more commonly and taught to generations of students in the post-war period, as the IS/LM/BP Keynesian model. In other words, the model is simply the one deployed to explain the short-run macroeconomic behaviour of *developed* countries. This immediately suggests doubts about its applicability.

Even if the model is appropriate for its intended purpose, there can be no presumption that its properties carry over satisfactorily to the short-run macroeconomics of developing countries. In short, developing economies are being treated theoretically as equivalent to developed economies. In addition, paradoxically, just as this model was being put forward for FP for developing countries, it was being discredited in its use for developed economies in a sort of pincer movement. With the stagflation of the 1970s, IS/LM analysis in such a simple form came under assault from Milton Friedman's revitalized monetarism. And the model was also subjected to considerable reassessment by those who questioned whether it accurately represented Keynes' own view of how markets would work imperfectly in the context of deficient demand.

But, what of the properties of the Polak–Argy model itself? First, as with the earlier version, it has an equilibrium solution. But it is now given by a complicated formula for nominal income, Y, in terms of a whole range of parameters represented by other letters:

$$Y = (BgX+bDC+gA+gX)/\{g(1-c+m+bk/h)+b(m-gk/h)\}$$

Despite its greater algebraic complexity, this is still an equilibrium. And, if we put each of the parameters equal to zero except for A and m, we retrieve the original Polak model. Thus, the later model is a generalization of the earlier one as a special case in which the other markets have no effects. The more complicated multiplier model that we now have essentially shows the interactions among markets, and the parameters multiplying or dividing one another imply a change in one market as an impact is felt from another.

This is, however, the only essential difference with the earlier model. And, once again, despite it being standard procedure, the model is not solved for its equilibrium. Instead, more attention is focused on the dynamics. These rely exclusively on the lagged adjustment of the money supply (currency reserves) to finance any balance of payments imbalance (trade and capital flows now). Interestingly, the dynamics could not be made simpler. As the authors report, 'For reasons of simplicity, this model makes no explicit allowance for reaction lags' (Polak and Argy 1971: 3; emphasis added). They are correct. If some of the other equations or relations were lagged – for example, if it takes time for consumption behaviour to catch up with changing income – the dynamics would become more complicated.

But, a crucial analytical point: a more complicated lag structure between the various markets and variables would not make any difference whatsoever to the underlying equilibrium. It would merely change, whether the equilibrium is stable or not, and the pattern of movement around it.[5] Given all of this, it follows that, as before and added complexity notwithstanding, the Polak–Argy model simply sets aside the issue of development as if short-run macroeconomics has no, or simply presumed positive, effect on longer-term prospects. The only difference is that many more parameters that need to be addressed in order to promote development are included and taken as given – those concerning levels of investment, how capital markets work, etc.

Washington Consensus as Marriage Model

Central to the Polak and Polak–Argy models is their dependence on short-run dynamics around a given static equilibrium, something that effectively precludes consideration of growth and development (including the effects on these of FP itself). That this was a problem was first recognized by those working with FP at the end of the 1980s. Significantly, as will be seen, it came at a time of peak influence of the Washington Consensus (between the IMF and the World Bank). In their attempt in the *IMF Staff Papers* to address the link between macroeconomic stabilization and longer-term economic growth, Khan and Montiel (1989) sought to construct 'a conceptual framework' for 'growth-oriented adjustment programmes'.[6] Khan and Montiel explicitly seek to bring together the growth model of the World Bank – known as the revised minimum standard model (RMSM) – and the Polak or FP model associated with the IMF. In a comment, Polak (1990) refers to a 'marriage' between the two models, a term accepted by Khan and Montiel (1990) in their response.

For Khan, Montiel and Haque (1990: 156), the motivation for the merging of the FP and RMSM models, which support the lending activities of the IMF and the World Bank, is 'because of the potential operational relevance – a starting point for the design of more realistic developing country models that deal with adjustment and growth'. The attempt to marry the two models rests on the premises: (1) the models are complementary and can be merged to formulate a general framework for linking the external sector with the real sectors of an economy; and (2) the task is straightforward as the FP focuses on monetary variables and the RMSM on real variables.

Khan, Montiel and Haque (1990: 172) also state that the model can be used for 'adjustment with growth' policy formulation, given the merged model's instrument and target variables: 'given chosen values for the target variables (price, output, reserves), two of the policy instruments (domestic credit and the exchange rate) can be chosen arbitrarily and the model will then determine values for the endogenous variables and the three remaining policy instruments. This is the model's "programming" mode.' The policy implication of the merged model is the same as the standard FP framework. In the short run, ceilings on the level of domestic credit and devaluation will stabilize inflation and the balance of payments. This process is complemented by improved tax revenue collection and reduction in the government deficit.

From this policy exercise, however, it is not clear where and how the RMSM features. The merged model's instrument and policy variables as well as its policy conclusions are the same as that of FP, which means that the short-run stabilization content of the model is still dominant, with no growth dynamics provided. Khan, Montiel and Haque (1990) ignore the emphasis of the merged model on the short run and focus on other limitations: for instance, the exclusion of an analysis of the interest rate and wages. However, the authors also claim inclusion of such variables complicates the model, for which simplicity is one important attribute.

The nature of the union, however, can be looked at from a number of perspectives. For Khan and Montiel, there is clear analytical attraction and synthesis. RMSM is what is known as a two-gap model, in which the level of foreign exchange that can be financed determines the potential level of output (growth) in the economy because it pays for the gap between investment and saving. It does, however, take the price level as exogenous.

On the other hand, FP is a model that determines the changes in the balance of payments and the level of nominal income, with the latter's division between real output and price left open for policy speculation. Consequently, each model can be closed in the mathematical sense by the contribution made by the other. RMSM determines output for FP, and FP determines prices for RMSM. As it were, irrespective of the conceptual basis of the two models and since they have variables in common, they are mathematical complements. A second feature of the merged model is to combine the short run of the FP with the long run of the RMSM. As already hinted, a third, closely related but separate feature is to link short-run macroeconomic equilibrium with long-run growth.

How does this, in many respects, appropriately motivated marriage turn out? First, incredibly but consistent with the earlier models, Khan and Montiel do not bother to identify long-run outcomes, despite this being both standard analytical procedure and logically compelling, given their objectives. Instead, they only carry the model forward for one or two periods of time. This is simply ridiculous because most models are capable of moving in a direction in a first period or two that is perverse in terms of signalling ultimate outcomes. Indeed, the logic of austere FP and neoliberalism more generally is 'no gain without pain'. Hopefully, for them, the pain is not indicative of longer-term outcomes.

Further, if the Khan and Montiel model is solved for the long run, the results are startling. The growth rate in per capita income falls to zero over time. This is because of one unreasonably pessimistic assumption after another in terms of what we know about growth and development. The contribution of productivity increase declines to zero over time; there is no growth in export demand through expansion of the world economy; and state expenditure does not contribute to growth through health, education and welfare, for example. If, however, the model is amended to allow for the possibility of steady-state balanced growth, it generally leads to unstable outcomes, unless holdings of foreign reserves start or adjust by chance to the right proportions, or unless the monetary authority has the capacity both to identify the long-run growth path and to adjust to it directly.

This implies that the table of results produced by Khan and Montiel, connecting shifts in exogenous and policy variables to adjustment in one period, are either totally meaningless or totally unnecessary. In case of imperfect monetary policy and instability, first-period shifts do not necessarily indicate subsequent direction of movement or changes in the underlying growth path, if any. For a perfect monetary authority, adjustment is irrelevant; it goes straight to the appropriate growth path. Not surprisingly, the marriage model has not found its way into the policy arena.

In many ways, the limitations of the marriage model revealed here are formalizations of the misgivings of Polak (1990) in debate with Khan and Montiel, reiterated in Polak (1997). For him, the FP model is only appropriate for examining the short run in stylized circumstances, to correct balance of payments rather than to target other objectives such as growth, and to leave the level of output to be assessed through iterative judgement rather than from formal modelling, especially from the RMSM that has been constructed for entirely different purposes. Indeed, in a personal communication commenting on the sorts of criticisms presented here, Polak suggests:[7]

My view is that (the marriage) is not a worthwhile project, and each subject should be approached on its own, provided the practitioners are fully aware of any recommended policies on the other objective (which to be sure has not always been the case between the Fund and the Bank). A possible simile, somewhat limping of course: the jobs of a schoolteacher and a pediatrician are both to do good to a child, and each should be aware of the other . . . but the professions should remain specialized for greatest efficiency in each field.

But what is true within his analogy surely does not hold for the stabilization and growth of an economy where the short and long runs are intimately and directly connected to one another. Khan and Montiel (1990) interpret Polak's critique as demanding a more complex marriage between the two models. Add more variables, disaggregate more, or introduce more behavioural relations. For example, they suggest that output could be made responsive to prices in the short run, rather than dependent upon the build-up of capacity through savings and investment.

In similar and cavalier fashion, Khan, Montiel and Haque (1990) assert that their analysis can be made more realistic by introducing more endogeneity into their model, through a variable capital–output ratio and investment function (ibid.: 166), and through a more complex monetary sector and lags in price and wage adjustments (ibid.: 176, 167). They pride themselves on having made the model available in view of 'the combination of widespread interest in Bank–Fund programs and the scarce existing literature on the methodology employed'. They confess 'that the simple model plays an important role when it comes to the quantitative macroeconomic analysis' (ibid.: 177). They explain the survival of such simple models on the basis of their limited informational requirements that can be 'supplemented by both qualitative and quantitative judgements . . . to work well in predicting outcomes for the principal macroeconomic variables' (ibid.: 178). Consequently, Khan and Montiel (1990: 191) feel able to close their debate with Polak as follows: 'The model . . . can serve as a basis for the development of more realistic models that capture the complexities of growth and adjustment, if only by focusing the discussion on precise identification of the model's shortcomings, thereby permitting superior, but equally policy-relevant, alternatives to emerge.'

These claims are nothing short of outrageous and monstrous for a model whose internal properties are such as to generate zero growth as presented, and unstable growth if corrected!

From FP to PRSPs

The IMF's FP has been with us for almost half a century. Recently, it has been subject to what appears to be a major change. Increased emphasis has been placed on poverty reduction and in a way that reflects sensitivity to the critical concerns gathered over the previous decade. As Ames *et al.* (2001), which ironically professes not to 'reflect the official policies or approaches of either the World Bank or the International Monetary Fund', put it:

> There has been an emerging consensus on how to make actions at the country level, and the support of development partners, more effective in bringing about sustainable poverty reduction. This consensus indicates a need for poverty reduction strategies that are: country-driven with broad participation of civil society, elected officials, key donors, and relevant International Finance Institutions; outcome-oriented; and developed from an understanding of the nature and determinants of poverty. Under the new framework, the country-led strategy would be presented in a Poverty Reduction Strategy Paper (PRSP), which is expected to become a key instrument for a country's relations with the donor community.

It might be thought that such a consensus, forged on the basis of past experience and research, would benefit from a sophisticated theoretical framework, elaborated in detail and subject to critical assessment of strengths and weaknesses. Nothing could be further from the truth. Consider the paper put forward to provide the new framework by Devarajan *et al.* (2000). At the time of its writing, this was the only theoretical paper explicitly offering an underpinning to PRSPs, and only a couple have been added since.[8] From what follows, it might be thought that it would be withdrawn and replaced by something more sophisticated and relevant. But two years later, it reappeared in amended form 'with an application to Zambia'. And it has been vigorously defended despite its considerable weaknesses because of its purported applicability across different countries (Bretton Woods Project 2003).

The paper begins by setting itself a number of objectives, including that of identifying 'critical trade-offs in poverty-reducing macroeconomic policies'. This is unduly pessimistic in assuming that poverty alleviation must come at the expense of something else, and in failing to seek out positive-sum outcomes. Further, it includes a bizarre requirement that 'the framework should be simple enough that operational economists can use it on their desktops. This means it should not make undue demands on data, it should be based on readily available software . . . and – most important – it should permit ready interpretation of model results.' It seems that the needs of economists, and their models, take precedence over those of the poor!

These polemics aside, the paper unquestioningly takes the FP model as a framework and reads it into the '1–2–3' model.[9] This is a general equilibrium model with no account taken of the possibility of externalities or multiple equilibria (poverty traps, for example). But, almost unbelievably, it is also assumed that there is full employment and a single labour market. In other words, although this is not made explicit, everyone who wants a job gets one and is paid the same wage. As the two major sources of poverty, wherever and however you care to define it, are low wages and unemployment, it is not clear how poverty can begin to be addressed within the model.

The answer is that, rather than examining low levels of and differentiated employment as sources of poverty, the latter is approached purely in terms of changes in relative prices (consumer goods might become cheaper with import liberalization) in a full employment one-wage economy. Otherwise, two options are offered for addressing poverty. One is to deploy Barro-type regressions for their growth coefficients, even though these have been shown to be entirely unacceptable for a whole range of reasons.[10] Still, the procedure allows poverty to be examined indirectly, for example, through the coefficient of 0.0055 for an increase in telephone lines per thousand people, or of –0.0092 for permitting a black market on foreign exchange. Accordingly, growth-induced poverty would be less if we had more telephones and less black market. Irrespective of the dubious merits of the associated empirical work, this has little or no causal content. This is made explicit in the second growth model option – to run a trivariate vector auto-regression between government policy (or shocks), the real exchange rate and growth. This is simply chart drawing writ large and complicated, without theoretical or causal content at all.

Concluding Remarks

The burden of this chapter has been to demonstrate how little FP has incorporated a content that reflects a preoccupation with growth and development, even when broaching the issue of poverty alleviation in developing countries. Where it has made some attempt to incorporate considerations of growth, these have been token, unexplored and fundamentally flawed.

But it is also possible to interrogate FP from another perspective. Forget development, how well does it stand up to the standards of developments within mainstream economics itself? Here, the answer is no less satisfactory. As already seen, FP took on Keynesianism as it was going into decline. It married itself to old growth theory just as new growth theory was emerging. It has been untouched by the major changes in macroeconomic theory, whatever their merits, even though developing countries continue to be treated as developed economies – for example, with the introduction of rational expectations by new classical economics. At most, over the past decade, it has slowly begun to converge with the long-established mainstream theory, most notably as represented by the text of Agénor and Montiel (1996).

Here, though, four points are of significance by way of conclusion. First, Agénor and Montiel (ibid.) explicitly argue that different theory is not required for developing countries. It is just necessary to recognize that they have a different composition of output and types and incidence of market and institutional imperfections. Second, fuller, more sophisticated models inevitably draw attention away from the imperatives of FP around correcting balance of payments and budget deficits, and towards labour market, agricultural and industrial policy. Third, the neglect of the weaknesses of the macroeconomic models underpinning FP is, in part, explained by their being so flawed and far behind the mainstream that the latter cannot even be bothered to consider them as worthy of critical attention. Finally, however much progress has been made in enhancing the theory of FP over the past fifty years, a huge step backwards has been taken with the introduction of PRSPs.

These conclusions are amply confirmed by the commentary of an 'insider', another to depart from the World Bank in a cloud for his apparently heretical views. For Easterly (2002: 4–5):

> Nor do I think that . . . financial programming is the same as evaluating IMF staff's knowledge of macroeconomics, which is quite sophisticated. The variables are projected with some combination of qualitative judgement and econometric equations. The program is usually arrived at iteratively as parameters change. Waivers of program conditions are frequently granted when variables do not evolve as expected. Fund economists have also commented that the practice of financial programming is different than what is portrayed in the written documentation.

Further, for purposes of transparency, political acceptance and accountability to a wide range of agents from governments to researchers:

> If the practice of financial programming departs in important ways from the published documentation on it, then it would seem desirable for the IMF to publish an accurate account of how it is applied in practice . . . Edwards as long ago as 1989 noted that financial programming:
>
>> has failed to incorporate issues related to the inter-temporal nature of the current account, the role of risk and self-insurance in portfolio choices, the role of time consistency and precommitments in economic policy, the economics of contracts and reputation, the economics of equilibrium real exchange rates . . . and the theory of speculative attacks and devaluation crises, just to mention a few of the more important recent developments in international macroeconomics.
>
> Presumably this list of omissions has grown even larger after another 12 years of research in international macroeconomics. Indeed, one curious thing about financial programming is how unchanged it has remained over the years despite these criticisms and the large changes in macroeconomic theory and empirics.

In short, much attention has rightly been directed at the negative impact of FP in practice through the imposed conditionalities attached to structural adjustment and stabilization. Less observed, and brought to the fore here, is that FP has rarely, if ever, been defended on the basis of fully elaborated analytical principles designed to address the problems of growth and development. Indeed, understanding of development within FP is notable for its absence unless it be tacked on as an afterthought. And the theory involved has, for almost fifty years, been little short of shambolic.

Appendix

The Polak–Argy model, using their equation numbers but a change of symbols, is as follows.

(9) $\quad Y = C + I + G + X - Z$

(10) $\quad C = cY$

(11) $\quad I = A - br$

(12) $\quad Z = zY$

(13) $\quad F = V + gr$

(14) $\quad hr = kY - M$

(15) $\quad B = X - Z + F$

(16) $\quad M_t - M_{t-1} = B + DC$

This reverts to the original model when $g=0$ (foreign flows are exogenous), $b=0$ (investment ditto), and $h=0$ (money demand is interest-inelastic). Note that (9)–(12) give us the traditional Keynesian IS curve; (14) is the LM curve; and (12), (13) and (15) make up the BP curve. This model is simply orthodox Keynesian macroeconomics applied to developing countries! It is recognized as such: 'The model . . . contains the major behavioural features to be found in macro-models of the industrial countries' (Polak and Argy 1971: 7). The only novelty is to be found in equation (16), which provides some dynamics for the model, as discussed in the text.

Notes

1 For a broader and more detailed treatment, see Fine and Hailu (2002).

2 See the chapters on 'The New Development Economics' and the Washington Consensus.

3 For discussion of this, especially but not exclusively in the context of the rise of 'social capital', see Harriss' chapter on Social Capital.

4 For his own retrospective, see Polak (1997).

5 In fact, to put it technically for those versed in linear difference equations, the dynamics are, essentially, not that much more complicated – depending on the largest of a number of solutions to an equation, rather than a single solution, as in the Polak model.

6 The quotes are taken from the sub-title and title of their article, respectively.

7 In his comment on the marriage of the IMF and World Bank models, Polak (1990) argues that the attempt, firstly, 'incapacitates each from doing its own job'; secondly, 'the simplicity that accounted for part of the attraction of the two models is lost in their merger' (ibid.: 184); and, finally, apart from intellectual curiosity, 'it adds little to our knowledge on the crucial issues of growth-oriented adjustment' (ibid.: 186). As far as the objective of raising output, Polak (1997) doubts that: 'With respect to the second dimension, it is curious that for their medium-term macroeconomic projections both the IMF and the World Bank continue to rely on highly mechanical growth models of the Harrod–Domar family, first developed in the late 1940s. In these models there is no place for what the two institutions themselves consider the most important factors determining the growth of developing countries, such as outward orientation, realistic prices, privatization, reform of the financial sector, and, in general, government attitude toward the economy. . . . In a formal sense, it would not be particularly difficult to introduce these three extensions into the model. But that would be essentially useless unless it were also possible to obtain some order of magnitudes of the coefficients for the variables in the newly introduced equations. And that, unfortunately, is not possible. In this setting, the IMF has had to forgo the comfort of its own model and base its conditionality on a set of ad hoc instruments that seemed plausible in the circumstances.'

8 See also Agénor (2003) and Agénor, Izquierdo and Fofack (2002), for more sophisticated models that allow for both unemployment and more than one labour market.

But growth is not integrated into these models theoretically, and the greater generality remains organized around a fixed, fundamental equilibrium.

[9] So-called for one (small) country, with two sectors (exports and non-traded) and three goods (imports also).

[10] See the chapter on 'New Growth Theory' in this volume. Ironically, these figures are drawn from the work of Easterly.

References

Agénor, Pierre-Richard (2003), 'The Mini-Integrated Macroeconomic Model for Poverty Analysis: A Framework for Analysing the Unemployment and Poverty Effects of Fiscal and Labour Market Reforms', World Bank, Washington DC; http://econ.worldbank.org/files/27033_wps3067.pdf.

Agénor, Pierre-Richard and Peter J. Montiel (1996), *Development Macroeconomics* (Princeton: Princeton University Press).

Agénor, Pierre-Richard, Alejandro Izquierdo and Hippolyte Fofack (2002), 'IMMPA: A Quantitative Macroeconomic Framework for the Analysis of Poverty Reduction Strategies', World Bank, Washington DC; http://www1.worldbank.org/wbiep/macro-program/age(r/pdfs/Immpa-text.pdf.

Ames, Brian, W. Brown, Shantayanan Devarajan and Alejandro Izquierdo (2001), 'Macroeconomic Policy and Poverty Reduction', International Monetary Fund and World Bank, Washington DC; http://www.worldbank.org/poverty/strategies/chapters/macro/macr0406.pdf.

Bretton Woods Project (2003), 'Macro-Models for Poverty Reduction Policies: Comparison of Key Features', Economic Policy Empowerment Program.

Devarajan, Shantayanan, William Easterly, Hippolyte Fofack, Delfin S. Go, Alejandro Izquierdo, Christian Petersen, Lodovico Pizzati, Christopher Scott and Luis Serven (2000), 'A Macroeconomic Framework for Poverty Reduction Strategy Papers', World Bank, Washington DC.

Easterly, William (2002), *The Elusive Quest for Growth: Economists' Adventures and Misadventures in the Tropics* (Cambridge, Massachusetts: MIT Press); http://www.worldbank.org/research/growth/pdfiles/devarajan%20etal.pdfhttp://www.worldbank.org/files/12937_TK_Paper_Chap_13_Devarajan_Go.pdf.

Fine, Ben (2001), *Social Capital versus Social Theory: Political Economy and Social Science at the Turn of the Millennium* (London: Routledge).

Fine, Ben and Degol Hailu (2002), 'Convergence and Consensus: The Political Economy of Stabilization, Poverty and Growth', Centre for Development and Policy Research, Discussion Paper 22, School of Oriental and African Studies, University of London; www.soas.ac.uk/cdprfiles/dp/DP22BD.pdf.

IMF (1977), 'The Monetary Approach to the Balance of Payments', International Monetary Fund, Washington DC.

—— (1987), 'Theoretical Aspects of the Design of Fund-Supported Adjustment Programs', IMF Occasional Paper 55, International Monetary Fund, Washington DC.

Khan, Moshin and Peter Montiel (1989), 'Growth-Oriented Adjustment Programs: A Conceptual Framework', *IMF Staff Papers*, 36 (2): 279–306.

—— (1990), 'A Marriage between Fund and Bank Models? Reply to Polak', *IMF Staff Papers*, 37 (1): 187–91.

Khan, Moshin, Peter Montiel and Nadeem Haque (1990), 'Adjustment with Growth: Relating the Analytical Approaches of the IMF and the World Bank', *Journal of Development Economics*, 32 (1): 155–79.

Polak, Jean-Jacques (1957), 'Monetary Analysis of Income Formation and Payments Problems', *IMF Staff Papers*, 6 (1): 1–50.

—— (1990), 'A Marriage between Fund and Bank Models?: Comment on Khan and Montiel', *IMF Staff Papers*, 37 (1): 183–86.

—— (1997), 'The IMF Monetary Model at Forty Years', IMF Research Department Working Paper 97/49, April, Washington DC.

Polak, Jean-Jacques and Victor Argy (1971), 'Credit Policy and the Balance of Payments', *IMF Staff Papers*, 18 (1): 1–21.

The Developmental State and the Political Economy of Development[1]

Ben Fine

The state has always been at the centre of the study of development. This is not just because of its overwhelming importance in promoting, or obstructing, development. In addition, how the nature and role of the state is understood is part and parcel of how the economy and development are conceived. In the nineteenth century, before development was acknowledged as such, policymakers became aware that economic development was essential to the survival and progress of nation-states, and that this required trade protection for infant industries, for example.[2] More recently, crudely simplifying, development in the post-war period was first understood through modernization, Keynesianism and welfarism, with socialist planning and Marxism as the alternative. Here, there is little difference over the immediate goals or outcomes of development. These include high levels of growth, industrialization, and the forging of a modern welfare state and socio-economic infrastructure. But there are considerable differences over how the state itself is conceived. For modernization, it is benevolent and pluralistic, promoting capitalism and ameliorating its excesses. By contrast, Marxism perceives the state as a reflection of class conflict, with socialist planning as the resolution of that conflict in favour of the working people, as opposed to the exploiting classes, whether these be landlords, merchants, financiers or capitalist entrepreneurs.

With the emergence of the neoliberal Washington Consensus in the 1980s, the state and development became understood completely differently. Far from being benevolent and representative (of pluralistic or class interests), the state was seen as being based upon the pursuit of individual self-interest through political as opposed to market means, most notably in the opportunities offered for rent-seeking and corruption.[3] Two propositions followed within this perspective. First, the state should be confined to a minimal level of activity. Second, development is an inevitable consequence of the liberation of, and reliance upon, market forces.

One effect of the Washington Consensus, not least because of its theoretical and empirical dogma, was to pose the issue of development in terms of the market versus the state. This was a break with the previous modernization/Marxist debate, with one seeing the state as complementing and promoting the market (not least, Keynesian manipulation of aggregate *market* demand), and the other perceiving both the state and the market as reflecting underlying class interests. In contrast and in particular, for the Washington Consensus and its critics, the issue was raised of the extent to which the East Asian economic miracle was a consequence of state policy or free play of the market. For those emphasizing the role of the state, the idea of the developmental state was put forward, its presence or absence presumed to explain success or failure (rather than reliance, or not, upon the market).[4]

The purpose of this chapter is to follow contributions around the developmental state as a partial attempt to address the role of the state in development. Essentially, the developmental state literature is concerned with two questions, corresponding to two different schools or approaches. One addresses the *economic* policies that should be adopted in order to promote development. The other focuses on the *political* or other conditions that enable appropriate policies to be adopted, whatever they might be. These two questions have tended to be subject to separate literatures, corresponding to the disciplines of economics and politics (and/or sociology), respectively. Their contributions are outlined in the next section. This is followed by an account of the rhythm of influence of the developmental state approach. As a leading idea in the critique of the Washington Consensus, the approach enjoyed considerable intellectual success and prominence.

Inevitably, though, its appeal declined to some extent with the eruption of the Asian crisis of 1997–98. But, for reasons to be explained, the picture is more complicated than this, with both the appearance of doubts about the approach prior to the crisis and some revival of it afterwards. The content of the developmental state approach has changed in response to the external environment, both material and intellectual, and to the anomalies it has itself thrown up. The political school, for example, has been forced to recognize the presence – for it, the emergence – of powerful class interests. Its response has been to delimit the life of the developmental state to historically contingent opportunities for state autonomy.

The economic school, on the other hand, has, in part, been analytically outflanked by the post-Washington Consensus.[5] The latter too suggests a limited life for the developmental state, but for different reasons than for the political school. Development is about handling the market, especially informational imperfections, through the efficacy of the financial system and institutions such as the state. Consequently, the developmental state is limited to late-comer catch-up, after which market imperfections are less pervasive and intervention, as opposed to market regulation, less necessary.

The partial capture of the economic school by the post-Washington Consensus will leave dissatisfied many of those who study development. This is because, as the political school has now been forced to recognize, the state involves questions of class, power and conflict. Inevitably, corresponding questions concerning the nature of contemporary capitalism as a system, and the role of classes, power and conflict, appear to evaporate, as market and non-market phenomena are reduced to the rationality of responses to market imperfections. As a result, there are bright prospects for radical political economy to contest the emerging orthodoxy, and this is explored in more detail in the last section by drawing out implications for the political economy of the state and development from the developmental state literature.

Political and Economic Schools

Literature on the development state has been interpreted through the prism of two distinct approaches or schools, the political and the economic (Fine and Stoneman 1996; Fine and Rustomjee 1997: Chapter 2). For the political school, focus has been concentrated on the nature and capacity of the state. In a nutshell, what is it that enables the state to adopt developmental policies *whatever they might be*? Kohli (1999: 94) recognizes the mission of the political school in terms of 'the prior question of *why* the South Korean state was able to do what it did'.

Such is one way of interpreting Johnson's (1982) founding contribution to the literature, his classic study of Japanese late development. His implicit attachment to the political school is confirmed by his recent retrospective, in which the decisive factor is perceived to be the relationship between the state and the private sector (Johnson 1999).[6] He reluctantly furnishes a 'model', but does so comprising four elements:[7] a small, elite, top-quality management within the state to select and promote industries, and to supervise competition; a political system that enables this; market-conforming methods of intervention; and an organization, such as MITI, to effect implementation. Further, Johnson explicitly praises Castells' (1992: 56–57) account of the developmental state, his definition having been widely cited by others:[8]

> *A state is developmental when it establishes as its principle of legitimacy, its ability to promote and sustain development, understanding by development the combination of steady high rates of growth and structural change in the productive system, both domestically and in its relationship to the international economy. . . . Thus, ultimately for the developmental state, economic development is not a goal but a means.*

So the developmental state concerns political legitimacy, with the economy as a sideshow. This definition borders on the tautological.

For the political school, the passage from Johnson, and his case study of Japan, to the present has been marked, as in his initiating work, by identifying decisive *characteristics* of the state and/or the *mechanisms* by which it becomes developmental, with an increasing range of case studies. As previously argued (Fine and Stoneman 1996; Fine and Rustomjee 1997), the explanatory (or descriptive) factors involved have expanded to accommodate a widening range of empirical case studies, successes or failures, that have not otherwise fitted comfortably within the narrower set of characteristics/mechanisms.

Starting with the autonomy of the state from vested interests, it was found that the state could either be developmental or use its freedom to be parasitical and siphon of the surplus that might otherwise be used for growth. Accordingly, autonomy as an essential feature of the developmental state also needed to be further qualified, somewhat inconsistently, by being 'embedded' in society in a functional, rather than dysfunctional, fashion (Evans 1992, 1995). But then we enter a universe of qualifications and extensions – (relatively) autonomous and embedded in what ways, and with whom? Thus, in pursuit of the democratic developmental state, White (1998) ranges over the following factors – consensus, institutions, political participation, authoritarianism, inclusion and exclusion, international environment, and social structure comprising class, gender, ethnicity, culture and religion.[9]

Similarly, Chan, Clark and Lam (1998: 1–4) add bureaucratic cohesion, depoliticization, weakness and strength, efficacy, adaptability, networks and politics in all its forms (leadership choice, regime maintenance, and interaction between economic performance and coalition formation). In the context of Japanese agriculture and national food supply, Francks (1998) and Francks (2000) emphasize the importance of a dedicated bureaucracy, giving rise to a bureaucratic developmental state. For Koh (1997), Singapore's developmental state is attached to a mission-oriented bureaucracy. Drawing upon the South Korean experience, Chibber (1999) insists that such a bureaucracy be of high quality and selective in its targeting.[10] But ideology is also crucial for such bureaucracies, as is more general opinion formation in Marsh's (1999) account of Asian developmental states, with Williams (1997) arguing that the failure of the developmental discourse to reach beyond an elite is crucial in explaining the failure of the Indian developmental state. Grabowski (2000: 274) points to the importance of national identity:[11] 'The developmental state is not rooted solely in the existing economic and social structure, but also in the future social and economic structure. This has generally involved the building or rebuilding of the national economic identity.'

The same issue is approached differently in terms of corporatism and consensus, central to the Riain (2000) and O'Hearn (2000) debate over the (flexible) Irish developmental state in an era of globalization. Xia (2000: a) perceives China as a *dual* developmental state, supported by both legislative and local political institutions, with structures at both central and local levels. Emphasis is placed on networks, with heavy analytical reliance on the transaction costs approach to the firm for understanding political hierarchy: 'although transaction costs analysis is a theory of the firm, it has utilities for our understanding of politics, international affairs, sociology, and law'.

In short, the political school focuses on the politics of economic policy with, paradoxically, little or no interest in economics as such. In contrast, the economic school is almost exclusively concerned with the necessity for economic policy at the expense of the political conditions that allow it to be identified and adopted. It is an approach to the developmental state inspired both by the notion of market imperfections and by an antipathy to neoliberalism. It is aptly summed up in the catchphrase associated with Alice Amsden of 'getting prices wrong', although this is symbolic of a more general commitment to state interventionism, especially in industrial policy involving state control of trade and finance.

Although Amsden (1989) and Wade (1990) are best known as leading representatives of the economic school, the most prolific and wide-ranging contributor in this vein has been Ha-Joon Chang, not least because he has addressed both theoretical and empirical issues, especially South Korea for the latter. Starting with Chang (1994), his work has covered most aspects of industrial policy, finance and 'cronyism'. For each, a clear case is made for the pervasive presence of market imperfections, the need for the state to intervene and correct or temper them, for the inappropriate perspective offered by the neoliberal Washington Consensus, and the latter's lack of correspondence to empirical realities.[12] Subsequently, Chang (2000) has emphasized how South Korea has coordinated investments within and across sectors, promoting complementary activity (economies of scope), but also proscribing excessive entry and competition within sectors so that economies of scale could accrue.

This is all to enter the world of industrial policy, a key element in industrialization and in demarcating the role of the state in development. In the past, simple prognoses have been offered, such as those of Little and Mirrlees (1969, 1974), in focusing upon individual projects, in isolation from one another and neglecting sources and transmission of productivity increase, even in a social cost–benefit analysis, through presumption that technologies can be picked off the shelf. More rounded was the approach taken by the World Bank under McNamara in perceiving the state and even, in part, public enterprise as agents of industrialization. But this remained aloof from the details of industrial change and from policy.

In contrast, the gathering experience and study of the East Asian newly industrialized countries (NICs), and their success in comparison with failure elsewhere, have increasingly revealed that the multiplicity and complexity of conditions required for industrialization (and, as such, the object of industrial policy) cannot simply be brought into play by some idealized reliance upon the market, the state, or some combination of the two. As revealed, for example, in the work of Sanjaya Lall, productivity increase, as a precondition of successful industrialization, depends upon appropriate *capabilities* being present and deployed in ways that vary from sector to sector and from country to country (for recent contributions spanning Africa and East Asia, see Lall 1992; Lall and Urata 2003; Lall and Pietrobelli 2002; and the chapter titled 'Analysis of Technology and Development' in this volume).

The source and application of these and other capabilities cannot be derived from an economic analysis alone. Accordingly, Chang has ultimately been drawn into emphasizing the institutional preconditions for a successful developmental state as part of a more general theory or political economy of development itself (Chang 2002b; Chang and Evans 2000). This, however, merely pushes back the issue of political capacity one step. For, in part, the political school is concerned with what makes developmental institutions possible. The economic school arrives where the political school begins. This confirms the division of the literature between the two schools, as has been neatly summarized by Cumings' (1999) simile of economic analysis as spider without the web, and of political analysis as web without the spider. This opens the option of each school complementing the other. But, to belabour the metaphor, how do we know that we have put the right spider in the right web? The two schools only offer a neat fit in the vacuous sense of occupying analytical terrains that do not overlap. Each has progressed within the confines of its own territory: the political school by refinement with an expanding range of case studies and evidence; the economic school by widening the scope of what constitutes market imperfections, and how they have or have not been appropriately handled.

A Complex Conceptual Rhythm

The developmental state approach has been at its strongest in charting the extensive role of the state in (East Asian) economic development and as a critique of the Washington Consensus. Its success was most marked by the apparent necessity for the World Bank to respond with its own report on the topic of the East Asian miracle (World Bank 1993). This was based on an extensive research programme and made some concessions to empirical realities in recognizing that the East Asian NICs had experienced considerable state economic intervention.

But the report was remarkable for the intellectual acrobatics by which it continued to support what was primarily a neoliberal posture. It contained two fundamental conclusions. First, it was argued, state economic intervention had been successful only when 'market-conforming', understood as doing what the market would have done had it been working perfectly. While there is an implicit recognition that the market had not worked perfectly, this posture retains the principle of relying upon the market. This was especially so in view of the second conclusion, that the East Asian success – and the role of the state in promoting it – was not replicable in other economies, and so its policies should not be emulated elsewhere.[13]

The report received a broad critical reception, not least because its existence owed more to the rise of Japan as an international donor and agent of development than to the felt need to respond to the developmental state approach.[14] Indeed, the World Bank study was financed by Japan, and it was disappointed with the results (Wade 1996). Wade shows in detail, against a background of intellectual sclerosis within the Bank, how irksome the Washington Consensus was for the Japanese in three respects. First, the increasing significance of Japan as donor suggested that it should have more influence over international donor financing through the World Bank and elsewhere. Second, it had become a major donor and foreign investor in the East Asian economies, and the Asia–Pacific region more generally, in ways that contradicted the Washington

Consensus in relying upon the states to support and coordinate industrial investment programmes. Third, the neoliberal posture on development was totally
inconsistent with the well-known history and continuing experience of the Japanese themselves, the classic case of a developmental state. In short, Japan could
hardly have been expected to fund a set of policies, and an underlying ideology,
which denied both its own experience and its own interests. In a sense, Japan was
looking to the state to promote industrialization and growth in other countries
where it was so heavily directing foreign investment, in part as a process of its
own industrial restructuring (towards more capital-intensive 'hi-tech' at home
and the converse, at lower wages, through overseas investments).

The World Bank's *East Asian Miracle* signalled the legitimacy crisis of
the Washington Consensus, rather than its resolution. In the mid-1990s, the prospects seemed bright for the developmental state approach. But such hopes were,
at least in part, rudely shattered within a couple of years by two factors, considered below – the East Asian crisis and the World Bank's putative turn away
from neoliberalism to the more state-friendly post-Washington Consensus. But
it is also important to recognize that doubts about the developmental state
approach began to gather before these two factors added their own weight
behind a less sanguine stance on the role of the state in East Asia's economic
development.

First, observe that the division between the political and economic
approaches has, if anything, been accentuated by the crisis of 1997. For, as the
political school tends to stand aloof from economic analysis as such, it is confronted most sharply by the analytical problem posed by the crisis – how is it that
a developmental state has proven incapable of safeguarding itself against crisis,
certainly of 1997 proportions?[15] The school has offered a particularly ingenious
answer, one already being formulated prior to the crisis itself.[16] This is to argue
that the developmental state is, by its nature, of limited duration. Specifically, it
is confined to *catch-up* by late-comer industrializers. The developmental state
can no longer be developmental once development has been achieved, if not
beforehand. As Moon (1999: 220) puts it:[17] 'The developmental state is a transitional phenomenon. It worked well in the earlier stage of economic development
and industrialization. As national economies become more mature and sophisticated, the state becomes a liability rather than an asset.'

The most significant factor in cutting off the life of the developmental
state is that its success undermines its own conditions of existence. More specifically, most notably for South Korea, the 'relative' or 'embedded' 'autonomy'
enjoyed by the state in its developmental phase gives rise to large-scale conglo-
merates, the chaebol, which eventually become too powerful to be subordinate to
the state. From being created instruments of the state, large-scale capital comes
into conflict with it (Lee 1997; Kim 1999). More generally, the developmental
state induces other interests and demands upon itself as development raises the
prospect of modernization in a western image.[18]

Development, for example, may increase pressure for democracy, but a common, if not universal, feature of the developmental state has been its authoritarianism. Trade unions and their demands are also a consequence. Accordingly, the developmental state is its own grave-digger, creating the demands and the organizations to achieve them, which undermine its developmental legitimacy. As White (1998: 44) suggests in the context of prospective democratic developmental states:[19] 'It is defined in terms that are potentially contradictory and difficult to achieve: autonomy *and* accountability; growth *and* redistribution; consensus *and* inclusiveness.' In addition, continuing or aspiring developmental states are, in deference to the major intellectual fashion of the 1990s (Fine 2004), taken to be subject to the constraints imposed by 'globalization' (Gereffi 1998; O'Hearn 2000).[20]

Thus, the political school views the developmental state as limited by its own internal dynamics and by increasing external pressure (to liberalize). Such limits on its life are complemented by those surrounding its birth. The emergence of a developmental state is perceived to be dependent upon the now analytically eponymous 'initial conditions', allowing the state to act both developmentally and, consequently, independently of special interests.[21] Thus, for Aoki, Kim and Okino-Fujimara (1998: 25–27):[22]

> Northeast Asian economies seem to have a unique initial condition of economic development: the absence of a dominant economic class. . . . Before the post-war development process took off in those economies, there were no individual capitalists who had amassed enormous assets and controlled the supply of financial and industrial capital. . . . Furthermore, political leaders and bureaucrats in these economies had no incentive to distribute political rents in favor of any particular economic class, because if that class were to become sufficiently powerful in the future, the favored class might thereby be able to threaten these leaders' autonomy someday in the future. Thus the 'shared growth' phenomenon in Northeast Asia seems to be a profoundly path-dependent phenomenon that evolved from the unique historical conditions prevailing immediately after the Pacific War. It was not something intrinsic to a Confucian tradition of the East Asian bureaucracy. Because of its apparent autonomy, the permanent bureaucracy in the East Asian state is sometimes characterized as 'strong'. Paradoxically, however, it may be also regarded as 'weak'. Both strength and weakness arise from the same source – the absence of a dominant economic class.

With the life-span of the developmental state hedged between fortuitous initial conditions and mounting internal and external pressures, the political school accommodates the crisis of 1997 by interpreting it as signifying the death throes of the developmental state as it undertakes transition to new state forms. What these are is rarely specified, but some sort of idealized western democracy is never far from sight. In this light, the developmental state is a temporary but beneficial aberration in the phase of catch-up, as if the 'catchees' were themselves free of state intervention, the exact opposite of the truth as far as the developed world is concerned. Inevitably, given the dramatic form taken by the

East Asian crisis, the political school emphasizes how financial liberalization has been damaging, appropriately weakening state control over finance, but without putting alternative forms of regulation quickly and securely enough into place.

Not surprisingly, this is a rare entry point of analysis, shared in common with the economic school. More generally, it has also needed to address the miracle/crisis syndrome – how could one so suddenly have become the other without having been anticipated? Limitations of previous analyses have rarely been acknowledged. The economic school has, however, offered new analyses for explanation of the crisis that fall into two types. One is to view the miracle and the crisis as entirely independent of one another, with the crisis explained by a fragile financial system, both created and destabilized by inappropriate financial liberalization and neoliberal macroeconomic policy. Such a stance is best represented by the work of Krugman, not least because he was also at the forefront in denying the miracle in the first place – with East Asian growth explained by growth simply of factor inputs.[23] In short, he merely needs to explain the crisis independently of longer-term economic performance.

This is admirably illustrated by Krugman's 'Analytical Afterthoughts on the Asian Crisis'. Essentially, his argument is that aggregate demand in an economy might not increase monotonically with a fall in the exchange rate, since the latter may lead to loss of confidence by foreign investors, and loss of net worth and investment by domestic firms; 'a loss of confidence by foreign investors can be self-justifying, because capital flight leads to a plunge in the currency, and the balance-sheet effects of this plunge lead to a collapse in domestic investment'. Krugman formalizes the model and discusses its implications. Analytically, the central property is the presence of two stable equilibria, one at a high (normal) and one at a low (crisis) exchange rate. Remarkably, considering the nature of the Asian crisis itself, both equilibria share the same level of real output![24] But the details of the model need not detain us, although it is indicative of the extent to which Krugman's approach is purely financial/macroeconomic. As a result, his primary concern is to redesign or reform international 'financial architecture'. In his model, at best, neoliberal policies reduce the level of equilibrium output, rather than address the problem of exchange rate confidence (for which he advises rapid balance of payments, support not least through controls on international capital flows).

Although they might hold to a different understanding of how the East Asian miracle was achieved, Krugman's approach is not too different from the alternative view of the crisis that is more attuned to the economic school's approach to the developmental state, in relation to which Krugman is a revisionist latecomer. In particular, for the economic school, emphasis is also placed upon the deleterious impact of financial liberalization (Wade 1998; Wade and Veneroso 1998), for example. But attention is also drawn to the dismantling of other forms of state intervention, especially those relating to elements of industrial policy. In part, such explanations complement the arguments of the political school, primarily blaming neoliberalism for the crisis and its depth, but also suggesting that its policies have not always been opposed by a maturing domestic industry seeking to free itself from the guidance and controls of the developmental state.

This is where the long-established developmental state literature meets the post-Washington Consensus. For, a more sophisticated approach within mainstream economics is to relate the financial crisis to the unfolding of the miracle underlying the real economy. This has been done by drawing upon the new development economics, whose leading representative has been Joseph Stigltiz, erstwhile chief economist at the World Bank, from where he launched the post-Washington Consensus as an explicit critique of the neoliberal Washington Consensus (Stiglitz 1998a).

Unlike the Washington Consensus, the post-Washington Consensus is based on the idea that markets are imperfect, especially in the light of informational imperfections and asymmetries. As a result, government intervention is justified as long as its own imperfections do not outweigh those of the market it is designed to remedy. Analytically, the new information-theoretic economics, upon which the post-Washington Consensus draws, explains both market and non-market outcomes as the rational response to market imperfections.[25] On this basis, it purports to explain, despite a continuing commitment to methodological individualism, institutions, customs, collective action, as well as economic and social structures. It also allows for history to matter in the form of path dependence, multiple equilibria and complex dynamics.[26]

In this light, the post-Washington Consensus understands the difference between the developed and the developing world in two complementary ways – by composition of output (with developing countries skewed towards primary production) and by institutional sophistication (with developing countries more primitive and more pervasive in response to higher incidences of market imperfections). Thus, Aoki, Kim and Okino-Fujimara (1998: 1) suggest that the 'developmental-state view regards market failures as more pervasive for developing economies . . . and thus looks to government intervention as a substitute mechanism for the resolution of these'. Consequently, extensive state intervention is warranted for those economies seeking to catch up. But the process of catching-up does itself render redundant the institutions that have enabled it. The Asian crisis is, then, explained as the end of the miracle, and the need to undergo a transition to more modern, market forms of regulation in correspondence to the more sophisticated level of economic performance (Lee 1999).

Such an account is supported by Stiglitz's (1998b) own discussion of the East Asian crisis. His main preoccupation is with the informational content of the domestic and international financial systems. There is suddenly 'the need for greater transparency and more information'. Related to this is the increasingly inappropriate allocation of finance by the state, a particular form of 'crony capitalism'. In this vein, Stiglitz raises the issue of the balance between the positive and negative impact of state intervention: 'Business–government interaction in the region . . . always included the danger that the fine line between consensus building and collusion, between partnership and political cronyism, would be crossed.' Not surprisingly, then, the new development economics is drawn to understand the East Asian crisis on the basis of three features – by finance and by cronyism, with both indicative of the impact of imperfect information and the structure of incentives, and through analytical generalization across countries, reading off selective empirical evidence in line with a preordained analytical framework.

The lead in this regard was taken up by Crafts (1999a, 1999b). He perceived economic performance as dependent upon factor inputs and 'social capability'. 'Catching-up is not automatic, therefore, and absence of social capability may be a crucial obstacle to growth and development' (Crafts 1999b: 112). He also stressed the role of imperfect information and financial systems. On the basis of highly questionable total factor productivity and other empirical work, he concluded, 'this analysis tends to reinforce the conclusion that the Asian developmental state has been much more successful in promoting high levels of investment than in achieving exceptional productivity performance.'[27] Thus, 'present problems are a result of earlier success which propelled the leading Tigers to a point at which more emphasis needed to be placed on strong productivity performance, and reform of the developmental state model seemed appropriate' (ibid.: 120).[28] Consequently, Crafts (1999a: 156–57) concluded:

> Initially backward countries have an opportunity for rapid catch-up if they take radical measures to promote development through institutional innovations and controlled capital markets . . . this would tend to leave a legacy of institutions different from the standard US model and that, especially in the longer term, there were a number of downside risks of this type of strategy. . . . A clear risk . . . is that it is perverted into opportunities for rent-seeking and corruption that ultimately undermine economic growth. . . . A second danger . . . is that it spawns government policies that serve the interests of special interest groups and actually inhibit economic growth by inducing misallocation of resources, for example, through so-called 'industrial policy'.

Crafts' explanatory reliance upon industrial policy, financial regulation and cronyism has been effectively demolished by Chang (2000) on simple empirical grounds. There is no evidence that these factors were sufficient or sufficiently different than from the past or from other countries to have generated the crisis. Across his own work, Chang seeks an explanation for the crisis, not in the persistence but in the dismantling of the core elements of the developmental state across industry and finance, not least through partial acceptance of the dictates of neoliberalism.[29] As Chang, Park and Gyue (1998: 735) argued:

> The crisis resulted from uncoordinated and excessive investments by the private sector, financed by imprudent amounts of short-term foreign debt, which in turn had been made possible by rapid and ill-designed financial liberalization

(especially capital account liberalization) and a serious weakening of industrial policy. . . . While it has some important shortcomings, Korea's supposedly pathological corporate governance system was neither the main source of the current crisis, nor something that has to be radically restructured if Korea is to regain its growth momentum, as many observers outside and inside Korea currently believe.

But it would be a mistake, from a methodological perspective, to exaggerate the differences between Crafts and Chang as leading representatives of the new post-Washington Consensus and old developmental state theory of the economic school. For, while the latter is considerably richer and deeper in theoretical and empirical scope,[30] there is *convergence* of analytical frameworks. Crafts (1999b), for example, perceives himself as incorporating the insights of Gerschenkron, Rodrik, Amsden and Wade. Chang (1999), on the other hand, is readily interpreted in one of the latest collections on the developmental state in the following terms (Woo-Cumings 1999: 3–4):

> The developmental state paradigm is often thought to be at loggerheads with both neoclassical economics and its cross-dressed version in political science, rational choice theory. The two chapters by economists working in England and Sweden show that this need not be so. Both Ha-Joon Chang and Juhana Vartiainen explain how some of the more recent ideas in economics – for example, the new institutional economics, evolutionary economics, the economics of increasing returns, and transactions theory – can be used to explain the rationality and efficiency of industrial policy.

Thus, for Crafts at least, the developmental state has a limited life just as for the political school. From an intellectual point of view, however, the post-Washington Consensus has the potential to appropriate the economic school on its own terms. Given its origins in taking the Washington Consensus as its critical point of departure, it is hardly surprising that its initial stance should remain cautious and guarded as far as the extent of market imperfections is concerned.[31] Further, as argued elsewhere, in becoming more state- and user-friendly, at least rhetorically, the World Bank and, to a lesser extent, the International Monetary Fund are keen to occupy and temper the analytical ground previously secured by the economic school (Fine 1999). They do so, however, without confronting its extensive theoretical and empirical work. Thus arises the process of diminishing the scope of the developmental state while retaining the term, as with Crafts, or its being displaced altogether by generalized reference to market imperfections. At best, the economic school survives, and is distinguished only by its limited, if more radical, stance on the extent of market imperfections and interventionism when compared to the Washington Consensus.

Indeed, the recently edited book by Ohno and Ohno (1998) reveals the extent to which there is a convergence between Japanese developmental thinking and the new consensus. Ohno and Ohno (ibid.: 4) highlight the following differences with the old consensus. First is the need to attach priority to the real economy:

> Most Japanese aid officials find such obsessions with finance and the macroeconomy narrow and unbalanced. True, inflation must be dealt with but not *at all costs* to the society, especially when the country is distressed by collapsing output, joblessness, political instability, ethnic conflicts, lawlessness, and public discontent. Under such adverse circumstances, the highest priority for Japan would be the *real* economy and *not* the financial side: how to arrest the fall in output, how to secure jobs, how to initiate revival and industrial restructuring, etc. These real concerns take precedence over money, budget, and inflation.

Second, the orientation of long-term plans needs to be attached to annual targets. Third, the positive impact of government needs to be emphasized in promoting the market and marketization, especially 'important in the early stages of development and in economic crisis' (ibid.: 7). Fourth, the process of development is slow and not subject to quick fixes. Finally, there is a need for specificity in dealing with particular countries, issues and sectors. Mainstream neoclassical economics is considered entirely unsuitable, in contrast to the welcome insights offered by Stiglitz, a view supported by Hara (1998), who praises the new information-theoretic economics for its capacity to design institutions to be compatible with incentives. Only a mild note of caution emerges in the 'Afterword' of Ohno and Ohno (1998: 310), who advise study of the different approaches to development economics prior to the emergence of the neoclassical orthodoxy.[32]

But, despite the pincer movement of crisis and post-Washington Consensus, the developmental state has refused to die. Indeed, reports of its death are exaggerated even if it has been less prominent than previously. There are three important reasons for this. First, despite the claims of the effects of globalization, especially in its neoliberal version, state economic intervention has continued to be extensive and demonstrably successful in achieving results. Whenever and wherever economies prosper, they are liable to be endowed with the label of developmental state. Close attention, for example, has recently turned to Singapore and China.[33]

Second, in line with the critical literature on globalization that continues to emphasize the salience of the nation-state, the developmental state approach has been applied at different levels of disaggregation than the nation itself, and to aspects other than industrial policy. Examples include skills in general and for construction in particular in Singapore, for Brown and Lauder (2001) and Debrah and Ofori (2001), respectively; public space and the port, also for Singapore, for Ling and Limin (2002) and Airriess (2001), respectively;[34] high-tech clusters in Beijing (Zhou and Xin 2003); the Tokyo waterfront (Saito 2003); differences across Indian states and Indian industries (Sinha 2003; Pinglé 1999); infant mortality (Shen and Williamson 2001); and public savings, as opposed to investment, in Brazil (Krieckhaus 2002).

Third, with the passing of the immediacy of the Asian crisis, and the generally neoliberal policy responses to it, there has been recognition that the old developmental states have not been dismantled and that state economic intervention remains significant. Thus, for Taiwan, Dent (2003) sees the developmental state evolving in response to liberalization, especially for trade and financial regulation, concluding that 'the Taiwanese experience demonstrates that liberalization can be most effectively implemented in an environment where comparatively high degrees of state capacity and institutionalized market order are evident' (ibid.: 481).[35] Yoshimatsu (2003: 120) concludes that the Japanese government 'has maintained and partially intensified the developmental state concept in its industrial cooperation programmes toward East Asia after the crises'.[36]

Towards an Alternative

The developmental state approach, then, has a shifting content and impact, as well as a mix of insights and limitations. It presumes the absence of class (to engender state autonomy), only for the state to create classes as a consequence of development. Its benevolent (embedded) interventions also become perceived as distorted by cronyism and/or international pressures whenever economic success turns sour. The result is for the developmental state approach to provide a selective organizational framework for describing the successes and failures of economic policy, generally from the separate perspectives of the economic and political schools.

What alternative approaches are there? First, a start can be made by rejecting the basis for the developmental state approach, that is, the dichotomy between market and state. Rather, both market and state are the consequence of or form taken by underlying economic and political relations and interests. Significantly, the political school suspends the (strength of the) presence of such interests in creating a limited space for the developmental state. But, while the school is correct to point to the changing nature of class relations as development proceeds, the state always reflects the balance of class forces and not their absence, as emphasized for South Korea by Koo and Kim (1992).

More generally, the critical work on the neoliberal approach to rent-seeking takes the view that it inappropriately sees it as being at the expense of development (see Khan and Jomo 2000 for a variety of theoretical and empirical studies). This is not necessarily so, since all economic change – ('Schumpeterian') productivity increase, for example – involves the creation, and possibly the destruction, of rents that can be, or were, appropriated. The incentives to promote or obstruct that change depend upon the economic and political positions of (class) agents. Corruption, cronyism or rent-seeking or whatever cannot be dismissed as sources of inefficiency in the abstract, but depend upon who is gaining or losing in what circumstances and with what consequences. This is not to praise and pursue rent-seeking, or even to view it as the predominant lever of development, but only to point to its dependence on the economic and political means by which rents are created and appropriated, or not.

Second, however, the representation of class interests through the state must always give rise to a specific system of accumulation – sectoral composition and levels of investment, financed and coordinated through private and public institutions. Such a system of accumulation, while not independent of external or international factors, is liable to be specific to each country, reflecting its history and dynamic as well as its evolving class structure.[37] In the case of South Korea, for example, real accumulation has primarily been undertaken by the chaebol, who have expanded and competed by diversification and conglomeration across sectors. State industrial policy has monitored performance, partially directed finance and tempered competition within sectors (Park 1999). Ultimately, the competition between chaebol has led them to press for deregulation in general and of (external) finance in particular, conforming to the dictates of neoliberalism (Kim and Cho 1999; Kang-Kook Lee 1999).[38] The system of accumulation prior to the crisis could no longer be sustained as it depended on excessive competitive penetration of chaebol across one another's sectors of operation. Neoliberal policies have only intensified that competitive process by weakening the constraints on the funding of intra-sectoral competition, while fuelling speculative investment and reliance upon foreign borrowing. This also explains the form taken by the crisis as seemingly unwise, unmonitored and even corrupt use of finance to support long-standing patterns of accumulation previously understood as miraculous.

The purpose here, however, is not to provide an alternative account of the South Korean or Asian crisis more generally.[39] Rather, it is to demonstrate that there are alternatives, both to the possibly expiring developmental state approach, and to the post-Washington Consensus as its putative, less radical successor. Debate over the developmental state has, at times, unwittingly brought the following problems to the fore, without being able to resolve them:

- What is the relationship between classes and the state, and how can they evolve and sustain a system of accumulation?
- What is the relationship between financial and industrial systems in the process of accumulation?
- What are national differences in systems of accumulation?
- Why are apparently miraculous and sustained periods of economic growth punctuated by crises?
- What is the relationship between economic and political systems, and how can they be addressed by a genuinely interdisciplinary approach?
- How do the new world order, US hegemony and the factors associated with 'globalization' impact upon the prospects for development?

In short, the role of the state in development, like development itself, needs to be situated in the context of class, power and conflict, each understood in both economic and political terms.

Notes

[1] This is an extended and updated version of Fine (2003).

[2] The classic reference is to Friedrich List and German industrialization in the nineteenth century. For a full discussion with relevance to present-day policy, see Chang (2002a).

[3] On which, see the chapter on 'Corruption, Governance and Economic Development' in this volume by Mushtaq Khan.

[4] Thus, Henderson and Appelbaum (1992) argue that dependency theory was displaced by the developmental state as the alternative to the mainstream.

[5] On which, see later.

[6] See also Johnson (1995: 99): 'The economists are unable to analyse the Japan problem because at root it is actually not an economic problem, but a matter of differing political institutions.'

[7] Johnson reports his reluctance in terms of his commendable wish to retain Japanese specificity and not to generalize unduly.

[8] See also Robinson's (2003: 25) description of Gordon White's (1998) definition of the developmental state as 'the deliberate construction of a set of institutions geared towards a clear vision of development under the guidance of a motivated political leadership.'

[9] See also, Trezzini (2001).

[10] See also, Chibber (2002) for a comparative study of bureaucratic rationality across India and South Korea.

[11] Note that Woo-Cumings (1999) emphasizes nationalism as crucial to Johnson's account of the Japanese developmental state, and the desire to break with both US and Soviet models of development.

[12] In case of destructive, duplicative competition, Carlile and Tilton (1998: 5) offer analysis typical of Chang: Private ownership is preferred over ownership by the state, but whereas Anglo–American liberalism views intense competition as a beneficial process that allows more efficient producers to replace less efficient ones, Japanese developmentalism holds that markets are prone to 'excessive competition', in which investment is wasted as firms overinvest and underutilize capacity as they drive each other out of business. In light of this, developmentalist policies have sought to economize on national investment resources by using public, private, or mixed regulation to limit competition.

[13] See Lukauskas (2002) for a more recent account of the market-conforming, non-replicable stance on the developmental state.

[14] Thus, it would be a mistake to see the shifts in thinking in the position of the World Bank over the last decade as primarily reflecting, let alone accepting, the overwhelming weight of research that has long been turned critically upon the old Washington Consensus. For, the developmental state literature as well as the new micro-foundations for development economics (or the basis for the post-Washington Consensus) have been around for two decades.

[15] Jones and Smith draw the parallel for the developmental state approach with Soviet studies and its failure to anticipate collapse.

[16] Thus, the death of the developmental state is anticipated in Chan, Clark and Lam, eds (1998), with earlier versions of the collection appearing in *Governance* in 1994.

[17] See also Jaymin Lee (1999) for South Korea, and Weyland (1998) for Brazil. For Singapore, Huff (1999: 234) concludes: 'The successful developmental state should obviate the need for its existence as the private sector, once nurtured by government, strengthens economically.'

[18] See Sum (2000) for the developmental state literature as a form of 'orientalism', how the west sees the east.

[19] Note that Cumings (1999) observes how such distinctions and oppositions are far from sharp.

[20] Although Lee (1997) argues that there are limits in response to globalization due to weaknesses in internal financial and ownership structures of East Asian economies,

Pang (2000) suggests that the financial crisis and globalization have the effect of dismantling the developmental state.

[21] Maundeni (2001), for example, suggests that Botswana has and Zimbabwe has not been developmental because of pre-colonial state culture – failing to mention the 'initial condition' of diamonds enjoyed by the former.

[22] See also Aoki (1998), Kim (1998), Woo-Cumings (1998) and Booth (1997). The roles of Japan as colonial power, followed by US aid, are important aspects of 'initial conditions'.

[23] Krugman (1994), drawing on the work of Young (1994, 1995).

[24] Presumably, however, future levels of investment would be lower in the crisis equilibrium.

[25] See the chapter titled 'The New Development Economics' in this volume.

[26] Thus, the developmental state is conceived in terms of game theory, especially a prisoners' dilemma, with problems of credibility and commitment (Huff, Dewit and Oughton 2001a, 2001b; Kang 2002).

[27] As Stiglitz (1998b) comments, 'I do not believe, however, that East Asia has grown through investment alone. Any visitor to the cities and factories in East Asia comes away impressed by the enormous technological progress in the last decades.'

[28] See also Crafts (1999b: 124): 'the 1997/8 crisis reflects weaknesses in the institutional arrangements of the East Asian developmental state model in the age of financial liberalization.'

[29] Note that Yeung (2000) correctly sees the crisis as strengthening state intervention in some respects.

[30] And in policy prescription.

[31] By taking the new consensus to its logical policy conclusions in favour of extensive interventionism, Stiglitz was forced to resign from the World Bank.

[32] In case those wedded to the new consensus become too heartened by the support they gain from the Japanese, it should be noted that authoritarianism is the preferred form of government to ensure an appropriate development state in the early stages of industrialization. See Murakami (1998) and Watanabe (1998).

[33] On Singapore, see Brown and Lauder (2001), Low (2001, 2003), Debrah and Ofori (2001), Airriess (2001), and Ling and Limin (2002), for example, and on China, Xia (2000) and Zhou and Xin (2003).

[34] In the context of Singapore's regional policy, Yeung (2000) perceptively sees the Asian crisis as in part strengthening the role of the developmental state.

[35] Of course, this throws into question what liberalization is, and whether it can exist other than as an influence on continuing state policies through pro-market ideology.

[36] See also Yoshimatsu (2002) for the synthetic fibre sector and earlier discussion of Japanese interest in the region.

[37] This approach was originally developed for South Africa in Fine and Rustomjee (1997). One implication, widely recognized in the literature, is that there is no single East Asian model. On this, in the context of the crisis and the developmental state, see Henderson (1999).

[38] For similar, if not identical, arguments for Taiwan, see Tsai (2001).

[39] See Cabalu (1999) for an overview. But note that Mathews (1998: 747) correctly sees three agendas at work in the Korean crisis: 'a conventional IMF agenda, a US trade and investment opening agenda, as well as a Korean-imposed institutional reform agenda'.

References

Airriess, C.A. (2001), 'Bureaucratic Rationality and the Developmental State', *American Journal of Sociology*, 107 (4): 951–89.

Amsden, Alice (1989), *Asia's Next Giant: South Korea and Late Industrialization* (New York: Oxford University Press).

Aoki, Masahiko (1998), 'Unintended Fit: Organizational Evolution and Government Design of

Institutions in Japan', in Masahiko Aoki, Hyung-ki Kim and Masahiro Okino-Fujimara, eds, *The Role of Government in East Asian Economic Development* (Oxford: Clarendon Press).

Aoki, Masahiko, Hyung-ki Kim and Masahiro Okino-Fujimara (1998), 'Beyond "The East Asian Miracle": Introducing the Market-Enhancing View', in Masahiko Aoki, Hyung-ki Kim and Masahiro Okino-Fujimara, eds, *The Role of Government in East Asian Economic Development* (Oxford: Clarendon Press).

Robinson, Mark (2003), 'Gordon White and Development Studies: An Appreciation', in Robert Benewick, Marc Blecher and Sarah Cook, eds, *Asian Politics in Development: Essays in Honour of Gordon White* (London: Frank Cass).

Booth, Anne (1997), 'Initial Conditions and Miraculous Growth: Why is South-east Asia different from Taiwan and South Korea?', Working Paper Series, 72, Department of Economics, School of Oriental and African Studies, London.

Brown, Phillip and Hugh Lauder (2001), 'The Future of Skill Formation in Singapore', *Asia Pacific Business Review*, 7 (3): 113–38.

Cabalu, Helen (1999), 'A Review of the Asian Crisis: Causes, Consequences and Policy Responses', *Australian Economic Review*, 32 (3): 304–13.

Carlile, Lonny and Mark Tilton (1998), 'Regulatory Reform and the Developmental State', in Lonny Carlile and Mark Tilton, eds, *Is Japan Really Changing Its Ways? Regulatory Reform and the Japanese Economy* (Washington DC: Brookings Institution).

Castells, Manuel (1992), 'Four Asian Tigers with a Dragon Head: A Comparative Analysis of State, Economy, and Society in the Asian Pacific Rim', in Jeffrey Henderson and Richard Appelbaum, eds, *States and Development in the Asian Pacific Rim* (London: Sage Publications).

Chan, Steve, Cal Clark and Danny Lam (1998), 'Looking Beyond the Developmental State', in Steve Chan, Cal Clark and Danny Lam, eds, *Beyond the Developmental State.*

Chan, Steve, Cal Clark and Danny Lam, eds (1998), *Beyond the Developmental State: East Asia's Political Economies Reconsidered* (London: Macmillan).

Chang, Ha-Joon (1994), *The Political Economy of Industrial Policy* (London: Macmillan).

—— (1999), 'The Economic Theory of the Developmental State', in Meredith Woo-Cumings, ed., *The Developmental State* (Ithaca: Cornell University Press).

—— (2000), 'The Hazard of Moral Hazard: Untangling the Asian Crisis', *World Development*, 28 (4): 775–88.

—— (2002a), *Kicking Away the Ladder: Policies and Institutions for Development in Historical Perspective* (London: Anthem Press).

—— (2002b), 'Breaking the Mould – An Institutionalist Political Economy Alternative to the Neoliberal Theory of the Market and the State', *Cambridge Journal of Economics*, 26 (5): 539–60.

Chang, Ha-Joon and Peter Evans (2000), 'The Role of Institutions in Economic Change', paper for the meeting of the 'Other Canon' group, Oslo, August.

Chang, Ha-Joon, Hong-Jae Park and Chul Gyue (1998), 'Interpreting the Korean Crisis: Financial Liberalization, Industrial Policy and Corporate Governance', *Cambridge Journal of Economics*, 22 (6): 735–46.

Chibber, Vivek (1999), 'Building a Developmental State: The Korean Case Reconsidered', *Politics and Society*, 27 (3): 309–46.

—— (2002), 'Bureaucratic Rationality and the Developmental State', *American Journal of Sociology*, 107 (4): 951–89.

Crafts, Nicholas (1999a), 'East Asian Growth Before and After the Crisis', *IMF Staff Papers*, 46 (2): 139–66.

—— (1999b), 'Implications of Financial Crisis for East Asian Trend Growth', *Oxford Review of Economic Policy*, 15 (3): 110–31.

Cumings, Bruce (1999), 'Webs with No Spiders, Spiders with No Webs: The Genealogy of the Developmental State', in Meredith Woo-Cumings, ed., *The Developmental State* (Ithaca: Cornell University Press).

Debrah, Yaw and George Ofori (2001), 'The State, Skill Formation and Productivity Enhancement in the Construction Industry: The Case of Singapore', *International Journal of Human Resource Management*, 12 (2): 184–202.

Dent, Christopher (2003), 'Taiwan's Foreign Economic Policy: The "Liberalization Plus" Approach of an Evolving Developmental State', *Modern African Studies*, 37 (2): 461–83.

Evans, Peter (1992), 'The State as Problem and Solution: Predation, Embedded Autonomy, and Structural Change', in Stephan Haggard and Robert Kaufman, eds, *The Politics of Economic Adjustment: International Constraints, Distributive Conflicts, and the State* (Princeton: Princeton University Press).

—— (1995), *Embedded Autonomy: States and Industrial Transformation* (Princeton: Princeton University Press).

Fine, Ben (1999), 'The Developmental State is Dead – Long Live Social Capital?', *Development and Change*, 30 (1): 1–19.

—— (2003), 'Beyond the Developmental State: Towards a Political Economy of Development', in Hitoshi Hirakawa, Makoto Noguchi and Makoto Sano, eds, *Beyond Market-Driven Development: A New Stream of Political Economy of Development* (Tokyo: Nihon Hyoron Sha, in Japanese).

—— (2004), 'Examining the Idea of Globalization and Development Critically: What Role for Political Economy?', *New Political Economy*, 9 (2): 213–31.

Fine, Ben and Zavareh Rustomjee (1997), *South Africa's Political Economy: From Minerals-Energy Complex to Industrialization* (Johannesburg: Wits University Press).

Fine, Ben and Colin Stoneman (1996), 'Introduction: State and Development', *Journal of Southern African Studies*, 22 (1): 5–26.

Francks, Penelope (1998), 'Agriculture and the State in Industrial East Asia: The Rise and Fall of the Food Control System in Japan', *Japan Forum*, 10 (1): 1–16.

Francks, Peter (2000), 'Japan and an East Asian Model of Agriculture's Role in Industrialization', *Japan Forum*, 12 (1): 43–52.

Gereffi, Gary (1998), 'More than Market, More than the State: Global Commodity Chains and Industrial Upgrading in East Asia', in Steve Chan, Cal Clark and Danny Lam, eds, *Beyond the Developmental State: East Asia's Political Economies Reconsidered* (London: Macmillan).

Grabowski, Richard (2000), 'The State and the Pursuit of the National Economic Interest', *Canadian Journal of Development Studies*, 21 (2): 269–93.

Hara, Yonosuke (1998), 'A Blueprint for Asian Economics', in Kenichi Ohno and Izumi Ohno, eds, *Japanese Views on Economic Development*.

Henderson, Jeffrey (1999), 'Uneven Crises: Institutional Foundations of East Asian Economic Turmoil', *Economy and Society*, 28 (3): 327–68.

Henderson, Jeffrey and Richard Appelbaum (1992), 'Situating the State in the East Asian Development Process', in Jeffrey Henderson and Richard Appelbaum, eds, *States and Development in the Asian Pacific Rim* (London: Sage Publications).

Huff, W.G. (1999), 'Turning the Corner in Singapore's Developmental State?', *Asian Survey*, 39 (2): 214–42.

Huff, W.G., Gerda Dewit and Christine Oughton (2001a), 'Building the Developmental State: Achieving Economic Growth through Cooperative Studies: A Comment on *Bringing Politics Back In*', *Journal of Development Studies*, 38 (1): 147–51.

—— (2001b), 'Credibility and Reputation Building in the Developmental State; A Model with East Asian Applications', *World Development*, 29 (4): 711–24.

Johnson, Chalmers (1982), *MITI and the Japanese Miracle* (Stanford: Stanford University Press).

—— (1995), *Japan: Who Governs, The Rise of the Developmental State* (New York: Newton).

—— (1999), 'The Developmental State: Odyssey of a Concept', in Meredith Woo-Cumings, ed., *The Developmental State* (Ithaca: Cornell University Press).

Jones, David and Michael Smith (2001), 'Is There a Sovietology of South-East Asian Studies?', *International Affairs*, 77 (4): 843–65.

Kang, David (2002), 'Bad Loans to Good Friends: Money Politics and the Developmental State in Korea', *International Organization*, 56 (1): 177–207.

Khan, M.H. and K.S. Jomo, eds (2000), *Rents, Rent-Seeking and Economic Development* (Cambridge: Cambridge University Press).

Kim, Soohaeng and Bokhyun Cho (1999), 'The South Korean Economic Crisis: Contrasting Interpretations and an Alternative for Economic Reform', *Studies in Political Economy*, 60: 7–28.

Kim, Yun-Tae (1998), 'The Origins of the Developmental State in South Korea, 1910–79', *Asian Profile*, 26 (6): 463–76.

—— (1999), 'Neoliberalism and the Decline of the Developmental State', *Journal of Contemporary Asia*, 29 (4): 441–61.

Koh, Gillian (1997), 'Bureaucratic Rationality in an Evolving Developmental State: Challenges to Governance in Singapore', *Asian Journal of Political Science*, 5 (2): 114–41.

Kohli, Atul (1999), 'Where do High-Growth Political Economies Come From?: The Japanese Lineage of Korea's "Developmental State"', in Meredith Woo-Cumings, ed., *The Developmental State* (Ithaca: Cornell University Press).

Koo, Hagen and Eun Mee Kim (1992), 'The Developmental State and Capital Accumulation in South Korea', in Jeffrey Henderson and Richard Appelbaum, eds, *States and Development in the Asian Pacific Rim* (London: Sage Publications).

Krieckhaus, Jonathan (2002), 'Reconceptualizing the Developmental State: Public Savings and Economic Growth', *World Development*, 30 (10): 1697–712.

Krugman, Paul (1994), 'The Myth of Asia's Miracle', *Foreign Affairs*, 73 (6): 62–78.

—— (1999), 'Analytical Afterthoughts on the Asian Crisis', http://web.mit.edu/krugman/ www/minicris.htm.

Lall, Sanjaya (1992), 'Technological Capabilities and Industrialization', *World Development*, 20 (2): 165–86.

Lall, Sanjaya and Carlo Pietrobelli, eds (2002), *Failing to Compete: Technology Development and Technology Systems in Africa* (Cheltenham: Edward Elgar).

Lall, Sanjaya and Shujiro Urata, eds (2003), *Competitiveness, FDI and Technological Activity in East Asia* (Cheltenham: Edward Elgar).

Lee, Jaymin (1999), 'East Asian NIE's Model of Development: Miracle, Crisis, and Beyond', *Pacific Review*, 12 (2): 141–62.

Lee, Kang-Kook (1999), 'The Change of the Financial System and Developmental State in Korea', WIDER, Research in Progress, 19, World Institute for Development Economic Research, United Nations University, Helsinki.

Lee, Yeon-ho (1997), 'The Limits of Economic Globalization in East Asian Developmental States', *Pacific Review*, 10 (3): 366–90.

Ling, Ooi and Hee Limin (2002), 'Public Space and the Developmental State in Singapore', *International Development Policy Review*, 24 (4): 433–47.

Little, I.M.D. and J.A. Mirrlees (1969), *Manual of Industrial Project Analysis in Developing Countries, Volume 2, Social Cost Benefit Analysis* (Paris: OECD).

—— (1974), *Project Appraisal and Planning for Developing Countries* (London: Heinemann Educational).

Low, Linda (2001), 'The Singapore Developmental State in the New Economy and Polity', *The Pacific Review*, 14 (3): 411–41.

—— (2003), 'Policy Dilemmas in Singapore's RTA Strategy', *The Pacific Review*, 16 (1): 99–127.

Lukauskas, Arvid (2002), 'Financial Restriction and the Developmental State in East Asia: Toward a More Complex Political Economy', *Comparative Political Studies*, 35 (4): 379–412.

Marsh, Ian (1999), 'The State and the Economy: Opinion Formation and Collaboration as Facets of Economic Management', *Political Studies*, 47 (5): 837–56.

Mathews, John (1998), 'Fashioning a New Korean Model out of the Crisis: The Rebuilding of Institutional Capabilities', *Cambridge Journal of Economics*, 22 (6): 747–60.

Maundeni, Zibani (2001), 'State Culture and Development in Botswana and Zimbabwe', *Journal of Modern African Studies*, 40 (1): 105–32.

Moon, Chung-in (1999), 'Political Economy of East Asian Development and Pacific Economic Cooperation', *Pacific Review*, 12 (2): 199–224.

Murakami, Yasusuke (1998), 'Theory of Developmentalism', in Kenichi Ohno and Izumi Ohno eds, *Japanese Views on Economic Development*.

O'Hearn, Denis (2000), 'Globalization, "New Tigers", and the End of the Developmental State?: The Case of the Celtic Tiger', *Politics and Society*, 28 (1): 67–92.

Ohno, Kenichi (1998), 'Overview: Creating the Market Economy', in Kenichi Ohno and Izumi Ohno, eds, *Japanese Views on Economic Development*.

Ohno, Kenichi and Izumi Ohno (1998), 'Afterword', in Kenichi Ohno and Izumi Ohno, eds, *Japanese Views on Economic Development*.

Ohno, Kenichi and Izumi Ohno, eds (1998), *Japanese Views on Economic Development: Diverse Paths to the Market* (London: Routledge).

Pang, Eul-Soo (2000), 'The Financial Crisis of 1997–98 and the End of the Asian Developmental State', *Contemporary Southeast Asia*, 22 (3): 570–93.

Park, Hong-Jae (1999), 'The Chaebol and Economic Growth in Korea', PhD thesis, School of Oriental and African Studies, University of London.

Pinglé, Vibha (1999), *Rethinking the Developmental State: India's Industry in Comparative Perspective* (New York: St. Martin's Press).

Riain, Sean (2000), 'The Flexible Developmental State: Globalization, Information Technology and the New "Celtic Tiger"', *Politics and Society*, 28 (2): 157–94.

Saito, Asato (2003), 'Global City Formation in a Capitalist Developmental State: Tokyo and the Waterfront Sub-centre Project', *Urban Studies*, 40 (2): 283–308.

Shen, Ce and John Williamson (2001), 'Accounting for Cross-National Differences in Infant Mortality Decline (1965–91) among Less-Developed Countries: Effects of Women's Status, Economic Dependency, and State Strength', *Social Indicators Research*, 53: 257–88.

Sinha, Aseema (2003), 'Rethinking the Developmental State Model: Divided Leviathan and Subnational Comparisons in India', *Comparative Politics*, 35 (4): 459–76.

Stiglitz, Joseph E. (1998a), 'More Instruments and Broader Goals: Moving Towards the post-Washington Consensus', 1998 WIDER Annual Lecture, Helsinki, 7 January.

—— (1998b), 'Sound Finance and Sustainable Development in Asia', Keynote Address to the Asia Development Forum, Manila, 12 March.

Sum, Ngai-Ling (2000), 'Globalization and its "Other(s)": Three "New Kinds of Orientalism" and the Political Economy of Trans-Border Identity', in Colin Hay and David Marsh, eds, *Demystifying Globalization* (London: Macmillan).

Trezzini, Bruno (2001), 'Embedded State Autonomy and Legitimacy: Piecing Together the Malaysian Development Puzzle', *Economy and Society*, 30 (3): 324–53.

Tsai, Ming-Chang (2001), 'Dependency, the State and Class in the Neoliberal Transition of Taiwan', *Third World Quarterly*, 22 (3): 359–79.

Wade, Robert (1990), *Governing the Market: Economic Theory and the Role of Government in Taiwan's Industrialization* (Princeton: Princeton University Press).

—— (1996), 'Japan, the World Bank, and the Art of Paradigm Maintenance: *The East Asian Miracle* in Political Perspective', *New Left Review*, 217: 3–37.

—— (1998), 'From "Miracle" to "Cronyism": Explaining the Great Asian Slump', *Cambridge Journal of Economics*, 22 (6): 693–706.

Wade, Robert and Frank Veneroso (1998), 'The Asian Crisis: The High Debt Model versus the Wall Street-Treasury-IMF Complex', *New Left Review*, 228: 3–23.

Watanabe, Toshio (1998), 'Designing Asia for the Next Century', in Kenichi Ohno and Izumi Ohno, eds, *Japanese Views on Economic Development*.

Weyland, Kurt (1998), 'From Leviathan to Gulliver? The Decline of the Developmental State in Brazil', *Governance*, 11 (1): 51–75.

White, Gordon (1998), 'Constructing a Democratic Developmental State', in Mark Robinson and Gordon White, eds, *The Democratic Developmental State: Politics and Institutional Design* (Oxford: Oxford University Press).

Williams, Glyn (1997), 'State, Discourse, and Development in India: The Case of West Bengal's Panchayati Raj', *Environment and Planning*, A 29 (12): 2099–112.

Woo-Cumings, Meredith (1998), 'The Political Economy of Growth in East Asia: A Perspective on the State, Market, and Ideology', in Masahiko Aoki, Hyung-ki Kim and Masahiro Okino-Fujimara, eds, *The Role of Government in East Asian Economic Development* (Oxford: Clarendon Press).

—— (1999), 'Introduction: Chalmers Johnson and the Politics of Nationalism and Development', in Meredith Woo-Cumings, ed., *The Developmental State* (Ithaca: Cornell University Press).

World Bank (1993), *The East Asian Miracle: Economic Growth and Public Policy* (New York: Oxford University Press).

Xia, Ming (2000), *The Dual Developmental State: Development Strategy and Institutional Arrangements for China's Transition* (Aldershot: Ashgate).

Yeung, Henry (2000), 'State Intervention and Neoliberalism in the Globalizing World Economy: Lessons from Singapore's Regionalization Programme', *Pacific Review*, 13 (1): 133–62.

Yoshimatsu, Hidetaka (2002), 'Japan and Industrial Adjustment in Asia: Overproduction Problems in the Synthetic Fibre Industry', *Pacific Affairs*, 75 (3): 377–98.

—— (2003), 'Japanese Policy in the Asian Economic Crises and the Developmental State Concept', *Journal of the Asia Pacific Economy*, 8 (1): 102–25.

Young, Alwyn (1994), 'Lessons from the East Asian NICs: A Contrarian Review', *European Economic Review*, 38 (3–4): 964–73.

—— (1995), 'The Tyranny of Numbers: Confronting the Statistical Realities of the East Asian Growth Experience', *The Quarterly Journal of Economics*, 110 (3): 641–80.

Zhou, Yu and Tong Xin (2003), 'An Innovative Region in China: Interaction between Multinational Corporations and Local Firms in a High-Tech Cluster in Beijing', *Economic Geography*, 79 (2): 129–52.

Analysis of Technology and Development

A Critical Review

Sonali Deraniyagala

Over the past two decades or so, significant advances have been made in the economic analysis of technology issues in developing countries. Prior to this, it was assumed that developing countries undertook limited technological change and that they remained dependent on foreign technology. This notion of technological dependence has been challenged by the more recent literature that has unravelled the varied and complex nature of technology generation in poor countries. These writings have also advanced our understanding of the factors that influence and determine technological change in these countries, as well as of the economic effects of technology development.

This chapter provides an overview of alternative approaches to technology and development. We show how technology issues that were previously considered as irrelevant to development have now been placed at the forefront of analyses of industrialization and growth. The first part of the chapter deals with older approaches to technology, and the early literature on technology and development. We show that this literature sheds very little light on the process of technology generation in developing countries. The second part examines more recent theoretical and empirical writings dealing with technology and development, which have proliferated since the late 1980s. The way in which this new literature questions many of the older assumptions relating to technology in developing countries is explored. Recent approaches to technology policy and its interaction with trade and industrial policy are also highlighted.

Changing Concepts of Technology and Technological Change

Technological change is defined as the creation or absorption of new products and processes. Early economic analyses of technology defined technological change as invention and innovation at the global technology frontier. Innovation in this sense was seen as distinct from the diffusion of innovations to new users. As shown later in this chapter, more recent analyses see the distinction between innovation and diffusion as increasingly blurred. Therefore, the first appearance of a product or process at the national, sectoral or organizational level, as well as the adaptation or modification of existing produce, are now commonly defined as comprising technological change.

The analysis of technology-related issues by economists has changed significantly over the past fifty years. Prior to the 1960s, technology and technological change were approached as being largely exogenous to the economy. Technology was treated as 'manna from heaven' and little attention was paid to the question of whether economic factors had any influence on technological change. According to this view, technological change was purely the result of scientific advance, which, in turn, was not driven by any economic motives or incentives. In the 1960s and 1970s, the endogenous nature of technological change was increasingly recognized and a variety of microeconomic models sought to identify the economic determinants of technological change (Arrow 1962; Gilbert and Newberry 1982).

Implicit in both the exogenous and early endogenous approaches to technological change was a specific conceptualization of the nature of technology. It was assumed that technology consisted of well-defined techniques and products. Information relating to the use of each technology was seen as easily and readily available to all potential users in the form of a 'blueprint' (Evenson and Westphal 1995). The blueprint was seen to contain complete information relating to the efficient use of a technology (Nelson and Winter 1982). This blueprint notion of technology was central to early neoclassical models of production and technical change in which the organization of production was determined by 'production possibility sets' describing 'the state of knowledge about the possibility of transforming commodities' (Arrow and Hahn 1971: 53). While these neoclassical models viewed the technological knowledge underlying the production set as changing over time as a result of 'technical progress', little attention was paid to unravelling the characteristics of such knowledge. Rather, the idea of technical progress was governed by its correspondence to the neoclassical theory of supply in terms of a (shifting) production function.

This conceptualization of technology had important implications for the analysis of technology issues in developing countries. Firstly, these early models defined technological change as invention and innovation at the global frontier. Given that this type of activity mainly takes place in advanced countries, it implied that technological change was largely absent in developing countries. Secondly, this approach presumed that technologies would diffuse from advanced countries to developing countries easily, with no more difficulty than within their countries of origin. It was assumed that developing countries could obtain and efficiently use technologies developed in advanced countries by merely accessing the relevant 'blueprint'.

Early Theoretical Approaches to Technological Change

Technological change was central to both early growth theory and to microeconomic models of innovation that emerged in the late 1950s and 1960s. The neoclassical model of economic growth developed by Robert Solow in 1957 posited that the growth of per capita output was only partly a function of the growth of factor inputs. Solow's discovery of a large 'residual' when estimating the determinants of growth led to the argument that this residual reflected 'technological progress'. Following Solow's initial formulation, a huge body of empirical research aimed to 'squeeze down' the residual. One way was to focus on improving measurement of the quality of variables included in the growth estimations, thereby reducing the size of the residual. Other studies sought to include inputs other than capital and labour, incorporating land, for example. The central characteristic of these growth models and growth accounting exercises was that technological progress was essentially treated as exogenous. Technology remained a 'black box', with little effort made to unravel its determinants.

Models of Induced Innovation

Early microeconomic models of innovation began to focus on the economic determinants of technological change. Models of 'induced innovation' (II) focused exclusively on developed countries, but were significant in that they treated technical change as endogenous (Bingswanger and Ruttan 1978). Their focus was on the direction of technological change – that is, on whether technological change was capital- or labour-saving. These models were based on the notion of an 'innovation possibility frontier' (IPF) that showed the set of possible innovations available. Innovations were realized through the R&D efforts of entrepreneurs and firms, and relative factor prices determined whether capital-saving or labour-saving innovations were produced. While R&D expenditures enabled firms to choose innovations from the IPF, there was little consideration of how this frontier came into existence. The assumption was that the frontier consisted of a set of blueprints determined by prior scientific advance and invention.

Diffusion Models

Diffusion models sought to explain how the use of a new innovation spread through an economy. Several types of diffusion models have been proposed (Mansfield 1961; Griliches 1957). 'Contagion' models of diffusion proposed that innovations spread through contact between existing and potential users, with there being some pre-specified criteria for adoption, such as firm size. If a potential user fulfilled these criteria, the adoption of the innovation upon 'contact' with an existing user was instantaneous. Here again, the assumption was that technological information was available in blueprint form and that assimilation of innovations by new users was a relatively straightforward process.

Search Models

Several authors applied search concepts to examine the nature of the invention process (Nordhaus 1969). The search process was modelled as a series of experiments consisting of trials or draws. These models assumed the existence of a distribution of potential inventions at the beginning of any research project. The uncertain outcome of research was treated as a random draw from this distribution. The distribution was seen as determined by factors endogenous to the economic sphere, such as the level of a country's technological skills, as well as factors such as the results of previous search efforts.

By focusing on the endogenous nature of technological change, these early microeconomic models made a significant contribution to the economic analysis of technology. However, their usefulness for analysis of technology and development was limited for several reasons. Firstly, their focus was confined to advanced countries that undertake invention and innovation at the global technology frontier. Secondly, they mostly analysed innovation within the framework of competitive equilibrium. In this sense, innovation was seen as responsive to market signals. The fact that a variety of market imperfections (such as information asymmetries, externalities and spill-over effects) impact upon the innovation process was not explicitly considered. Given the widespread existence of such market imperfections in developing countries, the relevance of these models to the analysis of technology and development was limited.

Technology in the Early Development Literature

While early economic models of technology paid little attention to technological change in developing countries, explicit analysis of technology issues was also absent in the early development literature. In much of this literature, it was assumed that developing countries were solely importers of foreign technologies and innovation, and technological change was seen as confined to advanced countries. Developing countries were seen to play little active role in independent technology generation.

The blueprint notion of technological knowledge was also implicit in the early development literature. As importers of foreign technologies, developing countries were seen as 'picking' suitable technologies from an exogenously given set of blueprints. This blueprint notion of technology had several implications for the analysis of technology in development. Firstly, given that blueprints contained all the information required for the efficient adoption and utilization of a given technology, the process of assimilating foreign technologies in developing countries was assumed to be relatively easy. Secondly, it implied that developing countries faced limited costs when introducing new technologies. Apart from the cost of purchasing new products or techniques, other costs (for instance, the costs involved in learning to use a new technology efficiently) were seen as minimal or non-existent. Finally, given the ready availability of information relating to each new technology, technological change in developing countries was seen as relatively risk-free. This was in contrast to the high levels of risk and uncertainty that characterized invention and innovation at the global frontier.

The 'blueprint' assumption of technology, therefore, meant that the supply-side of technological change was neglected in the early development literature. Given that all new technologies flowed from advanced countries to technologically backward developing countries, and given that the recipient countries had ready access to complete information relating to new technologies, there was little room for analysing the supply-side determinants of technological progress. The implication was that technological change was the outcome of demand conditions in developing countries; supply-side factors – such as the availability of skills, capabilities, institutions and infrastructure – had little effect on the adoption of new technologies.

The above points become clear when we examine key theoretical models in the early development literature.

Dual Economy Models

Much of the work on economic development in the 1950s and 1960s modelled long-run equilibrium economic growth in the context of surplus labour (Lewis 1954; Fei and Ranis 1964). These dual economy models increased awareness of the importance of technological change for economic growth and development. In these models, technological change was viewed from the point of view of structural change and choice of technique. They highlighted the role played by sectoral differences in technological change in promoting economic development. However, these models of development paid little attention to opening up the 'black box' of technological change. While they assumed the existence of a relatively technologically advanced modern sector, there was little analysis of how technological change in this sector was generated.

Models of 'Catch-up' and Convergence

While models of catch-up and convergence gained ascendancy in the 1990s (Barro and Sala-i-Martin 1992), these concepts were also central to the early development literature. Gerschenkron's (1962) analysis of the advantages of backwardness proposed that technological followers benefit from the technologies created by technological leaders. In some versions of the catch-up hypothesis, the scope for catch-up was proportional to the technological distance between leaders and followers.

However, these models generally contained limited analysis of the precise mechanisms by which technological catch-up took place, or of other factors that determined the possibility of catch-up. It was assumed that technologies developed elsewhere could easily be transferred to developing countries. The preconditions for successful technology transfer were factors seen as generally important for economic efficiency, such as the acquisition of human capital and infrastructure. Given the ready transferability of foreign technology, it was assumed that developing countries did not need to devote resources (such as research and development expenditure) specifically to technology development.

Infant Industries and Industrialization

Early discussions of industrialization in developing countries were also relevant to the analysis of technology and development. The literature of the 1960s and 1970s focused largely on arguments for inward-looking industrialization and on appropriate policy interventions to encourage it. The Prebisch–Singer hypothesis pointed to the secular decline in the terms of trade for primary commodities; the related export pessimism justified trade protection to nurture domestic industrialization. The 'capital goods fundamentalism' of the Mahalanobis model stressed the importance of import substitution in heavy industries.

Few of these infant industry models paid specific attention to the links between trade policy, technology development and industrialization. While these models were based on the need for independent industrialization in developing countries, no explicit attention was paid to issues relating to their own indigenous technology generation. Trade protection alone was seen as sufficient to nurture the growth and competitiveness of infant industries, and technological progress was seen to occur fairly automatically in protected sectors. The absence of import competition alone was seen as resulting in 'learning', which promoted technological change and productivity in nascent industries. This type of learning was seen to occur solely as a function of production experience, which itself was a function of time. These infant industry models largely assumed that developing countries did not require additional investment in technological learning, a point emphasized in more recent writings on technology in development, discussed below.

Early Models of Trade and Development
Technology issues also featured in many early models of international trade applied to developing countries. In models of dynamic comparative advantage, trade patterns were seen as determined by factor endowments, and the structure of production and trade was seen as evolving in response to changes in factor supplies and demand. These models of comparative advantage were based on specific assumptions relating to technological change. In relation to developing countries, it was assumed that new technologies would be adopted as production structures changed. There was little consideration, however, of the processes by which these new technologies were chosen and utilized. It was assumed that developing countries adopted foreign technologies from a given 'technology shelf'. The blueprint concept of technology, implicit in these models, meant that the need for additional investments to assimilate and efficiently utilize new technology was overlooked.

Technology-gap and product cycle models of international trade were also based on the assumption that developing countries were solely importers of technologies from advanced countries (Vernon 1966). In the technology-gap models, innovation was seen as confined to advanced countries, with developing countries imitating these innovations after a considerable time lag. In these models, therefore, international trade took place because of this 'innovation gap' between rich and poor countries. Product cycle models also posited the direction of international trade to be determined by the fact that new products are always invented in advanced countries, with production shifting to developing countries once the products become mature and standardized. In both these sets of models, therefore, technological change was unidirectional, originating only in advanced countries. Developing countries were seen as technological laggards, playing little role in generating independent technological activity.

Introducing Technology into the Development Literature:
Choice of Technique and Technology Transfer

Technology issues were first explicitly introduced into the development literature in the 1970s, with attention focusing on the question of appropriate technology choice. The aim of this 'choice of technique' literature was to examine the factor intensities of alternative techniques of production used in developing countries. Empirical studies typically showed a range of technology choices coexisting in specific sectors, with these techniques varying significantly in terms of their factor intensity (Stewart 1977). The dependence of developing countries on technology imports was shown to result in the use of 'inappropriate' (that is, capital-intensive) technologies. Many studies also showed the coexistence of appropriate or labour-intensive technologies, generally in the more 'traditional' industrial sub-sectors (for example, handlooms). A central conclusion of this literature was that technology choice in developing countries was often not compatible with an important policy objective – employment generation.

Several features of this 'choice of technique' literature are noteworthy for our analysis. Firstly, the notion of technological dependence is central to these studies, with developing countries seen as highly dependent on foreign technology. Secondly, it is assumed that foreign technologies are used in developing countries without any adaptation or modification. In this sense, technologies are essentially seen as well-defined and finite blueprints. Thirdly, while the existence of some 'indigenous' technologies was observed in several studies, little attention was paid to the processes by which these technologies themselves had been developed. Overall, therefore, this 'choice of technique' literature conceptualized technology in developing countries as being fairly static and unchanging. This conceptualization was challenged in later studies of technology and development, discussed below.

Questioning Notions of Technological Dependence:
The Post-1980 Literature on Technology and Development

Since the late 1980s, analysis of technology issues in the development literature has undergone significant change. A new body of literature has challenged many of the earlier assumptions relating to technology in developing countries (Lall 1987; Bell and Pavitt 1992; Pack and Westphal 1986). Contrary to earlier assumptions, this new literature has shown that technological change in developing countries is not confined to the use of foreign technologies in a 'passive' and 'static' manner. They have demonstrated that considerable technological activity takes place in developing countries, with relatively industrialized developing countries undertaking extensive technological change.

This new literature has also, for the first time, shed considerable light on the process of technology generation in developing countries. It has been emphasized that the types of technological change undertaken in many developing countries involve considerable effort and costs, exceeding those of merely purchasing foreign technologies. This has challenged the assumption that information relating to the use of existing technologies can easily be obtained in blueprint form. Investment in the acquisition of relevant technological skills and capabilities has been shown to be a critical ingredient for technological dynamism in developing countries. By highlighting some determinants of technological change, attention has been drawn to the supply-side of technology generation in developing countries, an issue hitherto ignored in the literature.

The rethinking of technology issues in the development literature has been the outcome of two factors. Firstly, the theoretical analysis of the effects and determinants of technological change advanced considerably in the 1980s, with a plethora of new models and theories focusing on these issues. Secondly, a significant and growing body of empirical literature unravelled the processes of technology generation in developing countries, and provided a much more dynamic account of technological change than had hitherto existed in the development literature. Both these developments are discussed below.

Technology and 'New' Theories of Economic Growth

The period since the 1980s saw the emergence of new theoretical approaches to technology and growth that addressed many shortcomings of the older neoclassical models. Theories of endogenous growth explicitly introduced investments in technology development as a determinant of long-run economic growth (Romer 1990). In these models, technology is essentially conceptualized as knowledge subject to externalities or spill-overs, resulting in increasing returns to investment. Empirical tests of these endogenous theories provide few generalizable conclusions, but highlight the contribution to growth of a range of technology investments such as investments in R&D and human capital.

Overall, however, while the contribution of endogenous technology investments to long-term economic growth is emphasized, these models do little to extend our understanding of the process of technology generation and the determinants of technological change. There is also little explicit consideration of the nature of technology generation or the relationship between technology and growth in developing countries. It is assumed that investment in R&D is an adequate indicator of technology generation in rich and poor countries alike, and that the trade–growth relationship is the same in both sets of countries.

Technology in 'New' Theories of International Trade

Technology and knowledge spill-overs are also key mechanisms that link international trade and growth in the 'new' theories of trade which emerged in the 1990s. In their classic work, Grossman and Helpman (1991) show how international trade can boost a country's R&D sector by transmitting technological information, increasing competition and expanding the size of the market. It is also acknowledged that trade can also have negative effects on the R&D sector by displacing innovative activities, thus making ambiguous the overall effects of trade.

Other new trade models emphasize the positive effects of openness by focusing on the role of capital goods imports in promoting economic growth (Coe, Helpman and Hoffmaister 1995; Lee 1995). In these models, technology spill-overs are generally proportional to capital goods imports. Imported capital goods embody information about new technologies, and producers who are exposed to this information are seen as more likely to innovate. Many of these models imply that increased amounts of resources will be devoted to R&D following trade liberalization.

The positive conclusion about openness in these models is dependent on specific assumptions about the nature of technology and technology transfer, and can be reversed when the definition of technology is refined. Most models implicitly assume that technology can be codified and easily transferred in blueprint form. If, in contrast, we acknowledge that learning by importing capital goods is partly dependent on the absorptive capacity of countries, then, gains from trade (especially for poorer countries) may be much more limited.

Microeconomic Theories of Market Imperfections and Informational Economics

At the microeconomic level, theoretical work in informational economics and market imperfections has questioned many assumptions about technology in standard neoclassical models, and highlighted the limits of the market mechanism in allocating resources for technology investment (Stiglitz 1989). This approach centres on the existence of market imperfections and has significant implications for the analysis of technology.

In this approach, information is always imperfect and markets are always incomplete, which means that the market does not yield an outcome that is even constrained Pareto-optimal (Greenwald and Stiglitz 1986). Contrary to the blueprint notion of technology, imperfect information and missing markets are seen as intrinsic to the acquisition of technology. If left to the market, this is likely to result in underinvestment in technology development, thus providing a rationale for government intervention to promote technological change.

These theoretical micro-foundations relating to information and technology are also used to analyse the process of industrialization. Industrializing in developing countries is seen as a move towards increasingly perfect markets. Technological change is placed at the heart of the industrialization process, particularly in developing countries. Given that industrialization involves continuously acquiring and managing new knowledge, overcoming market failures relating to asymmetric information, technological spill-overs and the public good properties of knowledge is seen as especially relevant.

While informational economics thus provides some theoretical micro-foundations for placing technology development as central to industrialization, problems with the manner in which technology generation is conceptualized remain (Deraniyagala 2001). The market failure approach largely assumes that correcting for imperfections will necessarily bring forth desired outcomes in the market for technology. However, imperfect understanding and heterogeneous capabilities among economic agents may mean that interventions (for instance, public provision of information on the availability of new technologies) have a varied and unpredictable outcome.

In addition, this emphasis on correcting for market distortions is also questioned by others who emphasize that market failures are intrinsic to production, and that dynamic technological change involves the creation, not the correction, of market failures (Amsden 1997). It is argued that East Asian governments often followed such an approach, correcting some market failures (for instance, in the market for long-term credit) while creating others (for instance, by erecting barriers to entry in specific sectors and protecting some forms of non-public knowledge) (Freeman 1994). Once the 'positive' role of market failures in promoting technology development is understood, therefore, reducing the process of technological change and industrialization to one of correcting market failures becomes problematic.

Evolutionary Theories of Technology

Some of the most important theoretical contributions to the analysis of technology in recent years has come from 'evolutionary' theories of technology and growth (Nelson and Winter 1982; Dosi 1997; Freeman 1994). These theories model economic growth as having its origins in technological decisions and actions undertaken at the micro level. They also highlight several characteristics of technology and make a significant positive contribution to the economic analysis of the way knowledge is produced, diffused and economically exploited.

Evolutionary theory defines technology as knowledge, and questions the notion that technological knowledge is well-defined and available in blueprint form. In contrast to neoclassical theory, knowledge is seen as 'fuzzy' and tacit, in the sense that it cannot be easily transmitted or communicated. For this reason, the innovative actions of economic agents are seen as being highly dependent on capabilities and skills necessary to absorb technological knowledge. It also means that a given technology will diffuse among potential users (for example, manufacturing firms) in a varied manner, depending on the absorptive capacity of each individual user.

Evolutionary theory models technological change as the outcome of a variety of supply- and demand-side factors. This contrasts with the older theories that focused exclusively on various inducements such as price incentives and demand. While inducements have some influence on the pace and direction of technological change, the notion that agents respond 'rationally' to inducements is rejected, and economic agents are seen to act with 'bounded rationality'. Technological change, therefore, is determined by the interaction of a variety of factors, including scientific opportunities, inducements and supply-side capabilities.

The emphasis of evolutionary theory on supply-side capabilities has been very relevant to the analysis of technology in developing countries, a point to which we return below. These theories posit 'learning', which determines the acquisition of capabilities, to be highly specific to individual agents such as manufacturing firms. Firms are seen as having 'learning routines' that are cumulative, in the sense that learning in one period impacts on learning in the next period. These learning routines essentially determine the pace and pattern of technological change at the firm level. Writers within the evolutionary tradition have also developed the idea of a 'national innovation system' (NIS), a concept that has gained intellectual and practical coherence over the past two decades or so. Analyses of technological and industrial dynamism in both developed and developing countries showed these countries to have well-functioning national innovation systems. An NIS has been defined as a network of public- and private-sector institutions which act to initiate, modify and diffuse new technologies (Freeman 1994), or, alternatively, as a set of institutions whose interactions determine the innovative performance of national firms (Nelson 1993).

The NIS approach, therefore, reflects the proposition that innovation is not simply a response to various inducements but is the outcome of a variety of economic, social and institutional phenomena. In this sense, innovation is viewed as intrinsically linked to macroeconomic and sectoral policies. The functions of an NIS include the creation of new knowledge, guiding the search for existing knowledge, supplying resources such as capital and skills, facilitating the creation of positive externalities, and facilitating the formation of markets (Lundvall 2000). Important actors within an NIS include the government, scientific and research institutions, universities, training centres and private firms. Again, the NIS concept is at odds with the neoliberal approach in that a key role for the government in promoting technology investment is emphasized.

The Post-1980s' Literature on Technology and Development

In the late 1980s, a few pioneering empirical studies shed light on the types of technological activities undertaken by manufacturing firms in countries such as India, Brazil and Argentina (Lall 1987; Katz 1987). These studies showed that technological activity in these firms was not confined to the use of imported technologies, and that considerable effort to adapt and modify foreign technologies was common. Some of these early studies focused on countries with protectionist trade policies, and it was shown that restricted access to technology imports led to various types of technological activity, such as the design of new products for domestic markets and 'innovative' efforts to extend the life of capital goods. Other studies of the rapidly industrializing East Asian economies also showed technological change playing an important role in the manufacturing success of these countries (Wade 1990, 2003; Chang 2002). Attention was drawn to the significance of efforts to 'reverse engineer' technologies developed in advanced countries; this type of reverse engineering was shown to have a significant positive effect on the productivity and international competitiveness of manufacturing firms in these countries.

Following these early pioneering case studies, a large body of empirical and conceptual research on developing countries has greatly enhanced our understanding of technology issues in the context of development (Evenson and Westphal 1995; Lall 2003; Bell and Pavitt 1992; Fransman and King 1984). While the early empirical studies focused on describing the nature of technological activities undertaken in developing countries, the literature that followed has dealt with a range of other issues, such as the patterns of technology development among developing countries, the determinants of technological change at the firm, industry and national level, and the economic effects of technological change in developing countries. Some of the key propositions of this new literature are as follows.

Significant technological change occurs below the global innovation frontier and developing countries actively undertake such technological change. This new literature has questioned the notion that technological change in developing countries only involves the purchase of foreign technologies. Focusing largely on manufacturing, it has shown technological change in developing countries to be varied and, sometimes, extensive. While acknowledging the fact that developing countries rarely innovate at the global scientific frontier, or even undertake much formal research and development, this literature has highlighted a range of technological efforts aimed at adapting and modifying existing technologies. Adaptation and modification of foreign technologies to suit domestic tastes, demand conditions and climatic conditions have been shown to be widespread among developing country firms.

It is also argued that, in contrast to innovation at the global frontier, technological change in developing countries is *minor* and *incremental*. The important point is that such minor technological change is also 'innovative', in that it involves technological efforts not previously undertaken by the firms or countries in question (Bell and Pavitt 1992). These findings, therefore, question the earlier blueprint notions of technology which imply that technology imports can be easily assimilated in a 'static' and unchanged manner.

Technological change in developing countries is a costly and cumulative process. It has also been emphasized that the cost of technological change in developing countries far exceeds the initial cost of purchasing foreign technologies. Adaptive technological change is shown to require much additional investment – for instance, investment to learn about alternative techniques, to modify process technologies and capital goods, to adapt product designs to suit domestic market conditions and to acquire the relevant technological skills necessary to undertake technological change. One important conclusion of this literature is that technological change in developing countries is both a *costly* and a *lengthy* process. For instance, the efforts of the East Asian economies to imitate and adapt existing technologies were partly determined by earlier investments that promoted the acquisition of relevant technological knowledge, capabilities and skills (Chang 2002). This emphasis on the costly nature of technological investments also enables us to go beyond the old blueprint notion, where the only costs involved in technological change are the costs of acquiring a new capital good (with its blueprint) or inventing a new blueprint.

Technologies are not easily transferable and technological knowledge is often tacit. This point, made at the theoretical level by evolutionary models, receives much support from the new development literature. Whereas the older 'choice of technique' literature assumed that technology imports could be easily absorbed and assimilated by developing countries, the more recent writings emphasize the fact that much technological knowledge is *tacit*, and remains embodied in individuals and organizations. When developing countries purchase foreign technologies, therefore, it is unlikely that they can obtain all the necessary information required for the efficient operation of that technology. For this reason, the importance of investments to develop the skills and knowledge required to choose, absorb, utilize and adapt technologies is emphasized. This is especially important in developing countries where the overall levels of skills and capabilities are low.

Technological change in developing countries is often 'innovative' and characterized by risk and uncertainty. The recent writings also highlight the fact that technologies are rarely static and absolute. It is argued that technologies are used in a manner that is highly specific to individual firms and countries. This characteristic of technology, referred to as *circumstantial specificity*, is the primary reason why developing countries adapt and modify imported technologies (Evenson and Westphal 1995). Such modifications are often seen as being 'innovative', in the sense that they involve changes previously not undertaken by the firm or country in question. Circumstantial specificity, together with the tacit nature of technological knowledge, also means that even relatively simple technological activities, such as the purchase of imported technology, can be risky and uncertain. These arise due to the difficulty of obtaining all the relevant knowledge about foreign technologies, and due to the need to adapt and modify them for domestic use. Therefore, many analysts argue that the distinction between innovation and diffusion of existing technologies is often blurred (Lall 2001).

Technological activity in developing countries is the outcome of a variety of factors. It is not merely an 'automatic' response to demand-side inducements or relative price changes. Supply-side factors – such as learning and the acquisition of relevant capabilities – have a crucially important influence on technological change. That the determinants of technological change in developing countries are varied and complex is a key theme of the literature. The role of learning and skill acquisition in promoting technology development in poor countries, has received much emphasis (Bell 1984; Bell and Pavitt 1992; Lall 2001). It is stressed that technological learning is important not only for countries that innovate at the global frontier, and various types of learning relevant to developing countries have been examined. While the older development literature largely assumed only the existence of 'learning-by-doing' effects that occur as output expands (as, for instance, in the infant industry models), learning has been shown to encompass a much wider range of activities. Apart from the formal acquisition of skills through education and training, acquisition of skills through searching for new technologies, operating and modifying new products and processes, interacting with buyers on export markets, and interacting with suppliers and competitors have been highlighted.

In terms of capability acquisition, the literature also differentiates between 'passive learners' and 'active learners'. 'Passive learners' are seen to absorb the capabilities for production using a 'black box' approach, while 'active learners' are seen as mastering technology and its improvements through deliberate effort. Active learning is seen as a critical ingredient for competitiveness and productivity growth. The importance of active learning in dynamic economies, such as in the rapidly growing East Asian countries, is emphasized.

Technological activities in developing countries have a significant positive effect on economic performance. This literature has also shown technological activity to have a positive effect on various indicators of economic performance. Econometric estimations have shown that both formal R&D and informal technical change boost productivity and efficiency at the firm and industry levels (Deraniyagala 2001; Katrak 1991). Technological dynamism has also been shown to be central to competitiveness in export markets. Poor technological performance of countries and regions (for instance, Sub-Saharan Africa) has also been shown as underlying poor economic performance in terms of growth and industrialization (Latsch and Robinson 1999).

Technological change in developing countries is subject to various types of market failure, thus providing a rationale for government intervention. Following both informational microeconomics and evolutionary theory, much of the research on technology and development argues that market forces alone are unlikely to result in an optimal allocation of resources for technology development. It is emphasized that the various market failures highlighted by these theories – such as 'missing markets' for technology and knowledge, problems relating to the appropriability of returns to technology investments, and the imperfect and asymmetrical nature of technological knowledge – are especially relevant to developing countries. The existence of pervasive market failures is seen as leading to underinvestment in technology. The need for government intervention in resource allocation is therefore emphasized, a point discussed in more detail below.

Debates on Technology Policy

Much of the literature on technological change in developing countries, therefore, pointed to the scope and need for public policy interventions specifically designed to promote technology development. Similarly, theoretical models – such as those dealing with market imperfections and evolutionary models –

also implied an active role for the state in affecting the allocation of resources for technological change. Despite this, technology policy issues have been largely ignored and overlooked by the dominant, orthodox approach to development policy that has prevailed since the 1980s.

The Washington Consensus Approach to Technology Policy

Since the mid-1980s, the dominant approach to development policy has been that of the 'Washington Consensus', and the area of technology policy is no exception. This approach was the outcome of several factors: the ascendance of neoclassical economics in advanced countries; the interpretation of the growth crises in developing countries in the 1980s as being caused by distortions to the market mechanism; and interpretations of the East Asian economic success as being the result of 'getting prices right'. This neoliberal Washington Consensus denoted a series of measures designed to result in greater growth and prosperity in developing countries. The suggested measures included fiscal and monetary austerity, elimination of government subsidies, moderate taxation, freeing interest rates, liberalization of foreign trade, privatization, deregulation and encouragement of foreign investment.

The Washington Consensus was based on the neoliberal premise that well-functioning markets can achieve efficient and optimal resource allocation in all sectors. State intervention, except in the provision of a limited number of public goods, was seen as essentially distortionary.

The Washington Consensus paid little attention to an analysis of technology policy. It was assumed that both technology development and industrial growth in developing countries are best nurtured by creating a correct set of incentives and by 'getting prices right'. There was little room for interventionist industrial policy in this approach, and its main task was seen as the creation of freely functioning factor and product markets. It was argued that industrial policy reform should focus on removing 'policy-induced' distortions arising from state intervention, privatization, removing entry and exit restrictions on private enterprise, and removal of price controls, discretionary taxes and subsidies (Frischtak 1989). Accordingly, the neoliberal approach saw any selective industrial policy that changes market-based resource allocation as distortionary. It was also argued that selective industrial policies are especially irrelevant to developing countries due to large informational requirements beyond the scope of developing country governments.

This approach to industrial policy assumed that technology generation in developing countries would take place solely in response to the creation of a correct set of incentives. There was little consideration of the complex nature of technological change and of the supply-side factors that generate it. It was assumed that *laissez-faire* industrial policies would result in optimal allocation of resources for technology development. Underlying this assumption was the neoclassical conceptualization of technology as being similar to any other good. There was little recognition of the specific characteristics of technology, highlighted by both evolutionary theories and the literature on developing countries. Characteristics, such as the tacit and imperfect nature of technological knowledge and the public good properties of innovation, that are likely to condition the response of economic agents to price incentives were also ignored.

The Washington Consensus approach to trade policy also had implications for technology. It was argued that trade protection, which was the dominant form of trade policy in developing countries until the 1980s, was seriously flawed (Bhagwati 1980; Balassa 1988). Inward-looking trade policies were said to have resulted in distorted price signals that caused inefficiencies in resource allocation, infant industries that never matured due to the lack of competitive pressures, and allocation of resources to unproductive activities, particularly rent-seeking. The policy prescription that followed was across-the-board trade liberalization.

Trade liberalization was seen to result in various static and dynamic gains for developing countries, and most important among these were gains in terms of technological change. Arguments relating to the positive effects on technology, in fact, dominate neoliberal discussions of the dynamic benefits of trade reform. However, in most of these discussions, the positive effects of trade liberalization are assumed, and no precise account of the mechanisms through which they materialize is given. Some studies argue that liberal trade policies induce 'the ability to take advantage of a wide range of innovations' (Thomas and Nash 1991: 34), while others assert that open economies are more efficient at absorbing exogenously generated innovations (Balassa 1988). It is also argued that trade liberalization creates competitive pressures sufficient to promote technology development.

All these arguments relating to trade policy and technology assume a smooth supply-side response to the 'improved' incentives that result from trade liberalization. Again, there is little consideration of the factors that determine this response, and that it may be constrained due to limitations on the supply side is completely overlooked. As discussed above, attention to the supply side is a key feature of both evolutionary theories and the post-1980s literature on technology and development, and a heterodox critique of the neoliberal approach to technology policy is provided by these writings.

Technology Policy: Heterodox Approaches

The heterodox critique of the Washington Consensus approach to technology policy focuses on both empirical and theoretical issues. Theories of informational imperfections, evolutionary theories and the development literature, all provide a variety of theoretical arguments to show that resource allocation in technological investments may not be optimal if left to the market alone. This conclusion is reached by analysis of the defining features of technology and technological change, and by questioning the simplistic notion of 'technology as blueprints' that dominates the neoclassical literature. In particular, the tacit and imperfect nature of technological knowledge, informational asymmetries, weak or non-existent markets for technology, the importance of cumulative and continuous active learning, as well as the existence of widespread spill-over effects and externalities, all highlight the limitations of a technology strategy that relies solely on the market mechanism.

In contrast to the neoliberal Washington approach, the heterodox literature argues for a much greater role for the government in technology development in developing countries. Three key policy interventions are proposed – selective intervention through industrial policy, strategic interventions in trade policy and the creation of dynamic national innovation systems. These three policy interventions are seen as complementary, interacting with each other to promote technological dynamism.

Industrial Policy

According to the heterodox approaches, rapid technology development in developing countries is unlikely to occur in the absence of interventionist industrial policy. The existence of informational imperfections is seen as requiring interventions to create relevant institutions and infrastructure, especially in relation to the provision of information and knowledge (Stiglitz 1998). The existence of positive technological externalities and spill-overs is seen as requiring *selective* industrial policies to identify and promote specific sectors where such externalities are widely prevalent (Lall 2003). Poorly functioning capital markets provide the rationale for interventions designed to increase investment in technology generation (Wade 2003).

The empirical case for intervention through industrial policy is made by analyses of the East Asian economies which show, contrary to orthodox interpretations, that the manufacturing success of these countries was partly a result of highly interventionist, strategic industrial policies (Wade 2003; Chang 2002). Industrial policy in these countries is shown to have promoted technology generation by identifying dynamic sectors, and providing incentives and resources for investment in these sectors (for instance, by limiting entry into specific sectors, thus allowing for the accumulation of 'rents' by early entrants and by provision of subsidized credit). Overall, this type of selective industrial policy is seen as instrumental in creating 'technological winners' – sectors that demonstrate high levels of competitiveness on international markets.

Trade Policy

The heterodox approaches also question the neoliberal stance that open trade policies alone are sufficient to induce technological dynamism. Neoliberal arguments relating to the technology-related benefits of liberalization remain at the level of casual observation with weak theoretical premises (Rodrik 1995). Thus, for instance, it is argued that the notion that openness leads to increased competition which induces cost-cutting technological change across all sectors is theoretically fragile and not empirically robust (Deraniyagala and Fine 2001). Schumpeterian and neo-Schumpeterian theories point to the role of oligopolistic market structures in promoting technological change. A well-established body of empirical research on market structure and innovation also throws doubt on an unambiguously positive relationship between competition and technological dynamism, but this too is ignored by the orthodox literature.

It is also argued that trade liberalization rarely leads to the costless flow of technological information to developing countries. The tacit and specific nature of technological knowledge partly prevents this. Further, the ability to absorb knowledge from international sources also partly depends on domestic skills and capabilities. For this reason, the responses of firms and organizations in developing countries to greater availability of knowledge are likely to be heterogeneous, and the overall effects – at the sectoral or national level – cannot be easily predicted.

Contrary to the orthodox approach, heterodox writings propose that strategic selective protection can promote technology development and knowledge creation in developing countries. Several arguments justify this. Firstly, openness can, in some instances, result in very high levels of competition that are destructive and serve as a disincentive for technological change. The negative effect of trade liberalization on manufacturing performance and technology upgrading in Sub-Saharan Africa during the 1990s is illustrative of this. Secondly, the cumulative and incremental nature of technological learning that is largely production-based means that production experience in some sectors needs to be accumulated without the constant threat of high levels of import competition. Thirdly, excessively high levels of import competition can be a disincentive to invest in capability acquisition, which is a key determinant of technology generation. Fourthly, selective protection may encourage (due to the absence of competition) technology development in sectors with pervasive externalities.

Overall, therefore, the heterodox literature provides arguments supporting infant industry protection for technology development. However, unlike the old infant industry literature of the 1970s, it is argued that technology is central to ensuring that infant industries do, in fact, mature. Hence, effective selection of strategic sectors for trade protection in terms of technological criteria is seen as essential. All this is not to say, however, that the benefits of openness are wholly denied by the heterodox literature. The fact that developing countries often obtain technological knowledge through exporting is a common theme in the literature, although it is noted that the learning effects of exporting are not universal, and vary according to sectors.

National Innovation Systems

That technology generation is determined by a complex interaction of a range of factors is the basis of the NIS approach to technology policy. As discussed, a national innovation system comprises a complex amalgam of state and non-state organizations, institutions, individuals, networks, and rules and regulations (Lundvall 2000). In this view, technology development cannot be promoted in isolation by trade policy or by industrial policy. The capacity to respond to any policy incentive ultimately depends on the effectiveness of the innovation system as a whole.

The NIS approach to technology policy, therefore, rejects the Washington Consensus view that effective technology development only involves getting prices right. It emphasizes the limitations of a purely market-based approach to technology policy, showing, instead, that non-market social and institutional factors are crucially important to technological dynamism. It also shows that technology policy cannot be considered in isolation from other macroeconomic and sectoral policies, all of which affect the incentive structure for building technological capacity. Accordingly, the aim of technology policy must be to develop and strengthen the entire innovation system. By broadening the scope of technology policy to include social, institutional, legal and cultural factors, the NIS approach highlights issues completely overlooked by the orthodox approach to technology policy, and correspond more closely to the empirical and historical realities of technological change itself (in which, for example, military capability has often been a decisive factor).

Conclusion

Over the past two decades, our understanding of technology issues in developing countries has advanced considerably. This chapter provides a brief review of some of the main themes in the literature relevant to technology and development. This body of literature is still evolving, and several issues need to be further investigated and resolved. New methodologies to empirically investigate technology in developing countries need to be developed and tested. Nevertheless, the fact that technology-related issues in developing countries require explicit attention and analysis has now been firmly established in the development literature.

References

Amsden, Alice (1997), 'Bringing Production Back In – Understanding Government's Economic Role in Late Industrialization', *World Development*, 25 (4): 469–80.

Arrow, Kenneth J. (1962), 'Economic Welfare and the Allocation of Resources for Invention', in R.R Nelson, ed., *The Diffusion and Direction of Inventive Activity* (Princeton: Princeton University Press): 609–25.

Arrow, Kenneth J. and Frank Hahn (1971), *General Competitive Analysis* (Edinburgh: Oliver and Boyd).

Balassa, Bela (1988), 'Interests of Developing Countries in the Uruguay Round', *World Economy*, 11 (1): 39–54.

Barro, Robert and Xavier Sala-l-Martin (1992), 'Economic Growth', processed, Yale University, New Haven.

Bell, Martin (1984), 'Learning and the Accumulation of Industrial Capacity in Developing Countries', in Martin Fransman and Kenneth King, eds, *Technological Capability in the Third World* (London: Macmillan), 187–209.

Bell, Martin and Keith Pavitt (1992), 'Accumulating Technological Capabilities in Developing Countries', Proceedings of the World Bank Annual Conference on Development Economics 1992, Supplement to *World Bank Economic Review* and *World Bank Research Observer*: 257–81.

Bhagwati, Jagdish (1980), 'Is Free Trade Passe After All?', *Welwirtschaftlichen Archiv*, 125: 17–44.

Bingswanger, Hans P. and Vernon W. Ruttan (1978), *Induced Innovation: Technology, Institutions and Development* (Baltimore: Johns Hopkins University Press).

Chang, Ha-Joon (2002), 'Kicking Away the Ladder: Development Strategy in Historical Perspective', *Oxford Development Studies*, 31 (1): 21–32.

Coe, David T., Elhanan Helpman and Alexander W. Hoffmaister (1995), 'North–South R&D Spillovers', CEPR Discussion Paper 1133, Centre for Economic Policy Research, London.

Deraniyagala, Sonali (2001), 'From Washington to Post-Washington: Does it Matter for Industrial Policy?', in Ben Fine, Costas Lapavitsas and Jonathan Pincus, eds, *Development Policy in the Twenty-First Century* (London: Routledge).

Deraniyagala, Sonali and Ben Fine (2001), 'New Trade Theory versus Old Trade Policy: A Continuing Enigma', *Cambridge Journal of Economics*, 25 (6): 809–25.

Dosi, Giovanni (1997), 'Opportunities, Incentives and Collective Patterns of Technological Change', *Economic Journal*, 107: 1530–47.

Evenson, Robert and Larry Westphal (1995), 'Technological Change and Technology Strategy', in Jere Behrman and T.N. Srinivasan, eds, *Handbook of Development Economics*, Vol. 3A (Amsterdam: North-Holland Press): 2209–299.

Fei, John and Gustav Ranis (1964), *Development of the Labour Surplus Economy* (Homewood: Irwin).

Fransman, Martin and Kenneth King (1984), *Technological Capability in the Third World* (New York: St. Martin's Press).

Freeman, Chris (1994), 'The Economics of Technical Change', *Cambridge Journal of Economics*, 18: 463–514.

Frischtak, Claudio (1989), *Competitive Policies for Industrializing Countries* (Washington DC: World Bank).

Gerschenkron, Alexander (1962), *Economic Backwardness in Historical Perspective* (Cambridge, Massachusetts: Cambridge University Press).

Gilbert, R.J. and David Newberry (1982), 'Pre-emptive Patenting and the Persistence of Monopoly', *American Economic Review*, 72: 514–26.

Greenwald, Bruce C. and Joseph E. Stiglitz (1986), 'Externalities in Markets with Imperfect Information', *Quarterly Journal of Economics*, 101, May: 229–64.

Griliches, Zvi (1957), 'Hybrid Corn: An Exploration of the Economics of Technological Change', *Econometrica*, 25: 501–22.

Grossman, Gene and Elhanan Helpman (1991), *Innovation and Growth in the Global Economy* (Cambridge, Massachusetts: MIT Press).

Katrak, Homi (1991), ' In-House Technological Efforts, Imports of Technology and Enterprise Characteristics: The Indian Experience', *Journal of International Development*, 3: 266–76.

Katz, Jorge, ed., (1987), *Technology Generation in Latin American Manufacturing Industries* (London: Macmillan).

Krugman, Paul (1984), ' Import Protection as Export Promotion', in Henryk Kierkowski, ed., *Monopolistic Competition and International Trade* (Oxford: Oxford University Press).

Lall, Sanjaya (1987), *Learning to Industrialize: The Accumulation of Technological Capability in India* (London: Macmillan).

—— (2001), *Competitiveness, Technology and Skills* (Cheltenham: Edward Elgar).

—— (2003), 'Symposium on Infant Industries', *Oxford Development Studies*, 31 (1): 14–20.

Lall, Sanjaya and Wolfram W. Latsch (1999), ' Import Liberalization and Industrial Performance: Theory and Evidence', in Sanjaya Lall, ed., *The Technological Response to Import Liberalization in Sub-Saharan Africa* (Basingstoke: Macmillan).

Latsch, Wolfram and Peter Robinson (1999), 'Technology and the Responses of Firms to Adjustment in Zimbabwe', in Sanjaya Lall, ed., *The Technological Response to Import Liberalization in Sub-Saharan Africa* (Basingstoke: Macmillan).

Lee, Jong-Wha (1995), 'Capital Goods Imports and Long-Run Growth', *Journal of Development Economics*, 58 (1): 91–110.

Lewis, W.A. (1954), 'Economic Development with Unlimited Supplies of Labour', *Manchester School*, 22: 139–91.

Little, Ian, Tibor Scitovsky and Maurice Scott (1970), *Industry and Trade in Some Developing Countries* (Oxford: Oxford University Press).

Lundvall, Bengt-Ake (2000), 'Introduction', in Charles Edquist and Maureen MacKelvey, eds, *Systems of Growth and Competitiveness* (Cheltenham: Edward Elgar).

Mansfield, Edwin (1961), 'Technical Change and the Rate of Imitation', *Econometrica*, 29 (4): 741–66.

Nelson, Richard (1993), *National Innovation Systems: A Comparative Study* (Oxford: Oxford University Press).

Nelson, Richard and Sidney Winter (1982), *An Evolutionary Theory of Economic Change* (Cambridge, Massachusetts: Harvard University Press).

Nordhaus, William (1969), *Invention, Growth and Wealth* (Cambridge, Massachusetts: MIT Press).

Pack, Howard and Larry Westphal (1986), 'Industrial Strategy and Technological Change: Theory Versus Eeality', *Journal of Development Economics*, 22: 87–128.

Rodrik, Dani (1995), 'Trade and Industrial Policy Reform', in Jere Behrman and T.N. Srinivasan, eds, *Handbook of Development Economics*, Vol. 3B (Amsterdam: North–Holland).

Romer, Paul (1990), 'Endogenous Technological Change', *Journal of Political Economy*, 98 (5): S71–S102.

Solow, Robert (1957), 'Technical Change and the Aggregate Production Function', *Review of Economics and Statistics*, 30: 312–20.

Stewart, Frances (1977), *Technology and Underdevelopment* (Boulder: Westview).

Stiglitz, Joseph E. (1989), 'Markets, Market Failures and Development', *American Economic Review*, 79 (2): 197–202.

―――― (1998), 'More Instruments and Broader Goals: Moving Towards the post-Washington Consensus', 1998 WIDER Annual Lecture, Helsinki, 7 January.

Thomas, Vinod and John Nash (1991), 'Reform of Trade Policy: Recent Evidence from Theory and Practice', *World Bank Research Observer*, 6: 219–40.

Vernon, Raymond (1966), 'International Investment and International Trade in the Product Cycle', *Quarterly Journal of Economics*, 80: 190–207.

Wade, Robert (2003), 'Symposium on Infant Industries', *Oxford Development Studies*, 31 (1): 8–14.

―――― (1990), *Governing the Market* (Princeton: Princeton University Press).

Privatization Theory and Practice

A Critical Analysis of Policy Evolution in the Development Context

Kate Bayliss

Over the past twenty-five years, development policies and practices have been fundamentally affected by a transformation in attitudes and approaches regarding the respective roles of the state and the private sector. The remit of the private sector has grown dramatically over this period. In addition to the transfer of ownership of state enterprises to private operators, governments have also encouraged the private sector to operate in areas which had previously been the preserve of the state, such as the supply of water, electricity, as well as health and education services. This policy shift emerged in response to perceived failures in the public sector, coupled with a growing prominence and refinement of theoretical arguments highlighting inefficiencies in the public sector and the superior performance of private ownership. Widespread privatization was part of a broader ideological shift in emphasis towards 'efficiency' and 'market-led' economic policies.

This chapter critically assesses key developments in the growing faith in both privatization and the private sector, with particular emphasis on developing economies. The chapter first outlines the theoretical framework underlying privatization and highlights some key weaknesses in these arguments. The subsequent section demonstrates how privatization theory is further undermined when translated to the developing country context, where the economic, institutional, historical and social conditions are vastly different from those in industrialized countries. The chapter evaluates empirical assessments of privatization and considers the meagre empirical evidence that relates to the low-income context.

In developing countries, privatization, in common with the wider neoliberal policy agenda, has failed to meet expectations. Privatization efforts have been undermined by various factors, including weak political commitment, poor investor supply response and institutional challenges. Since the late 1990s, the language of privatization has softened (as, for example, 'private sector participation' has replaced 'privatization'). Policy-makers have recognized the need for an effective state, even if only to create and maintain the rules for the market. However, despite a shift in tone, the underlying policy direction has remained unchanged as privatization has become so entrenched that it has been absorbed into general policy development. For donors and, in particular, the World Bank, which has been an important supporter of privatization in developing countries, the supremacy of the private sector in most areas of the economy is presented as virtually unquestionable.

Theory

The private sector was not always so highly regarded. In the 1960s and 1970s, state-led development was the orthodoxy in both industrialized and developing economies. Traditional growth models focused on the shift from agriculture to industrialization as developing countries began to adopt alternatives to specializing in primary commodities. Theories focused on the need for a 'big push' to catch up with the industrialized countries (Rowthorn and Chang 1995) and supported state-led development. In addition, for many countries, the immediate post-independence period was one where the domestic private sector was weak or virtually absent, so state ownership provided a means of 'indigenization', thus serving nationalistic political ideals, supported by orthodox theory promoting modernization. Throughout developing regions, 'import substitution industrialization' (ISI) was the widely adopted development strategy.

Initially, countries witnessed impressive growth rates in the first years of ISI, but faith in the state began to wane in the late 1970s when developing economies suffered major external shocks as the prices of exports declined and import prices, particularly of fuel, rose. Moreover, the debt crisis was looming. Previously high growth rates turned negative for many low-income economies. As the state had dominated economic activity in developing countries, attention turned to the performance of the public sector in an effort to account for, and remedy, economic decline. Countries were dependent, more than ever, on financial support from international donors and creditors, who increasingly influenced policy.

In parallel, a number of theories emerged pointing to the weaknesses and abuses of the state. Some had their origins in the new institutional economics (NIE), while others were rooted in the Austrian school. Brought together, the theories – described as the 'privatization synthesis' (Fine 1990) – developed arguments to support private, rather than public, ownership. There are two main strands to the theories underpinning privatization. The first relates to those that deal with incentive frameworks attached to different ownership structures. The second relates to the underlying motivation of individuals. All have questioned the effectiveness of the state sector and its ability to deal with market failure. Their theoretical constructs are outlined below, followed by a critical assessment.

Property rights theory gained increasing credibility during the 1960s. This approach originally centred on the internalization of externalities. According to the Coase theorem, in the absence of transactions costs, the clear definition of property rights would ensure that individuals face 'correct' (market) incentives, and free trade would lead to efficient resource allocation (Coase 1960). This core theoretical premise was later applied to the public sector by Alchian (1965), who demonstrated that property rights are more attenuated in the public than in the private corporation, the crucial difference being that owners in the public sector are unable to sell their shares.

In the context of privatization, according to property rights theory, the transfer to the private sector of the ownership rights of residual claimants results in greater efficiency in monitoring the enterprise. Ownership of a public company is not transferable, and this reduces incentives to monitor managerial behaviour. Even if the product market is not competitive, ownership in the private sector will still improve performance because of the discipline imposed by the capital market. Persistent poor performance by management would lead shareholders to trade their shares, lowering their value. There would be the threat of bankruptcy or of hostile take-over in the private sector, typically absent under state control.

Following from property rights came principal–agent theory that is central to theoretical analysis of privatization (Vickers and Yarrow 1988, for example). Principals, as owners of an enterprise, are faced with the challenge of ensuring that agents – enterprise managers – act in their interest. Under public ownership, the principal is the government, which, itself, in a democratic context, can be considered the agent of the electorate. Thus, ownership is dispersed and objectives are diverse. In the private sector, the principals are the private shareholders with the sole objective of profit maximization. Thus, with a single clear objective which involves personal interests, in the private sector, greater attention would be paid to monitoring financial performance and scrutiny of productivity and accountability, as principals exert more effective control over their agents.

A further dimension to privatization theory comes from the extension of the neoclassical concept of methodological individualism, which calls into question the motivation of public sector employees and provides further support for privatization. According to public choice theory, government bureaucrats are considered to be self-interested individuals set on maximizing their own welfare, and this is not likely to coincide with that of society or the political party in power. This depiction of the public sector is in stark contrast to the earlier position where governments were entrusted with maximization of social welfare.

According to Nisanken (1975), bureaucrats pursue their own self-interest and maximize their own utility, and a primary determinant of this is the size of the bureaucracy and of their discretionary budgets. This means that the more monopoly power a government or a bureaucracy has, the more likely governments will overspend. Douglass North introduced the concept of the 'predatory' state with the bureaucrat as a utility maximizer with a private objective function (North 1995). Public choice extends beyond the boundaries of the enterprises themselves, into the political structure. Politicians – who are supposed to monitor the activity of bureaucrats on behalf of the electorate – are considered to be interested only in getting re-elected, so the extent of their monitoring effort depends on how far this coincides with their gaining electoral support (Nisanken 1975). However, early public choice literature recognized that individuals were not purely utility maximizers, conceding that some aspects of human behaviour, such as ethics and moral values, cannot be explained by economics (Fine and Milonakis 2005).

Within the public choice framework comes the concept of rent-seeking, which is a further source of inefficiency associated with the motivations of individuals in the public sector. Rent-seeking was originally conceived to describe the efforts made by private firms to benefit from import protection measures such as currying political favour to obtain import licences (for example, Krueger 1974). Bhagwati (1982) expanded this to incorporate non-trading activity, and described efforts by economic agents to gain access to preferential status as directly unproductive activities (DUP). Rent-seeking has since been more widely applied to other aspects of government activity on the basis that distortions and inefficiencies emerge as a direct result of opaque public sector decision-making processes.

The supposed advantage of privatization, then, is that the scope for manipulation of government positions for private or political ends evaporates, as do the accompanying distortions and inefficiencies. Government officers are largely insulated from the discipline of competition, and from the need to contain costs and/or to improve productivity. Privatization is intended to shift attention to performance, with adverse consequences for non-achievement.

In tandem with the rise of theories of state weakness and abuse has been the apparent waning of the case for state ownership on grounds of pervasive market imperfections – 'the extent and permanence of market failure now seems to have been exaggerated' (Shirley and Nellis 1991: 2). This argument is widely applied to telecommunications as technological advances have increased competitive pressures in that sector. However, efforts to introduce competition in other sectors, such as electricity and water, have been less successful and 'market failure' continues to prevail.

The theoretical foundations for privatization have been subject to extensive criticism on numerous grounds. At the outset, the wider neoclassical framework applied to privatization has been criticized generally for being reductionist, apolitical and ahistorical (Shapiro and Taylor 1990). In practice, the incentives and motivations of both the public and private sectors are far more complex than the theory implies. For example, public choice theory attributes self-seeking motivation to all individuals, when there is evidence that bureaucrats do not always act in a self-interested manner (Chang and Singh 1992; Martin and Parker 1997).

The degree of bureaucracy within an organization has more to do with cultural norms and type of enterprise than whether it is privately or publicly owned. For example, a Japanese firm is likely to have fewer levels of delegation than an American firm. The underlying assumption that the state cannot be trusted is symptomatic of a more general mistrust of collective action in the neoliberal framework. However, there is an inconsistency in this approach as some groups – private corporations, for example – are regarded as legitimate, while others are not. Furthermore, entrepreneurship, in which neoliberal policy places substantial faith, is increasingly a collective rather than an individual effort (Rowthorn and Chang 1995).

Many problems that privatization is supposed to rectify are also to be found in the private sector. For example, the principal–agent problem persists in privately owned firms. Shareholders cannot be sure that directors will act in their interests (Aharoni 1991) and monitoring is difficult. The effectiveness of share-holder control is questionable as there is free riding of monitoring by sharehold-ers. The private sector is less preoccupied with efficiency than theory might suggest. Empirically, directors' pay is more closely related to size of firm than to performance. Capital markets are supposed to impose a disciplinary effect on private sector enterprises, but corporate control is more likely to be effective if shares are in large blocks. In reality, the likelihood of take-over has more to do with the size of an enterprise than its relative efficiency. Large firms do not so readily get taken over (Martin and Parker 1997).

Multifaceted relationships are narrowly depicted in privatization theory. Taking principal–agent theory, privatization creates a new principal–agent rela-tionship between the state, and enterprise owners and managers. According to orthodox theory, when the principal–agent framework is applied to privatiza-tion, the agents are typically the directors and managers of the enterprise, and the principal is either the government (if it is in the public sector) or the share-holders (if it is in the private sector). However, when it comes to the supply of an essential service, such as water, electricity or transport, the government has ulti-mate responsibility for provision of the service regardless of privatization, and effectively remains the principal.

The agents are, then, the private sector owners who have a separate principal–agent relationship with the enterprise directors. Privatization is inten-ded to simplify the complexities of the principal–agent relationship by replacing the diverse monitoring and incentive systems of the public sector with the one-dimensional, easy-to-monitor goal of profit maximization. However, when it comes to key sectors such as health or infrastructure, the non-profit objectives of service delivery remain, and the process of monitoring through an external regu-lator creates an additional layer of principal–agent dynamics and exacerbates informational asymmetries.

Private and public sectors are treated as static concepts, and the dyna-mic processes of growth and development are neglected. For example, the theory fails to consider how privatization relates to the transformation of a state-owned enterprise into a capitalist firm (Yamin 1998). The theory presents a false distinc-tion between the private and public sectors. In reality, there is more of a spectrum than a dichotomy (Martin and Parker 1997). Privatization theory presents a paradox in that the state which is performing so badly that its activities need to be privatized is entrusted with the task of implementing privatization. It is assumed that the public sector acts on the basis of self-interest except when carry-ing out privatization policies, but privatization itself provides ample opportunity for cronyism and patronage. In Chile in the 1970s, for example, the privatization programme was used to reward the upper-class groups that helped bring the regime to power (Aharoni 1991).

The process of privatization itself can exacerbate the declining performance of the public sector, partly through the adverse effect on morale. The impact of the constant pressure for privatization, or at least to be market-like, on the motivation and ethos of the public sector has been neglected, while there is no evidence that the private is any less corrupt than the public sector (Haque 1996). Generally, privatization theory fails to incorporate distributional considerations. By focusing on internal efficiency (that is, within the enterprise), there are no obvious direct consequences for the way in which resources are allocated on a sectoral or national basis.

The implications of privatization are different across enterprises, sectors and countries. Clearly, there are very different issues to consider when privatizing a monopoly as opposed to a small competitive enterprise. Competition (rather than privatization) may have a bearing on resource allocation (or 'allocative efficiency'), but there is no theoretical basis for associating privatization with competition. There is no guarantee that 'efficiency' will improve when a large number of factors prevent Pareto-optimal resource allocation (Commander and Killick 1988). The implications for long-term development may be adversely affected as on privatization, short-term political ends are substituted for by possibly even shorter-term financial ends as the over-riding objective becomes profit maximization for shareholders.

Finally, state intervention continues after privatization. According to theory, removing enterprises from government ownership prevents governments from using them for 'distortionary' political and social goals. However, the state intervenes substantially even where enterprises have been privatized. The boundary between the economic and the political is not something 'naturally' given, and there is nothing 'natural' or 'neutral' about a certain market outcome. All prices are potentially politically determined in most sectors, and the cost of some core inputs, such as wages and interest rates, are often politically set (Rowthorn and Chang 1995).

Privatization and Development

Privatization theory has been created on the basis of industrialized country experience and, as such, makes implicit assumptions about the policy context. For example, it is assumed that there are investors waiting to take over from the state; that there is an adequate financial sector that will allow ownership to be traded, thereby exercising monitoring of agents managing companies; that the public sector has the capacity to implement a transparent privatization programme. Such an environment is presumed to be so typical of economic life in industrialized countries that these parameters are taken for granted. When the policy is translated into the context of low and, to some extent, middle-income countries, where circumstances are very different, privatization outcomes can be affected.

Privatization theory assumes that the private and public sectors are substitutable, and that all that is required is for the state to step aside and private investment will be able to flow into areas previously blocked by the public sector. In practice, in developing countries, this is not the case, and the response from both domestic and international investors has been disappointing. Weak states tend to correspond with weak markets; so, where state performance has been poor, the private sector may also be fragile. Foreign direct investment flows to developing countries have fallen since peaking in 1999, and they are currently experiencing the most sustained fall since the global recession of 1981–83 (World Bank 2003). In the absence of investor interest, privatization initiatives become, in reality, an exercise in trying to entice investors. As many countries are privatizing at the same time, there is competition among governments to offer the best deals to foreign investors in terms of low prices, tax holidays and sovereign guarantees.

In developing countries, privatization can place considerable demands on an already stretched and weakened public sector, both in terms of implementation and regulation of the privatized enterprises. Industries are more monopolistic in smaller, low-income economies, due, in part, to a combination of technological dependence, market size, and economies of scale and scope (Mkandawire 1994). Privatization often entails turning a public into a private monopoly. Thus, there is a greater need for the state to fulfil a regulatory function at a time when it is weakest.

Governments have found it difficult to regulate large utilities. Regulatory capture (whereby the regulated enterprise is able to manipulate the decisions of the regulator) will arguably be more likely in an environment of weak institutions and donor pressure to privatize, and this may outweigh the benefits that privatization supposedly brings. Often, foreign companies have substantial market power and, as a result, they can exert considerable pressure on regulators (Adam, Cavendish and Mistry 1992).

Regulation requires more than just the creation of specialist institutions to monitor and check against monopolistic abuses, but incorporates the wider legal and institutional framework in which the private sector operates. Regulation includes such matters as enforceability of contracts and bankruptcy proceedings that are taken for granted in industrialized economies. Furthermore, there is always a gap between the letter and the interpretation of the law.

For example, property rights may not be clearly defined and, even if they are in place in principle, their treatment in practice may differ from that in industrialized countries. In Kenya, for instance, land registration takes precedence over customary rights but, in practice, multiple rights are recognized in rural communities and in courts (Berry 1993). Title transfer may not have a significant impact (Stein 1995). Unclear property rights can complicate privatization processes, as in some cases when enterprises were nationalized, it was not clear who owned the property. In other cases, it may be clear who had the property when it was taken over by the government but there are disputes over the terms on which it might be restored to previous owners.

Unlike industrialized countries, financial markets in many developing countries are thin and underdeveloped. For example, there are currently twenty active stock exchanges in Africa (UNDP 2003). The Johannesburg Stock

Exchange is the largest, with a capitalization of more than ten times that of all the other African markets combined (*African Business*, January 2001). Yet, it is only the world's eighteenth largest. Many developing country stockmarkets are light, only having opened in the last ten years as part of structural adjustment programmes. Thus, they lack adequate public information on corporate performance. They are also more volatile than those in advanced economies, and this can worsen financial instability.

Where financial systems are more sophisticated, there are more options for public enterprise reform. The use of capital markets and the existence of financial intermediaries contribute to the domestic capacity to participate. With more advanced systems for share-trading, capital markets can more effectively monitor the performance of listed companies (Demirguc-Kunt and Levine 1994). Equity is not really a viable means for raising finance in many developing countries and, hence, privatization tends more often to take the form of debt-based asset sales. Where absorptive capacity is weak, using the stockmarket can delay privatization sales. There is a danger that privatization issues will mop up all available equity at the expense of other private sectors (Commander and Killick 1988).

Where public flotations are possible, the diffused sale of shares may be problematic. Selling to a large number of shareholders who are inexperienced in the workings of capital markets will fail to create an effective means for monitoring the directors of private firms, and will undermine the principal–agent gain that privatization is supposed to achieve. Capital markets in Sub-Saharan Africa (SSA) are unlikely to be able to exert much in the way of disciplinary pressure on companies (Singh 1992, cited in Cook and Kirkpatrick 1995: 17).

Anything is Privatizable

The scope of privatization has widened since the early 1980s and it is now a core policy in most developing countries, despite the limitations outlined above. When attention first began to focus on the performance of the state, wholesale privatization of parastatals was not yet on the agenda. Management, rather than ownership, was deemed to have a greater impact on enterprise performance (World Bank 1981). Privatization in the form of divestiture received little attention in the early 1980s. At this stage, it was perceived as too problematic for several reasons. First, governments would only want to sell the loss-makers, and these would not be of interest to buyers. Second, weak domestic capital markets would mean that there would be few buyers. Third, sales would be concentrated in the hands of the already wealthy, thus reducing competition (World Bank 1983).

There was also concern that privatization was only likely to produce efficiency gains in a competitive environment, and privatizing state monopolies would bring little benefit. In the late 1980s, the argument for privatization faltered on the issue of competition. For example, in the widely cited work by Vickers and Yarrow (1988), the authors concluded that the case for preferring private to public ownership weakened considerably in a monopolistic situation.

However, in the early 1990s, the tone of the literature on privatization emerging from the World Bank shifted dramatically. State monopolies crept on to the privatization agenda as the Bank began to push the argument that ownership per se (rather than market structure) mattered for performance. Shirley and Nellis (1991) generated a sense of urgency by pushing the message that there would only be a temporary window of opportunity during which privatization would be possible. They suggested that it was the combination of the (then) current circumstances[1] that had created a favourable environment for reform of the state enterprise sector, and these circumstances would continue to exist only for a short time.[2] This urgency gave licence to the push for widespread privatization, even though some of the fundamentals that were regarded in the wider economic literature as essential prerequisites for privatization (such as a competitive environment and/or regulation, and social safety nets) were not in place.

The move towards widespread privatization was further boosted by a detailed World Bank empirical study in 1994 that attempted to estimate the welfare impact of privatization by generating a counterfactual position.[3] The study concluded that privatization of monopolies could bring about net welfare gains (Galal et al. 1994). This conclusion was cited (for example, Kikeri, Nellis and Shirley 1992; World Bank 1995) as evidence that privatizing monopolies can be beneficial despite the authors' warning that their findings should not be extrapolated to very poor countries (Galal et al. 1994). Thus, by the mid-1990s, the scope of privatization had widened. The small-scale private participation envisaged in the early 1980s was no longer considered adequate. It was now legitimate to privatize virtually anything.

Privatization programmes in developing countries became overloaded with objectives – and these have, at times, proven contradictory – as this was perceived as a policy that would bring widespread economic benefits.[4] At the World Bank, privatization began to filter into broader aspects of aid policy. Privatization began to be more specifically linked to aid disbursements than before. In an apparently subtle shift, privatization became absorbed into the private sector development (PSD) department in the Bank, but this was a significant development. Previously, the Bank had made some (limited) attempt to justify and debate the merits of privatization. Once the policy became categorized as one of a collection of policies to promote PSD (along with other less contentious policies such as small- and medium-sized enterprises [SME] support, micro-finance and legislative reform), there seemed no longer to be any need for discussion, as if the subject was closed and the argument won.

The rhetorical approach to privatization shifted slightly in the late 1990s with what became known as the post-Washington Consensus (PWC). The development of the PWC in relation to privatization is illustrated by two main outputs of the World Bank in the late 1990s. Firstly, the Bank's *1997 World Development Report* (*WDR*) marked a relaxation in the organization's anti-statist line that had blamed the public sector for all economic problems. The report titled *The State in a Changing World* made the observation that a strong institutional framework is needed for markets to work.

Secondly, the (then) chief economist at the Bank, Joseph Stiglitz (who had also managed the production of the *1997 WDR*), shed some light on the mania that had surrounded privatization earlier in the decade. In Stiglitz's view, most people at the time would have preferred to have proper regulatory systems and competition in place before privatization, but the reason it was pushed through was that 'no-one knew how long the reform window would stay open'. With hindsight, the idea of privatize now and regulate later 'seemed a reasonable gamble', although 'from today's vantagepoint the advocates of privatization may have overestimated the benefits of privatization and underestimated the costs' (Stiglitz 1998).

As with other aspects of the PWC (see Fine 2001), old ideas were presented as new, but the form, content and approach had been weakened. For example, according to Stiglitz, privatization had mistakenly become an end in itself, rather than a means to sustainable and equitable growth. Greater attention needed to be paid to institutional infrastructure and competition (Stiglitz 1998), echoing earlier concerns regarding market and regulatory failure that limited the extent to which privatization was implemented in the 1980s.

The words of Stiglitz and the theme of the *1997 WDR* appeared to offer a less aggressive stance on privatization, with a softening of the 'ownership matters/governments are inefficient' message that had previously dominated the Bank's approach. However, in practice, they masked a tougher policy line when it came to the role of the state in developing countries. Both Stiglitz and the *WDR* put forward the notion that states should match their role to their capability. While, at first sight, this may appear to be reasonable, when taken to its conclusion, it is the weakest states that should privatize most (and which, paradoxically, have the least capacity for regulation). For the poorest countries, states would be effectively consigned to an 'enforced minimalism' (Glentworth 1998).

The PWC marks a shift in the debate – from the state versus market dichotomy to an acknowledgement of the need for interaction between the two. However, the position with regard to low-income economies is essentially unchanged. It is the language and rhetoric that have become refined, while the policy implications are the same. While ostensibly more sympathetic to the needs of the public sector, the underlying thrust of the PWC continues to erode the authority and role of the state. While the language of privatization has softened, the genuine policy content of privatization continued much as before (Bayliss and Cramer 2001).

Empirical Analysis

There have been numerous attempts to assess the impact of privatization. These mainly take the form of regression analysis to compare public with private enterprises, or to assess the change in performance of privatized enterprises. Some empirical studies find that public sector performance is superior.

Others find that there is no significant difference but, on the whole, more studies find that private sector performance is better than the public sector (see, for example, Shirley and Walsh 2000, Megginson and Netter 2001, for tables listing and comparing findings from empirical analysis). However, the approach of such studies is often flawed as, for example, the performance indicators chosen are biased towards the private sector. These usually include profitability (return on sales), efficiency (net income per employee) and dividend payments (for example, D'Souza and Megginson 1999) – all of which are not likely to be priorities for the public sector.

Furthermore, rarely do such studies compare 'like-with-like'. An empirical analysis that compares changes in performance of enterprises, across sectors and from different countries, may encapsulate so many influences that it does little to isolate the impact of ownership change. Studies also tend to be static and micro in their perspective. That is, they look at one-off changes in performance without considering the wider macroeconomic impact (beyond, perhaps, the fiscal gains for governments). They typically fail to consider how privatization affects the wider allocation of resources in the economy.

Two major methodological difficulties confound such privatization research. Firstly, sample selection is biased in a number of ways. The privatization process itself is selective in that the most profitable and attractive enterprises are most readily sold. A sample of privatized firms will only incorporate firms that are visible and operating. Firms that have collapsed since privatization will not form part of the sample. Also, the sample is biased towards firms willing to cooperate with researchers. Some studies incorporate a different bias by limiting the sample to publicly listed firms.

Secondly, it is never possible to know what would have happened without privatization. Research can erroneously attribute all changes over a specified period to ownership change. Furthermore, where research does attempt to consider some kind of counterfactual possibility, this usually takes the form of continuation of the status quo. This may not be valid as privatization is just one of a number of policy reforms that may be undertaken.

Empirical studies are often especially weak in their assessment and treatment of 'developing countries'. This has become an umbrella term in much of the empirical literature, incorporating countries on an income scale ranging from very low to upper–middle. However, the issues and problems of the public and private sectors within these countries differ hugely at opposite ends of the income spectrum. Some studies do profess to analyse the impact of privatization in 'developing' countries, but the way in which countries are categorized means that the research fails to address the impact in the poorest countries.

For example, D'Souza, Megginson and Nash (2001) use a 'non-OECD' country grouping as a proxy for developing countries. Their study of privatization takes a sample of 118 firms from twenty-nine countries and twenty-eight industries privatized via public share offering between 1961 and 1995. One of their conclusions is that the level of development can have an impact on post-privatization performance as they find that 'stronger efficiency gains are observed for firms in developing nations'.

However, their methodology does not warrant such strong assertions. In their analysis, they compare firms from OECD countries with those that are non-OECD. The 'non-OECD' sample consists of a maximum of twenty-three firms, and includes four enterprises from Singapore, which is classified as a high-income economy,[5] and a number of upper–middle-income countries (Chile, Oman and Malaysia). None is from SSA. Aside from the empirical weaknesses of comparing across industries and countries, such findings are of little relevance to privatization in a low-income context. In other studies, authors group all low- and middle-income economies under one 'developing country' heading, in an attempt to show that privatization in poor countries can be beneficial. For example, Shirley and Walsh (2000: 38) make the observation (on the basis of four studies) that 'several major empirical studies have found marked improvements in post-privatization performance in developing nations'.[6]

However, a review of the supporting evidence indicates that this assertion is of little relevance to low-income economies. Three of the studies are entirely restricted to middle- and high-income countries like the UK, Chile, Malaysia, Mexico and Argentina. The fourth study, by Megginson, Nash and Randenborgh (1994), fails to include companies from any countries classified as 'low-income', and only one (Jamaica) classified as 'lower–middle-income', and this only accounts for two companies out of a sample of 69. The rest are at least 'upper–middle-income' or higher on the income scale. Thus, studies that claim to address privatization in development fail to do so.

What little evidence there is of the empirical impact of privatization in a low-income economy would seem to indicate that the gains achieved in industrialized countries might not be replicated. The dangers of applying conclusions from middle-income country research to a low-income country context were made clear by Galal *et al.* (1994: 560), following their research on monopoly privatization in Malaysia, Mexico, Argentina and Chile:

> These conclusions have to be extrapolated with caution to other countries. And nowhere does this cautionary note apply more than to the very poor countries of the world that are at a different level of development than any in our sample and therefore lack some of the institutions and markets our sample countries possess . . . the experience with divestiture could well be quite different from what we have observed in this study.

The developing country context was explored in more detail by Boubakri and Cosset (1998, 1999). Their findings indicated that privatization in a low-income economy will have weaker benefits. In their 1998 study, they attempted to assess the developing country impact of privatization by examining the change in financial and operating performance of 79 firms headquartered in twenty-one developing countries that experienced full or partial privatization over the period 1980 to 1992, including three low-income economies (Bangladesh, India and Pakistan). One SSA country (Nigeria) was also included. They found that privatization provided greater benefits for companies operating in developing countries with higher per capita incomes. This suggests that privatization brings less benefits for very low-income countries.

They then considered the impact of privatization on African enterprises (Boubakri and Cosset 1999). The sample consisted of sixteen large companies: ten from North Africa (five from Tunisia and five from Morocco), four from Nigeria, and one enterprise each from Senegal and Ghana. They used the same methodology as that adopted in the larger cross-country impact assessments carried out by Megginson, Nash and Randenborgh (1994), D'Souza and Megginson (1999), and Boubakri and Cosset (1998).

Contrary to these other studies, they found only a weak increase – that was not significant for the sample – in profitability after privatization. Furthermore, they found that after privatization, firm efficiency actually decreased, although this finding was also not significant. They documented efficiency improvements after privatization in just 47 per cent of their sample. They also found that sales (output) decreased by an average of 5 per cent from the pre- to the post-privatization periods for the sample.

Evaluation of privatization of core services needs to go beyond an assessment of the internal efficiency of the company as change in ownership has a far wider impact. The privatization of key services such as water and electricity, as well as health and education, have substantially different effects and implications, particularly in a low-income context, from the privatization of smaller-scale enterprises operating in more competitive sectors. Issues to be considered include access to services, pricing, quality and availability.

In addition, the focus on private sector participation (which usually means the involvement of international companies) creates new problems and issues in terms of regulation (with significant asymmetries in terms of information and resources) and financial sustainability. When it comes to infrastructure in low-income economies, privatization is constrained by limited investor interest largely because of perceptions of risk. Privatization, then, becomes a competition between governments to offer the best deal to investors that can hinge on the issue of transfer of risk. Contracts in water and energy are increasingly designed to minimize the risk to investors. However, this risk does not go away but rests with governments. For example, in the power sector, private firms construct power generation plants that sell electricity to the state transmission company. Contracts (known as power purchase agreements) are designed so that private companies do not face currency risk or demand risk, and are insulated from competition for long periods. Similar contractual arrangements are being devised in the water sector as with the proposed privatization of water and electricity in Ghana; an 'automatic tariff adjustment' has been proposed so that prices increase when the value of the currency falls.[7]

Such contracts are necessary if the private sector is to commit funds for long-term investment, but they arguably undermine some of the benefits that privatization is supposed to achieve. Firstly, privatization is expensive as companies seek to secure commercial rates of return. Secondly, the reduction of risk exposure can erode anticipated efficiency effects associated with privatization as companies are insulated from competition for the duration of the power or water contract. Thirdly, privatization can saddle governments with liabilities that are more onerous than debt as repayments are fixed in foreign exchange and quantities are predetermined. This is far more like international debt than equity investment as the government is required to pay the due instalments regardless of changing circumstances. As with debt, a fall in the currency value makes it very difficult to meet foreign payment obligations. However, payment guarantees for infrastructure may be more onerous than debt commitments in some respects, due to the far-reaching consequences that occur in the event of a breakdown in contractual arrangements. Where an organization cannot meet debt repayments to lenders, there are mechanisms to deal with this. Debt can be rescheduled or even bankruptcy might be an option. However, arrangements with private infrastructure providers through power purchase agreements (PPAs) do not attract debt relief, and conventional rescheduling arrangements may not apply (Wells 1999). While privatization may well reduce demands for normal debt repayments through a reduction in government borrowing, tax-payers will be saddled with alternative financial demands that may be more difficult to renegotiate, should circumstances change (Bayliss and Hall 2002).

The extent and impact of privatization has varied across regions. In Africa, for example, implementation of privatization has been slower than supporters would like, and has been shaped in some cases by the legacy of poorly performing state enterprises (Nellis 2003a). Nellis concludes that evidence from Latin America indicates that privatization has been a success in terms of improvements in firms' performance, extension of networks, and access and quality of service. However, privatization is not popular, but Nellis puts this down to perceptions and politics rather than research findings. Research by Djankov and Murrel (2002) which analyses findings from over 100 empirical surveys in transition economies indicates that, while privatization is associated with significant gains in Eastern Europe, there is no 'privatization effect' in CIS (Commonwealth of Independent States) countries.[8] Thus, the nature and effects of privatization would seem to depend, to a large extent, on the circumstances in which they are implemented.

Conclusion

The scope for privatization in developing countries has been growing over the past twenty years and looks set to continue, despite widespread criticism and disappointing results. Over the years, privatization has increased in prominence, despite weak empirical and theoretical foundations. The nature of the debate has also shifted. For a time, the privatization argument faltered on the issue of market failure as, in the absence of competition, it was not clear that privatization would be beneficial. This limitation has been recognized by privatization supporters. While the concerns over market failure still hold, it is the notion that public ownership is the solution to such failures that has come into question and is increasingly at the centre of the discussion. Thus, the debate is no longer focused on whether public or private is better or worse, but on whether the potential welfare losses from privatization of monopolistic enterprises outweigh the potential welfare gains from the increase in efficiency that privatization is purported to provide. With so much privatization already carried out, future policy decisions look likely to continue along this line.

In industrialized countries, privatization is not universal. For example, in Washington – the home of the World Bank and the International Monetary Fund – the municipal government opted not to privatize the water supply, deciding instead to work on improving internal incentives while retaining public ownership (Gutierrez 2002). Yet, this alternative perspective is largely ignored by the World Bank, which has constructed its own empirical and ideological support for privatization. Furthermore, the influence of the Bank, that has dominated development policy, means that developing countries have to implement policies which even the US has rejected.

Transfer of ownership to the private sector could bring benefits in some circumstances. Where long-term development is the over-riding objective, a policy that fosters enhancement of indigenous capacity through ownership transfer to the private sector may be viable. However, currently national privatization programmes tend to treat all state enterprises as candidates for privatization, with the future of firms determined by their 'saleability' or otherwise. Privatization, then, can be successful for enterprises that are relatively profitable or that operate in sectors where multinational corporations are interested in making acquisitions. However, for larger firms that operate in monopolistic markets, governments face difficulties implementing regulation.

Privatization can do little for firms where there is no interest from investors. According to the current approach to privatization, such enterprises are not considered viable, and, if restructuring efforts fail, stagnation and liquidation can be on the cards. This approach can be destructive in the long term. The level of investor interest in a firm scheduled for privatization is determined by many factors, including the access to credit, potential demand, level of competition (domestic and imported), historical relations between the private sector and the state, and the institutional and legal framework. These factors may be independent of the current 'viability' of the business. To allow such firms to collapse may prove myopic. There is a sense, particularly in World Bank literature, that privatization is about 'market forces' and efficiency of resource allocation. However, the circumstances of privatization are largely created, not by an 'invisible hand', but by government policies.

Privatization is just one reform option open to policy-makers in the light of poor performance by the public sector. It needs to be used selectively and evaluated alongside other alternatives (such as retention in the public sector, or allowing some form of self-management) which identify the specific needs of the enterprises and decide the best way of addressing these. Privatization cannot help but be shaped by the historical, economic and social context in which it is implemented, and this needs to come into policy decision-making. The policy needs to be examined closely and critically on a case-by-case basis, in the context of developmental needs rather than neoliberal ideology.

Notes

1 There was a sense that reform needed to be immediate because: 'A combination of circumstances has created a favourable environment for the reform of the state enterprise sector: the lesson of such reforms in developed countries and the successes of market-oriented strategies among developing countries; the acute financial crisis, which has raised the economic and political costs of doing nothing; and the installation of a number of new, reform-minded governments' (Shirley and Nellis 1991: 65).

2 'The resulting movement towards reform is inherently temporary; the momentum must be sustained' (Shirley and Nellis 1991: 65)

3 The study included enterprises from Malaysia, Mexico, Argentina, Chile and the UK.

4 For example, the Government of Malaysia's guidelines on privatization (1985, cited in Adam, Cavendish and Mistry, 1992: 23) state: 'privatization is expected to promote competition, improve efficiency and increase the productivity of the services. [In addition] privatization, by stimulating private entrepreneurship and investment, is expected to accelerate the rate of growth of the economy.'

5 Classification according to World Bank Country Classification on the basis of national income levels.

6 The studies cited are Megginson, Nash and Randenborgh (1994); Galal *et.al.* (1994); Ramamurti (1997); La Porta and Lopez-de-Silanes (1997).

7 See Citizens Network on Essential Services, www.servicesforall.org.

8 The Commonwealth of Independent States (CIS) is an association of former Soviet republics that was established in December 1991 by Russia, Ukraine and Belarus. Other members include Armenia, Azerbaijan, Georgia, Kazakhstan, Kyrgyzstan, Moldova, Tajikistan, Turkmenistan and Uzbekistan.

References

Adam, Christopher, William Cavendish and Percy S. Mistry (1992), *Adjusting Privatization: Case Studies from Developing Countries* (London: James Currey).

Aharoni, Yair (1991), 'On Measuring the Success of Privatization', in R. Ramamurti and Raymond Vernon, eds, *Privatization and Control of State-Owned Enterprises* (Washington DC: World Bank): 73–85.

Alchian, Armen (1965), 'Some Economics of Property Rights', *Il Politico*, 30: 816–29.

Bayliss, Kate (2001), 'Privatization and the World Bank: A Flawed Development Tool', *Global Focus,* 13 June.

Bayliss, Kate and David Hall (2002), 'Can Risk Really be Transferred to the Private Sector? A Review of Experiences with Utility Privatization', Public Services International Research Unit, University of Greenwich, London, www.psiru.org/reports/2000-11-U-WB.doc.

Berry, Sara (1993), 'Understanding Agricultural Policy in Africa: The Contributions of Robert Bates', *World Development*, 21 (6): 1055–62.

Bhagwati, J.N. (1982), 'Directly Unproductive Profit-Seeking (DUP) Activities', *Journal of Political Economy*, 90 (5): 988–1002.

Boubakri, Narjess and Jean-Claude Cosset (1998), 'The Financial and Operating Performance of Newly Privatized Firms: Evidence from Developing Countries', processed, Université Laval, Quebec, Canada.

—— (1999), 'Does Privatization Meet the Expectations? Evidence from African Countries', Plenary on 'Privatization and Corporate Governance', African Economic Research Consortium Biannual Research Workshop, Nairobi, Kenya, December.

Chang, Ha-Joon and Ajit Singh (1992), 'Public Enterprises in Developing Countries and Economic Efficiency: A Critical Examination of Analytical, Empirical and Policy Issues', UNCTAD Discussion Paper 48, United Nations Conference on Trade and Development, Geneva, August.

Coase, R.H. (1960), 'The Problem of Social Cost', *Journal of Law and Economics*, 3: 1–44.

Commander, Simon and Tony Killick (1988), 'Privatization in Developing Countries: A Survey of the Issues', in Paul Cook and Colin Kirkpatrick, eds, *Privatization in Less Developed Countries* (Hemel Hempstead: Harvester Wheatsheaf): 91–124.

Cook, Paul and Colin Kirkpatrick, eds (1995), *Privatization Policy and Performance: International Perspectives* (New York: Prentice Hall and Harvester Wheatsheaf).

D'Souza, Juliet and William Megginson (1999), 'The Financial and Operating Performance of Privatized Firms during the 1990s', *Journal of Finance*, 54 (4), August: 1397–438.

D'Souza, Juliet, William L. Megginson and Robert C. Nash (2001), 'Determinants of Performance Improvements in Privatized Firms: The Role of Restructuring and Corporate Governance' (March 2000), American Finance Association, New Orleans.

Demirguc-Kunt, Asli and Ross Levine (1994), 'The Financial System and Public Enterprise Reform: Concepts and Cases', Policy Research Department, Finance and Private Sector Development Division, World Bank, Washington DC, July.

Djankov, Simeon and Peter Murrell (2002), 'Enterprise Restructuring in Transition: A Quantitative Survey', CEPR Discussion Paper 3319, Centre for Economic Policy Research, London.

Fine, Ben (1990), *The Coal Question: Political Economy and Industrial Change from the Nineteenth Century to the Present Day* (London: Routledge).

—— (2001), *Social Capital versus Social Theory: Political Economy and Social Science at the Turn of the Millennium* (London: Routledge).

Fine, Ben and Dimitri Milonakis (2005), *Economic Theory and History: From Classical Political Economy to Economics Imperialism* (London: Routledge), forthcoming.

Galal, Ahmed, Leroy Jones, Pankaj Tandon and Ingo Vogelsang (1994), *Welfare Consequences of Selling Public Enterprises: An Empirical Analysis* (New York: Oxford University Press).

Glentworth, Garth (1998), 'A British Perspective', in 'Editorial Introduction' (by Alison Evans and Mick Moore), in 'The Bank, the State and Development', *IDS Bulletin*, 29 (2), April: 4–5, Box 1.

Gutierrez, Eric (2002), 'Washington DC's "Continuous Internal Improvement" Alternative – An Initial Inquiry on PSP in Water and Sanitation in the United States', Tearfund Case Studies on Private Sector Participation (London: WaterAid), http://wateraid.ellipsismedia.net/site/in_depth/current_research/411.asp.

Haque, M. Shamsul (1996), 'Public Service under Challenge in the Age of Privatization', *Governance*, 9 (2): 186–216.

Kikeri, Sunita, John Nellis and Mary Shirley (1992), *Privatization: The Lessons of Experience* (Washington DC: World Bank).

Krueger, Anne O. (1974), 'The Political Economy of the Rent-Seeking Society', *American Economic Review*, 64 (3): 291–303.

La Porta, Rafael and Florencio Lopez-de-Silanes (1997), 'The Benefits of Privatization: Evidence from Mexico', NBER Working Paper 6215, National Bureau of Economic Research, Cambridge, Massachusetts, http://papers.nber.org/papers/w6215.pdf.

Loftus, Alex and David McDonald (2001), 'Lessons from Argentina: The Buenos Aires Water Concession', Municipal Services Project Occasional Paper 2, Queen's University, Kingston, Canada, http://qsilver.queensu.ca/~mspadmin/pages/Project_Publications/Series/2.htm.

Martin, Stephen and David Parker (1997), *The Impact of Privatization: Ownership and Corporate performance in the UK* (London: Routledge).

Megginson, William and Jeffry Netter (2001), 'From State to Market: A Survey of Empirical Studies on Privatization', *Journal of Economic Literature*, 39 (2): 321–89.

Megginson, William, Robert Nash and Matthias van Randenborgh (1994), 'The Financial and Operating Performance of Newly Privatized Firms: An International Empirical Analysis', *Journal of Finance*, 49 (2), June.

Mkandawire, Thandika (1994), 'The Political Economy of Privatization in Africa', in G.A. Cornia and G.K. Helleiner, eds, *From Adjustment to Development in Africa: Conflict, Controversy, Convergence, Consensus?* (Basingstoke: Macmillan): 192–213.

Nisanken, W.A. (1975), 'Bureaucrats and Politicians', *Journal of Law and Economics*, 18 (3): 617–43.

Nellis, John (2003a), 'Privatization in Africa: What has Happened? What is to be Done?' Working Paper Number 25, Center for Global Development, Washington DC, February.

——— (2003b), 'Privatization in Latin America', Working Paper 31, Center for Global Development, Washington DC, August.

North, Douglass (1995), 'The New Institutional Economics and Third World Development', in John Harris, Janet Hunter and Colin M. Lewis, eds, *New Institutional Economics and the Third World* (London: Routledge): 17–26.

Peters, P.E. (1993), 'Is "Rational Choice" the Best Choice for Robert Bates? An Anthropologist's Reading of Bates' Work', *World Development*, 21 (6): 1063–76.

Ramamurti, Ravi (1997), 'Testing the Limits of Privatization: Argentine Railroads', *World Development*, 25 (12): 1973–97.

Rowthorn, Robert and Ha-Joon Chang (1995), 'The Role of the State in Economic Change: Introduction', in Ha-Joon Chang and R.E. Rowthorn, eds, *The Role of the State in Economic Change* (Oxford: Oxford University Press).

Shapiro, Helen and Lance Taylor (1990), 'The State and Industrial Strategy', *World Development*, 18 (6): 861–78.

Shirley, Mary and John Nellis (1991), *Public Enterprise Reform: The Lessons of Experience*, EDI Development Studies, Economic Development Institute, World Bank, Washington DC.

Shirley, Mary and Patrick Walsh (2000), 'Public versus Private Ownership: The Current State of the Debate', World Bank Working Paper 2420, World Bank, Washington DC.

Singh, Ajit (1992), 'The Stock Market and Economic Development: Should Developing Countries Encourage Stock Markets?', UNCTAD Discussion Paper 49, Geneva.

Stein, Howard (1995), 'Institutional Theories and Structural Adjustment in Africa', in John Harris, Janet Hunter and Colin M. Lewis, eds, *New Institutional Economics and the Third World* (London: Routledge), 109–32.

Stiglitz, Joseph (1998), 'More Instruments and Broader Goals: Moving towards the Post-Washington Consensus', WIDER Annual Lecture, Helsinki, Finland.

UNDP (2003), 'African Stock Markets Handbook', United Nations Development Programme, New York.

Vickers, John and George Yarrow (1988), *Privatization: An Economic Analysis* (Cambridge, Massachusetts: MIT Press).

Wells, Louis T. (1999), 'Private Foreign Investment in Infrastructure: Managing Non-Commercial Risk', paper presented at conference on 'Private Infrastructure for Development: Confronting Political and Regulatory Risks', Rome, 8–10 September.

World Bank (1981), *Accelerated Development in Sub-Saharan Africa* (Washington DC: World Bank).

——— (1983), *World Economic Recession and Prospects for Recovery* (Oxford University Press: World Bank).

——— (1995), *Private Sector Development in Low Income Countries* (Washington DC: World Bank).

——— (2003), *Global Economic Prospects 2003* (Washington DC: World Bank).

Yamin, Mo (1998), 'The Dual Risks of Market Exchange and the Transition Process', in Paul Cook, Colin Kirkpatrick and Frederick Nixson, eds, *Privatization, Enterprise Development and Economic Reform: Experiences of Developing and Transitional Economies* (Cheltenham: Edward Elgar).

From Washington to Post-Washington Consensus

The Triumph of Human Capital[1]

Pauline Rose

> A mere acquaintance with the history of economic thought is sufficient to show that the science of economics is almost as subject to fashions as the art of dressmaking. At the present time, 'human capital formation', 'human resource development', or, simply 'investment in human beings' is all the rage. As is so often the case with fads, the impetus has come from America. (Blaug 1968: 215)

While education has been receiving ever-increasing priority in recent years, one thing has remained consistently resilient to change amongst some education economists since the 1960s – an uncritical faith in the notion of human capital. This chapter begins by exploring the meaning of human capital, indicating the ways in which this has justified the involvement of economists in education. In particular, World Bank economists have had considerable influence over education policy in developing countries, particularly since the 1980s. The next part of the chapter explores the role the World Bank has played, and the effect this has had on ensuring an enduring emphasis on human capital. The implications of this emphasis are considered, particularly in relation to opening up the black box of education provision.

The Human Capital Revolution

The term 'human capital' was initially coined in 1960 by T.W. Schultz,[2] referring to the notion that people acquire skills and knowledge (assets perceived as a form of capital), and that such acquisition is a result of deliberate investment. Increased productivity, resulting from investment in human capital, is perceived to benefit individuals through increased future income, and society as a whole as a result of improved productivity and larger contributions to national income. As such, human capital is considered an important explanation for economic progress. According to its founder:

> I propose to treat education as an investment in man. Since education becomes part of the person receiving it, I shall refer to it as *human capital*. Since it becomes an integral part of a person, it cannot be bought or sold or treated as property under our institutions. Nevertheless, it is a form of capital if it renders

a service of value. The principal hypothesis underlying this treatment of education is that some important increases in national income are a consequence of additions to the stock of this form of capital. (Schultz [1960] 1993: 115)

A human capital approach implies that it is possible in principle to measure the profitability of, or rate of return on investment in, education. This is achieved by calculating the expected yield in terms of future benefits, compared with the cost of acquiring education. Private rates of return compare all direct and opportunity costs of education (earnings foregone as a result of time spent in school or college) to individuals, with their benefits in terms of increased lifetime earnings. Social rates of return measure the costs and benefits to society as a whole (Woodhall 1987). Ideally, social rates of return should include societal benefits in terms of higher productivity of educated workers and their contributions to national income (usually proxied by increased lifetime earnings), as well as allow for 'externalities' that are valued by society. Such externalities include, for example, improved health and reduced fertility. However, in practice, externalities are often not easily quantifiable, and so are usually not taken into consideration in the calculations of rates of return to education.

Schultz (1960) illustrated the importance of investment in human capital through the application of rates of return showing that, taking total costs of education into account (including opportunity costs), rates of return to education are relatively attractive and larger than returns in physical capital. In the early 1960s, Schultz's work was supported by Gary Becker (1964), who provided further evidence to reinforce the importance of human capital. Since the 1960s, proponents of human capital have continued to use calculations of rates of return as empirical justification to show that education is a good investment. As such, human capital has allowed an economic approach, based on the calculation of costs and benefits of education, to predominate.

Although Schultz (1960) and his followers do not deny the importance of the 'cultural purposes of education', or that education includes a 'consumption' as well as an 'investment' aspect, its property as a form of capital has driven economists, predominantly associated with the World Bank, to recognize its importance. This, in turn, has justified the World Bank's involvement in educational activities. The emphasis on human capital has shifted the focus on education from a traditional view of its role in cultivating social integration and cohesion, and forging new notions of national citizenship and identity, to a means of individual and collective economic advancement (Green 1997).

The World Bank as Self-Declared Leader in Education

In education, the World Bank has had the biggest influence over international and national priorities and policy-making, particularly since the 1980s. The World Bank is a self-declared leader in education, in terms of both its intellectual and financial roles. The self-perception of its intellectual role is exemplified by a statement made by George Psacharopoulos, a prominent education economist within the World Bank, particularly renowned for his meta-analyses of studies on rates of return to education that have had a central influence in setting the agenda for educational lending in the 1980s.[3] In his view, the 1980 World Bank Policy Paper on education deserved the full attention of the academic community as it represented the major explicit statement on applied educational policy in developing countries: 'It might not be an exaggeration to treat this Paper as a modern Bible on educational development' (Psacharopoulos 1981a: 141).

In terms of its financial role, the World Bank (1995) reports that it is the largest single source of external finance for education in developing countries, accounting for about a quarter of all external support by 1990. This share further increased to 30 per cent by the mid-1990s (World Bank 1999b). It acknowledges, however, that its spending is small compared to the spending on education by the developing countries themselves, and accounts for only 0.6 per cent of the total. It suggests, without apparent irony: 'This low share of total spending means that the Bank should concentrate on providing advice designed to help governments develop education policies suitable for the circumstances of their own countries' (World Bank 1995: 153). Thus, by its own admission, the World Bank's role cannot be ignored in setting education priorities and policy-making in developing countries.

A focus on the World Bank in this analysis does not intend to underplay the role played by other international agencies, but rather to highlight the central role played by a key actor in the global development process. Not all international agencies set their agenda according to economic criteria, and many also have an important influence over national priorities. As Mundy (1998) shows in relation to education, UNESCO played an important role, both financially and in terms of setting a rights-based agenda, in the 1960s and 1970s. At the outset of its involvement in education, the World Bank drew on UNESCO's expertise. However, by the 1980s, the World Bank had taken the lead, both in terms of its own research and superior access to other information and research, as well as in relation to the volume of loans to education that had grown substantially over this period. As a result, by the 1980s, the World Bank had an over-arching influence on both international and national policy-making in education (Mundy 1998; Jones 1992). Partnerships between the agencies have subsequently been revitalized as a result of the World Conferences on 'Education for All' in Jomtien and Dakar in 1990 and 2000, respectively, with international agencies converging on a common agenda of 'education for all'. Their different approaches towards this agenda remain evident, however (see, for example, UNESCO 2003; Bruns, Mingat and Rakatomalala 2003).

Pre-Washington Consensus and Education: Basic Needs

From the early 1960s, simultaneous with Schultz's development of the concept of human capital, the World Bank began a cautious exploration of the possibilities of involving itself in education.[4] From the outset, it was made clear that only economic factors should be taken into consideration for Bank lending in education, despite acknowledgement of its social and cultural objectives. In 1960, the prospect of introducing lending for education projects was initially dismissed, on the grounds that it was neither revenue-generating nor capital-intensive (Kapur, Lewis and Webb 1997a). Schultz's work, however, allowed this view to be refuted, as education could now be seen as an investment. However, the human capital revolution initially had little impact on the World Bank. Its staff was still reluctant to get involved in education, on the basis of the World Bank's perceived comparative advantage in other areas, the 'inherent subjectivities of a soft sector' and the potential influence of political issues (ibid.: 168–69).

Gradual acceptance that certain types of education were productive resulted in approval of investment in vocational and technical training at the higher and secondary levels. This was based on needs identified by manpower gaps revealed by other Bank projects in specific countries (Kapur, Lewis and Webb 1997a). Emphasis was placed on scarcities of technicians and engineers: 'this focus on one small part of the education sector became the first in a series of operational biases through which the Bank often sponsored, promoted and financed with borrower resources projects with distorted content' (Heyneman 2003: 317). At this time, primary education was not considered an appropriate area for World Bank investment: 'An initial antipathy towards support for primary education was apparent, based on the "bizarre rationale" that it would make unlimited demands as far as finance was concerned, and self-provision should be relied upon because of the high demand for it' (Jones 1992: 99).

A shift in emphasis to primary education only began in the 1970s, with expansion of the Bank's identity as a development agency and its adoption of the basic needs approach, in which education began to be taken more seriously. The phase was later called the 'McNamara revolution' in Bank policy toward education. McNamara opened up the possibility that, while continuing to emphasize projects linked with the need for trained manpower, financing of other projects with longer-term significance for economic development should also be considered (Jones 1992). Despite adoption of the basic needs approach, economic arguments in favour of education prevailed, with neither poverty nor equity entering into the case made for education during the early 1970s (Kapur, Lewis and Webb 1997a).

The increasing emphasis on education over the 1970s was evident in the changing priorities in World Bank lending. There was a notable expansion and diversification of lending for education during the early 1970s, including support for primary schooling and non-formal, adult and literacy training. Commitments for education increased considerably, from US$154 million per annum on average for the years 1963–69 to an average of US$528 million per annum in 1970–74. This continued to increase to US$794 million per annum on average during the latter half of the 1970s (see Table 1). Furthermore, greater priority to primary education was also apparent, with its allocation increasing from 4 per cent of education lending in the 1960s to almost 25 per cent by the late 1970s.

TABLE 1   *Trends in World Bank Lending to Education* (US$ million, average per year)

	1963–69	1970–74	1975–79	1980–84	1985–89	1990–94	1995–99
Total education (constant $)	154.0	528.0	794.0	977.0	1091.0	2024.0	1878.0
Education as % of total lending	3.0	5.1	4.4	4.5	4.5	8.2	7.6
% of education lending to pre-primary and primary	4.2	10.6	23.6	22.9	26.3	36.1	37.8

Source: Mundy 2002: Table 1.

Washington Consensus and Education: The Rise of Human Capital

Human capital took two decades to achieve prominence within the World Bank, finally coming into its own from the early 1980s. After cautious adoption of education using a manpower planning approach, analysis of rates of return to education became influential by the 1980s. The appointment of George Psacharopoulos to head the Education Department's Research Unit established in 1981 was instrumental in this significant shift (Jones 1992). The 1980 *World Development Report* and 1980 Education Sector Policy Paper highlighted the direct productivity benefits of primary education, drawing in particular on Psacharopoulos's studies of international comparisons of rates of return to education.[5] While the emphasis on a welfare focus in the 1970s continued to be evident in the 1980 Education Sector Policy Paper, a shift to emphasize education's role in promoting economic development was apparent, although the term human capital was not adopted in that paper.

Emphasis on the analysis of rates of return to education became increasingly evident within the Bank, supported in particular by Psacharopoulos's numerous surveys and summaries of studies (1973; 1981b; 1985; 1994; and, more recently, Patrinos and Psacharopoulos 2002). Investment in primary education, particularly of girls, was promoted on the basis that their estimated rates of return to education were the highest, and the difference between social and private returns the greatest, at that level. Rates of return to investment in education were also estimated to be above the 10 per cent yardstick used as the opportunity cost of capital in developing countries (Psacharopoulos and Woodhall 1985). As Jones (1992) suggests, Psacharopoulos brought to the Bank the type of educational research organizationally necessary for research to have an influence over the character and quality of lending in education.

In practice, however, lending decisions were rarely made on the basis of calculations of rates of return according to individual country circumstances. Rather, the conclusions drawn from Psacharopoulos's cross-country summaries of studies were used to provide generalized and prescriptive justification across countries for priority to primary education. This allowed the World Bank to conform to broader international prioritization of primary education, promoted by UN agencies, NGOs and some bilateral agencies from a rights-based perspective, rather than based on economic criteria.

Through application of rates of return analysis, the notion of human capital has enabled the World Bank to justify its role in education since the 1980s. This emphasis is not surprising, given that the Bank is regulated by rules that mean it has to find economic justification for its loans. However, as Jones (1992: 227) points out, the limitations of its contribution need to be understood in this light: 'Research needs to be driven by operational requirements and must reflect organizational values, aspirations and objectives. What becomes an issue is when researchers working in such contexts deny the institutional parameters that shape and dictate their work, and claim their research to be objective, untrammelled by institutional requirements.'

Furthermore, the narrow focus on economic aspects risks neglecting important features of education. As Lauglo (1996) notes, the 1995 World Bank review of education (*Priorities and Strategies for Education*) ignored the moral and social impacts of education, both in terms of the problems that schools might generate, as well as their potential for remedying the social dislocations of modernization and restoring social cohesion. The processes of teaching and learning, which transform inputs into outputs, tend to remain outside the scope of the Bank's approach to education, leaving the black box of educational provision firmly shut, as discussed below. In addition, emphasis on rates of return to education, with their measurement of returns focusing on years of schooling, has served to focus attention on the importance of increasing the quantity of education provided, potentially at the expense of quality, as experiences from developing countries such as Malawi indicate (Rose 2003b).

It is not coincidental that the ascendancy of human capital, in conjunction with the application of rates of return, corresponded with the advent of the Washington Consensus. Human capital provided the opportunity for the neoliberal agenda to be applied to education, allowing the World Bank to continue its involvement and even increase its influence in the education sector, despite austerity packages adopted as part of structural adjustment programmes. Basic education and health were seen as areas for public expenditure priority even during the Washington Consensus era. However, Williamson (1997), who first coined the term 'Washington Consensus', felt that the support given to these sectors in the Washington Consensus did not go far enough, and that less reform occurred in the area of public expenditure priorities than in other areas. The conflict between the Washington Consensus principle of prioritizing public expenditure on education and health, and conditions set by structural adjustment programmes for reducing overall government expenditure, meant that, in reality, education expenditure often suffered, even though governments made considerable efforts to protect the education budget where possible (Stewart 1994; Woodhall 1994).[6]

Even in the context of advocacy of more general austerity measures within the economy, the productivity benefits associated with human capital permitted an expansion of World Bank loans to education, despite a shift in focus away from the basic needs rationale of the 1970s. The global adoption of neoliberal principles and the associated rise of human capital corresponded with the demise of funding for education in UN organizations, including UNESCO and UNICEF, whose objectives were traditionally more related to social provision than productivity and economic growth. This provided further opportunity and legitimacy for the creation of more centralized mechanisms for setting and implementing international education policies by the World Bank (Mundy 1998).

While the UNESCO and UNICEF budgets for education remained unchanged at best between the 1970s and 1980s, World Bank lending to education increased dramatically – doubling from US$977 in 1980–84 to US$2,024 by 1990–94 (in constant 1994 prices) (Table 1). Furthermore, World Bank lending played an even greater role internationally, increasing from 16 per cent to 30 per cent of the amount spent on education by bilateral agencies (which remained relatively unchanged) over the period (Mundy 1998; World Bank 1999b) – indicative of the increasing financial dominance of the World Bank as international donor in education. The share of primary education remained relatively stable over the 1980s at around one-quarter of total education lending, despite proclamations of a focus on this level during the period.

The rise of human capital provided a rationale for the World Bank to reassess the role of states and markets in education, resulting in advocacy of cost recovery mechanisms in education, including at the primary level. World Bank-supported research put forward efficiency and equity arguments to justify setting a price for consumers (see, for example, Thobani 1984; Mingat and Tan 1986; Jimenez 1986, 1987; Psacharopoulos, Tan and Jimenez 1986). While payment of fees for education services was not new, market principles were formally adopted in the 1980s to justify cost recovery in public education. A total retreat of the state was, however, never supported in education, given the acceptance of presence of externalities, such as education's benefits to society through improved health, reduced fertility, etc., imperfections in capital and labour markets, and inadequate information about anticipated future benefits (Colclough 1996). As Fine and Rose (2001) argue, however, acknowledgement of externalities and market imperfections undermines the legitimacy of the human capital model, which views education as involving streams of costs and benefits in conditions equivalent to perfect competition and full employment.

Post-Washington Consensus and Education: Neoliberalism with a Human Face

The supposed post-Washington Consensus of the late 1990s provided an even greater opportunity for the prioritization of education, set within the context of its emphasis on more instruments and broader objectives. Thus, the emphasis given to the developmental role of education by the Washington Consensus has been perpetuated and reinforced by Stiglitz. Education was a recurring feature in Stiglitz's speeches during his tenure as chief economist at the World Bank, in which its role is extended to be not only an instrument required to achieve development, but also as a broader objective in itself. The justification for a focus on education, and the need for state intervention in it, continues to be based on the notion of human capital and its relationship with growth, as evident from the example of East Asian economies:

> The role of human capital in economic growth has long been appreciated. . . . The East Asian economies, for instance, emphasized the role of government in providing universal education, which was a necessary part of their transformation from agrarian to rapidly industrializing economies. . . . Left to itself, the market will tend to underprovide human capital. It is very difficult to borrow against the prospects of future earnings when the human capital itself is not collaterizable. . . . The government plays an important role in providing public education and using other methods to make education more affordable. (Stiglitz 1998a: 11)

Although Stiglitz recognizes trade-offs between some goals of development in other areas, education is seen as an area where there are complementarities with other goals. He proposes that promoting human capital can advance economic development, equality, participation and democracy. East Asia is again drawn upon, this time as an example of universal education creating a more egalitarian society, facilitating the political stability considered a precondition for successful long-term development (Stiglitz 1998a).

The emphasis on the East Asian miracle is not uncontroversial. Writers in the human capital tradition provide support for Stiglitz's claims, showing, for example, that heavy initial investment in human capital by households and governments, as well as heavy investment in physical capital, have been an important determinant of economic growth in the region (McMahon 1998). However, as Booth (1999) argues, East Asia comprises a diverse group of countries, each with very different colonial legacies with implications for different rates of educational progress between countries, as well as for income and wealth distribution. Her findings cast serious doubt on simple relationships between investment in education and economic growth in the East Asian context, as assumed in the human capital approach.

Stiglitz's broadened set of objectives includes democratic development that places emphasis on ownership and participation, which has had important implications for education. According to Stiglitz (1997: 6), development strategies in the 1980s saw development as a technical problem requiring technical solutions: they did not reach deep down into society, nor did they believe that a participatory approach was necessary. For him, participation is a means of improving educational outcomes, with education presumed to improve participation. On the one hand, 'in some cases – particularly as in education and health, where individual involvement is an essential part of the production process – participation can improve other outcomes (for instance, the amount of learning that occurs)' (ibid.: 5). On the other hand, 'for participation to be fully meaningful, it should be based on knowledge; hence the crucial role of education' (ibid.: 22).

Education is, therefore, given top priority by Stiglitz (ibid.: 31) in promoting development:

> Among the most important [priority] is *education*, because without education a country cannot develop, cannot attract and build modern industries, cannot

adopt new growing technologies as rapidly in the rural sector. But most fundamentally, if development represents the transformation of society, education is what enables people to learn, to accept and help engender this transformation. Education is the core of development.

These views of Stiglitz highlight what he considers to be new in his approach to education – namely, its importance as both an instrument and an objective of development; the complementarity between states and markets in education provision; and the importance of participation in both educational provision and outcomes. Stiglitz accepts that a focus on health and education, away from GDP measures, is far from revolutionary. The difference, for him, is that 'the whole is greater than the sum of the parts, and that successful development must focus on the whole – the transformation of society' (Stiglitz 1998b: 42). It is, however, also evident that the basis for his support for education remains firmly within the human capital paradigm, with the main contribution being an even greater emphasis on externalities.

The notion of human capital continues the motivation for investing in education, with rates of return analysis still deemed to be central in determining priorities in education. Burnett and Patrinos (1996: 273), lead authors of the 1995 World Bank *Priorities and Strategies of Education*, confirmed the Bank's uncritical adherence to human capital theory in the 1990s: 'Lauglo's claim that rates of return are controversial we believe, could be due to a confusion between rates of return and human capital theory. The latter is no longer considered controversial.'

The role of rates of return in shaping World Bank educational priorities has increased, rather than decreased, over time.[7] This has occurred despite the criticism of the studies, both methodologically as well as in relation to the time-span they cover, which make them outdated in the light of changing economic conditions as a result of economic crises and austerity packages in the 1980s (see, for example, Bennell 1996). It could be argued that analysis of rates of return is used for internal advocacy purposes within the Bank that members of staff do not necessarily believe themselves. This view is not supported, however, by public pronouncements of influential Bank staff who have been defensive of reliance on rates of return to education as a diagnostic tool (Burnett and Patrinos 1996; Psacharopoulos 1996).

Despite criticisms of the approach, the most recent World Bank (1999b) *Education Sector Strategy* continues to rely on rates of return to justify investment in education, albeit with reference to popular issues such as globalization, democratization and community participation. It, therefore, indicates a continued uncritical adherence to the importance of the notion of human capital and the application of rates of return analysis in the post-Washington Consensus era. It now also appears to confuse theory and application, perceiving neither as controversial: 'The rise of human capital theory since the 1960s, and its widespread acceptance now after thorough debate, has provided conceptual underpinnings and statistical evidence. Estimates by Nobel-laureate economists have shown that education is one of the best investments, outstripping the returns from many investments in physical capital' (World Bank 1999b: 6).

Primary education has continued as a central priority for the World Bank, with even greater emphasis given to the focus on poverty reduction in the 1990s, following severe criticisms of the negative effects of World Bank conditionalities in structural adjustment loans on the social sectors. This focus supports more general acceptance of the importance of primary education by international agencies and national governments, as articulated at the 1990 World Conference on Education for All in Jomtien, with both rights-based and economic-based arguments used in its favour. For the World Bank, the latter continue to predominate. Despite the apparent consensus on priorities within education, tensions are apparent within the World Bank's education department on the priorities set in recent years, with conflicts evident between educationists and education economists, and between central and regional staff (Heyneman 2003). On the one hand, Mundy (2002) notes, for example, that some senior education staff in the World Bank considered the 1995 *Review* as too focused on primary education. On the other hand, Heyneman (2003) reports that an earlier version of the *Review* called for all higher education to be privately funded, which created tensions with regional staff who insisted this should be taken out. While internally the World Bank's education sector was in revolt (Heyneman 2003), externally it continued to dominate.

The priority of primary education is also evident in changing lending priorities. Together with a doubling of total education lending between the 1980s and 1990s, the proportion allocated to primary education has also increased from one-quarter to one-third (see Table 1). However, according to Colclough *et al.* (2003), total World Bank lending for education has fallen dramatically over the 1990s (by 15.5 per cent), with lending to Sub-Saharan Africa being the most seriously affected (declining by 44 per cent), suggesting that it has not been possible to sustain the growth in lending, although a focus on primary education has remained evident.[8]

The increased prioritization of primary education, in principle at least, has allowed an image to be presented of the World Bank being more attuned to welfare, poverty alleviation, gender issues, and popular and community participation, in line with the post-Washington Consensus (see, for example, Ilon 1996; Puiggros 1997; Klees 2002). Already evident in the 1995 *Review*, this image was reinforced in the 1999 *Education Sector Strategy* that, Heyneman (2003: 330) suggests, resembled a 'laundry list of altruistic platitudes'. However, the focus continues to be integrated into the more traditional human capital dialogues, as evident in recent Bank literature: 'Since we accept human capital theory and the outcomes approach, then our focus naturally becomes poverty reduction. . . . Or in other words, empowering the poor by improving their productivity . . . is the World Bank's goal in education' (Burnett and Patrinos 1996: 276).

Neoliberalism with a human face in the post-Washington Consensus era is evident in the apparent softer approach to education in the 1990s, with a shift away from user fees to demand-side financing and community participation. The U-turn in primary school fees does not appear to be based on an acknowledgement of the problems associated with the theoretical basis of the 1980s' neoliberal model. While the model is no longer explicitly referred to in World Bank documents, the assumptions and concepts on which it is based are implicit in the more recent forms of cost-sharing advocated. Investment in human capital continues to be the driving motivation for pricing policy.

The role of the state, in this context, is unresolved and uncertain. While increasing attention is placed on the role of the private sector in education in the post-Washington Consensus, a role for the state continues to be envisaged in setting national objectives and maintaining educational standards (World Bank 1999b). Governments are still expected to play a part in financing education, particularly at the primary level. However, recognition that governments face financial pressures – which require alternative sources of resources, including at the primary level) – prevails: 'Fiscal considerations, including competing claims on the public purse, make it difficult for most governments – even those whose philosophies might push them in this direction – to be the sole provider of "free" education to all who seek it at every level' (ibid.: 18).

In this context, a change in cost-sharing approaches has occurred from a narrow focus on sharing costs between the government and households in the 1980s, to more diverse and indirect cost-sharing mechanisms in the 1990s. In particular, a shift in focus from the individual/household to the community as the unit of analysis is evident. For the World Bank (1995: 105):

> Public schools should not, of course, be prohibited from mobilizing resources, in cash or in kind, from local communities when public financing is inadequate and such resources constitute the only means to achieving quality. . . . *Cost-sharing with communities is normally the only exception to free basic education.* Even poor communities are often willing to contribute toward the cost of education, especially at the primary level. (Emphasis added)

As Dale (1997: 275) points out, a role for communities in school governance and financing has always been evident, with the state never solely responsible for funding, regulation and provision/delivery of education. However, as he suggests, the respective roles for states and communities are changing, with the role of communities becoming formalized and more responsibility passing to them. The post-Washington Consensus view has adopted a particular, top-down interpretation of community participation, formalizing it through inclusion in international agreements and promoting it in national policy. Although the rationale for community participation is couched in terms of ownership and accountability, the main objective for the World Bank is to mobilize, and make more efficient use of, resources. Furthermore, limited attention is paid to implications for equity within or between communities (Rose 2003a).

Community participation is likely to be most strongly advocated where the demand for schooling is high but government inputs are inadequate. It is not coincidental, therefore, that a more explicit emphasis on community participation has corresponded with economic crises that have adversely affected education systems in Sub-Saharan African countries since the 1980s, together with rapid expansion of school systems in the context of the drive for achieving universal primary education and advocacy of fees abolition in the 1990s. These changes necessitated the search for alternative sources of resources, with communities seen as a potential source (Bray 1996). In this context, community participation is being integrated into the market system by valuing contributions previously voluntarily made by communities (Rose 2003a). Such marketization is likely to affect the dynamics within a community and result in further fragmentation, as members compete for resources available, rather than encouraging cooperation (Sayed 1999). A shift in the perception of community participation as collective action to individual responsibility is promoted, contradicting the intended goals of accountability, ownership and empowerment. This implies that the focus on education in the post-Washington Consensus era continues to support neoliberal principles of individual responsibility for meeting social needs, as previously evident in the support for user fees in the 1980s.

After the Post-Washington Consensus? Global Education Industry

Education is increasingly seen as big business in the context of a global economy, in the twenty-first century. Presentations by World Bank staff, for example, point out that the global education marketplace is worth $2 trillion, with 15 per cent of the global education market in developing countries (Patrinos 2000). Most of the trade in education services has been in foreign students attending higher education and training institutions in other countries and, more recently, enrolled in distance education programmes at universities in other countries. Despite the apparent prioritization of primary education since the 1990s, the 'global education industry' has placed renewed emphasis by the World Bank on technical and higher education. This is evident, for example, in the 1998–99 *World Development Report* on *Knowledge for Development*, which proposes that basic education 'should not monopolize a nation's attention as it becomes a player in global markets' (World Bank 1999a: 42). Rather, it is proposed that higher levels of education deserve increased attention because of the need to adapt to and apply new information-based technologies. A shift away from what is now considered to be too narrow a focus on primary education in World Bank lending is also evident in the 1999 World Bank report on education in Africa:[9] 'Given the Bank's commitment to provide balanced support to all parts of the system in line with national priorities, there is a prima facie case for increasing support for post-primary education and developing a more balanced portfolio of education projects.' (World Bank 1999c: 66)

As a result of the focus on a global education industry, even greater emphasis has been placed on privatization of education in the international arena in recent years. This has occurred with respect to the promotion of free trade in goods and services (WTO 1998; Patrinos 1999). The World Bank (2000), for example, calls for a 'lighter touch' in regulating higher education, suggesting that countries remove restrictions on private provision of education services. The World Trade Organization's (WTO) General Agreement on Trade in Services (GATS) has been influential in promoting the market in education. Its memo on 'Education Services' (1998) indicates the intention to create conditions for greater liberalization of the trade in education and to create a market system of educational provision, particularly in higher education. The WTO and World Bank consider it important for countries to remove barriers to trade in education in order to promote competition (see, for example, Patrinos 1999). The WTO is, however, defensive about its intentions in the education sector (WTO 2001). As it points out, fewer than fifty WTO members have made commitments to education, which reflects the fact that education is essentially regarded as a function of the state in many countries. While little is known of the implications of the WTO's role in the education sector in practice, that it is supporting a discourse of a market for education goods and services is evident.

Inside the 'Black Box' of Educational Provision

The almost universal acceptance of human capital theory is due, in part, to the influence of the World Bank itself in promoting reliance upon it. According to Jones (1992: 234), if it had not been for the World Bank, human capital theory would probably not have achieved such prominence:

> The flame of human capital theory has been kept alight in the corridors of the Bank partially through the devotion of those analysts committed to manifesting its pertinence through cost-benefit analyses of educational expenditures . . . human capital theory has served a useful institutional purpose, irrespective of its dated and limited theoretical character.

However, human capital theory has not been as uncontroversial as World Bank documents imply. Despite the uncritical adherence of the World Bank to the notion of human capital in the context of the Washington and post-Washington Consensus, as shown above, major criticisms have been raised against the ways in which the human capital approach was adopted in the 1980s. T.W. Schultz (1960) himself aimed to pre-empt criticism that seeing humans as capital goods might be perceived as akin to slavery and reducing people to property. However, such criticism has been less forthcoming than might be expected, allowing the hegemony of human capital to continue.

Although an initial ardent supporter of human capital, Mark Blaug became increasingly disillusioned, in particular of its application, such that, by the mid-1980s, he prematurely proposed its epitaph:

> There are certainly grounds for thinking that the human-capital research program is now in something of a 'crisis': its explanation of the private demand for education seems increasingly unconvincing; it offers advice on the supply of

education, but it does not begin to explain either the patterns of educational finance or public ownership of schools and colleges that we actually observe . . .; its rate-of-return calculations repeatedly turn up significant, unexplained differences in the yields of investment in different types of human capital. (Blaug 1987: 849)

Among economists, concerns have been raised that the apparent relationship between increased years of schooling and productivity is actually 'screening' for innate productive ability, rather than actually contributing to increased productivity directly. More fundamentally, treating educational provision as streams of costs and benefits, both to individuals and society as a whole, ignores social relations within and around education (and presumes labour markets to be perfect). As such, human capital proponents show no understanding of the educational process. On the one hand, the 'black box' of how education is provided remains firmly shut other than in the labelling of financial costs and benefits.[10] On the other hand, the notion of human capital has neither historical nor social specificity. The rise of human capital theory within the World Bank grew out of the more specific application of cost–benefit analysis to calculation of rates of return. As such, it has nothing to do with education specifically. Exactly the same methodology can be applied to any factor with an economic effect (Fine and Rose 2001).

With its focus on costs and benefits, human capital is unable to address questions of how and why national education systems emerge, and how and why did they evolve differently. Bowles and Gintis (1976) have provided a strong critique of the notion of human capital. In their view, the school is analogous to a mini factory in which the social relations of dominance, hierarchy, respect for authority, punctuality, etc., are replicated.[11] This is in order to socialize future workers into accepting positions they are expected to occupy in the future. As such, schooling reinforces the socialization process, for example by strengthening gender stereotypes, rather than challenging power relations, as discussed below. By contrast, for human capital:

> the systemic and endemic presence of racism and sexism within educational provision and subsequent outcomes tends to be set aside as a residual. This is a consequence of orthodoxy in the economics of discrimination in which this is taken as a deviancy from what is normal rather than the norm itself. (Fine 1998: 23)

This implies the need to open up the black box of educational provision. As described in Fine and Rose (2001), education, as well as training and skills, is understood to be attached to a 'system of provision' (Fine and Leopold 1993) with the following elements. First, education is indeed provided through a series of economic and other activities, from building schools to setting curricula and training teachers. Second, educational provision is potentially interactive with the full panoply of economic, social, political and cultural relations. Third, the educational process is heavily embroiled in social structures, relations and processes, and their associated conflicts, which are themselves attached to underlying economic and political interests. Finally, as a result, the formation and evolution of education systems are historically contingent. In other words, national educational systems need to be allowed to define themselves, and to be understood in light of underlying economic and political interests.

Interestingly, the post-Washington Consensus is, in principle, capable of accepting and analysing the presence of socio-economic systems. Analytically, however, for it to do so depends upon reducing such systems to market and information imperfections. The reductionism attached to such principles is incapable of doing justice to the rich complexity of educational systems. In effect, the failure of the post-Washington Consensus to understand education systemically is a sharp reflection of an approach to education in terms of market failures. So pervasive are market imperfections and their mutual spillovers that the education system and its socio-economic determinants increasingly appear as the necessary analytical starting points, rather than some generalized notion of market failure, as the (post-) Washington Consensus implies.

Gender Inside the Black Box

Economic arguments used by the World Bank to justify a focus on female education provide a good illustration of the problems associated with the human capital perspective. As discussed below, the approach neglects the broader historical, social and political context in which gender relations are constructed. Emphasis on economic efficiency arguments in favour of investment in female education, with a deliberate neglect of the broader context in which gender relations are formed, was highlighted, for example, by Lawrence Summers (1994: 20), a former chief economist at the World Bank:

> In making an economic argument for investing in female education, I have tried to steer clear of the moral and cultural aspects unavoidably involved in any gender-related question. Partially this reflects my comparative advantage as an economist, but it also reflects a conviction that helping women be better mothers to their children is desirable whatever one's view of the proper role of women in society.

In making his case for female education, Stiglitz relies on these arguments put forward by Summers, his predecessor. In particular, Stiglitz (1996: 167–68) considers the importance of female education to be one of the lessons from East Asia:

> The emphasis on female education led to reduced fertility, thus mitigating the adverse effects of population pressure felt in so many developing countries, and it directly increased the supply of educated labour. Most studies suggest that a worker's wage performance is more directly related to non-school factors, such as home background, than to education in school. Education of women can be

thought of as a roundabout but high-return way of enhancing labour force productivity.

Here, female education is considered important not for enhancing women's own position in the labour force but for influencing the productivity of their offspring. In a subsequent paper, Stiglitz (1998b: 24) does consider the increased labour force opportunities for educated women. However, he focuses on the effect that their increased wages will have on the family. He, therefore, perceives that women will maintain their role in the household while playing an increased role in the work force, without considering the implications of this on their work load. As Stromquist (1998: 36) points out: 'When the defense for attention to women is based on the principle of efficiency, such an argument downplays the fact that women are productive but exploited under current conditions. The call for "utilizing women's resources in development" often translates into giving them double and triple working duties.'

Expectations of the benefits of female education not only assume that women are not otherwise productive, but also do not challenge the traditional gender division of labour within the household and society. For, women who are not in a position to afford child care and who are expected to play an increased role in the productive sphere could only do so by increasing their own work burden, or by keeping girls out of school to substitute for them in the home. As in the education sector more generally, the justification for incorporating gender into World Bank policy and project work on education continues to be heavily based on rates of return to education, which suggests that social returns to education are stronger for girls than boys.

Recent evidence on rates of return to female education is not, however, as clear-cut as suggested (Kingdon 1998; Appleton *et al.* 1995). Furthermore, problems of measuring rates of return also apply to gender comparisons. For example, there will probably be selectivity bias since calculations of rates of return are based on the observed wages of women working in the labour market. These women often account for a very small proportion of the female population, and those who have access to employment opportunities are likely to exhibit particular characteristics that cannot be generalized. There is, therefore, a problem that educated females included in the sample are not selected randomly. In addition, the calculations assume perfectly competitive labour markets, whereas, in practice, there are many forms of structural constraints including, in many countries, gender discrimination in employment opportunities.[12] As employment opportunities expand for women, those currently in the labour market, and the wages and conditions they experience, are not liable to be representative of outcomes for substantially increased female labour market participation. Moreover, the process is not likely to be incremental but, rather, linked with substantial structural change, as evident from the experiences of developed countries (Fine 1992).

Further justification is given to investment in female education by virtue of the anticipated additional social benefits, in terms of reduced fertility, improved child health and so on. However, the externalities associated with girls' education are difficult to value in monetary terms and, therefore, estimation of social returns is problematic. In addition, the linkages are contested. T.P. Schultz (1995: 48) points out, for example, that it is difficult to determine causality in the relationships between market, labour force commitment, decline in fertility and the educational attainment of women. More importantly, the arguments for female education do not address whether and how women's control over resources and decision-making within the household is improved as a result of increased education. Schooling can, in fact, reinforce the subordinate position of women, and may not be sufficient to ensure empowerment. For example, despite massive increases in women's formal schooling, in many countries, men continue to dominate economic and political life (Swainson 1998; Longwe 1998).

Studies, particularly in South Asia, have questioned the validity of the posited direct relationship between female education and fertility decline (Jeejeebhoy 1995; Jeffrey and Basu 1996; Kumar and Vlassoff 1997, for example). The relationship between female education and fertility decline is found to be highly variable and context-specific, with reference to both the level of development and the nature of gender relations in the society. The results of these studies suggest that autonomy is crucial to women's control over their fertility, and that the relationship between education and autonomy is mediated by the cultural relations of patriarchy (Heward 1997). Weaknesses detected in the relationship should not be used to suggest that priority to female education is misguided, as suggested by Knodel and Jones (1996). Rather, it highlights the need to ensure that the quality and type of schooling received by boys and girls requires attention. Where schooling, either intentionally or unintentionally, ignores economic and social relations, the desired outcomes are not likely to be attained.

It is undeniable that World Bank efforts have been successful in raising the profile of gender disparities in education and have provided justification for investment targeted at girls. However, reliance on economic arguments is inadequate and misleading. As Baden and Goetz (1997: 10) note: 'Tenuous evidence on the relationships between female education and fertility decline, or female education and productivity, can easily be challenged, weakening the justification for addressing gender issues, with a danger that resources will be withdrawn.' Such a fear is not without foundation (Knodel and Jones 1996). Rates of return to human capital are an extremely fragile basis on which to justify investment in female education, quite apart from providing little or no guidance on how to succeed in achieving expansion of, and parity in, educational provision.

Thus, an improved understanding is required to ensure that gender relations in education continue to receive attention, regardless of fads in interpretation and calculation of economic returns to education. As Stromquist (1994) notes, studies that do not attempt to construct a theoretical understanding of how women's inferior condition emerges and is maintained in society, recommend actions as if there are no societal constraints on their attainment. Without a fuller analysis, it is not certain that the desired goals (for example, lower fertility and increased labour productivity) would be attained. Even if they were, the incidence of gender inequality could continue to be reproduced, as is so sharply evident in the developed world. To be effective, analysis of constraints and formulation of interventions have to be situated within the economic, political and social environment that shapes the nature of gender relations in education and society more broadly.

Conclusion

The first lesson of this educational history is that the Bank has been recommending faulty education policies since the beginning of the sector in 1962. This is not to suggest that all Bank education policy recommendations have been faulty; nor is it to suggest that the benefits of the lending have not been substantial. It is only to point out that poor education recommendations have a long tradition in the Bank, and thus far, no one has been able to answer the question of who is accountable. (Heyneman 2003: 331)

This chapter has shown the important role that the World Bank has played in framing an agenda for education economists in development contexts. Despite apparent shifts from broader objectives of development to a narrower focus on economic growth objectives and back again to broader objectives, in practice, there has been an unswerving adherence to human capital in World Bank thinking. Just as the post-Washington Consensus has permitted a populist notion of neoliberalism more generally, within education, the terms 'participation' and 'empowerment' are touted to provide a human face to World Bank operations in education, although economic outcomes of education associated with the notion of human capital continue to be stressed. As observed by Jones (1997: 111), the World Bank's intellectual position towards education over time has remained unchanged: 'What has changed is the Bank's [sic] perception of its own role, the most dramatic changes being corrections of earlier arbitrariness rather than any shift in fundamentals . . . the Bank's [sic] rationale has barely changed in 35 years, a celebration of the elegance of human capital theory.'

The chapter has illustrated the ways in which the human capital approach has allowed the World Bank to emphasize economic returns to education, with a focus on calculations of streams of costs and benefits. This analysis is shown to take education out of the analysis and then bring it back in, with the effect of undermining the approach itself. The more broader issues are incorporated (as evident in the post-Washington Consensus era, in particular), the more the need to take account of socio-economic processes, structures and relations, showing how they fit together to reproduce or transform society. As such, rather than viewing education systems as a stream of costs and benefits, the chapter argues for the need to see education as attached to a system of provision. This approach recognizes that any education system, as the outcome of historically and socially evolved socio-economic practices, is specific to the particular country in which it is located.

Notes

1 This chapter draws on earlier work by Fine and Rose (2001).

2 T.W. Schultz (1961) acknowledged that Adam Smith had previously recognized acquired and useful abilities to be a form of capital.

3 A recent special issue of *Economics of Education Review* [22 (5), 2003] in honour of Psacharopoulos reasserts the influence he has had over education within the World Bank.

4 Jones (1992) suggests, however, that the timing was coincidental, rather than a result of the discovery of education by economists.

5 Education's role in promoting economic development was also seen more broadly – in reducing fertility, and improving health and nutrition (see Colclough 1982 for a detailed review of the evidence).

6 In recognition of this, Williamson adds improved education as one of two topics (in addition to institutional building) that he considered the Consensus should address. His rationale for doing so was based on the need to reduce birth rates in order to control pressures on the environment, and that it would be good for growth and income distribution, as well as promoting overall human development (Williamson 1997).

7 Bennell (1996) notes that the 1980 World Bank policy paper refers to rates of return to education only once, whereas the 1995 World Bank *Review* refers to it over thirty times in order to substantiate, support and qualify a number of key statements about different types of educational investments, and the appropriate roles of the public and private sectors.

8 The reasons advanced by the World Bank for this slowdown include political turmoil in some of the larger countries, the weak absorptive capacity of key institutions throughout the region, and the reluctance of some governments to introduce (education) policy reforms (World Bank 1999c). Thus, blame is placed on problems within the countries themselves.

9 An important reason for the shift in emphasis from lending to primary education is that this proved difficult in practice (see Colclough *et al.* 2003).

10 See Blaug (1987) and Samoff (1996) for their discussions of schooling as a black box.

11 Thus, Bowles and Gintis substitute a different view of production, the socially situated and contested work place, for the human capital production function of neo-classical economics.

12 For example, Kingdon (1998) shows that wage differentials between men and women in her sample are determined more by labour market discrimination than by differences in educational attainment, which invalidates the calculation of rates of return as attempted.

References

Appleton, Simon, *et al.* (1995), 'Gender Differences in the Returns to Schooling in Three African Countries', *Economics Energy Environment*, Milano.

Baden, Sally and Anne-Marie Goetz (1997), 'Who Needs [Sex] When You Can Have [Gender]? Conflicting Discourses on Gender at Beijing', *Feminist Review*, 56: 3–25.

Becker, Gary (1964), *Human Capital: A Theoretical and Empirical Analysis with Special Reference to Education* (Chicago: University of Chicago Press); third edition, 1993.

Bennell, Paul (1996), 'Using and Abusing Rates of Return: A Critique of the World Bank's 1995 Education Sector Review', *International Journal of Educational Development*, 16 (3): 235–48.

Blaug, Mark (1968), 'The Rate of Return on Investment in Education', in Mark Blaug, ed., *Economics of Education 1* (Middlesex: Penguin Books).

—— (1987), *The Economics of Education and the Education of an Economist* (New York: New York University Press).

Booth, Anne (1999), 'Initial Conditions and Miraculous Growth: Why is South East Asia Different from Taiwan and South Korea?', *World Development*, 27 (2): 301–21.

Bowles, Sam and Herb Gintis (1976), *Schooling in Capitalist America: Educational Reform and the Contradictions of Economic Life* (London: Routledge and Kegan Paul).

Bray, Mark (1996), *Decentralization of Education: Community Financing* (Washington DC: World Bank).

Bruns, Barbara, Alain Mingat and Ramahatra Rakatomalala (2003), *Achieving Universal Primary Education by 2015: A Chance for Every Child* (Washington DC: World Bank).

Burnett, Nick, and Harry Anthony Patrinos (1996), 'Response to Critiques of Priorities and Strategies for Education: A World Bank Review', *International Journal of Educational Development*, 16 (3): 273–76.

Colclough, Christopher (1982), 'The Impact of Primary Schooling on Economic Development: A Review of the Evidence', *World Development*, 10 (3): 167–85.

—— (1996), 'Education and the Market: Which Parts of the Neoliberal Solution Are Correct?', *World Development*, 24 (4): 589–610.

Colclough, Christopher, et al. (2003), *Achieving Schooling for All in Africa: Costs, Commitment and Gender* (Aldershot: Ashgate Press).

Dale, Roger (1997), 'The State and the Governance of Education: An Analysis of the Restructuring of the State-Education Relationship', in A.H. Halsey et al., *Education, Culture, Economy and Society* (Oxford: Oxford University Press).

Fine, Ben (1992), *Women's Employment and the Capitalist Family* (London: Routledge).

—— (1998), 'Human Capital Theory: Labour as Asset?', in Ben Fine, ed., *Labour Market Theory: A Constructive Reassessment* (London: Routledge).

—— (2002), *The World of Consumption: The Material and Cultural Revisited* (London: Routledge).

Fine, Ben and Ellen Leopold (1993), *The World of Consumption* (London: Routledge).

Fine, Ben and Pauline Rose (2001), 'Education and the Post-Washington Consensus', in Ben Fine, Costas Lapavitsas and Jonathan Pincus, eds, *Development Policy in the Twenty-First Century: Beyond the Post-Washington Consensus* (London: Routledge).

Green, Andy (1997), *Education, Globalization and the National State* (London: Macmillan).

Heward, Christine (1997), 'The Women of Husseinabad and the Men in Washington: The Rhetoric and Reality of "Educating the Girl Child"', paper presented at the Oxford Conference on Education and Development, Oxford.

Heyneman, Stephen (2003), 'The History and Problems in the Making of Education Policy at the World Bank 1960–2000', *International Journal of Educational Development*, 23 (3): 315–37.

Ilon, Lynne (1996), 'The Changing Role of the World Bank: Education Policy as Global Welfare', *Policy and Politics*, 24 (4): 413–24.

Jeffrey, R. and A. Basu (1996), *Girls' Schooling, Women's Autonomy and Fertility Change in South Asia* (New Delhi: Sage Publications).

Jejeebhoy, S. (1995), *Women's Education, Autonomy and Reproductive Behaviour: Experience from Developing Countries* (Oxford: Oxford University Press).

Jimenez, Emmanuel (1986), 'The Public Subsidization of Education and Health in Developing Countries: A Review of Equity and Efficiency', *World Bank Research Observer*, 1 (1): 110–29.

—— (1987), *Pricing Policy in the Social Sectors: Cost Recovery for Education and Health in Developing Countries* (Baltimore: Johns Hopkins University Press).

Jones, Phillip (1997), 'On World Bank Education Financing', *Comparative Education*, 33 (1): 117–29.

—— (1992), *World Bank Financing of Education, Lending, Learning and Development* (London: Routledge).

Kapur, Devesh, John P. Lewis and Richard Webb (1997a), *The World Bank: Its First Half-Century, Volume 1: History* (Washington DC: Brookings Institution).

Kingdon, Geeta (1998), 'Does the Labour Market Explain Lower Female Schooling in India?', *Journal of Development Studies*, 35 (1): 39–65.

Klees, Stephen (2002), 'World Bank Education Policy: New Rhetoric, Old Ideology', *International Journal of Educational Development*, 22 (5): 451–74.

Knodel, John and Gavin Jones (1996), 'Post-Cairo Population Policy: Does Promoting Girls' Schooling Miss the Mark?', *Population and Development Review*, 22 (4).

Kumar, A. and C. Vlassoff (1997), 'Gender Relations and Education of Girls in Two Indian Communities: Implications for Decisions about Childbearing', *Reproductive Health Matters*, 10: 139–50.

Lauglo, Jon (1996), 'Banking on Education and the Uses of Research: A Critique of World Bank Priorities and Strategies for Education', *International Journal of Educational Development*, 16 (3): 221–33.

Longwe, Sarah (1998), 'Education for Women's Empowerment or Schooling for Women's Subordination?', *Gender and Development*, 6 (2): 19–26.

McMahon, W. (1998), 'Education and Growth in East Asia', *Economics of Education Review*, 17 (2): 159–72.

Mingat, Alain, and Jee-Peng Tan (1986), 'Expanding Education through User Charges: What Can Be Achieved in Malawi and other LDCs?', *Economics of Education Review*, 5 (3): 273–86.

Mundy, Karen (1998), 'Educational Multilateralism and World (Dis)Order', *Comparative Education Review*, 42 (4): 448–78.

—— (2002), 'Retrospect and Prospect: Education in a Reforming World Bank', *International of Journal Educational Development*, 22 (5), 483–508.

Patrinos, Harry (1999), 'Market Forces in Education', processed, World Bank, Washington DC.

—— (2000), 'Global Education Market', http//www.worldbank.org/edinvest.

Patrinos, Harry and George Psacharopoulos (2002), 'Returns to Investment in Education: A Further Update', World Bank Policy Research Working Paper 2881, World Bank, Washington DC.

Psacharopoulos, George (1973), *Returns to Education: An International Comparison* (Amsterdam: Elsevier).

—— (1981a), 'The World Bank in the World of Education: Some Policy Changes and Some Remnants', *Comparative Education*, 17 (2): 141–45.

—— (1981b), 'Returns to Education: An Updated International Comparison', *Comparative Education*, 17 (3): 321–41.

—— (1985), 'Returns to Education: A Further International Update and Implications', *Journal of Human Resources*, 20 (4), 583–604.

—— (1994), 'Returns to Investment in Education: A Global Update', *World Development*, 22 (9): 1325–43.

—— (1996), 'Designing Educational Policy: A Mini-Primer on Values, Theories and Tools', *International Journal of Educational Development*, 16 (3): 277–79.

Psacharopoulos, George, Jee-Peng Tan and Emmanuel Jimenez (1986), *Financing Education in Developing Countries* (Washington DC: World Bank).

Psacharopoulos, George and Maureen Woodhall (1985), *Education for Development: An Analysis of Investment Choices* (Oxford: Oxford University Press).

Puiggros, Adrianna (1997), 'World Bank Education Policy: Market Liberalism meets Ideological Conservatism', *International Journal of Health Services*, 27 (2): 217–26.

Rose, Pauline, (2003a), 'Community Participation in School Policy and Practice in Malawi: Balancing Local Knowledge, National Policies and International Agency Priorities', *Compare*, 33 (1): 47–64.

—— (2003b), 'From the Washington to the Post-Washington Consensus: The Influence of International Agendas on Education Policy and Practice in Malawi', *Globalization, Education and Societies*, 1 (1): 67–86.

Samoff, Joel (1996), 'Which Priorities and Strategies for Education?', *International Journal of Educational Development*, 16 (3): 249–71.

Sayed, Yusuf (1999), 'Discourses of the Policy of Educational Decentralization in South Africa since 1994: An Examination of the South Africa Schools Act', *Compare*, 29 (2): 141–52.

Schultz, T.P. (1995), *Investment in Women's Human Capital* (Chicago: University of Chicago Press).

Schultz, T.W. (1960), 'Capital Formation in Education', *Journal of Political Economy*, 68 (6):

571–83; reproduced in T.W. Schultz (1993), *Investing in People: The Economics of Population Quality* (Berkeley: University of California Press).

—— (1961), 'Investment in Human Capital', *American Economic Review*, 51 (1): 1–17.

Stewart, Frances (1994), 'Education and Adjustment: The Experience of the 1980s and Lessons for the 1990s', in Renee Prendergast and Frances Stewart, eds, *Market Forces and World Development* (London: Macmillan).

Stiglitz, Joseph E. (1996), 'Some Lessons from the East Asian Miracle', *World Bank Research Observer*, 11 (2): 151–77.

—— (1997), 'An Agenda for Development for the Twenty-First Century', Ninth Annual Bank Conference on Development Economics, World Bank, Washington DC.

—— (1998a), 'More Instruments and Broader Goals: Moving towards the Post-Washington Consensus', The 1998 WIDER Annual Lecture, WIDER, Helsinki.

—— (1998b), 'Towards a New Paradigm for Development: Strategies, Policies and Processes', The 1998 Prebisch Lecture, UNCTAD, Geneva.

Stromquist, Nelly (1994), 'Gender and Basic Education in International Development Cooperation', UNICEF Staff Working Papers 13, UNICEF, New York.

—— (1998), 'Agents in Women's Education: Some Trends in the African Context', in Marianne Bloch, Josephine Beoku-Betts and Robert Tabachnik, eds, *Women and Education in Sub-Saharan Africa: Power, Opportunities and Constraints* (Colorado: Lynne Rienner Publisher).

Summers, Lawrence (1994), 'Investing in All the People: Educating Women in Developing Countries', EDI Seminar Paper 45, World Bank, Washington DC.

Swainson, Nicola (1998), 'Background Paper on Gender and Education', processed, Oxfam.

Thobani, Mateen (1984), 'Charging User Fees for Social Services: Education in Malawi', *Comparative Education Review*, 28 (3): 402–23.

UNESCO (2003), *Education for All: The Leap to Equality* (Paris: UNESCO).

Williamson, John (1997), 'The Washington Consensus Revisited', in Louis Emmerij, ed., *Economic and Social Development into the XXI Century* (Baltimore: Johns Hopkins University Press).

Woodhall, Maureen (1987), 'Human Capital Concepts', in George Psacharopoulos, ed., *Economics of Education: Research and Studies* (Oxford: Pergamon Press); reprinted in A.H. Halsey *et.al.*, eds (1997), *Education: Culture, Economy and Society* (Oxford: Oxford University Press).

—— (1994), 'The Effects of Austerity and Adjustment on the Allocation and Use of Resources: A Comparative Analysis of Five Case Studies', in Joel Samoff, ed., *Coping with Crisis, Austerity, Adjustment and Human Resources* (London: Cassell).

World Bank (1995), *Priorities and Strategies for Education: A World Bank Review* (Washington DC: World Bank).

—— (1999a), *World Development Report: Knowledge for Development* (Washington DC: World Bank).

—— (1999b), *Education Sector Strategy* (Washington DC: World Bank).

—— (1999c), *A Chance to Learn: Knowledge and Finance for Education in Africa* (Washington DC: World Bank).

—— (2000), *Higher Education in Developing Countries: Peril and Promise* (Washington DC: World Bank).

WTO (1998), 'Education Services', Background Note by the Secretariat, S/C/W/49, 23 September, WTO, Geneva.

—— (2001), *GATS – Fact and Fiction* (Geneva: WTO).

Social Capital

John Harriss

Social capital – referring to resources inherent in social relationships that, for those who are able to access them, enhance the possible outcomes of their actions (after Lin 2001) – is an idea that has a long history in the social sciences. It has been mentioned from time to time in a metaphorical sort of a way by several scholars, and was then put forward in a more rigorous and considered manner by Glenn Loury in the 1970s, in work that was concerned with explaining racial income differences in the United States (1977), and a little later, each in a different manner by Pierre Bourdieu (1980, 1986) and then by James Coleman (1988, 1990). But the astonishing explosion of its use and influence over the last decade has been due, unquestionably, to the work of the political scientist Robert Putnam from Harvard University. His book, written with Roberto Leonardi and Rafaella Nanetti, on regional government in Italy, entitled *Making Democracy Work: Civic Traditions in Modern Italy* (1993a), was described at the time in a review in *The Economist* as the most important work of social science since Pareto and Max Weber. The tidal wave of interest in social capital was probably stimulated as much, however, by the articles that Putnam published at about the same time (1993b, 1995) on the decline of social capital in the United States, summed up in the epigrammatic title of one of them, 'Bowling Alone' – which reappeared as the title of a book, sub-titled 'The Collapse and Revival of American Community', in 2000.

In regard to his home country, Putnam's ideas had the great merit of appealing to politicians and thinkers of both right and (in so far as the category has application in the United States) 'left'. These ideas both tapped into and encouraged a current of thinking about the significance of variations in culture and social organization in different societies for economic outcomes, and they have also proven a capacious peg on which it has been possible to hang a great range of interests and of subject matter. And, as we now know from an account given by several of the leading proponents of how the idea of social capital was taken up in the World Bank, Putnam's personal influence as an advisor to both Michael Bruno, then chief economist and senior vice president of Development Economics, and Ismail Serageldin, vice president of Environmentally Sustainable Development, was very significant (see Bebbington, Guggenheim, Olson and Woolcock 2004). By 1997, the concept of social capital was described in one publication from Serageldin's department as 'the missing link in development' (Grootaert 1997; see also Harriss and de Renzio 1997). It has, since then, become *the* concept *par excellence* of the new development economics in so far as it seeks to address the non-economic.

Putnam at first defined social capital as 'trust, norms and networks that can improve the efficiency of society by facilitating coordinated actions'. Later he clarified this definition by arguing that it is in social networks, especially those built up through people's participation in horizontal, voluntary associations, that a sense of mutual obligation is established amongst them, and norms of reciprocity are developed. As he says in *Bowling Alone*, 'associations and less formal networks of civic engagement instil in their members habits of cooperation and public-spiritedness' (Putnam 2000: 338). This experience, and the habits of thought to which it gives rise, make for generalized reciprocity or widespread trust running through a society, even amongst strangers. This kind of 'social capital' is therefore a characteristic of whole societies.

Putnam's is a rather bolder statement than appears in the work of the scholar who seems most to have influenced his thinking – James Coleman, the sociological rational choice theorist. Coleman suggests that social capital 'inheres in the structure of relations between persons and among persons', and that it facilitates actions of the persons who are connected by 'the structure of relations'. Using a number of examples – like that of traders in a Cairo market who share information about customers – he shows how the reciprocity and trust that may be an aspect of social relationships are of value to people because they help to reduce many of the costs of transacting, through communication of information and the kinds of insurance that are created in social networks (in which people recognize some obligations to help each other).

Lin has subsequently elaborated upon these arguments, suggesting that, in addition to information, networks of social relationships may supply certification (or credentials) for individuals, which is of value to them in economic or other transactions; they may enable them to exert influence; and they can provide what he refers to as 'reinforcement', meaning 'being assured of and recognized for one's worthiness as an individual and a member of a social group . . . emotional support (and) also public acknowledgement of one's claim to certain resources' (Lin 2001: 20). In these accounts social capital is an asset of individual social actors, rather than an attribute of society as a whole, though it is recognized that there may be positive social externalities arising from some social networks; and social capital is assumed usually to be an unintended outcome of social relations. Putnam goes beyond these positions when he argues that 'networks of civic engagement' give rise to *generalized* reciprocity, or generalized trust.

In view of the influence of Putnam's ideas, I shall first provide a critical consideration of them (following mainly from Tarrow's outstanding critique of Putnam's Italian book, 1996; see also Levi 1996, Fine 2001, Harriss 2001 and

Szreter 2002 – on *Bowling Alone*). I will then discuss the earlier formulations of
the concept by Bourdieu, which in fact address the limitations of Putnam's
approach and lead to different conclusions. I illustrate these arguments in considering the uses of the idea in international development. The chapter concludes
with an assessment of the status and analytical value of the concept of social
capital.

'Civic Engagement' in Italy and America

Putnam sought to demonstrate statistically in his research on regional
governments in Italy that variations in *both* government performance (which is
what his book is essentially concerned with, rather than the 'democracy' of its
title) and levels of economic development in different regions of Italy are most
strongly explained by a factor that he calls at first 'civic involvement' or 'civic
engagement', and only later, in a concluding chapter, where it appears almost as
an afterthought, 'social capital'. Civic involvement is measured by an index that
combines evidence on political participation, on newspaper readership and on
the density of membership in voluntary associations of diverse kinds – most
famously, choirs, football clubs and bird-watching societies.

There is a confessed circularity in the argument: the experience of association gives rise to habits of thought that promote association and cooperation.
Following from this construction, there has been a great deal of emphasis in
development practice on 'horizontal, voluntary associations' that are more readily
observed and counted than 'trust, norms and networks'; and the way in which the
concept of social capital has been sought to be operationalized has commonly
been through interventions to encourage the formation of voluntary associations.[1]
The idea has thus come to be used almost interchangeably (as Mike Edwards has
told us from his experience in the World Bank) with the idea of 'civil society' as
the sphere of voluntary association between the state, on the one hand, and
ascriptive groups such as families or castes, on the other.

On the basis of Putnam's statistics it is concluded that the Italian south is
locked into 'underdevelopment' not because of structural conditions (such as
those of land tenure or the history of its relations with power centres in the north
of the country) but because of its relative lack of social capital. Prosperous
regions in Italy had abundant civic organization and poor regions did not,
because the prevalence of hierarchical, vertical social relations within them has
tended to preclude such organization. These differences are shown to have deep
historical roots, going back to the formation in the Middle Ages of city republics
in north-central Italy (characterized by high civic engagement) and to the establishment of a feudal kingdom in the south (low civic engagement). Without much
civic organization the poor lacked social capital, which, in turn, undermined
political and economic development. Therefore, government efforts should be
directed at facilitating the development of self-help through civic organization in
the poor regions. This is the message that has been picked up by developers.
'Civic organization' or 'the development of civil society' seems to be a remark-

ably potent factor – 'the missing link' indeed. The possibility that some redistribution of resources in a region like the Italian Mezzogiorno might have a significant part to play, *both* in facilitating local organization *and* in assisting political and economic development, is studiously ignored.

There are so many problems with Putnam's method (for example, 'civic community' as defined by Putnam's index does not explain variations *within* either north or south, which it should do if it has the explanatory power that is claimed for it), with his theory and with his history that it is surprising the book should have been so influential. The important criticisms are as follows more.

1. He ignores contrary historical evidence, both that showing the vitality of civic organizations in the Italian south over a long period and how the south was in fact systematically 'underdeveloped' by the north in the nineteenth century. He ignores, too, evidence demonstrating a strong connection between the development of progressive left-wing politics in north-central Italy and the elements that make up the index of civic involvement. Putnam himself notes what is for him a rather odd correlation between social capital and support for the Communist Party (PCI), never taking account of the fact that the PCI encouraged precisely those activities that are captured in his measure of civic involvement. In other words, there is an alternative historical explanation for Putnam's own observations: one that shows how politics and the actions of governments drive developments in civil society, rather than the reverse.

2. There is a logical flaw in the argument that the experience of cooperating with others in local associations aggregates up into society-wide generalized trust. It is readily understandable how knowledge of others that is built up through social networks may give rise to cooperation and to trust. But how does personalized trust built through networks give rise to generalized trust? There is evidence, for instance, from research on business organization in India, that the strength of the 'specific trust' that is generated in family and caste groups constrains the development of generalized reciprocity and trusting behaviour (Harriss 2003; and see Platteau 1994 for a more general argument on these lines). Why should we trust strangers from outside our personal networks of social relationships? Putnam's argument, quoted earlier, that generalized trust is built up from the experience of 'networks of civic engagement', is at best a weak one (see Levi 1996).

Another answer to this question, though not one that is entertained by Putnam, except in passing in *Making Democracy Work*, is that it is when there is a framework of institutions, notably laws, in which we have confidence – and in the implementation of which we also have confidence. As Szreter (2002: 585) has argued, 'The state plays a vital role in sanctioning the ground rules for respect [the prior condition for the establishment of trust, he argues] among citizens.' This answer to the question of the sources of generalized trust in a society places the causal weight on the sphere of government, and hence of politics, instead of within civil society.

A further possible answer to the question of how trust is built up outside personal social networks is that it can derive from ideological commitment, such as may be established by religion or in mass political organizations. People are ready to trust each other and to practise generalized reciprocity because of shared beliefs. But Putnam is always reluctant to recognize any role for ideology, or the possibility that the significance of membership in a political or a religious association is substantially different from that of membership in choirs or sports clubs. He seems to believe, for instance, that people are recruited into social movements on the basis of friendship ties and social networks, rather than because of ideological commitment. This is one of the aspects of his work that has recommended it so much to choice-theoretic economists, operating as they do with a very simple construction of human beings (as 'economic man') in which people are represented as *responding* to the external world but not as *interpreting* it. Such mainstream economists seek to subsume the complexity of the idea of trust under decision-making and exchange theories (see Dasgupta 1988).[2]

3. Following from the last points, it is far from clear that the social capital that accrues to individuals by virtue of their participation in particular social networks neatly aggregates up into a societal total, in the way which Putnam suggests. Indeed, to the contrary, 'my social capital', generated through my participation in particular social networks may be associated with 'your social exclusion'. There is a 'dark side' to social capital, both because of such social exclusion and because social capital may be an important characteristic of frankly anti-social organizations – such, paradigmatically, as the mafia. There *may* be socially positive externalities from the social capital that is built up in particular social networks (from that of a parent–teacher association, perhaps) but, equally, there may *not* be.

Putnam's work on America, which uses the idea of people now 'bowling alone' instead of taking part in bowling teams, as a metaphor for the decline of associational life (*aka* social capital) and of community, suffers from similar limitations. In the first place, it is not clear that associational life really has declined. There is certainly evidence of the relative decline of a large number of older organizations that have been dominantly or exclusively male, white and middle class, or of organizations of women as housewives; but there is also evidence of the rise of newer, less exclusive organizations, and of an increase in 'volunteering' in America. Secondly, Putnam's analysis demonstrates a strong (negative) spatial correlation between social capital as he defines it and levels of social inequality. It also appears that the decline of social capital, latterly, coincides with increasing inequality in American society. But the possibility that the phenomena which Putnam associates with relative strength of social capital might be explained as well, or more effectively, in relation to inequality, does not enter into the analysis. He prefers the argument that the decline of social capital in America has to do, notably, with the impact of television-watching upon everyday sociality, and his prescriptions include an injunction that Americans should spend less time watching TV. Finally, just as there is an alternative historiography for Italy to that which Putnam elaborates, so there is for America. Theda

Skocpol has shown how the rise of civic associations in the United States has been facilitated by institutions established by government (like the US Postal Service), and has been associated with periods of national crisis (like the Civil War, World War I, the New Deal and then World War II). She argues that 'Putnam is wrong to assume, as he often seems to, that social capital is something that rises or declines in a realm apart from politics and government' (quoted from Fiorina and Skocpol 1999).

In both his Italian work and in that on America, therefore, Putnam's analysis is society-centric, proposing that qualities of politics and of the state follow from features of social relationships – rather than allowing for the possibility of the opposite direction of causality or of relations of mutual determination. As Szreter (2002) has also argued, Putnam systematically downplays the role of the state, even in the examples that he gives of successful community development. But this feature of his analysis helps to account for the way in which it has been taken up so extensively in public policy in both rich and poor countries, and by influential development agencies – most notably, the World Bank – because it fits so well with the neoliberal agenda of sidelining the role of the state. It resonates with antipathy towards trade unions and the pervasive disillusionment with political parties, and implicit and explicit hostility to those of the left in particular; and it chimes perfectly with ideas about the improvement of governance by means of 'participation' that 'empowers' people, and may be facilitated and encouraged through decentralization and through the development of civil society (usually including, most notably, non-governmental organizations). It is rhetorical ideology, in other words, serving either to promote or to veil intensification of neoliberal policies. The idea of social capital is a powerful part of a depoliticizing discourse (that is, in fact, profoundly political: see Harriss 2001).

From 'Civic Engagement' to 'Embedded Autonomy' and 'Linking Capital'

In his work on America, Putnam implicitly acknowledges some of the criticism of his initial explorations of the idea of social capital – at least the idea that it might have a 'dark side' – when he follows Gittell and Vidal (1998) in distinguishing between 'bonding' and 'bridging' capital. The former refers to social networks that build upon and reinforce a sense of shared identity – social capital that binds the members of a self-conscious group, therefore, or 'sociological superglue', as Putnam calls it figuratively. The latter refers, on the other hand, to networks of relationships that connect people from different social groups, where shared identity is not the organizing principle. Putnam's own political project for America – in which he aims to 'reconnect' American citizens with each other and with democratic politics – emphasizes this sort of social capital, that brings people from different social backgrounds together. It is, he says, in another memorable metaphor, a kind of 'sociological WD–40'.[3]

The distinction between closed social networks and open networks, which is another way of conceptualizing that between 'bonding' and 'bridging capital', is certainly significant, and it has been built upon by some development theo-rists. Both are necessary for development, they argue. The idea has been put most influentially by Peter Evans (1995) through the (apparently oxymoronic) notion of 'embedded autonomy'. Evans found in empirical research on industrial policy in South Korea, India and Brazil, that the more successful case (that of Korea) involved the combination of the 'relative autonomy' of the bureaucrats concerned with devising and implementing the policy (they are bound together in a closed network of relationships, in other words, and are fairly well insulated from the influence of particular interest groups), with their also being 'embed-ded' in policy networks with industrialists and technologists. That is, they were also engaged in open social networks (the basis of 'bridging capital') through which they secured information and entered into dialogue with other significant policy actors. Evans found that part of the problem of industrial policy in India, in comparison with South Korea, was that while the senior bureaucrats con-cerned enjoyed significant autonomy in relation to pressure from particular inter-ests, they were also not sufficiently involved in policy networks with industry actors.

Somewhat later, Evans argued that developmentally positive results can follow from what he described as 'synergy' across the public–private divide, between state agencies and communities or groups of people as citizens. 'Social capital', he suggests, 'inheres not just in civil society, but in an enduring set of relationships that span the public–private divide' (1996: 1122). He, and several co-researchers, show that the implications of the primary social ties and local social networks that were sought to be elevated into 'the missing link' in develop-ment, depend upon the wider socio-political context. Michael Woolcock (1998) then developed Evans's ideas into a more general statement about the relation-ships amongst citizens and their associations, and with the state and other 'exter-nal' agencies, in which he argues that in order to optimize the prospects for sustained and equitable development, it is necessary that there should be a good balance between autonomy, or 'bonding capital', and embeddedness, or 'bridg-ing capital'. People in poor neighbourhoods, for example, may well have lots of bonding capital, which provides them with some minimum insurance against the hazards they confront. But their prospects for development are likely to be much greater if they also have bridging capital in the form of connections with other social groups.

Woolcock (2000) has subsequently extended his analysis by adding a new concept, that of 'linking capital', or 'vertical' as opposed to 'horizontal' capital. This refers to social connections between the relatively weak (like those of poor neighbourhoods, just referred to) and relatively powerful people 'in posi-tions of influence in formal organizations (banks, agricultural extension offices, the police)'.[4] The idea of 'linking capital' is said to have been developed in *response* to the recognition that 'A theory of social capital that focuses only on relations within [bonding] and between [bridging] communities opens itself to the criticism that it ignores power.'

Yet, the response, while recognizing the exclusion of poorer people 'by overt discrimination or lack of resources from the places where major decisions relating to their welfare are made', is a suggestion that accepts existing differences of wealth and power. It is certainly possible that the kind of linking between unequal agents to which Woolcock refers can have a positive, empowering character *if* 'those involved are endeavouring to achieve a mutually agreed, beneficial goal . . . on the basis of mutual respect, trust, and equality of status, despite the manifest inequalities in their respective positions' (Szreter 2002: 579). This seems to have occurred in the 'islands of sustainable development' that Bebbington (1997) has identified and analysed, in different parts of the Andes. But there is also a wealth of evidence to show how social connections between particular groups of poorer people and, say, the police (but not only the police) may contribute to the reproduction of oppression and of poverty. The protagonists of this idea seem to overlook or to downplay certain of the arguments of *Making Democracy Work*. In describing social relations in the Italian south, Putnam emphasizes the importance of patron–client relations, which link some poor people with those in positions of power and influence. These are relations that are seen, rightly, as serving to reinforce existing power relations and, therefore, as militating against 'civic engagement' and all that is held to follow from it.

There could hardly be a more vivid demonstration of the ways in which the language of social capital is depoliticizing, than that which appears in the passages just quoted, taken from the World Bank's *World Development Report 2000–2001*. Existing power structures are taken as given, and the politics that are likely to be involved in creating circumstances in which social actors in unequal positions achieve 'mutual respect, trust, and equality of status' are not addressed – even though, as Szreter (2002: 581) argues, 'The possibility of respectful linking social capital is the most difficult and highly contingent form of social capital. It clearly refers to a relationship that is not easy to achieve.' The possibility that through political organization and mass mobilization poorer people might struggle against 'exclusion' and 'lack of resources', and so bring about change in the distribution of power and resources, or that through these means they may succeed in realizing 'respectful linking capital', does not enter into consideration.

Bringing Power Back In

The foregoing discussion of the arguments about social capital that have been most influential, certainly in regard to international development, has shown how the idea (notably as it has been elaborated by Putnam) systematically downplays the role of the state and of political agency, and how analysis of the role of social capital in different contexts has ignored alternative historiographies, showing up precisely the centrality of the state and of politics, including the contribution of political parties. This idea of social capital takes no account of power, or of ideology, but it fits well with contemporary liberalism, and with policy discourses following from it that seek to limit the role of the state and celebrate the virtues of 'community' when the 'free' market is deemed to be insufficient. It is not surprising, therefore, that neither Putnam nor those who have been influenced by his conceptualization of social capital make much – if any – reference to the formulation of the idea by Pierre Bourdieu, showing how social capital is an aspect of, and must be understood in the context of, the exercise and reproduction of power.[5]

Bourdieu's central interest was in the ways in which social classes are reproduced, especially through the construction of meanings. In the course of his investigations he came up with the idea that 'connections' play a part in the reproduction of classes, and he pointed out that investment, for example, in membership in a prestigious club builds a sort of social capital that may be converted into economic capital. The 'possession' of particular durable social relationships, in other words, may provide for differential access to resources. In this view, social capital is certainly not an attribute of 'society' as a whole but it is an aspect of the differentiation of classes. Social capital is understood as an instrument of power.[6] Bourdieu (1993: 32–33) says of 'social capital' that:

> One can give an intuitive idea of it by saying that it is what ordinary language calls 'connections' . . . by constructing this concept one acquires the means of analysing the logic whereby this particular kind of capital is accumulated, transmitted and reproduced, the means of understanding how it turns into economic capital and, conversely, what work is required to convert economic capital into social capital, the means of grasping the function of institutions such as clubs or, quite simply, the family, the main site of accumulation and transmission of that kind of capital.

Bourdieu has a rather chaotic conception of 'capital' that leans in some ways towards the conventional view of it as 'stuff used to produce things', or as 'assets', but also holds that it comes in different forms. He is especially concerned with 'cultural capital' – referring to socially constructed qualifications of one sort or another, to which rank is attached – and with 'symbolic capital', which refers to prestige or honour. Social capital (the 'possession' of particular, durable social relationships), for Bourdieu, is intimately linked to these forms of capital that enter significantly into the formation and reproduction of class relationships. Cultural/symbolic/social capital is, quite evidently, 'socially and historically limited to the circumstances that create them . . . they are contextual and constructed'. Thus, while his concept of social capital as 'connections' seems to put him in sympathy with 'the new economic sociology' and its emphasis on social networks, for Bourdieu it is not enough to establish the existence of a network, but essential also to examine its cultural/ideological content and context. As I argued above, a very important aspect of Putnam's reworking of the idea of social capital, on the other hand, is that content and context are stripped out. Bourdieu's concept is not one that recommends itself to most of the World Bank specialists who have adopted it so enthusiastically.[7] The concept that has proven attractive to them – as I pointed out earlier, with reference to ideas about trust – is not of phenomena that are ideologically or contextually and therefore historically dependent but, rather, of phenomena that are both conditions and outcomes of rational calculation by individuals. 'Social capital can only reign supreme by excising the cultural, the symbolic – and Bourdieu' (Fine 2001: 17).[8]

'Social Capital' Put to Work in Development Practice: A Story of Contradictions

The importance of the context of power, and of the content of social relationships, is brought out in one World Bank study that leads to conclusions which are quite sharply critical of the Putnam view – and the basis for so many policy recommendations – that social capital lies especially in 'horizontal, voluntary associations'. The study, *Exploring the Concept of Social Capital and its Relevance for Community-Based Development: The Case of Coal-Mining Areas in Orissa, India*, is by Enrique Pantoja of the South Asian Infrastructure Unit of the World Bank.[9] At the outset he pays due respect to Bank social capitalizing when he says that 'The potential contribution of social capital, or in simple terms civic engagement and social connectedness to development appears to be immense'; but then he goes on almost immediately to note that 'The celebratory tone surrounding the notion of social capital must be dealt with cautiously, and the concept investigated rigorously', not least because there is a lot of uncertainty about its meaning. The significance of social capital, he notes, is supposed to be that it facilitates access to other resources (such as basic services) that are, in turn, instrumental in bringing about poverty alleviation. This is the main reason for attempting to support and promote it, and why it is held to be such 'an important new dimension in community development'. But what about access to social capital resources themselves, Pantoja wonders, suggesting that 'under scarcity conditions . . . it (may) also become an integral part of the structures of constraint created by gender, class, ethnicity' (the exclusion of some others that is associated with bonding capital). The relevance of social capital, then, 'cannot be fully assessed unless one considers the power relations that mediate social interaction'.

The study is based on research in a number of villages in two somewhat contrasted coal-mining areas in Orissa, and many of Pantoja's observations are familiar, from earlier Indian village ethnographies. There is a lot of 'social capital' about in the Orissa villages he studied, in the sense that there are strong horizontal networks amongst people – but they are fragmented on caste lines: 'mutual trust exists in abundance, but it is highly fragmented, as a mechanism of inclusion/exclusion [essentially those principles on which the differentiation of castes rests] tends to operate very strongly among residents of the study areas to create closed groups . . . there might actually be an oversupply of certain forms of social capital [he is referring to what might now be called 'bonding capital'] (while there are no) large, continuous and interlocking networks of support [or 'bridging capital']'. The interventions of Coal India Limited (CIL) have tended to accentuate and exploit divisions amongst people in local communities.

Unsurprisingly, in these circumstances in which residential 'communities' are cross-cut by such differences of identity and of power, what associational life there is (outside gender, caste and such class-based groups as there are) reflects the existing social structure: 'the decision-making process is usually dominated by the most powerful members, with the exception perhaps of the youth clubs'. The community development programmes that CIL is now undertaking involve the establishment of 'village working groups' which are supposed to ensure participation and build a sense of ownership of the assets that are provided amongst beneficiaries. 'These working groups are intended to have a village-wide membership, representative of all castes and tribal population, and to be concerned with the development needs of all the habitations within the boundaries of the (project) villages. . . . The village working groups, however, have tended to reproduce the existing social structure and power relations.' Pantoja points out that any attempt at 'building' social capital in a context like that of the coal-mining villages of Orissa has to contend with the problem of establishing cooperation amongst very unequal partners (recognized in the discussion of 'linking capital', above, as being particularly difficult); and also that the formation of ('bridging') social capital involving articulations between groups – in a union, for example – or across villages, may well be opposed by CIL because of its potential for triggering collective action liable to interfere with the company's interests.

Pantoja argues finally – like some of those who studied the community development programmes of the 1950s – that

> the standard approach to community development has been based, at least in the Indian context, on unrealistic notions of the nature of community in the villages and of the possibilities and democratic content of collective action . . . there are three critical issues missing from these assumptions: (a) social capital is not inherently beneficial to all members of the community; (b) horizontal forms of social capital are important, but without vertical articulations [that 'linking social capital' which is recognized as being 'the most difficult and highly contingent form of social capital': see above] the impact of community development efforts will be very constrained; and (c) external agents can help in facilitating the creation of social capital, but their presence can create dependency . . . (and). . . sustainability of (such) induced social capital may be low.

The standard approach has been lacking because it has been assumed that communities are inherently democratic. They are not; *and without 'interventions to democratize community life'* (emphasis added), 'village-wide groups are not effective mechanisms for democratic planning and decision-making'.

Pantoja's 'general discussion' in the conclusion of his report is strikingly at odds with so much that is claimed about social capital by the World Bank (as on its social capital website). His basic points are these: 'Our analysis seems to indicate (that) it would be limiting to approach social capital by focussing exclusively on associational membership and norms of reciprocity and trust and by

assuming that social capital always produces beneficial forms of civic engagement or that more of it is always better'; and 'civic society and its social capital
matter for community development, but in the context of government institutions
and the general institutional framework of society at large'.

Pantoja's study, and his discussion of it, bring out very well the limitations of the idea of social capital established by Robert Putnam, while also showing how and why it has been so attractive to the protagonists of the contemporary
liberal development discourse. The neutral terminology of 'bonding', 'bridging'
and 'linking' erases categories of social analysis such as race, caste, class and
gender that necessarily feature strongly in Pantoja's analysis, and it has the effect
of setting aside the ways in which these 'old' categories cut across so-called
bonding, bridging and linking capital. The new terms share in the contextual
vacuousness of their parent – Putnam's idea of social capital – and similarly
evade the aspects of power and meaning, and the conflicts, attached to social
relations.

Conclusion: Weighing Up 'Social Capital'

The idea of social capital engages with questions about the economic
and political implications of variations in culture and social organization between different societies, that are now recognized as being of great significance
across the social sciences. The argument that there are resources inhering in
social relations is a compelling one; and that there are differences between societies in terms of generalized reciprocity and trust is empirically demonstrable (see
Platteau 1994). But the particular concept of social capital that has been most
influential so far, that of Robert Putnam – who treats it as a synonym for 'civic
involvement', and this as being more or less equivalent to the 'density of voluntary associations' – suffers from serious flaws. It systematically downplays the
significance of state action and of ideas, and hence of politics, assigning causal
primacy to social networks in a way that appears untenable in light of the study
of the history of the particular societies that Putnam himself has studied, or the
analysis presented, for instance, by Peter Evans (1996). It ignores the significance
of the context and content of the relationships in social networks, and thus evades
questions of power. It offers a consensual view of social relationships, downplaying
conflict. Yet, these features are precisely the ones that have made this particular
idea of social capital so attractive in development agencies, both practically
(because they find it difficult to address problems of power and of class relations
directly) and ideologically (in the context of the dominance of neoliberalism and
of hostility to even moderate left politics). They also help to account for the
attractiveness of the idea to some neoclassical economists. Bebbington,
Guggenheim, Olson and Woolcock (2004: 16), in their article on the social capital debates at the World Bank, explain how 'the argument that a discussion of
social capital should be linked to themes in institutional economics (à la [Mancur]
Olson) more than to themes in political economy [as the political scientist Jonathan
Fox had proposed] slowly won the day'. The concept of social capital taken from

Putnam lent itself to treatment especially within information-theoretic economics, and it has provided a neat way for this paradigm to further extend itself across the terrain of sociology and politics, as Ben Fine (2001) has argued. It has also given rise to a lot of rather dubious, positivistic social science. As Fine notes, the manner of much of the work follows lines established earlier by James Coleman, and then by Putnam, and it has by now been replicated many times. A measure of social capital is found (some measure, say, of the density of voluntary associations) and it is then shown to be strongly correlated with an 'output' such as a measure of health. In studies of this kind there may be, but there often is not, an attempt to explain, and less frequently an attempt to test, why the correlation indicates causality. Even careful studies that attempt to measure the effects of social capital are often unsatisfactory because 'social capital' remains a statistical artefact, and the questions of what causes what and by what mechanisms or social processes remain unanswered.

Criticism of the Putnamian idea of social capital is by now well established and acknowledged as 'serious' even by those who have been responsible for encouraging the use of the idea within the World Bank (see Bebbington, Guggenheim, Olson and Woolcock 2004). The recognition that 'building social capital' through trying to set up the likes of 'village organizations' is potentially misplaced and counter-productive – because it ignores power, as Enrique Pantoja shows[10] – may be beginning to creep into development agencies. The question remains, however, as to whether a conceptualization of social capital that is in line with Bourdieu's ideas, and, perhaps, makes use of the distinctions between 'bonding', 'bridging' and 'linking' (as Szreter suggests), is not a valuable contribution to social science. The recognition of the significance of 'connections' in the manner of Bourdieu surely is imperative, and it does provide one way into the analysis of politics and power. Similarly, there is value in ideas about the implications of different types of social networks, *when* these are analysed in terms of their context and content. What the description of 'social capital' adds to such analysis is, however, less apparent. The ideological uses of the term outweigh such analytical value as it has.

Notes

[1] An example is in the East India Rainfed Farming Project that encouraged people in the villages where the project was working to form community development organizations. Such organization was seen as being the key to improved, sustainable livelihood security. In practice, as Kumar and Corbridge (2002) have shown, because membership in the organizations was made a requirement for accessing inputs made available by the project, they have come to be dominated (unsurprisingly) by those who were already relatively wealthy and powerful. It is possible, in this case, that the livelihood security of poorer people has actually suffered as a result of the formation of these associations.

[2] Trusting behaviour involves more than expectations based on information about others; it requires a kind of a leap of faith because of the absence of complete information. See Möllering (2001).

[3] 'WD–40' is an agent used, for example, for loosening tight nuts and bolts.

[4] This quotation and those that follow come from the *World Development Report 2000–2001* (World Bank 2000: 128).

[5] There is a difference of opinion on this point. Ben Fine (2001) argues strongly that the 'balloon' of social capital only went up after the jettisoning of Bourdieu's ideas, although he recognizes a subsequent process of 'bringing Bourdieu', and associated omissions, 'back in', albeit at the expense of the conceptual generality of the idea of social capital (Fine 2004). Nonetheless, Simon Szreter (2002: 616–17) accuses Fine of 'slipperiness' and asserts that there are several scholars, including himself, interested in social capital, who are engaging with Bourdieu's concepts. My own review (2001) of work done in the World Bank – which seems rather studiously to ignore Bourdieu – inclined me to support Ben Fine's view, and some of the work published since Fine wrote his book reflects the 'bringing back in' of 'power, politics and history' (the title of Szreter's paper), partly through reference to Bourdieu's ideas.

[6] Bourdieu's point is made very clearly in work by a group of French sociologists on the big bourgeoisie in France (reported in *Le Monde Diplomatique* in September 2001). The authors describe world cruises as '*les hauts-lieux de gestion du capital social*' ('pinnacles for the formation of social capital'). They note that 'Entering the grande bourgeoisie is accomplished through the accumulation of wealth. But this is not sufficient in itself. It takes time to build up the network of social relations that is the guarantor of social standing.' 'Connections' that count involve status distinctions that may be seen, as Szreter has suggested, as reflecting the existence of 'bonding capital' and the more or less deliberate disavowal of bridging capital.

[7] Michael Woolcock, who does treat Bourdieu's ideas seriously (in Woolcock 1998), may well have found it expedient strategically to 'jettison' them once he got to the Bank. This seems to be the purport of the account of the adoption of social capital thinking in the Bank, of which he is a joint author (see Bebbington, Guggenheim, Olson and Woolcock 2004).

[8] A perspective that draws on Bourdieu's, though set in the frame of social network analysis, is provided by Nan Lin (2001). For him, social capital refers to resources embedded in social relations. But then, accessing these resources depends upon actors' structural positions (within society), their locations in particular social networks and the purposes of their actions. It is immediately evident that the possibilities for many people to access resources are constrained by their social positions (for example, as blacks or dalits or women) and thus that social capital is an aspect of power–class differentiation. Key arguments in his exposition may be summed up in the following propositions: (a) Individuals have differential social resources depending on the extent and the diversity of their social connections, and the other resources of the persons included amongst their social connections. (Critical factors, then, are: (i) the number of persons amongst their connections who are prepared to or obliged to help; (ii) the strength of the relationships involved; and (iii) the resources of those persons). (b) It is possible that certain groups of people develop and more or less maintain social capital (durable social relations) as a collective asset, which enhances the group members' life chances (which is Bourdieu's argument).

[9] All quotations in the text come from Pantoja (1999).

[10] See also Kumar and Corbridge, cited in note 1.

References

Bebbington, Anthony (1997), 'Social Capital and Rural Intensification: Local Organizations and Islands of Sustainability in the Rural Andes', *Geographical Journal*, 163 (2): 189–97.

Bebbington, Anthony, Scott Guggenheim, Elizabeth Olson and Michael Woolcock (2004), 'Exploring Social Capital Debates at the World Bank', *Journal of Development Studies*, 40 (5): 33–64.

Bourdieu, Pierre (1980), 'Le capital sociale: notes provisoires', *Actes de la Recherche en Sciences Sociales*, 31: 2–3

——— (1986), 'The Forms of Capital', in J. Richardson, ed., *Handbook of Theory and Research for the Sociology of Education* (New York: Greenwood Press).

—— (1993), *Sociology in Question* (London: Sage Publications).

Coleman, James S. (1988), 'Social Capital and the Creation of Human Capital', *American Journal of Sociology*, 94, Supplement: S95–S120.

—— (1990), *Foundations of Social Theory* (Cambridge: Harvard University Press).

Dasgupta, Partha (1988), 'Trust as a Commodity', in Diego Gambetta, ed., *Trust: Making and Breaking Co-operative Relations* (Oxford: Blackwell): 49–71.

Evans, Peter B. (1995), *Embedded Autonomy: States and Industrial Transformation* (Princeton: NJ: Princeton University Press).

—— (1996), 'Government Action, Social Capital and Development: Reviewing the Evidence on Synergy', *World Development*, 24 (6): 1119–32.

Fine, Ben (2001), *Social Capital versus Social Theory: Political Economy and Social Science at the Turn of the Millennium* (London: Routledge).

—— (2004), 'Social Capital for Africa?', *Transformation*, 53: 29–52.

Fiorina, Morris P. and Theda Skocpol, eds (1999), *Civic Engagement in American Democracy* (Washington DC: Brookings Institution Press).

Gittell, Ross J. and A. Vidal (1998), *Community Organization: Building Social Capital as a Development Strategy* (London: Sage Publications).

Grootaert, Christiaan (1997), 'Social Capital: "The Missing Link"', in *Expanding the Measure of Wealth: Indicators of Environmentally Sustainable Development* (Washington DC: World Bank).

Harriss, John (2001), *Depoliticizing Development: The World Bank and Social Capital* (Delhi: LeftWord). (Also London: Anthem Press, 2002.)

—— (2003), 'Widening the Radius of Trust: Ethnographic Explorations of Trust and Indian Business', *Journal of the Royal Anthropological Institute*, 9(4): 755–73.

Harriss, John and Paolo de Renzio (1997), '"Missing Link" or Analytically Missing?: The Concept of Social Capital, An Introductory Bibliographic Essay', *Journal of International Development*, 9 (7): 919–37.

Kumar, Sanjay and Stuart Corbridge (2002), 'Programmed to Fail? Development Projects and the Politics of Participation', *Journal of Development Studies*, 39 (2): 73–103.

Levi, Margaret (1996), 'Social and Unsocial Capital: A Review Essay of Robert Putnam's *Making Democracy Work*', *Politics and Society*, 24 (1): 45–55.

Lin, Nan (2001), *Social Capital: A Theory of Social Structure and Action* (Cambridge: Cambridge University Press).

Loury, Glenn (1977), 'A Dynamic Theory of Racial Income Differences', in P. Wallace and A. Le Mund, eds, *Women, Minorities and Employment Discrimination* (Lexington, Massachusetts: Lexington Books).

Möllering, Guido (2001), 'The Nature of Trust: From Georg Simmel to a Theory of Expectation, Interpretation and Suspension', *Sociology*, 35(2): 403–20.

Pantoja, Enrique (1999), 'Exploring the Concept of Social Capital and its Relevance for Community-based Development: The Case of Coal-Mining Areas in Orissa, India', World Bank Social Capital Initiative Working Paper 18, World Bank, Washington DC.

Platteau, Jean-Philippe (1994a), 'Behind the Market Stage Where Real Societies Exist (Part One)', *Journal of Development Studies*, 30 (3): 33–77.

—— (1994b), 'Behind the Market Stage Where Real Societies Exist (Part Two)', *Journal of Development Studies*, 30 (4): 753–817.

Putnam, Robert D (1993a), *Making Democracy Work: Civic Traditions in Modern Italy* (Princeton, NJ: Princeton University Press).

—— (1993b), 'The Prosperous Community: Social Capital and Public Life', *The American Prospect*, 13: 35–42

—— (2000), *Bowling Alone: The Collapse and Revival of American Community* (New York: Simon and Schuster).

Szreter, Simon (2002), 'The State of Social Capital: Bringing Back in Power, Politics and History', *Theory and Society*, 31: 573–621.

Tarrow, Sidney G. (1996), 'Making Social Science Work Across Time and Space: A Critical Reflection on Robert Putnam's *Making Democracy Work*', *American Political Science Review*, 90 (2): 389–97.

Woolcock, Michael (1998), 'Social Capital and Economic Development: Toward a Theoretical Synthesis and a Policy Framework', *Theory and Society*, 27 (2): 151–208.

—— (2000), 'Managing Risks, Shocks and Opportunity in Developing Economies: The Role of Social Capital', in Gustav Ranis, ed., *Dimensions of Development* (New Haven: Yale Center for International and Area Studies).

World Bank (2000), *World Development Report, 2000–2001* (Washington DC: World Bank).

Corruption and Governance

Mushtaq Husain Khan

Corruption and governance have come to the fore in contemporary discussions of reform in developing countries. Many of the problems to which corruption and governance refer are significant and long-standing. Yet, the way in which mainstream economics has analysed them simply provides support for a programme of market-enhancing reforms. These seek to reduce the role of the state to the delivery of a small range of core services that cannot be delivered by the private sector. The mainstream analysis is not only misleading in failing to identify many of the most important determinants of corruption and of apparent governance failures in developing countries. By offering wrong diagnoses and solutions, these mainstream approaches waste time and resources in programmes that are unlikely to provide reductions in corruption and improvements in governance. Even worse, by promoting reforms that lessen the ability of the state to accelerate development, they may paradoxically *reduce* the prospects of substantial and lasting improvements in corruption and other desirable features of 'good governance' such as democracy.

The first section of this chapter outlines the definitions of corruption and governance used in the literature. The second section describes the comparative evidence on corruption and governance that has driven the contemporary interest in these issues as determinants of the prospects of developing countries. The third section outlines the mainstream analysis and its limitations. It argues that the neoclassical analysis of corruption and governance and its policy conclusions is based on a model of market-driven development that is inappropriate for analysing a number of critical problems faced by developing countries in their transitions to more productive societies. The fourth section provides an alternative approach to corruption and governance, drawing on different segments of the heterodox literature on the role of the state during the social transformations that developing countries are going through. It identifies four different types of corruption with very different causes and implications, and with different policy implications. The neoclassical analysis of corruption is at best relevant for understanding and responding to one of these types of corruption, and this is not the most important type of corruption affecting developing countries. The other types of corruption are associated with processes more critical for explaining the success or failure of developing countries, but here neoclassical policy prescriptions actually hinder the construction of more effective developmental policies that are necessary for sustainable reductions in corruption. These conclusions apply to the neoclassical analysis of good governance as well. That analysis is also based on the assumption that the governance tasks of the state should be limited to providing the basic conditions for a market economy to work. It ignores the political and economic transformations that developing countries are going through, and the state capacities necessary for success in this transformation. As with neoclassical anti-corruption policy prescriptions, its good governance policy prescriptions are damaging because they can weaken those state capacities that are vital for the social transformations that developing countries are going through. The fifth and final section summarizes the implications of this analysis for policy in developing countries.

Defining Corruption and Governance

Most economists and social scientists define corruption in a narrow way, and I will follow this definition in addressing the literature and its implications. According to this definition, corruption takes place when public officials (including both bureaucrats and politicians) violate formal rules of conduct in pursuit of their private benefit, whether for wealth, in the form of bribes, or for political advantage (Nye 1967; World Bank 1997). Corruption is therefore defined as an exchange between a private individual (or group) and a public official (or officials), where the public official breaks formal rules of conduct and provides something to the private individual or group that would not otherwise have been received. The benefit that the public official gains is technically illegal because it violates a formal rule of conduct (for the act to be corrupt). But the benefit the private individual receives in exchange may be either a legal entitlement that he would not otherwise have received or an illegal benefit that confers greater advantage than otherwise. The differences between these cases are important and will be discussed further later.

A number of points are noteworthy about this definition. Firstly, corruption is defined in such a way that its analysis does not involve moral judgements about the act. This is an advantage of the definition, since, if corruption is defined as acts that are 'wrong', this would result in different acts being identified as corrupt by different people according to their different moral standards. For instance, a public official who gives a job to a nephew in exchange for maintaining his own political influence over his clan may not be considered as corrupt by someone who thinks that it is a moral duty to promote one's family. But it would be corrupt according to the definition here, as long as formal rules of conduct for public officials in that country rule out such acts. There is still the possibility that there may be differences in legal or formal rules of public conduct across countries, but, in general, in virtually every country, rules of public conduct do not allow the acceptance of bribes, nepotistic allocations or diversions of public resources for economic or political benefit. This makes it easier to identify corruption according to this definition, without engaging in debates about morality. Nevertheless, the problem remains that in everyday usage people do make moral judgements when discussing corruption, and the difference between the everyday sense of corruption and the definition that is commonly used in economic and social analysis needs to be kept in mind.

Secondly, corruption is deliberately defined as a *process*, rather than an *outcome*. If corruption were to be defined to include only acts that have damaging *outcomes* for the public, then, this would rule out cases where a process is corrupt but its overall effects are neutral or even positive. Thus, the definition we use is useful in analysing differences in the effects of corruption across countries. But, once again, in common usage corruption often describes actions by public officials that are against the 'public interest', whether or not any rules of conduct are violated, while actions where rules *are* violated but the 'public' does not suffer (or even benefits) are often not described as corrupt. Once again, the difference between everyday conceptions of corruption and its definition in economics and social analysis needs to be kept in mind.

Finally, the definition of corruption that we follow places public officials at the centre of the analysis. According to this definition, corruption does not take place where public officials are not involved; in this sense, corruption is simply a lens through which to examine the operations of the state. This, too, is somewhat at odds with common usage where corruption can refer to reprehensible behaviour by anyone, including interactions exclusively between private individuals or agents. According to the social science definition, if a private person steals from another, that is *theft*, not *corruption*. However, even in the case of theft corruption may be implicated because the state is the ultimate protector of property rights, and theft may take place with the connivance or even involvement of public officials. Note that using this definition does not mean accepting that corruption is more important than theft, only that the focus of corruption analysis is on the functioning of the state.

Nonetheless, there are important grey areas that we need to keep in mind. If a small shopkeeper gives a job to a relative without following proper procedures or charges a fee for providing the job, these acts would very likely be described as nepotism or extortion rather than corruption in common usage, and here common usage conforms to the economist's definition. But if the chief executive of a large quoted company does the same thing, this would be commonly described as corruption and would very likely be treated as a corrupt act in the literature on corruption. This is because many authors treat private sector executives in important economic positions as having semi-public roles. A more consistent position would be to argue that their activities are regulated by the state, so that theft, extortion or fraud by executives in important private sector positions often involves either a failure of public governance or direct corruption and collusion by public officials. It is important to keep in mind that a definition of corruption is not making a statement about the relative importance of the private and public sectors in explaining economic and social problems but, rather, is a lens through which to analyse the operation of the state. In this sense, heterodox analysis can contribute to the debate while keeping to a definition of corruption that puts the state at the centre of the analysis.

The definition of governance is also deeply connected to the state. Governance is what the state does, but identifying the areas of governance on which to focus is problematic because it requires specific assumptions about what the state is supposed to be doing. The conventional analysis of 'good governance' is explicitly based on a neoclassical analysis of the role of the state in economic development. The assumption in neoclassical analysis, in its neoliberal form, is that all that the state is required to do is to protect stable property rights, achieve low corruption, and restrict itself from expropriation by committing itself to democracy and protection of majority interests. This, in turn, is based on the assumption that the market is sufficient to ensure rapid development, and that as long as the state maintains stable property rights and an environment of low transaction costs and low expropriation risk, the market will work efficiently. This model of the economy and of the role of the state then leads to the conclusion that reducing corruption, improving property rights stability, lowering expropriation risk and deepening democracy are *preconditions* for rapid economic development (Khan 2002a, 2002b).

The Comparative Evidence

Each of the variables in mainstream neoclassical analysis of 'good governance', such as corruption, the stability of property rights, expropriation risk and the depth of democracy, are regularly 'measured' in cross-country surveys that collect subjective judgements of these variables by investors, ordinary citizens or other target groups. These survey-based indices have serious problems that are well known. First, these are subjective indices and so are likely to be biased by local economic performance. For instance, investors or ordinary citizens are likely to report greater property rights stability or lower risk of expropriation and perceive lower corruption if the economy is performing well, rather than if it is stagnating.

Second, these indices are only available for the last couple of decades, and this makes it difficult to assess causality. The problem in assessing causality is that we expect corruption and governance to improve anyway with greater prosperity. As economies become richer, they spend more on law enforcement, they can afford higher salaries for public officials, and, most important, as the capitalist class becomes entrenched and acquires legitimacy, it begins to buy influence through legal processes of lobbying, political contributions and so on, which converts illegal influence-buying in the form of corruption into legal influence-buying of different sorts. As a result, corruption is reduced, even though influence-buying by the rich is not. Therefore, to see if prior reduction of corruption is a precondition for development, data over longer periods are required to determine the *sequence* of changes in corruption, governance and economic development. If low corruption and 'good governance' are preconditions of growth, only those poor countries that *first* reduced corruption or improved on these specific governance indicators would achieve high growth subsequently. If, however, corruption is reduced and 'good governance' is achieved only after growth is achieved for some time, the sequence observed would be reversed. But these different hypotheses about the relationship between corruption, good governance and economic development cannot be tested with data for very short periods.

Despite the weaknesses in these indices, they are widely used in mainstream analysis and, in particular, to support policy prescriptions which suggest that focusing on these variables will help to create the preconditions for an efficient market and, therefore, for rapid development. The empirical evidence is quite strong, keeping in mind the shortcomings in these indices. It shows that, in general, countries that have lower corruption and better scores on property rights stability, expropriation risk, democracy and other 'good governance' characteristics perform better in terms of growth rates and other economic indicators (for instance, Hall and Jones 1999; Kauffman, Kraay and Zoido-Lobatón 1999; Johnson, Kauffman and Zoido-Lobatón 1998; Clague *et al.* 1997; World Bank 1997; Knack and Keefer 1995, 1997; Barro 1996; Mauro 1995). But the problem is that this correlation does not tell us much about causality. In other words, the correlation does not tell us whether some countries perform better because they *first* achieved lower corruption and better governance as defined in the good governance analysis, or whether they have lower corruption and better governance because they developed first.

The standard statistical regression does not answer this question, but a closer look at the data shows that the causality suggested in the neoclassical analysis of corruption and governance is seriously flawed (for an extensive discussion, see Khan 2002a and 2002b). Figure 1 summarizes the data on corruption and governance observed over the last two decades that underpins most of the statistical results apparently supporting the mainstream position. Most developing countries are in group 1, with relatively low growth, and poor governance and corruption indicators. Most advanced countries are in group 3, with moderate growth, and much better governance and corruption indicators. Because most countries are clustered in either group 1 or group 3, the statistical regression relationship shows a positive relationship between better governance and lower corruption, on the one hand, and growth and other economic performance indicators, on the other.

The problem for the conventional view is the existence of a small number of high growth developing countries that were actually growing fast enough to begin to converge to the living standards of the advanced countries. These high growth developing countries are located in group 2 in Figure 1. They had the highest growth rates of all countries, since, by definition, they were catching up with the advanced countries, but their corruption and governance indicators were not distinguishable from the developing country average. This raises a serious question for conventional wisdom. Even with the very limited periods over which there is data, it is possible to argue that a move from group 1 to

FIGURE 1 *Empirical Relationships between Corruption, Governance and Economic Performance*

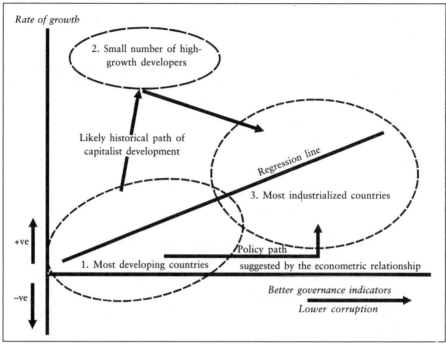

Source: Khan 2002a: Figure 2.

group 3 cannot be achieved by trying to first emulate the governance characteristics of group 3 countries (as neoclassical theory prescribes). This is simply
because it is not possible to find any example of a high-growth developing country that had achieved high growth by first acquiring advanced country governance or corruption characteristics. The only feasible route for sustained reductions
in corruption, and even for achieving some of the 'good governance' characteristics of group 3 countries, is likely to involve first emulating the governance
characteristics of group 2 countries, which may then allow group 1 countries
eventually to catch up with the advanced countries in group 3. The relevant
governance characteristics of group 2 countries that allowed them to grow
rapidly are different from the 'good governance' characteristics of property rights
stability, democracy, low corruption and so on, even though all of the latter may
be desirable goals in their own right. What is important is that achieving these
desirable goals may require first achieving the social transformations that group
2 countries are successfully achieving because of governance characteristics that
neoclassical approaches are not well suited to identifying.

In contrast to the neoclassical analysis of corruption and governance,
heterodox theories provide a very different diagnosis and identify very different
priorities for reform. These theories fit in better with the feasible route to development suggested in Figure 1, of a transition from group 1 to group 3 *via* group
2. The role of the state in heterodox analyses of this transition is significantly

different. The state in successful developing countries is identified as playing a much more important role than simply maintaining property rights stability and providing some key services. The state is recognized as a key set of institutions playing a role in the social transformation of pre-capitalist societies into capitalist ones, in assisting the acquisition of technology and in maintaining political stability (Amsden 1989; Aoki, Kim and Okuno-Fujiwara 1997; Khan and Jomo 2000; Lall and Teubal 1998; Rodrik 1995, 2002; Wade 1990; Woo-Cumings 1999). All of these processes require significant interventions in pre-existing property rights, so that the neoclassical requirements of low corruption and 'good governance' are typically not met in any developing country, regardless of their relative economic performance (Khan 2002a, 2002b). At the same time, there is no reason to be sanguine about property rights instability or corruption in developing countries. In most developing countries, property rights instability and corruption are, indeed, associated with very poor economic performance, and by studying the *types* of corruption and property rights instability that are involved in specific countries, valuable insights can be gained into the processes that are blocking the transition of the country from group 1 to group 2.

The Mainstream Analysis and its Limitations

The weakness of the neoclassical economic analysis of corruption and governance is that it ignores many of the most significant causes and effects of different types of corruption. In the same way, it ignores some of the most important types of governance failure relevant for developing countries and concentrates on an analysis of governance failure (described as failures of 'good governance') that is at best relevant for economies that have already achieved the transition to a developed economy. Misleading use of statistics is then used to find support for these simplistic economic models. In fact, a considerable literature exists on different types of corruption, and their causes and effects (significant contributions to the debate are available in Williams 2000; Williams and Theobald 2000; Heidenheimer and Johnston 2002). This complements the equally substantial literature on the role of the state in economic development, which shows that the role of the state in successful developers has typically gone well beyond the relatively limited tasks of property rights maintenance and service delivery that neoclassical theory suggests.

Here, it will be argued that the mainstream approach to corruption and governance identifies a number of general effects of corruption and some specific governance failures that are potentially damaging in theory, but these effects are not the most important for most developing countries. In contrast, a number of very important damaging effects of corruption as well as many serious types of governance failure are ignored and downplayed. This makes the mainstream analysis both misleading and potentially damaging.

Any corrupt transaction is a type of 'exchange' and, therefore, has two components. First, there is the bribe or the political support that is offered by the private sector individual or firm to the public official, and this has a measurable cost in terms of lost investment or higher costs of business. The cost of this part of the transaction includes the cost of the resources used up in unproductive activities like lobbying, bargaining and other activities that seek to identify and influence the relevant public officials. It also includes the possible social cost implicit in transferring resources (the bribe) from productive users (if the bribe-givers are productive investors) to less productive ones (bureaucrats or politicians). The overall effect of this part of the transaction is therefore very likely to be negative, increasing the costs of doing business and the uncertainty for investors. In general, therefore, the first effect of any corrupt exchange is typically negative since bribe-giving or offering political support usually (though not always) transfers resources (the bribe) from more productive to less productive resource users, and the organization of the transfer or the support can itself be very costly and increase the uncertainty faced by investors.

But giving the bribe or political support to the public official is only one part of the corrupt transaction. The public official offers something in return to the individual or firm offering the bribe or the political support, in the form of an action or decision affecting resource allocation. For instance, the official can allow the person or firm giving a bribe to get access to some resources, or make a decision that favours that individual or firm, and all these decisions also have an economic effect. Thus, corrupt transactions always have a second economic effect, since there is always some public decision affecting resource allocation that would not otherwise have been made. But this effect is not always negative. If the intervention that the public official offers in exchange adds to the productivity of the economy, the effect of this second component of the corrupt transaction is positive, and if it reduces social productivity, this effect is negative. Our judgement of the second effect of corruption depends on an analysis of the types of intervention, whether they are productivity-enhancing or productivity-reducing. That is why any analysis of corruption involves an analysis of the role of the state in economic development. Some interventions by corrupt public officials can clearly have damaging consequences for the economy. Examples would be the creation of monopolies or decisions that allow bribe-givers to corner markets or engage in fraud. In these cases, the second effect of corruption is negative, adding to the first negative effect discussed earlier. But, in other cases, the second effect may be positive and this could, in some cases, outweigh the first effect so that the overall effect of corruption can be positive. Examples would be cases where public officials transfer resources to productive uses or make decisions that raise productivity but charge a bribe for doing so. In these cases, the positive effect of a productivity-enhancing decision may outweigh the negative effect of the cost of organizing the bribe.

For the mainstream neoclassical analysis, corruption is always damaging because the effects of both components of the corrupt transaction are deemed to be negative. The first effect, associated directly with the organization and transfer of the bribe, is always likely to be negative because it increases the cost of doing business. But in the mainstream analysis, the interventions offered to the private sector in exchange (typically in the form of creating private monopolies and transfers) are also judged to be damaging for the overall economy. The two negative effects of corruption then add up to explain why corruption can have serious economic consequences. Mainstream economists recognize that corruption can sometimes allow investors to avoid socially damaging regulations and restrictions, like unnecessary restrictions on imports and exports. But they argue that even in these cases, the best policy would be to remove the unnecessary restrictions directly, rather than hope that corruption would enable the economy to function. The mainstream policy conclusion is, therefore, to fight corruption with a combination of liberalization (to remove these restrictions and interventions), and direct anti-corruption measures. Policies to attack corruption directly include raising bureaucratic salaries (to reduce the incentive to be corrupt), setting up independent anti-corruption agencies with the power to prosecute and punish, and encouraging civil society organizations to act as watchdogs (World Bank 1997, 2000). These policies also form an important part of what has come to be known as the 'good governance' agenda. While this analysis appears to be plausible, it is based on the implicit assumption that there is an underlying competitive market economy that would work ideally in the absence of any state intervention, which only creates opportunities for corruption. This leads to the conclusion that if only these unnecessary interventions and opportunities could be removed, the underlying market would drive faster economic growth and development.

But the historical evidence shows that only relatively advanced capitalist countries have been successful in significantly reducing corruption, and that there are virtually no poor developing countries with low corruption. Why is this so? Moreover, contrary to neoclassical theory, observation of developing countries shows that the mix between public and private sectors, the presence or absence of democracy, and the types of economic policies developing countries adopt have very little effect on the overall extent of corruption. Developing countries that follow policies of low intervention and have active civil society participation in politics tend to have just as much corruption as those that have more interventions or authoritarian political regimes (Treisman 2000; Khan 2002a). Yet, the economic performance of developing countries can vary dramatically. To make sense of this evidence and to come up with better policy responses, a more refined analysis is necessary.

An Alternative Framework: Four Types of Corruption

Implicitly, the neoclassical analysis of corruption focuses on opportunities for corruption created by state interventions that are not themselves necessary for economic development. Examples would be unnecessary red tape and restrictions on private sector activities that serve no useful purpose except to create opportunities for public officials to extract bribes from private citizens seeking to avoid these restrictions. In these cases, not only is the intervention unnecessary, but the corruption imposes additional costs on society.

But not all state activities are of this type and, by making this distinction, some sense can be made of the historical evidence. While bribing and other ways of illegally influencing the state imposes costs on society, the net economic effect of corruption also depends on the type of intervention or subversion of policy that is achieved through the bribe. Many interventions of the state are critical for accelerating development, as heterodox analysis of the state in developing countries has pointed out. In these cases, corruption can have ambiguous effects. If the state can intervene in ways that accelerate development, even if these interventions create opportunities for corruption, as long as the cost of organizing the corruption does not snowball, corruption can coexist with substantial economic dynamism.

On the other hand, if corruption results in useful interventions being subverted, the overall effect of corruption would be unquestionably damaging for the economy. Moreover, in addition to these types of necessary interventions that can potentially be legally regulated, other necessary interventions are more problematic because they cannot be sanctioned and regulated by law. For instance, in developing countries, often there are interventions that *cannot* be legally sanctioned for political reasons, even though they are necessary for maintaining political stability or economic growth. In these cases, too, the economic effects associated with the corruption can be ambiguous, because the benefit of the intervention for growth or political stability can sometimes outweigh

TABLE 1 *A Typology of Corruptions affecting Developing Countries*

	The Required Interventions *Are* Legally Allowed	The Required Interventions are *Not* Legally Allowed
Interventions that *are* required for economic development or political stability	(ii) This type of corruption may be associated with growth or stagnation, depending on how seriously necessary interventions (market regulation, promotion of industries, subsidies for political stabilization) are subverted. Anti-corruption policy should seek to improve implementation and reduce corruption, but not to remove the interventions.	(iii) All such interventions are likely to involve corruption. These types of corruption may be associated with growth or stagnation, depending on the nature and extent of these interventions (political stabilization using off-budget transfers, preferential access to resources for emerging capitalists). Policy should focus on legalizing necessary interventions and reducing damaging interventions.
Interventions that *not* required for economic development or political stability	(i) These types of corruption are associated with dysfunctional interventions (unnecessary paper work and permissions, protection of inefficient industries) and always have negative effects. Policy should seek to remove these state 'functions' (through liberalization and privatization). This has been the focus of mainstream anti-corruption strategies.	(iv) Predatory extortions. This type of corruption predominates in failed or failing states where armed groups can extort from society, regardless of political stability or economic performance (Afghan warlordism, extortion by political mafias). Effective policy to counter this type of corruption has to strengthen the centralized coercive power of the state.

the costs associated with bribing and influencing. These distinctions between types of corruption are important for understanding both the economic and political effects of corruption, and the appropriateness of different anti-corruption strategies.

Based on this discussion, at least four types of corruption can be distinguished. The differences between them depend on whether the underlying interventions are potentially necessary for economic or political reasons, and whether the interventions in question are legally allowed or not. While all corruption involves the violation of some formal rules of conduct, the underlying interventions with which they are associated may themselves be legal or illegal, and they may be harmful or beneficial for economic development. These distinctions are important for identifying the types of policies that may be appropriate for dealing with different types of corruption, and to identify some types of corruption that may not be amenable to any simple policies. This classification is shown in Table 1.

Only the first type of corruption is relevant for the anti-corruption policies that are widely promoted by multilateral agencies following the neoclassical analysis. These corrupt acts are associated with laws that enable interventions which have no potential to assist economic development. Classic examples are tariff protection for industries that have no catching-up potential, or excessive regulation and requirements of permissions that have no purpose except to enable bureaucrats to extract bribes from businessmen. These dysfunctional interventions cause not only direct economic damage, but also secondary damage through corruption as entrepreneurs attempt to capture monopoly profits or circumvent unnecessary restrictions. They include, in particular, the 'petty corruption' involving low-level officials extracting small bribes for performing their duties (red-tapism and speed money), for not harassing the innocent by deliberately misinterpreting very complex and unclear regulations (customs officials or police engaging in petty extortion). This is the most visible face of corruption and, in opinion surveys, public irritation with these types of corruption often dominates. Police corruption, for example, often takes top position in popular perception, largely because the police in developing countries have the powers to gain from widespread petty corruption when implementing complex and badly defined laws.

While these types of corruption are very irksome and can affect the greatest number of people, they are not necessarily the *most* damaging type of corruption from an economic perspective. Nevertheless, these types of petty corruption are damaging; they are regressive in that the victims are very often the poor, and they increase transaction costs and the general perception of lawlessness in developing countries. It is for this type of corruption that the neoclassical analysis of corruption is most appropriate. Here, not only are public officials extracting resources from society, the 'services' or decisions that they are providing, or threatening not to provide, usually have further damaging effects on society. Moreover, the ability of the state to define unnecessary laws can encourage the creation of more and more artificial restrictions, and more and more red tape to increase opportunities for extraction (Myrdal 1968: 937–51).

For this type of corruption, the liberal prescription of liberalization and privatization would, in theory, be the most appropriate, together with direct anti-corruption measures such as higher salaries for public officials and more effective punishments. But it is doubtful if this is the most important type of corruption in most developing countries. If this is only a part of the corruption problem and if, in addressing this, the policies involved damage the potential of accelerating development through state intervention, then, these policies may hinder, rather than help, the reduction of corruption in the long run. A better approach would be to target these types of corruption separately, rather than with general anti-corruption strategies that may, at best, make sense for particular types of corruption but may make economic performance worse if other types of corruption predominate.

The second type of corruption shown in the table is associated with the implementation of interventions that are potentially necessary for the economy or polity, *and* which are allowed and regulated by law. These include such things as managing taxes and tariffs to promote catching-up by domestic industry, the regulation of financial markets, the allocation of land and the licensing of land use, and the allocation of credit or the prioritization of infrastructure construction. These are precisely some of the types of interventions that heterodox theories of the state have identified as critical in developing countries going through rapid transitions and catching up with advanced countries. Clearly, corruption in these areas can have a much more significant effect on the economy, both in terms of growth and distribution.

Nevertheless, the simple neoclassical prescription of fighting corruption through liberalization can have problematic consequences as soon as we look at these cases. The difference is that for this category of corruption, the service or decision that the public official is providing or making is *potentially* beneficial for the economy, though, in practice, the decisions may often be damaging because corruption may subvert the type of decision or allocation that is being made. But here, the correct approach cannot be, in general, to remove or even reduce the capacity of the state to engage in these interventions. A more involved analysis is now required that distinguishes between those functions of the state that are never likely to play a useful role, and those that can. The policy response to the two should be very different. For those functions that are never likely to be of any use, the neoclassical policy prescription would still apply. But for a range of state functions that are critical for development, the appropriate policy response must be to *strengthen* the capacity of the state to intervene, and to reduce the susceptibility of state decisions to subversion by corruption or political processes, rather than to remove the interventionist capacity itself.

If the decisions that are being 'sold' are the right ones in terms of accelerating economic development, then, all that needs to be done is to reduce or eliminate the corruption, perhaps by paying bureaucrats and politicians more, or by setting up better monitoring and greater sanctions for the corrupt. On the other hand, if corruption is subverting decision-making and resource allocation, so that potentially important state functions are being subverted by corruption the policy has to be a more aggressive one. It can involve insulating key state agencies from the pressures of particular unproductive groups or encouraging the organization of productive groups and weakening unproductive groups. For instance, it may be potentially very beneficial for society to provide emerging entrepreneurs with tax breaks or other resources to accelerate technology acquisition.

But if their political power allows inefficient capitalists to use corruption and other methods of exerting pressure to capture subsidies without engaging in technology acquisition, a potentially critical economic mechanism is subverted by corruption. In these cases, it is important to have specific policies to improve the implementation of these critical state functions, for instance, by weakening the political organization of capitalists. Thus, if inefficient capitalists lose the political power to resist subsidy withdrawal by the state, corruption on its own will not prevent states from withdrawing subsidies from inefficient capitalists, because public officials can extract even bigger bribes by allocating subsidies to productive capitalists (Khan 1996).

This is where heterodox approaches can effectively identify a significantly different, and wider, set of governance issues than those in the neoclassical approach. The heterodoxy accepts the importance of state capacities and powers to encourage the emergence of local capitalists, of assisting their technology acquisition, and of vigorously pushing their interests in international trade and investment. If these tasks have not been effectively carried out in the past, the heterodox approach would identify the political and institutional problems that have prevented this, and target these for policy attention in the future.

In contrast, the neoclassical approach to governance observes the failure of most developing country states to prevent the subversion of critical state tasks by corruption, and argues that these interventionist capacities should therefore be removed. This is clearly an extreme and counterproductive 'solution' that is not likely to work if the state capacities in question are indispensable for development. Unfortunately, most anti-corruption strategies in developing countries are aimed at removing the capacity of states to intervene in these areas, rather than assisting states to intervene better to accelerate catching up by encouraging technology acquisition, promoting local capitalism and regulating incentives to achieve these goals.

The third type of corruption shown in the table refers to a much more problematic area associated with the implementation of necessary interventions that are not, or cannot be, regulated by law. These include processes of political stabilization through off-budget transfers, and interventions to accelerate and promote emerging capitalism through processes of 'primitive accumulation'. Primitive accumulation describes non-market processes (both legal and illegal) through which the emergence of a capitalist economy is accelerated in countries going through a transition to capitalism. Primitive accumulation includes, in particular, the changes in property rights in favour of an emerging capitalism, and the asset transfers facilitated by state actions that tilt the playing field in favour of emerging capitalists (or particular factions of emerging capitalists). Some of these state actions can be legal, in the form of changes in relative prices, taxes, land licensing and so on, but others cannot be legalized because the underlying processes are too politically unpopular, unjust or unfair for it to be possible to codify and regulate them. In extreme, primitive accumulation can take the form of outright theft or occupation of public or common assets by factions or individuals, often exploiting political connections to facilitate this process.

Not surprisingly, when states are engaged in primitive accumulation, corruption is endemic. Conversely, the absence of primitive accumulation to anything like the same extent in countries that are already significantly capitalist is part of the explanation for systemically lower levels of corruption. But, as noted earlier, lower corruption does not mean that influence-buying is less in advanced capitalist countries. The process of primitive accumulation has not been sufficiently analysed, even in heterodox analysis. The outcome of primitive accumulation does not necessarily have to be a dynamic capitalism. Much of the resources that are transferred to potential 'emerging capitalists' may be wasted because the appropriators may fail in the end to become capitalists and instead prove to be unproductive consumers of stolen assets. This is part of the explanation for the very high degree of variation in the outcomes of primitive accumulation, ranging from the rapid emergence of dynamic capitalism in countries like China after the 1980s to the waste and collapse within many economies in Asia, Africa and Latin America as a result of failed processes of primitive accumulation.

While processes of primitive accumulation do not always lead to the emergence of viable capitalist economies, it is difficult to envisage how the transition from pre-capitalist to capitalist economies can be organized without primitive accumulation. By definition, developing countries have large segments of their economies that are unviable in terms of the technologies and prices set by the world market. As a result, developing countries are typically forced to go through rapid economic and social transformations simply because pre-existing economic formations are often rapidly collapsing. In the fortunate cases, new and more dynamic social formations have rapidly emerged, but it is scarcely credible that such transformations could be organized while observing all the legal requirements characteristic of, and now demanded by, the developed countries. In other countries, social transformations have been much slower, even though the collapse of pre-existing formations was just as rapid. In the least fortunate cases, there is growing social chaos and conflict, and viable alternatives have failed to emerge. But in all developing countries, pre-existing property rights and class structures have been rapidly eroded or changed by powerful processes that cannot be easily stopped or reversed. These processes are not just market processes where more productive producers buy out less productive ones. They also include significant non-market processes simply because more productive producers and efficient markets do not already exist, and resources are captured by political entrepreneurs of different types who may or may not become dynamic capitalists over time.

The important observation from this perspective is that corruption is unlikely to be controllable in a context of rapid non-market changes in property rights where political power is being used to change rights, grab resources and rewrite the rules of the game. These processes are in turn likely to predominate in contexts of transition and primitive accumulation. The important point is that economic and social transformation, and primitive accumulation, are not processes that are simply the product of any 'intention' on the part of public officials who want to profit from the opportunities they create for corruption. Rather, transitions in developing countries are typically driven by the growing non-viability of pre-capitalist rights and production processes, and the internal political conflicts and struggles that this generates. If the ensuing transition takes society in the direction of a viable capitalist economy that can produce a significant economic surplus, this can eventually pay for the protection of the new structure of rights. Once this happens, both primitive accumulation and corruption can be significantly reduced. But before this happens, the existing structure of rights is *not* viable in the typical developing country. Surplus generation is low, and the state is unlikely to have the resources to protect property rights, and ensure that voluntary and legal market transfers predominate. Moreover, in such a context, powerful groups and factions in society are likely to be engaged in a struggle to restructure ownership and the organization of production or simply capture resources using their political power as a tool. In this context, the corruption associated with primitive accumulation is a systemic process and not one that can be limited or bypassed by policies such as limiting the role of the state, increasing public awareness or paying bureaucrats more. A focus on these policies assumes that corruption is largely due to the *intentions* of public officials, and that if their incentives and opportunities can be changed, corruption can be reduced.

Thus, during this period, regardless of the incentives facing public officials, a significant part of the activities involved in protecting and transferring assets in developing countries are likely to be non-market, illegal and unjust. Anti-corruption policies which assume that states can be made to stabilize essentially unviable property rights and establish a rule of law in this context are not likely to work. If states tried to do this, given that the existing structure of rights is not productive enough to pay for such a scheme, the likelihood would be that such policies would be rapidly abandoned. Indeed, this is precisely what we observe in developing countries that have adopted, for a time, a serious commitment to across-the-board anti-corruption strategies. This explains why the 'political will' to combat corruption appears to be systematically lacking across the entire swathe of developing countries.

Another type of intervention that falls within the category of necessary interventions which cannot be legalized is intervention aiming to achieve political stabilization in the absence of significant fiscal resources. In advanced capitalist countries, political stabilization is typically organized using fiscal transfers through the budget. This process is legal, and the rent-seeking (or influence-buying) that it generates is, therefore, also legal, typically in the form of lobbying, political contributions and other legal or semi-legal means to influence the allocation of subsidies and transfers. Once again, note that influence-buying and rent-seeking can be widespread in advanced countries. It is only that most of it is legal.

In contrast, in developing countries, the fiscal space for political redistribution is limited for a number of reasons. The modern sector of the economy that can be taxed to redistribute to others is small. At the same time, the political conflicts faced are often more serious than those in an advanced country. In many cases, the taxes collected are insufficient even for paying the salaries of bureaucrats. Capital expenditures in the development budget often depend on aid and other foreign capital inflows. Thus, the fiscal reality in most developing countries (apart from a few resource-rich ones) leaves little scope for significant redistribution through the budget. But the political survival of the regime requires that powerful groups are accommodated.

These powerful groups are typically not the poorest. Their political accommodation often requires off-budget 'redistribution' through patron–client networks to achieve political stabilization (Khan 2000b). The corrupt exchange here involves politicians (the public officials in question) transferring resources to powerful clients and receiving, in exchange, their political support. In some cases, clients can provide more than simple political support, by acting as thugs and musclemen for patrons. It is impossible to regulate these off-budget transfers legally for two inter-related reasons. First, by definition, these transfers go to buy off the most dangerous or troublesome sections of society and cannot be given to everybody. This inherent inequity based on the potential power to disrupt cannot be legally recognized. Second, given the absence of fiscal resources, financing these 'transfers' involves patrons in public office engaging in acts of corruption to raise resources for their political survival, even in the extreme cases when there is no individual greed. Of course, if political survival requires corruption, this attracts a particular type of individual to public office, and few political leaders in developing countries can refrain from individual enrichment. It is therefore not surprising that political stabilization through patron–client networks in developing countries is inherently clandestine and is often closely linked to the processes of primitive accumulation described earlier.

None of the processes raised – the primitive accumulation that follows from collapsing pre-capitalist production structures and the political stabilization that has to take place clandestinely because of fiscal constraints – is significantly affected by the presence or absence of democracy, civil society pressures, or the integrity of individual public officials. Nor is there any government function that can be removed to reduce this type of corruption. If corruption were largely due to the greed of public officials or the absence of public awareness, political mobilization would indeed succeed in reducing the problem.

But if the problem is that any ruling group is unable to stabilize property rights that are not viable, and has to engage in political corruption to survive, then, political mobilization, democratization and demands for integrity will do little to reduce this type of corruption. In fact, developing countries that have attempted to root out corruption through public mobilization have uniformly failed to make a lasting dent on the problem. In most cases, this has done little to reduce the problem in the long term, though there have sometimes been short-term reductions in corruption because of public pressure.

Lasting reductions in corruption in developing countries going through a capitalist transformation generally only take place once a viable capitalist economy has been established, defined as one where the modern or capitalist sector is generating enough surpluses to finance the effective protection of its property rights by the state. At the same time, the growing surplus generated by a viable capitalist sector allows the tax share in the economy to be significantly increased, allowing political stability to be maintained through transparent and legal transfers to broadly defined social groups. As soon as political corruption is no longer structurally necessary for the political survival of a regime, pressure from powerful interest groups that are hurt by corruption can begin to make rapid progress in reducing the extent of corruption. Of course, having the resources to avoid political corruption is not *sufficient* for corruption to come down. It is easy to find examples of very rich countries that continue to suffer from corruption. Popular pressure is also necessary. Nevertheless, pressure alone is not sufficient to reduce corruption if existing property rights are not feasible and if political power cannot be maintained using fiscal strategies of redistribution.

Thus, for this type of corruption (type iii in our table), it would be futile to target the corruption directly since its removal would paradoxically be detrimental to the stability of the state and would, therefore, not be sustainable. Here, feasible policy has the more limited task of damage limitation in the short run and of ensuring rapid progress to a position where it would be possible to legalize some of these interventions, while other interventions would no longer be necessary. This, too, is an area where discussions of feasible anti-corruption strategies are most deficient. To some extent, while these types of corruption are very undesirable because they are associated with unfair and inequitable processes, they are unlikely to be tackled using the conventional mechanisms of liberalization, democratization and criticisms coming from civil society. The long-term answer must be to achieve a viable economy, increase tax collection, and gradually shift to maintaining political stability through fiscal transfers and property rights stability through enforcement mechanisms financed by taxation. The viability of these strategies depends on the success of the state in promoting economic development, rather than its immediate success in implementing 'good governance' reforms. This is particularly important because there is little evidence, as we have argued, to show that stable property rights and 'good governance' can be meaningfully achieved *before* the conditions for rapid growth have been set in place.

Finally, the worst type of corruption is the fourth type shown in our table, where the social order has broken down completely and corruption is associated with illegal interventions that have no economic or political rationale for any group, apart from the predatory 'officials' involved. This type of corruption is based solely on the coercive power of small groups to extort from the majority, and may appear to occupy a grey area since, if the state fragments sufficiently, individual warlords lose any state-like quality and become more like private individuals stealing from other private individuals. The distinction is largely semantic in this case, because warlords in such a society *are* the state, and if they deliver 'security' only to those who are willing to pay for it, this is clearly a type of corruption rather than an example of theft. While there are aspects of such extortions in every society, it only takes on significant proportions in failed or failing states, which are characterized by the failure of higher levels of the state to discipline lower levels. If the state is not in a process of collapse, some degree of extortion can always take place at lower levels of the state, but higher levels have no interest in allowing this extortion to continue when they discover it because it is unlikely to aid their own accumulation and stabilization strategies. This is because if the state can actually enforce discipline, then, even if higher-level bureaucrats and politicians are interested in personal enrichment, they will do better by promoting development rather than through predation (Khan 1996). This is why predation and extortion are usually endemic in fragmented and weak states, and, paradoxically, much less in evidence in strong and centrally coordinated ones. The latter are more likely to engage in what we have described as type (ii) corruption, associated with the management of developmental interventions, and these are likely to be more rewarding for politicians and bureaucrats in these societies than attempts at predation. If a significant amount of extortion takes place without higher levels of the state reacting, this is usually evidence of a much more serious underlying problem that can be described as actual or impending state collapse. The policy response in these cases has to be very different from the others, simply because, here, the priority must be to construct the political and institutional conditions to re-establish the state as an institution with a monopoly of legitimate violence. Far from liberalization, democratization and civil society pressure, the priority in these cases has to be a much more fundamental political one of constructing the political basis for creating the state's monopoly of legitimate violence, and establishing the institutions to exercise the centralization of violence capacity in society.

Implications for Policy

By breaking down corruption into a number of different problems in this way, it is possible to explain why the *prior* reduction of corruption has never been a precondition for rapid capitalist development. Some types of corruption are simply not going to be significantly reduced in societies going through social transformations, even in societies where such transformations eventually turn out to be successful. At the same time, this is not to deny that corruption is a problem. Very few developing countries have graduated to become dynamic capitalist economies. In poorly performing economies, corruption is damaging because it subverts critical state functions or is associated with failing processes of primitive accumulation or political stabilization. In extreme cases, corruption can be associated with state collapse and descent into warlordism.

However, our analysis suggests that in each case, the policy response has to be based on a proper analysis of the types of corruption that dominate and target the strengthening of state capacities that are most important for creating the governance capacities required for achieving rapid transformation and high growth rates. Here, heterodox analysis of governance capacities in high growth developing economies can play an important role in identifying critical transformational state capacities that may be subverted by specific types of corruption which dominate in particular countries. If the necessary state capacities for accelerating transformation can be achieved, a low-growth economy can transform into a high-growth one. Paradoxically, corruption may persist and coexist with growth if the state is able to provide the necessary interventions and regulations, even if it extracts resources through corruption, both for political stabilization and for the personal enrichment of individuals within the bureaucratic and political structures.

Yet, even if corruption can *coexist* with rapid growth, this should not be interpreted to mean that corruption in these countries is *functional*. This is not the case because, even if some interventions were useful, it would be even better if these could be organized with less corruption. Recall that all corrupt transactions have two components, and that the first component, that is, bribe-giving and all forms of rent-seeking, is usually a cost. If necessary state interventions could be organized without this cost, or with lower cost, economic output would be even higher. Heterodox analysis is not arguing that corruption is functional, but only that if the attempt to remove corruption results in the removal of useful interventions, the outcome may be even more serious economic damage. If corruption simply allowed investors to work their way around unnecessary legal restrictions, it is even less convincing to argue that corruption was functional. Accordingly, some earlier mainstream analyses which suggested that corruption could be functional – if it allowed businessmen to sidestep restrictive regulations (for instance, Leff 1964) – were misleading because they ignored the fact that such unnecessary regulations could themselves be removed as part of an anti-corruption policy. The outcome would then be even better.

While corruption does not, therefore, play any functional role in driving economic development, heterodox analysis points out the danger of making anti-corruption strategies a precondition for economic development, and an adjunct of liberalization and privatization strategies. This analysis suggests that attempts to fight all types of corruption in developing countries through these mechanisms will not only fail to reduce corruption, but may also seriously damage long-term efforts to enhance the capacity of developing country states to carry out the interventions that, in the end, are essential for accelerating development and creating viable economies. The analysis of corruption helps us to understand that the state capacities required during processes of social transformation are far removed from the market-enabling capacities that neoclassical analysis focuses on. The key governance capacities of the developmental state are related to its political and institutional capacity to carry out the necessary developmental interventions that enable a dynamic capitalism to rapidly emerge. But for this to be possible, the state's political and institutional conditions must allow political stabilization and primitive accumulation in the direction of a viable capitalism. In some developing countries, the most important task may be the even more basic one of consolidating a state and imposing control over fragmented predation. Thus, the political and institutional priorities for different countries cannot be generalized into a blueprint of reforms. These priorities are bound to depend on pre-existing political, social and institutional configurations.

If a developmental state can be constructed in a developing country, some types of corruption can coexist for a while with high rates of accumulation and growth. But even a developmental state in a developing country will be located in a context of rapid social transformation. It is therefore unlikely, by definition, to be able to enforce stable property rights and low expropriation risk for all social groups (though dynamic capitalists are likely to face low expropriation risk in high-growth economies). This is why it is not surprising that high-growth early developers do not fit into the expectation of good governance theories in having stable property rights, high levels of democracy, low levels of corruption and so on.

While neoclassical analysis is wrong to identify corruption and 'good governance' as necessary preconditions for growth, it would be wrong to deny that the reduction of corruption and the achievement of democracy are, in particular, important aspirations for many people in developing countries. Heterodox analysis is important for pointing out that the achievement of these aspirations requires successful social transformation of these societies and, therefore, the achievement of a very different set of transformation capacities for the state from the ones identified by neoclassical analysis. An analysis of the types of corruption that predominate in particular developing countries can provide a useful lens for examining the accumulation processes and the political constraints that different countries face. This, in turn, can help to identify the most important areas where policy should concentrate to strengthen the capacities required for successful transformations. Thus, the analysis of corruption and of different types of governance capacities remains important in helping to identify appropriate policies for accelerating growth in particular countries, even if there may be no immediate general strategies to reduce corruption significantly across the board in most cases. Lasting reductions in corruption and expropriation risk, improvements in the stability of property rights and the deepening of democracy are all likely to depend on whether policy can be used to ensure that growth and development are accelerated and sustained over time. None of these goals is likely to be promoted, and their eventual achievement may even be damaged, by the uncritical adoption of mainstream anti-corruption and good governance policies.

References

Amsden, Alice (1989), *Asia's Next Giant: South Korea and Late Industrialization* (Oxford: Oxford University Press).

Aoki, Masahiko, Hyung-Ki Kim and Masahiro Okuno-Fujiwara, eds (1997), *The Role of Government in East Asian Economic Development: Comparative Institutional Analysis* (Oxford: Clarendon Press).

Barro, Robert (1996), 'Democracy and Growth', *Journal of Economic Growth*, 1 (1): 1–27.

Clague, Christopher, Philip Keefer, Stephen Knack and Mancur Olson (1997), 'Democracy, Autocracy and the Institutions Supportive of Economic Growth', in Christopher Clague, ed., *Institutions and Economic Development: Growth and Governance in Less-Developed and Post-Socialist Countries* (Baltimore: Johns Hopkins University Press).

Hall, Robert and Charles Jones (1999), 'Why Do Some Countries Produce So Much More Output per Worker than Others?', *Quarterly Journal of Economics*, 114: 83–116.

Heidenheimer, Arnold J. and Michael Johnston, eds (2002), *Political Corruption: Concepts and Contexts*, third edition, (New Brunswick: Transaction Publishers).

Johnson, Simon, Daniel Kauffmann and Pablo Zoido-Lobatón (1998), 'Regulatory Discretion and the Unofficial Economy', *American Economic Review*, 88 (2): 387–92.

Kauffman, Daniel, Aart Kraay and Pablo Zoido-Lobatón (1999), 'Governance Matters', World Bank Policy Working Paper No. 2196, World Bank, Washington DC.

Khan, Mushtaq H. (1996), 'A Typology of Corrupt Transactions in Developing Countries', in Barbara Harriss-White and Gordon White, eds, 'Liberalization and the New Corruption', *IDS Bulletin*, 27 (2): 12–21.

—— (2000a), 'Rents, Efficiency and Growth', in Mushtaq H. Khan and Jomo K.S., eds, *Rents, Rent-Seeking and Economic Development: Theory and Evidence in Asia* (Cambridge: Cambridge University Press).

—— (2000b), 'Rent-Seeking as Process', in Mushtaq H. Khan and Jomo K.S., eds, *Rents, Rent-Seeking and Economic Development: Theory and Evidence in Asia* (Cambridge: Cambridge University Press).

—— (2002a), 'State Failure in Developing Countries and Strategies of Institutional Reform', in Bertil Tungodden, Nick Stern and Ivar Kolstad, eds, *Towards Pro-Poor Policies: Aid, Institutions and Globalization: Proceedings of the World Bank's Annual Bank Conference on Development Economics* (New York: Oxford University Press, for World Bank).

—— (2002b), 'Corruption and Governance in Early Capitalism: World Bank Strategies and their Limitations', in Jonathan Pincus and Jeffrey Winters, eds, *Reinventing the World Bank* (Ithaca: Cornell University Press).

Khan, Mushtaq H. and Jomo K.S., eds (2000), *Rents, Rent-Seeking, and Economic Development: Theory and Evidence in Asia* (Cambridge: Cambridge University Press).

Knack, Stephen and Philip Keefer (1995), 'Institutions and Economic Performance: Cross-Country Tests Using Alternative Institutional Measures', *Economics and Politics*, 7 (3): 207–27.

—— (1997), 'Why Don't Poor Countries Catch Up? A Cross-National Test of an Institutional Explanation', *Economic Inquiry*, 35: 590–602.

Krueger, Anne (1974), 'The Political Economy of the Rent-Seeking Society', *American Economic Review*, 64 (3): 291–303.

Lall, Sanjaya and Morris Teubal (1998), '"Market-Stimulating" Technology Policies in Developing Countries: A Framework with Examples from East Asia', *World Development*, 26 (8): 1369–85.

Leff, Nathaniel (1964), 'Economic Development through Bureaucratic Corruption', *American Behavioral Scientist*, 8: 8–14.

Mauro, Paolo (1995), 'Corruption and Growth', *Quarterly Journal of Economics*, 110 (3): 681–712.

Myrdal, Gunnar (1968), *Asian Drama: An Inquiry into the Poverty of Nations,* Vol. II (New York: Twentieth Century).

Nye, Joseph S. (1967), 'Corruption and Political Development: A Cost-Benefit Analysis', *American Political Science Review,* 61 (2): 417–27.

Rodrik, Dani (1995), 'Getting Interventions Right: How South Korea and Taiwan Grew Rich', *Economic Policy,* 20: 55–107.

—— (2002), *Institutions, Integration, and Geography: In Search of the Deep Determinants of Economic Growth* (Princeton, NJ: Princeton University Press).

Treisman, Daniel (2000), 'The Causes of Corruption: A Cross National Study', *Journal of Public Economics,* 76: 399–457.

Wade, Robert (1990), *Governing the Market: Economic Theory and the Role of Government in East Asian Industrialization* (Princeton, NJ: Princeton University Press).

Williams, Robert, ed. (2000), *Explaining Corruption* (Cheltenham: Edward Elgar).

Williams, Robert and Robin Theobald, eds (2000), *Corruption in the Developing World* (Cheltenham: Edward Elgar).

Woo-Cumings, Meredith, ed. (1999), *The Developmental State* (Ithaca: Cornell University Press).

World Bank (1997), *World Development Report 1997: The State in a Changing World* (Washington DC: World Bank).

—— (2000), *Helping Countries to Combat Corruption: Progress at the World Bank since 1997* (Washington DC: World Bank).

Agriculture and Development

Towards a Critique of the

'New Neoclassical Development Economics'

and of 'Neoclassical Neo-Populism'[1]

Terence J. Byres

Neoclassical economics comes in different forms. Two currently influential variants of neoclassical theorizing on 'development', whose essential concern has been with agriculture, are considered in this chapter. The first is the so-called 'new development economics', which, I suggest, might more appropriately be termed the 'new neoclassical development economics', and whose outstanding exponent is Joseph Stiglitz. Here the central focus is upon Stiglitz's formulations. The second I have called 'neoclassical neo-populism'. Its major representatives have been Michael Lipton and Keith Griffin. It is the ideas of the latter that are considered.

Both approaches have possible appeal beyond the usual constituency of neoclassical economics because they depart from the extreme position of the 'Washington Consensus' economists and seem to show neoclassical economics with a 'human face': the former, for example, opposing the virulent anti-state position of the neoclassical views that underpinned the Washington Consensus, and strongly critical of the International Monetary Fund (as indicated elsewhere in this book); and the latter advocating a seemingly ultra-radical, egalitarian, pro-poor redistributive land reform. Here they are both considered critically from the viewpoint of Marxist agrarian political economy.

This chapter is about *agriculture* and the two approaches in question are set in historical context, in the second section, by considering the unavoidable salience of agriculture from the very beginnings of post-1945 development economics; and by identifying the central issues at stake, including the perceived desirability of land reform. It is also about *competing paradigms* in the field of development economics. The two approaches are then further contextualized, in the third section, by viewing them in relation to the post-1945 history of development economics and the changing fortunes of different paradigms within that history. The following are then described: the initial dominance of a form of classical economics with which neoclassical economists concurred; the wresting of hegemony from those of a classical bent by a new and uncompromising neoclassical economics from the late 1960s onwards; and the emergence of the less uncompromising 'new neoclassical development economics' and of 'neoclassical neo-populism', with its concern for the poor and disadvantaged. Other paradigms are also noted, but are not discussed in detail.

In the section that follows, the major components of the 'new neoclassical development economics', according to Stiglitz, are identified; and in the subsequent section, that approach is given critical scrutiny. It is argued that the 'new neoclassical development economics' is seriously inadequate in the following respects: its assumption of the existence of a homogenous peasantry rather than of differentiated peasantries; its positing of relationships of mutuality rather than exploitation in the countryside; its assumption of parity of economic power rather than asymmetry of economic power among social classes; its neglect of the causes of economic backwardness; and its defective view of the state. In both this approach and the extreme neoclassical view that it sought to replace, land reform virtually disappears as a desirable policy initiative.

In the two final substantive sections, first redistributive and tenurial land reform are distinguished and the Griffin case for the former presented; and then a critique of neo-populism is offered. In this critique, the nature of neoclassical neo-populism is identified and two of its contradictions indicated. That approach is unusual among neoclassical economists in its espousing of a political economy framework. Its political economy is criticized for its deployment of inadequate social categories. The approach is further criticized for its ignoring of the development of capitalism and for its ahistorical nature. At the centre of the case for redistributive land reform lies the positing of an inverse relationship between land productivity and size of holding. While such a relationship has certainly existed pervasively in the past, it disappears with the development of capitalism in the countryside; and so the central support for the case for redistributive land reform collapses. In the brief concluding section, it is suggested that in ignoring the contemporary realities of poor countries, both approaches perform an essentially reactionary role.

The Dawn of Development Economics:
The Need for Agricultural Growth and a Case for Land Reform

Development economics emerged as a distinct sub-branch of economics in the immediate aftermath of World War II. Its purpose was to identify and theorize, on the one hand, the character of economic backwardness and the mechanisms that perpetuated it, and, on the other, the nature of economic development and the means by which it might be secured. In economically backward economies, distribution was very unequal and material poverty was deep and massively pervasive. Development economics, by uncovering the basis and origins of economic backwardness, and clarifying the means by which development might be made to proceed, might help with the reduction and, ultimately, the eradication of poverty.

The nature of the problem confronted and the possible solutions, as envisaged by the initial small band of 'development economists', were stated in two important public documents, both published in 1951: *Measures for the Economic Development of Under-Developed Countries*, and subtitled *Report by a Group of Experts appointed by the Secretary-General of the United Nations* (United Nations 1951a); and *Land Reforms: Defects in Agrarian Structure as Obstacles to Economic Development* (United Nations 1951b). Those documents expressed the current orthodoxy of the time. The authorship of the latter is not stated. But the 'group of experts' responsible for the former included three economists who would become prominent in the then fledgling field of development economics: W. Arthur Lewis (1915–1990), then at the University of Manchester; Theodore W. Schultz (1902–1998), of the University of Chicago; and D.R. Gadgil (1901–1971), Director of the Gokhale Institute, Poona. Lewis's ideas, formulated within the analytical framework of classical political economy, dominated development economics in the first era of its operation, in the 1950s and 1960s. Schultz was prominent in the attack on classical ideas by neoclassical economists in the 1960s, which resulted in the wresting of dominance from the classical economists by the neoclassical economists. Lewis and Schultz were jointly awarded the Nobel Prize in Economics in 1979 for their contributions to the field of economic development. Gadgil was prominent in important economic debates in post-1947 India and was a prolific writer on planning.

From the very outset, agriculture, of necessity, loomed large in the sights of development economists. In developing countries, in Asia and Africa, from country to country, more than 70 per cent and up to 90 per cent of the working population were in agriculture, and between a half and two-thirds of national income might be generated there. Agriculture, by its massive presence, forced itself on to the agenda. It was here that economic backwardness was most obvious and the great bulk of the poverty was located. One might contemplate neither the terrain of economic backwardness nor the possibility of development without immediate confrontation with agriculture. Assuming no structural change in the economy, then, *ceteris paribus* (for example, without any shift in the distribution of income), the output/income necessary to reduce that poverty would have to come from a *growing agriculture*, while the increased food essential to poverty reduction (the demand for food was likely to grow *pari passu* with income) required agricultural growth (whether to supply the food domestically, or to earn the foreign exchange to allow it to be imported). It was an agriculture, however, that was either stagnant or growing very slowly. As the first document had it, in a chapter entitled 'Development Planning Priorities', 'agricultural improvement', that is, agricultural growth, was essential (United Nations 1951a: 59). These were issues that development economics faced most starkly as that discipline emerged and grew after 1945.

Manufacturing industry, by contrast, was of negligible importance. Might the solution, or part of it, lie in structural change in the economy, via industrialization, in which labour was transferred from low-income agriculture to higher-income industry? The first document embraced that position very strongly – this being especially the case, it argued, in those many poor countries characterized by large amounts of surplus labour in agriculture. But such a solution could not be secured with a backward agriculture that continued to stagnate. Agriculture was a source of the labour that would man the factories. Such labour transfer was unlikely to be secured with a stagnant agriculture. Agriculture supplied, critically, food, the wage good *par excellence*, the demand for which would grow significantly as industry grew. Agriculture was the source of the raw materials necessary for certain important industries (most notably textiles); of foreign exchange needed for certain strategic imports (for example, in the first instance, machinery of one kind or another); of the investible surplus that would allow accumulation in industry in the early years of industrialization, before industry could finance itself; and, in those early years, of the bulk of the home market for industrial goods. A stagnant agriculture simply could not meet these needs.

But what was preventing agricultural growth? There were two distinct levels of obstruction: levels that were not isolated from one another, but which were closely articulated. At one level, the productive forces in agriculture, that is, agricultural technology, were very poorly developed. There were backward means of production – say, wooden rather than iron ploughs; inadequate inputs – seeds that gave low yields, an absence of assured irrigation and inorganic ferti-lizers; primitive techniques/backward methods of cultivation – for example, in rice cultivation, sowing by the broadcast method rather than sowing in rows. This was so while known superior possibilities existed. This meant, inevitably, low agricultural productivity, low yields per unit of land and low output per head. It also meant that, as agriculture had reached the limits of its productive potential, the scope for agricultural growth was limited. Agricultural growth required that this must change. Development of the productive forces that would bring a far more productive agriculture, with the potential for significant growth, was essential. But what might prevent such change?

At a second level, the existing relations of production were seen as a formidable obstacle. It was the received wisdom, as expressed in the second document (but also in the first), that:

> for many countries the agrarian structure, and in particular, systems of land tenure, prevent a rise in the standard of living of small farmers and agricultural labourers and impede economic development, both by preventing the expan-sion of the food supply and by causing agriculture – usually the major eco-nomic activity – to stagnate. (United Nations 1951b: 89)

That is to say, there was a powerful case for land reform, both for reasons asso-ciated with agriculture itself and for inter-sectoral reasons. Such land reform might release the springs of growth in economically backward economies.

Although the documents in question might not have expressed it in quite the following way, one might say that within the existing agrarian structure, relationships were such as to dull the *incentive* to produce for most cultivators, because of the degree of surplus appropriation by dominant classes; while that same appropriation removed the *wherewithal* to invest. This was so because, for example, of existing tenure systems, and most notably sharecropping, which killed incentives; high levels of rent, which left little for investment; absentee landlordism; fragmented land holdings; very high levels of rural interest rates and heavy levels of indebtedness, which deterred borrowing for productive purposes. All of that would have to change.

Development Economics, Contending Paradigms and Switching Hegemony: From Classical to Neoclassical Dominance

In development economics, in the first two decades after 1945, a *modern variant of classical political economy* was hegemonic. The two decisive texts were Rosenstein–Rodan's 'Problems of Industrialization of Eastern and Southeastern Europe' (1943) and Arthur Lewis's 'Economic Development with Unlimited Supplies of Labour' (1954). The influence of Rosenstein–Rodan (1902–1985) was clear in both aforementioned documents, while Lewis's ideas – given powerful, concentrated expression in his article, the celebrated 'Lewis model', and then more extended and discursive treatment in his book, *Theory of Economic Growth* (1955) – were clearly influential. Indeed, one might date the *birth of modern development economics* with the publication of the former's article; while one might identify the beginnings of its remarkable growth with the appearance of the Lewis article (his book, curiously, had very limited impact). There has been no more influential text in the whole history of post-war development economics than the Lewis article.

Both Rosenstein–Rodan and Lewis conceived of what would later be termed a 'developmental state' and development planning as essential. Both assumed the existence of a large quantum of surplus labour in agriculture. Both laid central stress on the need for industrialization, with surplus labour shifting from agriculture to constitute industry's labour force. In his book, Lewis (1955: 120–27) made a strong case for land reform and had much to say about agriculture. Rosenstein–Rodan's concern was not primarily with agriculture but his essential approach did influence thinking on agriculture. The great thrust of development thinking, in the classical tradition, was in favour of the measures recommended in the two cited United Nations documents.

Both of the aforementioned economists were clearly in the classical tradition. Both denied the relevance, for economically backward economies, of neoclassical economics. Rosenstein–Rodan, when he came to assess his views as one of the 'pioneers in development' some forty years after the publication of his celebrated article, entitled his paper, in continuing defiance of the relevance of neoclassical economics, 'Natura Facit Saltum: Analysis of the Disequilibrium Growth Process' (1984). *Natura Non Facit Saltum* (Nature does not make a jump) was the motto that Marshall placed on the frontispiece of his *Principles*, the first polished statement of neoclassical economics. Rosenstein–Rodan denied this. 'Nature' could and would make a jump; and if the jump were to be made, the state would have to intervene. Then, recall the opening paragraph of Lewis's article: 'This essay is written in the classical tradition, making the classical assumption, and asking the classical question. The classics, from Smith to Marx, all assumed, or argued, that an unlimited supply of labour was available at subsistence wages ([1954] 1958: 400). Neoclassical economics was, Lewis (ibid.: 401) insisted, irrelevant for the analysis of underdeveloped economies. Again, intervention by the state was essential.

Neither Rosenstein–Rodan nor Lewis was dismissive of neoclassical economics in any general, or ultimate, sense. It would come back into its own when development had been secured (cf. ibid.). Nor was either sympathetic to Marxism. Nevertheless, here was a profoundly non-neoclassical approach. The classical approach remained dominant probably until the middle or end of the 1960s. Already, however, by the 1960s, the centre of gravity had begun to move quite decisively from classical to neoclassical economics. That was as true in relation to agriculture as it was more generally.

For present purposes, I would distinguish four distinct manifestations of the neoclassical paradigm in the post-war era, with respect to 'development'. The exponents of each have had distinctive and differing views on agriculture, to which I come later. Here, let me note their more general views. The third and fourth will be the object of my detailed attention.

The first of the four is the 'old neoclassical development economics', henceforth ONCE. Until the late 1960s, neoclassical economics had lived perfectly happily, on the whole, with development planning in poor countries, and, indeed, many of its practitioners were closely associated with such planning. Markets did not work, and the state needed to intervene to ensure that the initial steps towards development might be taken, before, ultimately, the market could come into its own. There was agreement, too, on the existence of surplus labour. The need for land reform – essentially *tenurial land reform* – was accepted. Prominent, indeed, in the ranks of ONCE economists was the aforementioned Theodore Schultz, at least as indicated by his signing the United Nations 1951 report, *Measures for the Economic Development of Under-Developed Countries*.

One may pause, however, to observe that in that first era of development economics (roughly from 1945 until the mid- to late 1960s), there were in contention paradigms other than classical and neoclassical economics. These were: *Marxism*, which focused upon the nature of both capitalist and socialist transformation, and whose influence was widespread; *structuralism*, which originated in, and was especially influential in, Latin America; and *variants of Keynesianism*, in particular, the *Harrod–Domar model*. They were important and must not be ignored. I can, however, do no more than note them here.

Outstanding among Marxist economists were Maurice Dobb (1900–1976), famous as the progenitor of the Dobb–Sweezy debate (through his *Studies in the Development of Capitalism*, 1946, to which Sweezy reacted, thus initiating the debate) on the transition from feudalism to capitalism in Europe, whose Delhi lectures of 1951 (Dobb 1951) and *An Essay on Economic Growth and Planning* (1960) were significant; Michal Kalecki (1899–1970), who, within a rigorous framework, consistently stressed the social determinants and social consequences, that is, the class dimensions, of economic phenomena (all of his incisive writing on development is conveniently gathered together in a single volume [Kalecki 1993]); Paul Baran (1910–1964), with his book *The Political Economy of Growth* (1957), and its stress upon the generation and utilization of economic surplus; while the famous model of the Indian physicist and statistician, P.C. Mahalanobis (1893–1972), which made the case for the development of a capital goods sector (1953, 1955), was Marxist in its inspiration.

Structuralists, among whom the leading spirit was the Argentinean economist, Raul Prebisch (1901–1986), stressed the importance of different historical situations and national contexts – qualitatively different structures; deployed a centre–periphery model; pointed to the unequal division of the gains from trade, manifested in deteriorating terms of trade between centre and periphery; and emphasized the importance of the 'developmental state' (see Kay 1989, Chapter 2 for an excellent treatment of structuralism). Their numbers included the Brazilian, Celso Furtado, who posited the notion of structural stagnation. The Harrod–Domar model was used to provide the logic underpinning planning exercises; for example, the Indian First Five Year Plan.

The second neoclassical manifestation is what would become the Washington Consensus (henceforth WC) view, to use Williamson's expression (1990). From the 1960s, this consolidated, hardened and became hegemonic, reaching its full dominance in the 1980s. It argued strongly against the existence of surplus labour. It was relentlessly anti-planning, anti-state and pro-market. With state withdrawal, and a leaner, non-interventionist state, an untrammelled market would secure development. With the state dismantled, all that was necessary for development was 'getting prices right'. Many of the former neoclassical advocates of planning adopted this view and metamorphosed into fervent proponents of liberalization. It became the dominant view within both the IMF and the World Bank, and among neoclassical development economists, and remained so until the late 1990s. Land reform of any kind disappeared from the neoclassical agenda. A succinct and uncompromising statement of this view may be seen in Deepak Lal's (1983) pamphlet, *The Poverty of 'Development Economics'*.

The third variant is so-called 'new development economics', which set the terms for the 'post-Washington Consensus', and whose major proponent has been Joseph Stiglitz. It was, I think, Stiglitz (1986) who coined the term 'the new development economics'. In doing so, he was clearly not referring to the replacement of any non-neoclassical development economics but, rather, to an apparently marked revision of the WC view. He might, more appropriately, have referred to 'the new neoclassical development economics' – henceforth NNCDE. This, as it happens, has taken agriculture very much as its focus, although it had little to say about surplus labour. The state is not lambasted with such ferocity. There is something of a case for positive state intervention. The market, unaided, will not necessarily deliver the goods. 'Getting prices right' may not be enough. But land reform does not figure in its concerns. In accordance with the theme of this book, this will be the first focus of my critical attention here.

A final neoclassical form is what has been termed 'neoclassical neo-populism'. Again, agriculture is at its centre. Its major exponents have been Michael Lipton (1968, 1977) with his urban-biased thesis (see Byres 1979 for a critique) and Keith Griffin [1974] 1979; and Griffin, Khan and Ickowitz 2002) with his advocacy of *redistributive land reform*, but not tenurial reform. In the latter case, via the deployment of the standard apparatus of neoclassical economics, a radical egalitarianism, characteristic of populist/neo-populist views, with the advocacy of extreme redistributive land reform, is embraced. A remarkable role for the state is envisaged. This departs markedly from the WC and seems to show that neoclassical economics can be deployed to embrace dramatically radical initiatives. The argument, as presented in an article by Griffin, Khan and Ickowitz (2002), is subjected to critical scrutiny in a special issue of the *Journal of Agrarian Change*, entitled *Redistributive Land Reform Today*.[2] This is the second focus of the critical treatment below.

One may also note that, as neoclassical economics, in its different forms, became hegemonic from the late 1960s onwards, heterodox views were in clear evidence. Agriculture attracted increasing attention. Again, I must be very brief. Thus, for example, a powerful classical statement, with agriculture at its centre, was developed by the Indian economist, Krishna Bharadwaj (1935–1992), some of whose writing I will note presently. Marxists gave increasing attention to the agrarian question, much of which may be seen in the *Journal of Peasant Studies* (founded in 1973) and the *Journal of Agrarian Change* (established in 2001 by the previous editors of the *Journal of Peasant Studies*). Structuralism gave way to dependency theory (see Kay 1989, Chapters 5 and 6, for a lucid treatment of dependency theory).

The New Neoclassical Development Economics according to Stiglitz

In the 1960s, in the growing literature on 'agriculture and development', a powerful challenge was mounted by neoclassical economists against the dominance of the classical paradigm. As this happened, so ONCE was replaced by a new neoclassical variant, that would become the standard orthodoxy. The WC view became predominant. But elements were there that eventually would form part of NNCDE. One may trace these metamorphoses briefly.

Exponents of ONCE did not demur at the central classical postulate of the existence of surplus labour or at other classical views. They argued strongly for land reform. They saw high rates of rural interest in informal markets as 'unreasonable' (even 'exploitative'); condemned sharecropping within a Marshallian framework; and perceived peasants as possibly not responding to price movements. While stressing the importance of markets/prices, they were preoccupied with market imperfections, seeing them as a possible justification for planning. Planning might clear the way for the ultimate operation of the market. They did not, necessarily, see relationships between economic agents as being mutually advantageous. The state might play a significantly positive role.

A fundamentally different neoclassical view emerged. Its exponents departed from the foregoing, root and branch. In 1964, Schultz's *Transforming Traditional Agriculture* was published – a key text in the questioning of ONCE. The neoclassical economists were on the march: Chicago had had enough of classical economics, with its absurd assumptions and policy prescriptions. What one witnessed, then, was resistance to the idea that economic agents in poor countries are anything other than allocatively efficient. If they are not allocatively efficient, the state might have to step in on a significant scale. One sees the embracing of 'the economic efficiency hypothesis' (Schultz 1964: 36). Land reform disappeared from the analytical and policy agenda. It was not necessary. Indeed, it might be positively harmful, inasmuch as it involved top–down intervention by the state, with accompanying high costs, corruption, rent-seeking and distortion of land markets.

The first 'revision' was over surplus labour. It was now assumed that disguised unemployment was non-existent (for example, Jorgenson 1961). In Schultz's (1964, Chapter 4: 53–70) book , 'The Doctrine of Agricultural Labor of Zero Value' is dismissed. The latter was bound up with the strongly held classical position that the state was necessary to get development going: in this instance, to mobilize surplus labour, but also more generally. That could not be so since, *contra* Lewis, there *was no* surplus labour.

A further blow was struck in the 1960s on relative price movements. The Indian economist, Raj Krishna (1963: 486), showed that 'while the elasticity of acreage of wheat in the Punjab was much lower than that in the United States, the elasticities of cotton and maize acreage in the Punjab were significantly higher'. So here were rational actors – rational peasants – behaving as rationally as North American farmers. Such evidence would later be used as part of the argument that the strategy of 'getting prices right' had a sound basis in poor countries, and should replace the hopelessly inefficient government intervention and planning, with its accompanying, rampant rent-seeking.

In the new WC view, what Stiglitz (1989b: 20) has referred to as 'the efficient markets hypothesis and the Coase theorem' prevail. This is the proposition that, left to themselves, 'individuals would quickly get together to eliminate any inefficient resource allocation (or inefficient institutional arrangement)', and are prevented from so acting only by '(harmful) governmental intervention since economic forces naturally lead to economic efficiency' (ibid.: 20). To this, Stiglitz, as indicated below, took exception. His departure in this respect, in part, distinguishes NNCDE from ONCE.

The next major assault is related to rural interest rates. In a series of articles in the 1960s, Bottomley (1963a, 1963b, 1964a, 1964b, 1969, all reprinted in 1971) challenged the idea that the very high interest rates observed in informal credit markets were exploitative. They could be explained in terms of the costs associated with making the loans (administrative costs, opportunity costs, etc.). – he did not use the term 'transaction costs' but the idea was there; and, very important, the risks associated with them – that is, the risk of default. He stressed the significance of so-called lender's risk. Rural interest rates were not 'unreasonably' high. The 'institution' of unorganized money markets, or the 'village moneylender', supplies credit at interest rates that are perfectly reasonable, in the given circumstances.

One sees the beginnings of an approach to 'agrarian institutions' that views them in a far more favourable light. *Contra* the ONCE view, unorganized money markets are desirable and efficient: they supply credit that would not otherwise be supplied, at rates that reflect relevant costs. They are to the mutual advantage of both parties. From this, Stiglitz does not demur.

The next battleground was over sharecropping. Such a tenancy form was observed to be widespread in poor countries. Until the late 1960s, it had been condemned as inefficient by a line of economists running from Adam Smith down through Alfred Marshall to those who considered it in post-war developing countries. The ONCE view of sharecropping was that suggested by Marshall (1979: 534–37). It was inefficient because of the disincentive associated with only a partial share accruing to the producer, and the Marshallian proposition was maintained that share tenancy would yield lower input per acre and lower output per acre than peasant proprietorship or fixed money rent or wage-based agriculture.

But, if it were so inefficient, how did one explain its prevalence and its tenacity? In 1969, Cheung gave an answer. Transaction costs were important but it was sharecropping's *risk-dispersing property*, more or less ignored earlier, that was crucial. Its prevalence and its tenacity, then, might be explained in a dramatically new

> view that it represented an efficient institutional arrangement for risk-sharing in an environment where other forms of insurance were not available: the landlord and the tenant shared in the risks associated with the fluctuations in output caused by weather, disease etc. as well as those associated with the vicissitudes in the prices of marketed commodities. (Stiglitz 1989a: 309)

To this, Stiglitz (1989b: 21) added a novel argument: 'that contrary to the standard view that criticized sharecropping as inefficient because it dampened incentives, sharecropping was desirable because it increased incentives'.

Risk was a new element in the explanation; and sharecropping was seen to be mutually advantageous to landlord and tenant, as rural credit in informal markets was to lender and borrower. Risk had already been given central emphasis by Bottomley, with respect to interest rates. Now it was seen to be of primary significance in tenancy markets. This emphasis on risk was taken up by Stiglitz and was a crucial part of the NNCDE.

Risk further entered the scene when another phenomenon was 'discovered' that lent itself to the new approach. Previously, a recurring phenomenon had been observed. For example, those from whom loans were taken might be landlords or traders, as well as moneylenders. Moreover, these activities might be formally linked. A landlord who was also a moneylender might stipulate what crops were to be grown, or might insist that all the crop above the rent must be sold to him. Or a moneylender-cum-trader might insist, as a condition of the loan, that the crop be sold to him at pre-fixed prices. Until the 1960s, although this had been observed, it had not attracted any great attention from economists. That now changed.

It was, in fact, Krishna Bharadwaj who first drew attention rigorously to this relationship, herself an outstanding economist in the classical tradition. She conceived it in terms of 'interlocking of markets' (Bharadwaj 1969, 1974), although, within her framework, it might more accurately be identified as 'interlocking modes of exploitation'. She would later develop her analysis (Bharadwaj 1979) and provide a magisterial treatment (Bharadwaj 1985). Bhaduri (1973), too, analysed it, with some power. Neoclassical economists were attracted to the issue, although they would give it a very different treatment. The phenomenon was given analytical attention in the NNCDE. Interlinkage was seen to be the outcome of market imperfections, which had associated with them particular costs, for both parties. Interlinked markets were a way of minimizing these costs, to the mutual advantage of both parties. One particular cost is that deriving from risk. High risks, rooted in endemic uncertainty, are characteristic of poor agrarian economies. Interlinkage serves to disperse those risks and is the preferred solution for both parties. This includes: the risks associated with agricultural production itself, the risks involved in seeking employment, the risks involved in seeking a loan, the risks involved in seeking a labour force, the risks of default on interest on loans (or the loans themselves), the risk of rent not being paid.

Having identified some of the building blocks of the NNCDE, one may briefly state Stiglitz's rendering of this variant of the neoclassical paradigm, before turning to a critique. Stiglitz conveniently provides a lucid and brief statement. In two of his texts (Stiglitz 1986, 1989b), that theory is encapsulated in seven tenets.

First, the land in poor countries is worked by peasants, whether tenants or owner–cultivators, who are rational in that 'they act in a (reasonably) consistent manner, one which adapts to changes in circumstances' (Stiglitz 1986: 257). There is much 'econometric evidence, showing that peasants respond to market forces' (ibid.): not least the large amount of evidence on price responsiveness. Stiglitz works with the category 'peasants', or 'individuals' (ibid.). In this neoclassical universe, classes as such do not exist. There is no hint that peasantries might be socially differentiated. One sees here a tension in the methodological individualism that lies at the heart of the neoclassical approach. While, in principle, every individual is potentially different, in practice, each is treated as if the same and, indeed as representative of all others.

Second, while peasants are rational, 'they are not fully informed about the consequences either of their actions, or of the institutions through which they operate' (Stiglitz 1989b: 23). Information is costly and imperfect 'and hence . . . behaviour may differ markedly from what it would have been . . . [with] perfect information' (Stiglitz 1986: 257). Further, there is likely to be information asymmetry. Thus, say, a landlord or a moneylender may be in possession of information that a peasant does not have, or vice versa. There is no suggestion that rich and poor peasants may differ significantly in their access to information, or in the quality of information they have. Those categories, indeed, do not exist in this universe.

Third, 'one of the distinguishing characteristics of LDCs is the absence of certain markets . . . [or the existence of markets that are] thin' (Stiglitz 1989b: 23), and the absence, therefore, of a central driving force in the economy. Stiglitz denies the 'efficient markets hypothesis'. While certain kinds of government intervention may be an 'impediment to development' (ibid.: 20), he insists that the stark view of the Coase theorem that 'markets by themselves would take care of matters . . . have done a disservice . . . for they fail to take note of the important, seemingly positive, role of government in the case of so many of the developed countries' (ibid.).

The fourth tenet encompasses a positive view of 'agrarian institutions' in general: that is to say, crucial 'institutions' like rural money markets, share-cropping, interlinked markets. Previously denounced as 'inefficient' by old-style neoclassical economists (ONCE), these are now seen as 'functional but imperfect' (Stiglitz 1986: 257). They are far more flexible than previously thought. Thus: 'Institutions adapt to reflect these information (and other transaction) costs. Thus, institutions are not to be taken as exogenous, and changes in the environment may lead with a lag to changes in institutional structure' (ibid.). This remarkable 'flexibility', of advantage to all parties involved, seems to be a powerful attribute.

These 'agrarian institutions' have a yet further powerful feature, enshrined in the fifth tenet: their capacity to deal with risk. He stresses: 'in the absence of insurance markets . . . this is clearly an important function' (Stiglitz 1989b: 21). This is one of the major 'discoveries' of the NNCDE school. These institutions are far more effective and efficient than was thought previously. In the *given objective circumstances*, they probably produce the optimum solution. They perform important economic functions 'better than alternative institutional arrangements' (ibid.).

The sixth tenet is: 'The fact that individuals are rational and that institutions are adaptable does not, however, imply that the economy is (Pareto) efficient' (Stiglitz 1986: 257). For it would require 'a complete set of markets and perfect information' (ibid.). Absurd as that might be in an advanced economy, it is *a fortiori* so in a poor one. Anyway, from this he derives the conclusion that 'there exists a set of taxes and subsidies which can make everyone better off' (ibid.).

Stiglitz (1986: 257) uses this, along with the third tenet, to derive the seventh one: that 'there is a potential role for the government'. It is, however, a cautious endorsement of a circumscribed role. He stresses that the market itself cannot eradicate economic backwardness and generate development. But he remains more than a little suspicious of government. The following might seem bold and radical in the company of extreme, pro-market, anti-state neoclassical economists of the WC persuasion:

the government could effect a Pareto improvement if (i) it had sufficient knowledge of the structure of the economy; (ii) those responsible for implementing government policy had at least as much information as those in the private sector; (iii) those responsible for designing and implementing government policy had the incentives to direct policies to effect Pareto improvements, rather than, for instance, to redistribute income (either from the poor to the rich or vice versa, or from everyone else, to themselves), often at considerable loss to national output. (ibid.: 257–58)

But it is hardly a clarion call for a developmental state.

Towards a Critique of the New Neoclassical Development Economics
Differentiated versus Homogeneous Peasantries

There are, in the NNCDE universe, *divisions*: between producers with land, landless labourers, landlords, traders, moneylenders. These are not, however, antagonistic divisions: divisions of class. Moreover, it is further assumed that the peasantry is a homogeneous one. This is so in the literature on price responsiveness, on rural credit markets, on interlinked markets, on sharecropping and so on.

The appropriate assumption, however, is that of antagonistic class relations and of socially differentiated peasantries. It is useful to think in terms of a poor peasantry, a middle peasantry and a rich peasantry. These strata need to be identified with care, in concrete historical situations. Their precise characteristics will vary with time, place and circumstance, and according to the degree of capitalist penetration of the countryside. They may, for example, be identified in terms of holding size; whether they produce a regular surplus and what kind of surplus; whether they are net hirers in or out of labour, or are family-based with the need to do neither; whether they are heavily indebted, at usurious rates of interest; whether they are compulsively involved in interlinked markets; and so on. Size of holding will be a useful, if imperfect, stratifying variable. Of all this, NNCDE is innocent. One might illustrate the need to proceed in terms of socially differentiated peasantries and antagonistic relations of production with respect to any of the major issues addressed by the NNCDE.[3] Here, I will concentrate on the problematic of the need to secure agricultural growth, identified at the outset, and some simple propositions.

Such growth requires agrarian transformation. The form taken by that transformation will vary. Historically, it has often had at its centre either a landlord class transformed into a class of capitalist farmers (capitalism from above) or a rich peasantry that may be so transformed (capitalism from below), and the emergence of a class of wage labour, a rural proletariat. In each case, the relationship between capitalist farmer and wage labour, and the subsequent struggle between capital and labour in the countryside, are crucial. In contemporary developing countries, both capitalism from below and capitalism from above may be seen (see Byres 2002: 65–80). Whichever tendency predominates, it is particularly important to focus on the nature of socially differentiated peasantries and the extent to which rich peasantries are accumulation-oriented; and, if one's concern is with poverty, on the fate of middle and poor peasants, and of wage labourers. The analytical categories of the NNCDE are incapable of capturing this. They abstract from such questions. That being so, its practitioners simply ignore the major tendencies at work in the countryside.

Relationships of Exploitation rather than Mutuality

The second questionable NNCDE assumption is that of mutuality between producers and non-producers, and among producers themselves; with the relevant 'agrarian institutions' acting powerfully to disperse risk for all parties. Stiglitz (1986: 261) strongly resists the idea of exploitation: arguing that 'the exploitation hypothesis . . . fails to explain the detailed structure of rural organization'. But, in a political economy approach, in considering those 'agrarian institutions', exploitation/surplus appropriation is far more important in explaining their operation than risk. In a capitalist situation, a relationship between a capitalist employer and wage labour involves exploitation, appropriation of surplus value. That, of course, is vehemently denied by the neoclassical of any stripe. In circumstances of economic backwardness, exploitation is equally emphatically denied. But a tenancy relationship, a relationship with a moneylender, a relationship with a trader, or a relationship between an employer and labour, all involve exploitation, that is to say, appropriation of surplus. Even more starkly than in the capitalist situation, these are relationships of exploitation: there are relentless pressures to appropriate all surplus above bare subsistence. These will be intensified where there are interlinked modes of exploitation. Thus, the essence of the sharecropping relationship, in which a percentage of the crop, gross or net, 50 per cent or more, automatically goes to the landlord, is the appropriation of surplus. If a poor peasant takes loans at very high rates of interest, for whatever reasons, that he or she is unable to repay – that is, is saddled with debt – then, the moneylender is appropriating surplus. If a poor peasant is locked into a relationship with a trader whereby he or she is paid for his produce less than the market price, then, surplus is being appropriated. If a poor peasant, as part of interlocked markets, supplies labour to a landlord at less than the market wage or at no wage at all, then, surplus is being appropriated. It is very difficult to see these as relationships of mutuality. One need make no moral judgement. Quite simply, dominant classes are able to appropriate much of the surplus above subsistence.

Because the NNDCE ignores exploitation, it ignores (i) the crucial matter of surplus appropriation and its associated mechanisms, and the implications for those from whom surplus is appropriated; and (ii) the manner of its utilization by the classes that appropriate surplus. A political economy approach immediately focuses on these matters. The crucial issues are why, in circumstances of economic backwardness, such surplus is used unproductively (that is, in ways that do not enhance the economy's productive base), and how a shift takes place towards more productive use on a regular and expanding basis. NNDCE has little to offer on this. Again, then, critical tendencies are simply missed.

Asymmetry of Economic Power

Embedded in the assumption of mutuality is the assumption of parity of economic power among the different agents/classes. That is inappropriate. NNCDE makes much of information asymmetry, and the remarkable ability of 'agrarian institutions' to deal with it. What it ignores completely is asymmetry of economic power. One might illustrate this pervasively (for a treatment in the context of sharecropping, see Byres 2003: 246–48).

The universe invoked by Stiglitz *et al.* is one in which there is active bargaining, conducted between parties of more or less equal bargaining power. It is not a convincing one. As Bhaduri (1983b: 88) has observed: 'Bargaining is a meaningful concept only if both parties enjoy more or less symmetrical economic power. This is hardly the case when a landlord confronts a pure landless tenant with meagre and uncertain alternative employment opportunities.' Where a powerful landlord confronts either a pure landless tenant or a heavily indebted poor peasant with a tiny holding over whom considerable power is exerted – perhaps as a moneylender as well as a landlord – 'negotiation costs' will be minimal, or non-existent. They are a neoclassical fiction.

The same is so with respect to 'the cost of enforcement' (Cheung 1969: 62). This supposedly represents the costs associated with 'enforcing the stipulations of the contract' (ibid.: 63), the 'costs of controlling inputs and distributing input according to the terms of the contract' (ibid.: 67). High enforcement costs of the kind suggested again imply some parity of bargaining power and economic strength. If, however, there is no 'symmetry of economic power'; if, indeed, one has a powerful landlord, in relationship with a poor peasant, desperately fearful of losing his land, then, 'enforcement costs' will be very low. The fear itself of losing the land will be sufficient enforcement. Again, one is in the presence of a neoclassical fiction.

What emerges is the incapacity of this approach to identify the reasons for the tenacity of 'agrarian institutions' like sharecropping, or informal money markets/usurious moneylending, or interlocked markets. Those reasons lie, surely, in the sheer scale of the asymmetry in question and the gains it provides for dominant classes. If one seeks to understand why economic backwardness persists, one must seek to grasp this and to contemplate how it might be broken, so that a new kind of asymmetry of economic power might arise, on a more productive basis.

The Causes of Backwardness

Stiglitz (1989b: 27) himself raises 'that most fundamental of questions with which we as development economists are concerned, the persistence of massive differences in standards of living and the means by which those means may be reduced'. There is a prior question: wherein lie the *causal roots* of economic backwardness and *why is that backwardness reproduced*? The practitioners of NNCDE have remarkably little to say about that. Indeed, if what they say about the relevant 'agrarian institutions' is valid, it is difficult to see why there is any economic backwardness at all. Within these remarkably functioning agrarian institutions – with their flexible adjustment to 'thin' markets, their capacity to deal with risk, etc. – economic backwardness should have gone long ago.

There is, by contrast, within the agrarian political economy tradition, a concern with the roots of economic backwardness and how it is reproduced. This one may see, for example, in the treatment of interlinked markets. Here, the effects are clear: upon the generation, form and character of surplus; its utilization; and the pace of accumulation. This is absent from NNCDE.

Thus, the poverty that prevails in a 'backward agriculture', and which is intensified by interlinking modes of exploitation, and the dependency that interlinking secures, are crucial. They encourage particular forms of capital investment: a specific pattern of investment. Accumulation takes on a particular character. 'Unproductive', 'usurious', 'mercantile' and 'speculative' forms of investment are the norm: because, for dominant classes, those who extract and control the surplus, tenancy, usury, trade and speculation pay handsomely. Poverty and dependency make high rents and very high rates of interest possible; make profit on trade high because of the low prices at which commodities can be bought; make speculation attractive because commodity markets are 'unformed'. The rate of return on these is far higher than any alternative rate of return (Bharadwaj 1985: 15). The consequences are: 'investment goes into unproductive channels. Productive investment, meaning investment that enhances output growth is at a disadvantage. . . . Where possibilities of exploiting labour become almost limitless there is less incentive to improve productive forces, that is, undertake productive investment' (ibid.). So it is that the rate of reinvestment of surplus and, hence, 'the growth of surplus itself' (ibid.) are influenced. They are far less than they would be if a greater incentive to undertake productive investment existed. These are powerfully sustained by interlinked modes of exploitation. The central question – the 'agrarian question' – then becomes: under what circumstances might these conditions be overcome and a transition to a capitalist agriculture be secured; whether that transition is via a capitalism from above or a capitalism from below (see Byres 1996 for a full-scale treatment of such transitions in the nineteenth and early twentieth centuries, in two cases: capitalism from above in Prussia and capitalism from below in the USA). It is the case that such a transition is well under way in many developing countries. That is the question addressed by agrarian political economy.

The State

The NNCDE economists have a problematic, and ambiguous, view of the state. One may focus upon Stiglitz, as the major intellectual force in NNCDE and as one who has been preoccupied with the issue. With Stiglitz, indeed, it seems promising enough to attract the criticism of extreme neoclassical free marketeers.

But how 'state-friendly' is NNCDE? 'One must', Stiglitz (1986: 258) insists, be 'cautious in recommending particular government actions as remedies for certain observed deficiencies in the market'. Is it simply 'a set of taxes and subsidies' that can make everyone better off? If that is so, it is not very much. While, indeed, he wishes to stress government's *potential* role, he never really spells that out. He tells us, in a footnote, with respect to its role in the earlier phases of capitalist development in the now advanced countries: 'Though Japan is the case that inevitably comes to mind, one should not forget the role of the federal government in the development of American railroads' (Stiglitz 1989b: 27, n.4). That is inadequate. It needs to be replaced with a more positive, a more nuanced and a more informed view of the state.

There is an essential ambivalence. Even as he warms to the task of identifying the senses in which state intervention is essential, he seriously qualifies his argument and distances himself from anything resembling advocacy of a 'developmental state'. Sender (2002: 192–97) addresses incisively Stiglitz's view of the state, with respect to the latter's apparently fundamental critique of the WC: 'In sum, the post-Washington Consensus, like the old Washington Consensus, retains a very limited conception of the role of the state in promoting growth in poor economies.' Sender then notes of the architect of the post-Washington Consensus: 'The grudging and qualified tone of the critique is evident in the following speculative conclusion: "Perhaps had these [East Asian] countries followed all of the dictums of liberalization and privatization, they would have grown even faster" (Stiglitz 1998: 120).'

The heterodox view of the state is a more positive one. It does not deny the problems associated with an interventionist state, and how, in some circumstances, state intervention can go disastrously wrong. It is sensitive, moreover, to the difficulties that derive from the state's representation of the interests of dominant classes, to the detriment of subordinate classes. Intervention by the state is neither unproblematic nor guaranteed to generate successful development. History is littered with too many contrary instances for such a position to be sustained.

Yet, in agriculture, there are certain essential tasks that only the state can undertake. Sender (2002: 192) points out that Stiglitz and other representatives of NNCDE in effect focus upon 'the familiar limited menu . . . [of] education, health, roads, law and order'. But the state has a far wider, crucial part to play, in agriculture and more generally. This includes the pursuit of protectionist trade policies and import-substituting industrialization to allow for the structural transformation that has been a critical part of all major historical instances of capitalist development. In agriculture, it is so in the pursuit of land reform: which, deriving from the very different view of the nature and functioning of 'agrarian institutions', would include the *replacement* of the much-vaunted, flexible 'agrarian institutions', such as sharecropping and interlinked markets. It further entails a massive programme of formal credit, with credit provided at non-usurious interest rates. And it is so with respect, for example, to substantial

initiatives in the creation of modern irrigation facilities, the generating and disse-
mination of other forms of new technology, the control of inter-sectoral prices,
and comprehensive poverty alleviation schemes. Without such an interventionist
state, it is difficult to conceive of dynamic agrarian transformation in economically backward economies; or transformation in which the interests of subordinate classes are served. State intervention is a necessary condition for successful
development, but the state that intervenes must be one that is genuinely 'developmental'. Here lies one of the central problems of development. It is not a problem
upon which the new neoclassical development economics casts much light.

The Neoclassical Neo-Populist Case for Redistributive Land Reform
Different Kinds of Land Reform
There are, indeed, different kinds of land reform. Abstracting from, for
example, government-sponsored settlement schemes, and distinguishing collectivization (the socialist attempt to resolve the agrarian question) from land
reform (more usually a non-socialist initiative, and sometimes a moment in the
development of capitalist agriculture), there are two basic types: *tenurial reform*
and *redistributive reform*. Both, in the post-1945 era, have been the initiatives, or
potential initiatives, of 'developmental' states.

Tenurial reform concerns the terms on which the operated holding is
held and worked, and seeks to eliminate those aspects of the tenurial relationship, or the form of operated holdings, that are held to dull incentives, reduce the
wherewithal to invest and impede efficiency: and so prevent the emergence of an
efficient, dynamic and growing agriculture. In the ideal, tenancy itself may be
abolished, with a policy of 'land to the tiller'. In that instance, all (or almost all)
tenurial obstacles to a dynamic agriculture would be swept away. Where tenancy remains, such land reform has included the following strands: the abolition
of absentee landlordism, held to be inferior to resident landlordism, on the grounds
that the absentee has no interest in productive investment in the land; the eradication of a particular tenancy form, sharecropping, held to be especially pernicious because of its effects on incentives and its heavy appropriation of surplus
(so removing from the producer the means to invest); the introduction of fixed
money rents and 'fair' rents (that is, controlled rents), which commercializes
agriculture and controls the rent burden; the elimination of insecure tenure since
it is a disincentive to that investment whose benefits accrue in the longer term.
One may also include the rooting out of land fragmentation (where an operated
holding is held in several physically separate pieces) via a programme of consolidation of holdings, although owned as well as tenanted holdings may be fragmented. Such fragmentation is held to lead to an inefficient use of land, labour
and capital. In theory, such tenurial reform, in its various manifestations, could
proceed without any change in the distribution of operated holdings: with both
large and small holdings (rich, middle and poor peasants) benefiting. In practice,
the most likely beneficiaries have been larger/richer peasants.

Redistributive land reform is, in principle, more radical, and seeks to redistribute operated holdings, taking land from those with large operated holdings and transferring it either to those with no land at all (landless peasants and wage labourers) or those with tiny holdings (poor peasants), and imposing ceilings on the size of operated holding. A crucial part of its *economic* rationale has been that there is an inverse relationship between land productivity and size of holding, with a gap of as much as 50–60 per cent between the largest and the smallest holdings. This has sometimes been held to show that small holdings are more 'efficient' than large; that, certainly, redistribution would bring about a significant once-and-for-all rise in output; and probably that redistribution would bring a more quickly growing agriculture. It has been further argued that such redistributive land reform would reduce the incidence of widespread rural poverty: by providing land – the means of subsistence, security for borrowing and the source of employment – to those without it or with inadequate amounts. Redistribution, where it has been pursued, has required 'ceiling' legislation, itself a matter of considerable controversy, over what the size of a 'viable' holding might be and what the 'optimum' size of holding is. To be successful, it has been assumed to require simultaneous tenurial reform, so that the operated holdings will be worked to maximum effect: with the necessary incentives in place. It is *redistributive land reform* that is the focus of neoclassical neo-populism.

The Prominence, Eclipse and Reappearance of Land Reform on Policy Agendas

Land reform was prominent on the development agendas of the 1950s and 1960s, in both socialist and non-socialist states, with both tenurial reform and redistributive land reform figuring in the land reform programmes of a variety of poor countries. In socialist countries it proved to be a prelude to collectivization, and disappeared with the advent of collectives. In non-socialist countries it achieved limited success, with tenurial reform pursued more robustly and with greater success than redistributive land reform, and largely to the benefit of richer peasants. In those countries land reform was swept away as a major policy initiative by the late 1960s, in the wake of the 'new technology' and its 'betting on the strong' philosophy – in the belief that much-needed agricultural growth in countries in which growth had slowed to very low levels could only thus be secured. That 'new technology' was often adopted by those larger peasants who had benefited from tenurial reform. The adoption of that 'new technology' produced increasingly unequal structures. Land reform receded into the background from the late 1960s onwards, although it never disappeared.

In the meantime, the demise of the 'developmental' state has been signalled, with its replacement by supposedly leaner and meaner neoliberal states in poor countries. Land reform, after the eclipse of its earlier prominence in a variety of poor countries, has recently returned to policy agendas, but often, now, in a form more attuned to the market. The World Bank has been urging 'market-friendly land reform' as altogether more appropriate for such neoliberal states, which involves creating incentives and providing the means for large landowners to sell part of their holding. It is an approach that is hostile to state-led agrarian reform, with its supposedly large bureaucracy and top–down methods, and, as indicated above when discussing the WC view, its postulated high costs, corruption and distorted land markets. This reappearance of land reform as an issue has been true of both non-socialist and former socialist countries.

The GKI Intervention

The case for redistributive land reform has been made most recently in an article by Griffin, Khan and Ickowitz (2002) (henceforth GKI), 'Poverty and Distribution of Land'. A theoretical argument is proposed for truly radical redistributive land reform, which would take land from large landowners and vest it in small holdings, with those who would work it as owner-operated, family-based farms.

The case for *tenurial reform* is dismissed, on the grounds that it cannot produce a superior outcome, and might even worsen matters. The logic is very similar to that deployed by Stiglitz in his stipulation of flexible 'agrarian institutions'. To that extent it has a certain kinship with NNCDE. But, in its advocacy of radical redistribution, it departs markedly from what might be seen as an NNCDE policy agenda.

GKI note the World Bank's 'market-friendly', 'negotiated' land reform. This they reject as a realistic solution to problems of inequality, poverty and growth because 'the financial cost to the government of a "market friendly", full compensation land reform is bound to be onerous and the government is likely to feel compelled to shift as much of the financial burden as possible on to the beneficiaries' (Griffin, Khan and Ickowitz 2002: 321). It is too expensive and could only have very limited impact. They argue: 'The inescapable conclusion is that a major redistributive land reform is impossible if land transfers are based on free market prices; either government must act to depress land prices or there must be outright confiscation of some kind' (ibid.).

The land reform advocated, it is argued, would produce a more efficient and a more dynamic agriculture, and would soon eliminate rural poverty. That case is made theoretically: concisely, rigorously and cogently, and with great clarity, within a neoclassical framework. And, in its treatment of the 'power of landlords' who mobilize to 'extract effort from their workers and tenants' (Griffin, Khan and Ickowitz 2002: 287, 288), it seems to embrace a political economy that transcends usual neoclassical treatment.

In the very broadest terms, in the pre-reform situation, monopsonistic landowners confront rural labour in circumstances of significant inequality. The existing land concentration is shown to give markedly inferior results to a perfectly competitive situation, and this is taken to show a strong case for redistribution. Fragmented factor markets (for land, labour and capital) and powerful systems of labour control generate underemployment and pervasive rural poverty. Because of these fragmented factor markets, small farmers (for whom labour is relatively cheap, and land and finance capital relatively expensive) adopt lower capital–labour ratios/higher labour–land ratios, and large farmers (for whom labour is relatively expensive, and land and capital relatively cheap) adopt higher capital–labour ratios/lower labour–land ratios; and it is clearly the case that small farms produce significantly higher output per acre – are more efficient – than large farms (the explanation of the inverse relationship is a clearly neoclassical one, couched in terms of 'imperfections in factor markets'). A redistributive land reform would increase agricultural output significantly and would accelerate agricultural growth. It would, concomitantly, get rid of rural poverty.

The foregoing is geared to the microeconomic context. There is treatment also of 'Land Reform in a Macroeconomic Context', where it is argued that redistributive land reform will lead to an acceleration of *overall* economic growth. This will be so, however, only if certain conditions are met. The pernicious influence of 'urban bias' is argued and it is insisted that 'the removal of urban bias is . . . a necessary condition for a successful redistributive land reform' (Griffin, Khan and Ickowitz 2002: 317), and, therefore, for the postulated more rapid economic growth. So, too, must what GKI refer to as 'landlord bias' be removed.

The GKI paper seems dramatically radical and may be very attractive for those in the development field normally hostile to neoclassical approaches (among them, academics, intellectuals, students, NGOs, if not representatives of governments). Its considerable appeal lies in its appearing to hold out the promise – *if it could be implemented* – of eradicating rural poverty, and accelerating both agricultural and overall growth; and doing so with a case that is rigorously and confidently presented. In its boldness, it seems to embrace a potent iconoclasm that is powerfully at variance with the recommended land reform policies of the World Bank and, clearly, on the side of the poor. Moreover, it has a political economy content that neoclassical texts usually lack, and which seems to give it a relevance that appears absent from more purely technical exercises. If it is not a variant of Stiglitz-style NNCDE, it does draw on its logic (in dismissing the case for tenurial reform), and it is, surely, a very distinctive form of neoclassical development economics, which demands attention.

Towards a Critique of Neoclassical Neo-Populism
Neoclassical Neo-Populism

I have termed the GKI approach neoclassical neo-populism. It is neoclassical in that it deploys the conceptual apparatus of neoclassical economics. In its stress upon factor market imperfections and 'efficiency', and its resort to the notion of perfect competition, it is quintessentially neoclassical. At the same time, in its quest for egalitarian solutions to the problems of developing countries, and in its advocacy of the cultivation of the land with household labour by peasant owner–operators, it is archetypally neo-populist; in the latter regard, bearing a strong family resemblance to the arguments of the father of neo-populism, A.V. Chayanov (on populism and neo-populism, in a related context, see Byres 1979). I have elsewhere provided a detailed critique of the GKI logic (Byres 2004). Here, drawing upon that critique, I present a very brief treatment and focus upon a limited number of relevant issues.

Some Contradictions and Some Absences

The GKI approach is fraught with contradictions. Let me note two.

Firstly, at its very core, and its central contradiction, is the simultaneous pursuit of *equality*, its compelling populist goal, and *efficiency*, its disciplining neoclassical force. Its advocacy of massive intervention by the state to achieve equity, is derived via an undiluted neoclassical treatment that should, on strict neoclassical logic and in the interests of efficiency, oppose such state action. Moreover, how such a cataclysmic redistribution might be *implemented* is no-where considered. It lacks any convincing view of the state and is devoid of any political dimension.

Secondly, it embraces a 'new' neoclassical treatment of tenurial forms, which posits the efficiency of existing 'rural institutions', such as share tenancy. At the same time, it advocates ownership of the redistributed land by the cultiva-tors that, in effect, finds no support in such logic.

The GKI Political Economy

The GKI approach is to be distinguished from that of all the other neo-classical economists already noted in that it seeks to operate within a clear politi-cal economy framework. It is, however, a framework that is limited in scope. I have noted the absence of any treatment of the state and of a political dimension. To that I would add the following.

I would stress the social categories used: 'large private landowners', 'small peasant farmers' and 'landless agricultural workers'. Indeed, the last-named, that is, wage labour, hardly figure prominently, so that it is, in effect, a dichotomous class structure that is portrayed. There is no mention of capitalism or capitalist farmers, or of peasants other than 'small peasant farmers'. There is no hint of differentiated peasantries – of rich, middle and poor peasants; or where, on that continuum, 'small peasant farmers' might fit. The peasantry is, in effect, homogeneous. One is, most clearly, in a neo-populist universe.

As I have suggested already, one cannot capture the reality of the countryside without some notion of differentiated cultivators; and of a develop-ing capitalism and class relationships in the countryside – a more complex class situation than is suggested by the simple landlord/small farmers dichotomy. GKI nowhere consider the possibility that the redistributive land reform they advocate might, if it were successful, lay the basis for capitalism from below; might create structures within which processes of differentiation flour-ished and a class of capitalist farmers emerged. This is a possibility of consider-able significance.

The Development of Capitalism and an Ahistorical Approach

The analytical framework in which this needs to be discussed is that of the development of capitalism in the countryside. GKI do not operate within such a framework. They simply abstract from it. Yet, a clear historical perspective would suggest the compelling need for such a framework. Their approach, in effect, is resolutely ahistorical. That, one might say, is a defining characteristic of neoclassical neo-populism, as it is of all neoclassical analysis. To be ahistorical is to run the risk of failing to see history changing before one's very eyes. That is precisely the case here.

It ignores the historical role of capitalist industrialization and its accompanying structural change, which has been a crucial means by which massive rural poverty has been eradicated in the past. It denies the need for structural inequality of access to resources as a prerequisite for capitalist acceleration in the countryside, which has characterized past transformations. It can posit the staying power, viability and superiority of peasant agriculture vis-à-vis capitalist agriculture only by failing to acknowledge the existence and nature of capitalism. Methodologically, its shortcoming is that it is a static approach in a dynamic context that does not and cannot capture the relevant change and its contradictions.

The Inverse Relationship

Crucial to the whole GKI case for redistributive land reform is the inverse relationship. One may, then, consider that in a little more detail.[4] Part of the explanation of the inverse relationship in those agricultures with a highly unequal distribution of operated holdings and holdings worked by non-owners may be as follows: that an essential reason for the heavy application of labour by small cultivators, which produces the inverse relationship, is that their very survival requires this; that they are locked into surplus appropriation relationships that push them down to bare subsistence; and that they are forced to apply labour very intensively in order to maximize output and so achieve a tolerable existence. These relationships include tenancy and especially sharecropping, usurious credit, highly unequal trade, and, indeed, interlinked modes of exploitation. This GKI resolutely ignore as the causal mechanism. It is what Dyer (1997: 47) refers to as 'a class-based approach to understanding the inverse relationship' that is necessary. Dyer (ibid.: 53) insists, I think rightly, that 'it is thus misguided to treat the inverse relationship as a sign of relative efficiency rather than of distress'. But if, with redistributive land reform, these relationships of appropriation were eradicated, part of the reason for heavy labour application would go, too.

It is likely to be the case that, where the inverse relationship exists, it is the outcome of far heavier application of labour by small farmers, in circumstances in which large and small farmers use essentially the same technology. Large farmers will not have access to a technology that might countermand that 'advantage' possessed by small farmers: either a perhaps scale-neutral superior technology to which small farmers did not have access or a technology with clear economies of scale. GKI deny the existence of economies of scale. But the arrival of such a superior technology, with the capitalist penetration of the countryside and its adoption by 'large farmers' (that is, capitalist farmers/rich peasants) will cut at the basis for the inverse relationship.

A central fallacy in this whole approach is the assumption that the *inverse* relationship holds for all times and all places. It clearly does not. Here is an obviously static approach. But, widespread as the inverse relationship has been, there are circumstances in which it breaks down and disappears. To maintain such a static approach in a dynamic context is clearly methodologically inadequate. Where the 'new technology' has spread and, as part of that, mechanization has been adopted, the economies of scale associated with that have given large farmers a clear advantage. The former 'advantage' of small farmers in being able to apply labour very intensively, where large farmers had no clear technical superiority, gave rise to the inverse relationship. The new, technical advantage of large farmers brings a new *direct* relationship between land productivity and size of holding. It is in this sense that there is a contradiction between equity and efficiency, whose twin pursuit lies at the core of neoclassical neo-populism; or, if not, between equity and efficiency, between equity and growth.

What happens to the case for redistributive land reform? Its central prop has gone. Large farms now have higher land productivity and, indeed, must be seen, in neo-classical terms, to 'maximize total factor productivity'.

Conclusion

I would not wish to question the genuine desire of the practitioners of both of the neoclassical variants considered here to find a solution to the problem of an agriculture that lacks dynamism and fails to grow, and to put an end to the obscenity of pervasive rural poverty. In the case of neoclassical neo-populism, a truly radical solution appears to be suggested, and is argued with some passion.

The solutions offered by both of the neoclassical approaches considered are, however, fatally flawed. The fundamental weakness lies in the failure to confront the realities of either capitalist industrialization (which is ignored more or less completely), or of capitalist penetration of the countryside. Both approaches ignore the actual class structure of the countryside. Both fail to capture the existence of differentiated peasantries. Neither addresses the struggle between capital and labour in capitalist agriculture. Both are weak in their treatment of the state.

In so proceeding, they act to conceal the realities of contemporary poor countries and so, paradoxically, in their earnest break with extreme forms of neoclassical theorizing, and, in the Griffin case, the genuinely radical intent and apparent pursuit of egalitarianism, they perform an essentially reactionary function. They do so in the NNCDE case by romanticizing the operation and effects of the 'agrarian institutions' theorized, and obscuring their harsh realities, and in the GKI instance by the advocacy of solutions that are unattainable.

Notes

1 Here I present other versions of arguments developed earlier (Byres 2003, 2004a, 2004b). I am grateful to Ben Fine and Jomo K.S. for their editorial suggestions. They helped eliminate some obscurities and secure certain improvements. They are, of course, not responsible for any errors or ambiguities that might remain.

2 See the Introduction, where the arguments are contextualized and summarized (Byres 2004a), and Byres (2004b) for a full explanation of the term 'neoclassical neopopulism'.

3 See Byres (2003: 243–44), which draws on Bhaduri (1983: 33) on price responsiveness, in particular.

4 Here, I summarize my own treatment of the inverse relationship (Byres 2004). The inverse relationship receives detailed critical scrutiny by Dyer in the aforementioned special issue of the *Journal of Agrarian Change* on *Redistributive Land Reform Today* (Dyer 2004).

References

Baran, Paul (1957), *The Political Economy of Growth* (New York: Monthly Review Press).

Bhaduri, Amit (1973), 'Agricultural Backwardness under Semi-Feudalism', *Economic Journal*, 83 (329), March: 120–37.

—— (1983a), *The Economic Structure of Backward Agriculture* (London: Academic Press).

—— (1983b), 'Cropsharing as a Labour Process: Size of Farm and Supervision Cost', *Journal of Peasant Studies*, 10 (2 and 3), January and April: 88–93, special issue on *Sharecropping and Sharecroppers*.

—— (1986), 'Forced Commerce and Agrarian Growth', *World Development*, 14 (2): 267–72.

Bharadwaj, Krishna (1969), *Production Conditions in Indian Agriculture: A Study Based on Farm Management Surveys*, mimeo, Department of Applied Economics, Cambridge.

—— (1974), *Production Conditions in Indian Agriculture: A Study Based on Farm Management Surveys*, University of Cambridge Department of Applied Economics Occasional Paper 33 (London: Cambridge University Press).

—— (1979), 'Towards a Macro-Economic Framework for a Developing Economy: The Indian Case', *Manchester School*, 47 (3): September, 270–301.

—— (1985), 'A View on Commercialization in Indian Agriculture and the Development of Capitalism', *Journal of Peasant Studies*, 12 (4), July: 7–25.

Bottomley, Anthony (1963a), 'The Cost of Administering Private Loans in Underdeveloped Rural Areas', *Oxford Economic Papers*, 15, July: 154–63.

—— (1963b), 'The Premium for Risk as a Determinant of Interest Rates in Underdeveloped Rural Areas', *Quarterly Journal of Economics*, 77, November: 638–47.

—— (1964a), 'The Structure of Interest Rates in Underdeveloped Rural Areas', *Journal of Farm Economics*, 46 (2), May: 313–22.

—— (1964b), 'Monopoly Profit as a Determinant of Interest Rates in Underdeveloped Rural Areas', *Oxford Economic Papers*, 16, July: 432–37.

Bottomley, Anthony (1971), *Factor Pricing and Economic Growth in the Underdeveloped Rural Areas* (London: Crosby, Lockwood and Son).

Bottomley, Anthony and D. Nudds (1969), 'A Widow's Cruse Theory of Capital Supply in Underdeveloped Rural Areas', *Manchester School*, 37 (2), June: 131–40.

Byres, Terence J. (1979), 'Of Neo-Populist Pipe Dreams: Daedalus in the Third World and the Myth of Urban Bias', *Journal of Peasant Studies*, 6 (2), January: 210–44.

—— (1996), *Capitalism from Above and Capitalism from Below: An Essay in Comparative Political Economy* (Basingstoke and London: Macmillan).

—— (2002), 'Paths of Capitalist Agrarian Transition in the Past and in the Contemporary World', in V.K. Ramachandran and Madhura Swaminathan, eds, *Agrarian Studies: Essays on Agrarian Relations in Less-Developed Countries* (New Delhi: Tulika Books).

—— (2003), 'Agriculture and Development: The Dominant Orthodoxy and an Alternative View', in Ha-Joon Chang, ed., *Rethinking Development Economics* (London: Anthem Press).

—— (2004a), 'Introduction: Contextualizing and Interrogating the GKI Case for Redistributive Land Reform', *Journal of Agrarian Change*, 4 (1 and 2), January and April: 1–16, special issue on *Redistributive Land Reform Today*.

—— (2004b), 'Neoclassical Neo-Populism 25 years on, *Déjà Vu* and *Déjà Passé*: Towards A Critique', *Journal of Agrarian Change*, 4 (1 and 2), January and April: 17–44, special issue on *Redistributive Land Reform Today*.

Cheung, Stephen N.S. (1969), *The Theory of Share Tenancy* (Chicago and London: University of Chicago Press).

Dobb, Maurice (1946), *Studies in the Development of Capitalism* (London: Routledge and Kegan Paul).

—— (1951), *Some Aspects of Economic Development* (Delhi: Delhi School of Economics).

—— (1960), *An Essay on Economic Growth and Planning* (London: Routledge and Kegan Paul).

Dyer, Graham (1997), *Class, State and Agricultural Productivity in Egypt: A Study of the Inverse Relationship between Farm Size and Land Productivity* (London: Frank Cass).

—— (2004), 'Redistributive Land Reform: No April Rose, the Poverty of Berry and Cline and GKI on the Inverse Relationship', *Journal of Agrarian Change*, 4 (1 and 2), January and April: 45–72, special issue on *Redistributive Land Reform Today*.

Griffin, Keith ([1974] 1979), *The Political Economy of Agrarian Change* (London: Macmillan).

Griffin, Keith, Azizur Rahman Khan and Amy Ickowitz (2002), 'Poverty and Distribution of Land', *Journal of Agrarian Change*, 2 (3), July: 279–330.

Jorgenson, Dale W. (1961), 'The Development of a Dual Economy', *Economic Journal*, 71 (282), March: 309–34.

Kalecki, Michal (1993), *Collected Works of Michal Kalecki, Volume 5, Developing Economies* (Oxford: Clarendon Press).

Kay, Cristóbal (1989), *Latin American Theories of Development and Underdevelopment* (London: Routledge).

Krishna, Raj (1963), 'Farm Supply Response in India–Pakistan: A Case Study of the Punjab Region', *Economic Journal*, 73 (291): 477–87.

Lal, Deepak (1983), *The Poverty of 'Development Economics'* (London: Institute of Economic Affairs).

Lewis, W. Arthur ([1954] 1958), 'Economic Development with Unlimited Supplies of Labour', *The Manchester School* 22 (2), May: 139–91; reprinted in A.N. Agarwala and S.P. Singh, eds, *The Economics of Underdevelopment* (London: Oxford University Press).

—— (1955), *The Theory of Economic Growth* (London: Allen and Unwin).

Lipton, Michael (1968), 'Strategy for Agriculture: Urban Bias and Rural Planning', in Paul Streeten and Michael Lipton, eds, *The Crisis of Indian Planning* (London: Oxford University Press).

—— (1977), *Why Poor People Stay Poor: A Study of Urban Bias in World Development* (London: Temple Smith).

Mahalanobis, P.C. (1953), 'Some Observations on the Process of Growth of National Income', *Sankhya, The Indian Journal of Statistics*, 12 (4), September: 307–12.

—— (1955), 'The Approach of Operational Research to Planning in India', *Sankhya, The Indian Journal of Statistics*, 16 (Parts I and II), December: 3–130.

Marshall, Alfred (1979), *Principles of Economics*, eighth edition, (London: Macmillan).

Rosenstein–Rodan, P.N. ([1943] 1958), 'Problems of Industrialization of Eastern and South-eastern Europe', *Economic Journal*, 53, June–September: 202–11; reprinted in A.N. Agarwala and S.P. Singh, eds, *The Economics of Underdevelopment* (London: Oxford University Press).

—— (1984), 'Natura Facit Saltum: Analysis of the Disequilibrium Growth Process', in Gerald M. Meier and Dudley Seers, eds, *Pioneers in Development* (New York: Oxford University Press).

Schultz, Theodore W. (1964), *Transforming Traditional Agriculture* (New Haven: Yale University Press).

Sender, John (2002), 'Reassessing the Role of the World Bank in Sub-Saharan Africa', in Jonathan Pincus and Jeffrey A. Winters, eds, *Reinventing the World Bank* (Ithaca: Cornell University Press).

Stiglitz, Joseph E. (1986), 'The New Development Economics', *World Development*, 14 (2): 257–65.

—— (1989a), 'Sharecropping', in John Eatwell *et al.*, *The New Palgrave: Economic Development* (London: Macmillan), 308–15; this was published originally in John Eatwell *et al.*, *The New Palgrave: A Dictionary of Economics* (London: Macmillan), 1987.

—— (1989b), 'Rational Peasants, Efficient Institutions, and a Theory of Rural Organization: Methodological Remarks for Development Economics', in Pranab Bardhan, ed., *The Economic Theory of Agrarian Institutions* (Oxford: Clarendon Press).

United Nations (1951a), *Measures for the Economic Development of Under-Developed Countries* (New York: United Nations).

—— (1951b), *Land Reforms: Defects in Agrarian Structure as Obstacles to Economic Development* (New York: United Nations).

Williamson, John (1990), 'What Washington Means by Policy Reform', in John Williamson, ed., *Latin American Adjustment: How Much Has Happened* (Washington: Institute for International Economics).

Development and Geography

Current Debates in Historical Perspective

Hugh Goodacre

A 'geographical turn' has now been under way in mainstream economics for more than a decade, exemplified by Paul Krugman's 'new economic geography', as well as the contributions of other influential representatives of the
discipline such as Robert Barro, Paul David and Jeffrey Sachs. Yet, no constructive interchange or cooperation has been established with geographers, who have,
on the contrary, merely taken the opportunity to extend and elaborate a critique
of the economic mainstream that has long been sustained from within their discipline. The field of development economics provides particularly suitable terrain
on which to survey the issues under debate, not only because development issues
have figured prominently in the subject matter now increasingly addressed 'geog-
raphically' by economists (most obviously in the case of Sachs), but also due to
the close theoretical affinity that exists between Krugman's geographical initiative and the 'post-Washington Consensus' in development economics, sharing as
they do much of the same analytical approach.

The disciplines and sub-disciplines concerned in these debates have followed very different paths during the past half-century and more. In what follows, the current geographical turn in the work of Krugman and Sachs will be
examined against this historical background, along with an assessment of critical reactions from both mainstream economists and economic geographers. Next,
it will be shown that a comparison of these two contrasting geographical initiatives also provides the opportunity to address some wider issues regarding the
current situation of economics, both internally and in its relations with its
neighbouring disciplines. In conclusion, it will be argued that to advance beyond
the current situation of inter-disciplinary stand-off, and to forge a more inclusive
and constructive approach to the geography of development, it is necessary to
centralize the fundamental issues of the political economy and historical legacy
of colonialism.

Economic Geography and Development Economics

Economic geography has a distinctive identity within the wider field of
geographical studies, with its own traditions of theory, methodology and research. These traditions have been developed in the course of an explicit

rejection of the theoretical and methodological principles prevailing in the neighbouring discipline of economics. Indeed, the economic geography literature has, in many ways come to constitute, in itself an immanent critique of the economic orthodoxy, to which it aims to provide an empirically oriented and theoretically pluralistic alternative.

This situation perpetuates the effects of a traumatic rupture in the sub-discipline's history that occurred in the late 1960s. Prior to that time, geographers had been devoting much effort to assessing and incorporating formalistic models of spatial-economic behaviour, notably those inherited from an approach, developed largely by German writers, known as 'location theory'. This enterprise gave economic geography the aspect of a positivistic discipline, ripe for closer theoretical and methodological association with mainstream economics.

This orientation was, however, abruptly repudiated as a result of a sharp turn towards a radical approach with roots in Marxian, Myrdalian and other such historically oriented and discursive bodies of theory. The paradigmatic case of this anti-positivistic turn occurred in the field of regional studies, but other sub-fields of economic geography were also affected, each in its own way. For example, the field of resource economics, the first in which economic geography had achieved a foothold in the academic world, was from the time of the so-called 'first oil shock' of the early 1970s subjected, within mainstream economics, to reductionist modelling, most notably the celebrated textbook model of 'OPEC as cartel'; in contrast, economic geography has kept alive a more empirically oriented and conflictual approach to oil and other resource issues. Meanwhile, transport studies, almost by virtue of the very tractability of the subject to quantitative modelling, became unappealing to economic geographers, and it is only recently that their interest has returned to the field as an element in the wider sphere of 'transport and communications. (Sheppard and Barnes, eds 2000, chapters by Barnes, Hanink, Watts and Castree [resources], and Warf and Hanson [transport]).

The outcome of these distinct, though related and largely synchronous, developments in the various sub-fields of economic geography, has been the consolidation within the sub-discipline as a whole of a core literature that remains fiercely defensive of its anti-positivist traditions. (See the three handbooks or 'companions' – Lee and Wills 1997; Sheppard and Barnes, eds 2000; and Clark, Feldman and Gertler, eds 2000; and the two readers, Bryson *et al.*, eds 1999; Barnes *et al.*, eds 2004.) By the same token, while mathematical modelling was advancing towards its present dominance within the economics discipline, it was becoming a minority pursuit within economic geography (see Sheppard and Barnes, eds 2000: Chapter by Plummer). Instead, the sub-discipline has been swept by a series of waves of theoretical and methodological initiatives expressed in discursive form – Marxism and its derivatives such as regulation theory, a postmodernist 'cultural turn', an 'institutional turn', with associated debates around concepts such as flexible specialization – none of which has found a place in mainstream economics.

The history of development economics has followed a very different trajectory from that of economic geography. Historically based, the structural approaches to development were already firmly established during its early formative years as a sub-discipline in the early post-war period, long before the anti-positivistic turn within economic geography. Furthermore, this latter turn was accomplished with only limited reference to the debates within development economics and the economic heterodoxy.[1] Thus, the incorporation of Marxian and Myrdalian theory was overwhelmingly accomplished in relation to issues such as regional (under)development within the countries of the west, rather than international issues, while the prioritization within economic geography of theoretical and methodological debate has contrasted with the centralization of policy issues that characterizes development economics.

It was from development economists that the economic orthodoxy faced much of its most-determined criticism during the period when it largely endorsed the neoliberal policy environment of the 1980s, the so-called 'Washington Consensus'. The ensuing 'post-Washington Consensus' has been an essentially defensive move, designed to coopt as much as possible of the heterodoxy by subsuming elements of its criticisms (see chapter by Ben Fine in this volume). Development economics has thus played a relatively prominent role in the history of the economics profession as a whole. In contrast, the field of economic geography continues to this day to be preoccupied (at any rate in its approach to development issues) with theory and methodology rather than policy; as a result, it has been perceived as little or no threat to the orthodoxy, which has, in consequence, largely ignored it.

Development Issues in Paul Krugman's 'New Economic Geography'

Krugman's 'new economic geography' would appear to offer a promising opportunity to establish an approach to development issues that could be acceptable within the mainstream, while at the same time sufficiently critical of some aspects of its established theoretical framework to open up the possibility for genuine interchange with radical currents of thought hitherto dismissed or ignored within this notoriously conservative discipline. In particular, Krugman gives grounds for such optimism by launching his initiative in tandem with a call for a return to the historically oriented approach of pioneers of development economics such as Myrdal and Hirschman. He argues that the reason their insights failed to gain the attention they deserved was that their theories were not formulated in the mathematical, 'maximizing–minimizing' terms regarded as essential within the economic mainstream (Krugman 1995: Chapter 1). Such formalization is, he claims, now possible, due to subsequent technical advances in economic methodology, and it is these theories, reformulated in mathematical terms and extended from the field of development to economics as a whole, which form the basis of the modelling strategy of his geographical initiative.

A corollary would appear to be that a mutually beneficial avenue of cooperation is thereby opened up between economics and economic geography, a sub-discipline where such historical orientation has long been firmly entrenched,

and which has, moreover, traditionally been incomparably more hospitable to
radical and critical currents of thought than economics. The fact that Krugman
has, in his journalistic writings, taken a strongly oppositional stand on a number
of economic and political issues of current concern offers yet more grounds for
hope that his geographical initiative might help radical currents of thought gain
a foothold within the economic mainstream. The outcome has not, however,
been so fortunate, for as will now be shown, Krugman's concept of history has
turned out to be drastically reductionist, his attitude to geographers dismissive to
the point of hostility and his commitment to the established principles of mainstream economics inflexible to the point of dogmatism.

   For all its mathematical mode of presentation, the fundamental principles of Krugman's initiative are simple. The basic building block is a two-
sector (manufacture–agriculture) 'core–periphery' model. In this model, an initial
equilibrium situation exists, in which manufacturing is distributed symmetri-
cally between the two locations, since high transport costs do not allow significant trade to occur between them. Transport costs then fall, trade increases and
one of the two locations gains an advantage in manufactures. A process of cumulative causation now sets in: more firms move into the advantaged location to
benefit from economies of scale in production there and this results in market
effects – 'forward and backward linkages' – which, in turn, attract yet more
firms. Eventually a new equilibrium emerges, in which this location becomes the
exclusive site of manufacturing, or the 'core', reducing the 'periphery' to agricultural production only. (Fujita, Krugman and Venables 1999: Chapter 5; Krugman
1995, 1998, 1999, 2000; Venables 1998; Schmutzler 1999; Meardon 2002.)

   That such a simple concept was formerly considered intractable to incorporation within a neoclassical framework was due, Krugman argues, to the problem of how to model monopolistic competition: firms must have free entry and
exit to and from locations, and yet increasing returns to scale when they get
there, something that requires reconciling the apparently irreconcilable free competition and monopoly models. Now, however, claims Krugman, this has become possible with the use of new 'analytical tricks' developed in the course of
the 'increasing returns revolution in economics'.[2]

   Using this methodology, Krugman models development issues very largely
in terms of the effects of the long-term reduction in transport costs – 'first caravels,
then steamships and railroads, then air freight' – though these are, by extension,
used to represent transaction costs as a whole. It is shown that the transition from
symmetrical to core–periphery equilibrium is not necessarily the end of the story
told by this model. For, a further phase may subsequently occur in which transport (or transaction) costs decline so far that manufacturing firms desert the core
to benefit from lower production costs in the periphery – an effect that Krugman
labels globalization. At this point, the driving force of Krugman's model can be
seen to merge with another current of thought that is deeply rooted in the neoclassical approach to international economics, which is that of 'factor price equal-
ization', or international convergence in income and wealth.[3] Krugman's model

effectively restates this as a process in which 'declining trade costs first produce, then dissolve, the global inequality of nations'. To provide a rationale for the fact that such convergence does not proceed evenly across the periphery as a whole, further ingenious modelling is carried out to represent a situation of 'sequential and rapid industrialization by countries in turn' (Venables 1998: 5), which is intended to provide a more realistic account of how globalization effects have been observed in recent decades (Fujita, Krugman and Venables 1999: 253, 259–60, Chapter 15).

Krugman's regression to a traditional neoclassical approach is further illustrated by a model of the effects of international trade on Mexico's domestic economic geography. In this model, Krugman and his co-authors argue that the relocation of that country's export industries to regions along the US border not only mitigates the congestion diseconomies consequent on the previous concentration of industry around Mexico City, but also provides advantages of 'industrial clustering' to the industries in the new locations. The authors admit that 'intuition' suggests that this not only endorses the standard arguments regarding 'gains from trade', but adds a further 'pro-competitive' effect in the spatial sphere. The outcome is, in effect, no more than the addition of a geographical twist to the argument that Mexico's path to development can only lie through the further liberalization of its trade with the US (Fujita, Krugman and Venables 1999: Chapter 18).

Within the field of mainstream economics itself, it is still too early to say whether Krugman's initiative has stood what he calls 'the test of the intellectual market place' (Krugman 1995: 41). Its drastically reductionist representation of firm behaviour has drawn critical comment (see the special issue of *Economic Geography*, 77 [4], 2001), while its attempt to model geographical developments in terms of economic categories that are derived aspatially has drawn some searching questions: it has been asked, for example, how the wide-ranging supply-side functions of the city can be captured by a model that portrays urbanization merely in terms of the agglomeration of firms (Isserman 1996: 38; David 1999; Machado Ruiz 2001: 22–28; Olsen 2002: 156); it has also been pointed out that Krugman defines locational externalities at city level, and yet 'switches' the resulting framework to the regional and even global scale, where externalities thus defined become meaningless (Yeung 2002: 289–92; Olsen 2002: 158). It has also been objected that the initiative displays an unusually low 'ratio of data to models' (David 1999: 162), that its mode of justifying its achievements has hitherto been 'self-referential' (Meardon 2002); while it has even been suggested that these achievements lie not so much in actual theoretical advance as in the generation of a new 'high-tech glossary' (Machado Ruiz 2001). The consistency of Krugman's standpoint on policy has also been questioned; for, while he insists that it would be premature to draw policy conclusions from his models, it has been pointed out that his 'Mexico' model of the advantages of industrial decentralization and clustering is nevertheless prescriptive, at least by implication[4] (David 1999: 167–68; Machado Ruiz 2001: 21–22).

Despite the trenchant nature of much of this critical comment from economists, it is commonly advanced from a generally supportive standpoint, since Krugman's initiative, whatever its perceived shortcomings, undoubtedly provides a ringing endorsement of the fundamentals of mainstream economic analysis. It is otherwise with the reaction of geographers, which has predictably been far more sweeping and negative. They flatly reject Krugman's claim to have incorporated the historical orientation of the pioneers of development economics, seeing this claim as founded on his irremediably reductionist conception of what history is. As for the relation of his initiative to geography, they see it as neither 'new' nor a re-launch of 'lost' traditions but, rather, as an attempt to resurrect the formalistic models of location theory that had long been discarded by geographers on theoretical and methodological grounds.

Geographers do not, in fact, acknowledge Krugman's 'new economic geography' to be geography at all, preferring to label it 'geographical economics', since its advocacy of the *a priori* construction of abstract and scale-independent geometrical landscapes represents the very opposite of the geographical project, which is to substantiate the specificity of 'real places' at different levels of scale (Martin 1999; Dymski 1996; Martin and Sunley 1996; Clark 1998; Boddy 1999; Sheppard 2000; Thrift 2000; Olsen 2002: 154; Barnes 2003). For geographers, space is 'socially constructed', or 'part of a larger social narrative' (Barnes *et al.* eds 2004: 172). For example, from their point of view, the analysis of globalization cannot meaningfully be approached in such terms as those of Krugman's model of the effects of declining transport costs; rather, a range of methodologies must be brought to bear, to explain how globalization results in 'landscapes of socio-economic power, where islands of extreme wealth are interspersed with spaces of poverty, social exclusion, and the erosion of the socioeconomic fabric' (Swyngedouw in Clark, Feldman and Gertler eds 2000: 543).

Such a wider frame of reference had long been applied within development economics to a core–periphery (or 'centre'–periphery) concept which, in strong contrast to its namesake in Krugman's 'new economic geography', is rooted not in abstract or deductive theoretical constructs, but in descriptive generalizations drawn from the history of international colonialism and trade since the sixteenth century. This 'dependency theory' – advanced by writers including Frank and Wallerstein from the 1960s onwards – has long served to counter the parochialism of much western social science. However, by concentrating its focus on the cumulative effects of centuries of unequal trade, it has had the effect of presenting core–periphery relations as ensnared in an effectively static situation. From there it is only a short step towards over-emphasizing other seemingly insuperable obstacles to development, such as physical geography. But to explore such issues further in the present connection, it is first necessary to consider another manifestation of the geographical turn in economics distinct from that of Krugman – the more recent and less theoretical intervention by Jeffrey Sachs.

The Geographical Turn in the Development Economics of Jeffrey Sachs

It has now been seen that Krugman's 'new economic geography' has provoked considerable critical response from within economic geography. It has, however, been of much less interest to development economists, primarily concerned as they are with questions of policy than with theoretical and epistemological debate. Rather, their most immediate experience of the 'geographical turn' in economics has been at the hands of Jeffrey Sachs, the substance of whose position is contained in the statement that 'levels of per capita income, economic growth, and other economic and demographic dimensions are strongly correlated with geographical and ecological variables such as climate zone, disease ecology, and distance from the coast' (Sachs 2003a), a statement that is extended to embrace the even stronger claim that 'perhaps the strongest empirical relationship in the wealth and poverty of nations is the one between ecological zones and per capita income' (Sachs 2001: 1).

Though his frame of reference extends to cases in many parts of the world, including China and the US (on which see, respectively, Jian, Sachs and Warner 1996; Rappaport and Sachs 2003), Sachs's main focus in this connection has been on Africa. In a major co-authored article (Bloom and Sachs 1998), a list is presented of six factors that are often adduced as adversely affecting that continent's economic development – the history of slavery and colonial rule, primary export dependence, adverse internal political institutions, poor economic policy, population increase, and social conditions characterized by deep ethnic divisions and low levels of social capital. It is argued, however, that 'an even bigger truth' lies in the continent's 'extraordinarily disadvantageous geography', notably the 'high disease burden' and low agricultural productivity due to its tropical ecology, as well as the high proportion of its territory that is landlocked and lacking in transport facilities. Though this last point is embellished with citation of Smith's *Wealth of Nations* ([1776] 1976: 35–36), the argumentation is developed in quantitative terms with Barro-type cross-country regressions (see the chapter titled 'New Growth Theory' by Ben Fine in this volume), on the basis of which it attributes 'about two thirds of the weight of Africa's growth shortfall to . . . "noneconomic" conditions and only one third to economic policy and institutions' (Bloom and Sachs 1998: 210–11, 271).

This approach is generalized in the work of Sachs and his co-authors to apply to all regions of the world. They find only one other factor to be of sufficient influence to over-ride these effects, which is that such geographical variables 'generally do not eliminate the evidence for the curse of natural resources', which they explain by the standard argument that positive wealth shocks lead to excess demand for non-traded goods and consequently squeeze profits in traded activities.[5] This exception does not, however, affect his overall conclusion that 'coastal and temperate-zone economies significantly and consistently outperform landlocked and tropical regions. . . . Temperate ecozones proximate to the sea account for eight per cent of the world's inhabited land area, twenty-three per cent of the world's population, and fifty-three per cent of the world's GDP.' His aim is thus to develop an approach that can 'better integrate physical geography into the study of long-term economic development' (Mellinger, Sachs and Gallup 2000: 169).

Though this turn in Sachs's work might give the impression of engagement with the geographical literature on a broad front, it is in fact underpinned intellectually by a very narrow geographical current within the field of world history. One evident and acknowledged influence is Landes (1998), which sets the scene for what is represented as the ineluctable advance of the west by giving an account of its geographical and climatic advantages; from there, the work goes on to provide a compendium of views upholding the doctrine of 'Western exceptionalism', in explicit repudiation of 'multi-cultural' approaches. Aimed at readers who, in the author's terms, 'prefer truth to goodthink', this work has, despite its ostensibly scholarly mode of presentation, attracted widespread criticism for ignoring debates on the issues concerned which have, in a number of cases, been proceeding in the relevant fields of scholarship for generations.

The other main intellectual source of Sachs's geographical turn is the work of a number of writers, including McNeill, Curtin and Crosby, who assert the paramount influence of human disease ecology on the course of history, the principal work he singles out being the best-selling Diamond (1997). This work argues that the demographic catastrophes suffered by indigenous Americans and other peoples following contact with the west in early modern times were the inevitable result of development in neolithic times, when those who first moved from hunting and gathering to food production gained a head start of many millennia in developing immunity to a number of fatal diseases which migrated to humans from domesticated animals. Thus, the geographical pattern of today's global inequality is represented as the outcome of biological and ecological influences, rather than of the history of colonial conquest as such, let alone of the emergent capitalist social formation of which colonialism was a mutually necessary concomitant. Diamond's thesis has been contested on immunological and epidemiological grounds, let alone in terms of historical methodology, historians attributing these catastrophes to a far wider range of causes, including 'wars and genocide, enslavements, removals and relocations, and changes in American Indian societies, cultures, and subsistence patterns accompanying European colonization' (Fetter 2002: 434–36, citing a study by the population historian Russell Thornton). Though Diamond insistently claims that his intention is to counter racist interpretations of history by showing that differences in environments, rather than peoples, are decisive, parallels have been drawn between his approach to the effects of population movement and those advanced in the *Bell Curve*, a work notorious for its assertion that black and Latino immigration puts 'downward pressure on the distribution of intelligence' in the US (Herrnstein and Murray 1994: 360–61).[6]

The field of world history, whose central focus is commonly taken to be the global divergence in economic fortunes between rich and poor countries since early modern times, is poorly represented by these two works by Landes and Diamond singled out for attention by Sachs. This is a field that has accommodated wide-ranging debate, from the work of dependency theorists and their critics, such as Brenner, to recent works such as Pomeranz (2000). The latter in particular has demonstrated that analysis of the effects of geographical and climatic factors can constructively be interwoven with a narrative which, rather than continually seeking to extend the chain of causation back to previous millennia, sustains its focus on social and economic developments during the past two centuries – which is, after all, the period when the global divergence has emerged.

Sachs has, then, selected from a multifarious literature only those elements which convey the simplistic impression that the geography of world inequality is determined not by social and historical but by impersonal geographical and biological factors. His turn towards geography is thus, at the same time, a turn away from social theory, with consequences that will now be further explored.

Development, Geography and Institutions

Sachs's conclusions on the preponderant influence of geography have been challenged on his own chosen ground of statistical inference by a series of studies co-authored by Acemoglu, which argue that he fails to allow for the influence of institutional factors, in particular those originating in different experiences of early modern colonialism.[7]

The first of these studies (Acemoglu, Johnson and Robinson 2001, usefully summarized in Acemoglu 2003) finds that the mortality rates of bishops, soldiers and sailors stationed by the European powers in their colonies from the seventeenth to the nineteenth centuries show strong negative correlation with today's GDP in the countries concerned. They associate this finding with the observation that the disease environment most adverse to Europeans resulted in the development of the most exploitative forms of colonial state (the so-called 'extractive states'), while the most favourable such environments resulted, in contrast, in the establishment of 'neo-Europes'. They argue that the form of state, and associated weak or strong property rights and other institutional features, had effects that persist till today. Furthermore, they hold that these effects override geographical or any other possible influences (such as religion) and thus explain the first great divergence in the global economy in early modern times, and, by extension, the geographical pattern of inequality in the world today. In a further study (Acemoglu, Johnson and Robinson 2002a), the same authors argue that the countries colonized by European powers have undergone a 'reversal of fortune', with those that were initially relatively poor being those that were subsequently to become relatively rich, and *vice versa*. They link this phenomenon to institutional changes resulting from colonization and argue that a reversal such as this, once again, 'weighs against a view that links economic development to geographic factors'.[8]

Sachs disputes the results of his critics' regressions by showing that they are not robust to the substitution of alternative geographical data, namely, those indicating the risk of malaria. (For response and counter-response, see Sachs and McArthur 2001; Sachs 2003a, 2003b: 39; Acemoglu, Johnson and Robinson 2001: 1391–93.) He also objects that the idea of 'a single-factor explanation of something as important as economic development' has proved so 'alluring' to his critics that it has drawn them into a line of reasoning that is 'dangerously simplified' (Sachs 2003b: 38). Sachs insists that there is more to this standpoint than the principle that attack is the best means of defence, holding that no country is 'fated to be poor' for geographical reasons and that 'economic policy matters' (Bloom and Sachs 1998: 212). He draws the conclusion that 'rather than focus on improving institutions in sub-Saharan Africa, it would be wise to devote more effort to fighting AIDS, tuberculosis, and malaria' and other 'direct interventions' to address 'disease, geographical isolation, low technological productivity, and resource limitations that trap [the Sub-Saharan countries] in poverty'; such interventions, he states, 'require much more than lectures about good governance and institutions (Sachs 2003b: 38). This declamation is significant in bringing to the fore the motivation for Sachs's repudiation of the 'institutions' school of thought, showing that it forms part of his long-standing critique of the World Bank's policy orientation in favour of structural adjustment (see further in Bloom and Sachs 1998: 270).

The impression that emerges from this debate is that Sachs and the propo-

This explicitly critical policy standpoint makes it all the more reasonable to expect Sachs to put forward an appropriately innovative alternative policy framework, particularly since he makes the strong claim that 'efficient economic policies' are nothing less than a 'sufficient condition' for 'convergence' of today's poor countries with the rich. However, his proposed policy package rests on nothing more innovative than a reiteration of the call for policies that promote 'mainly open trade and protection of private property rights' (Sachs and Warner 1995a), so that the unquestionably worthy causes he advocates may be 'financed privately in a competitive market setting' (Bloom and Sachs 1998: 272).

The only innovative features in this otherwise all-too-familiar policy orientation are some geographical trimmings in its presentation: he argues, for example, that technical, medical and other policies must be 'customized' to accommodate geographical conditions, taking account of the fact that 'technological innovations do not always cross the ecological divide' (Mellinger, Sachs and Gallup 2000: 192; Sachs 2000: 33), while at the same time acknowledging that the pattern of geographical advantage is not unchanging, being affected by technological developments (Gallup, Sachs and Mellinger 1999: 186). He also adds further policy prescriptions with a less specifically geographical flavour, including, in the case of Africa, the encouragement of export-led manufactures by means of tax havens and export promotion zones on Southeast Asian lines, the promotion of tourism and of the exemplary experience of Botswana and Mauritius, and the establishment of a data services sector (Bloom and Sachs 1998: 212, 263–64, 267–72).

The impression that emerges from this debate is that Sachs and the proponents of the 'institutions' critique only apply their statistical tests to data and relationships which have already been filtered through the preconceived theoretical or policy orientation they each claim to be 'testing'. It is consequently difficult to avoid the conclusion that what is in contention is not actually the statistical validity of opposing hypotheses at all but, rather, a clash between deeply held convictions regarding policy, which their advocates would, in any case, refuse to relinquish on principle, let alone on technical–statistical grounds.

The same unconvincing mode of proceeding characterizes a further critique of Sachs advanced by Rodrik and others, which, while generally supporting the arguments of Acemoglu, Johnson and Robinson, extends the discussion beyond the spheres of geography and institutions to embrace a third range of variables – international trade or 'integration' – and argues that such market variables are also discounted by Sachs (Rodrik and Subramanian 2003; Rodrik 2003). The implications of this critique are indeed ironic, since what stands revealed is that Sachs, whose policy prescriptions are so explicitly market-oriented, at the same time lays himself open to challenge for neglecting to take market effects into consideration in his approach to historical geography. This shows how far he has departed from any aspiration to theorize the economy in an integrated way; it is enough to recall the rigorously cohesive market-based structure of Krugman's initiative to realize what a fundamental contrast there is between their respective forays into the field of geography, a contrast that will now be explored in more detail.

Development, Geography and Economic Theory

The contrast between the approaches of Krugman and Sachs to geographical issues in economic development conveniently illustrates some wider aspects of the current situation in and around economics as a discipline.

The most obvious contrast is between Krugman's 'reticence' towards policy issues and the overwhelming predominance of precisely such issues in Sachs's geographical writings. Indeed, Sachs's preoccupation with policy sometimes even goes to the extent of implicitly downgrading economic theorizing as such; in his own words, 'economists ought to lift their gaze above macroeconomic policies and market liberalization, in order to deepen their understanding of the linkages between the physical environment and social outcomes' (Bloom and Sachs 1998: 271). Such linkages lie in 'the interactions of tropical diseases and growth, or tropical agricultural productivity, nutrition, human capital accumulation, and development', which are to be analysed by a number of 'cross-disciplinary research approaches' (Mellinger, Sachs and Gallup 2000: 193). There could be no greater contrast with the unrelentingly unified and theoretical character of Krugman's 'new economic geography', and his intolerance of economic geographers and others who advocate a plurality of approaches, instead of the inflexibly unitary approach of neoclassicism.

Direct debate between the two writers has been meagre. A discussion organized by the World Bank in 1998 only served to highlight the lack of substantial interchange; ironically, the main protagonists themselves referred to each other's standpoints only cursorily (Krugman 1999: 142, 156–57; Gallup, Sachs and Mellinger 1999: 213), leaving it to others to make the principal contributions on the issues in question (David 1999, and also a contribution by Venables). In his brief comment on the work of Sachs, Krugman argues that there is room for reconciliation of their respective approaches on the basis that geography sets initial conditions, while subsequent cumulative causation operating through market linkages can magnify or diminish its effects. He cites the examples of Mexico City and New York, which owe their original foundation to a lakeside and a canal-side location respectively, and yet have both continued to grow inordinately long after the lake has been drained and the canal has become no more than a tourist attraction.

He concludes that though the two approaches 'seem to take diametrically opposed positions', what in fact divides them is only a 'false dichotomy'. In a subsequent co-authored article, Sachs accepts this position and concedes that 'the two approaches are potentially complementary'. However, the concepts and processes in question are in fact accorded a fundamentally different epistemological status in the work of the two authors: for Krugman, they are immediately and unproblematically incorporated into his theoretical analysis; for Sachs, in contrast, they are categorized, in inductive style, as 'hypotheses' that require further analysis and testing in the light of the relevant data (Mellinger, Sachs and Gallup 2000: 171–73, 192–93).

It is of course Krugman, rather than Sachs, whose standpoint best represents the present situation prevailing in economic theory, both within the discipline and in its relations with its neighbouring social sciences – a situation that is, to a great extent, characterized by the promotion of precisely the kind of analytical approach used by Krugman in his 'new economic geography'. A prime example of the kind of formal feature involved is the presence of multiple equilibria as a means of endogenizing processes that could previously only be modelled as consequences of exogenous events. This has already been illustrated in the case of Krugman's 'globalization' model, where falling transport costs generate three equilibria (symmetrical, core–periphery, symmetrical again) without any recourse at all to explanations exogenous to the model itself. Models exhibiting these and related features have been termed 'location-theoretic', a derivative term which refers to the fact that their formal structure is essentially the same as that of the wider family of models termed 'information-theoretic'. Such models provide the fundamental modelling strategy of a whole range of initiatives taken from within economics that seek, like Krugman's 'new economic geography', to 'colonize' neighbouring disciplines and re-cast them in accordance with the methodological principles prevailing within economics itself, a strategy that has been termed the 'new economics imperialism'.

Krugman has been particularly unabashed in making it clear that the intention of such 'imperialism' is nothing less than utterly to supplant the traditions native to the social science concerned, finding the incumbent discipline of economic geography a particularly suitable target for such extirpation, due to its long-term and inveterate criticism of neoclassical economic doctrine. His standpoint towards its practitioners is consequently dismissive in the extreme and he brands its endeavours in recent decades as nothing but an 'anti-model, anti-quantitative backlash', making it clear that, in his eyes, this is effectively synonymous with a wilful rejection of scientific method.[9] Geographers are, of course, eager to give as good as they get, the result being that both sides now hold positions that are highly developed and logically impregnable in their own terms, with economic geography firmly established as a determined exponent of empirical orientation and theoretical pluralism in the social sciences, and Krugman conversely being an 'exemplar of progress in social science', in so far as this is seen as the systematic modelling of the economy in logically consistent (preferably mathematical) terms (Meardon 2002: 217).

Yet, paradoxically, there is also a sense in which the two sides in this debate have something in common, which is their shared prioritization of theoretical and methodological questions at the expense of policy issues. For, Krugman can hardly fail to be aware that the informality and popularizing character of his economic journalism, to say nothing of its increasingly radical content, might easily be taken to indicate an incipient repudiation of market-based economics as such.[10] His 'new economic geography' provides him with the opportunity to demonstrate that this is not so, and that not only can he sustain a project which meets the standards of formal elaboration expected within the economics profession, but, furthermore, that his frequently radical standpoints on issues of current concern should not be taken to indicate any relaxation in his determination that his theory should ultimately rest on the bedrock of the market-based principles of neoclassical economics. His critics from within economic geography also have their own reasons for keeping the focus on theoretical and methodological issues, for it is here that they consider much of the strength of their sub-discipline to lie. The two sides are thus, for utterly different reasons, ideal sparring partners, each taking the opportunity to promote the principles on which they defend the identity, cohesion and traditions of their respective disciplinary heritage – Krugman, by insisting on the strict application of the inflexible principles of neoclassical economics, and the economic geographers, by tirelessly asserting the benefits of their diverse and pluralistic experience, not least through the publication of their handbooks, 'companions', readers and other multi-author (and multi-perspective) compilations.

In contrast to Krugman's fundamentalist 'economics imperialism' and unconcealed antagonism to the discipline of geography, Sachs adopts a relaxed (if not particularly engaged) standpoint towards neighbouring disciplines, without any particular discrimination against concepts that are commonly formulated without regard to the search for micro-foundations, such as 'resource curse' (Sachs and Warner 1995b: 2–7, 1999: 43–46) and 'delayed demographic transition' (Bloom and Sachs 1998: 239). A corollary of this detachment from debate on the foundations of economic theory and methodology has been that his geographical work, unlike Krugman's 'new economic geography', has provoked little reaction, critical or otherwise, from within economic geography, irrevocably focused as that sub-discipline is on precisely such debates.

Such is the opposite significance of the geographical turns by Sachs and Krugman in their respective intellectual trajectories, with Krugman turning to geography as a means of intensifying his efforts to develop a systematic theorization of the economy and Sachs, on the contrary, turning to geography in a manner that effectively entails the abandonment of any such ambition.

Economic Geography and the Legacy of Colonialism

While the geographical turn in the work of Krugman and Sachs has now been seen to assume a significance that is in many ways opposite, their respective contributions are nevertheless united in endorsing market-based solutions to economic problems, their emphasis being on theory and on policy application, respectively. It is sufficiently understood within critical social science traditions that the 'market', as represented from such a point of view, is by no means left to its own devices, as the customary iteration by market enthusiasts of quaintly worded passages from Smith's *Wealth of Nations* is intended to suggest. (See Peck and Yeung 2003: Chapter by Tickell and Peck)

It is a matter of concern in this connection that the various branches of orthodox economics that address international issues commonly move directly from the observation that economic transactions increasingly over-ride the barriers posed by state frontiers, to the wider political–economic conclusion that state sovereignty has thereby become an essentially obsolete concept. This standpoint inherits the perspective adopted by Ohlin in his seminal work of 1933, in which international trade theory is simply location theory raised to the international level. Krugman further elaborates this point of view, asserting that national borders 'do not introduce qualitatively new issues' over and above those existing at the regional and urban levels; he accordingly refers to them as 'arbitrary lines called borders', advances models of 'a world in which borders are irrelevant', and questions the 'inherent importance in drawing a line on the ground and calling the land on either side two different countries' (Krugman 1991: 71–72, 8; Krugman 1998: 14; Fujita, Krugman and Venables 1999: 239–40, 259, 309).

It is disappointing that the economic geography literature has shown itself as reluctant to acknowledge the legitimacy of the assertion by peripheral states of their territorial integrity as neoliberalism is to tolerate it. Economic geographers routinely portray the state as an entity that is supposedly dwindling in significance, without making any reference to the fundamental difference in its political–economic status in core and peripheral countries. (See Martin and Sunley 1996: 260; Lee and Wills 1997: 149–51; Sheppard and Barnes, eds 2000: Chapters by Swyngedouw, Rigby and Painter, particularly 52, 202 [discussing Storper, Scott and others], 360–61, 371, 374–75.) Such a standpoint paralyses any approach in normative or legal terms to the international context in which the pattern of global inequality has in reality been determined, since efforts to mitigate or counter this inequality inevitably involve state action from within the periphery.

This shortcoming in the geographical critique of orthodox economics reflects the predominantly occidentalist context in which it has been formulated. To take just one example, the concept of flexible specialization has minimal application outside 'relatively developed countries' (a shortcoming acknowledged by Asheim in Clark, Feldman and Gertler 2000: 428, as well as, explicitly or implicitly, in Barnes *et al.*, eds 2004: 58 [Amin], 86 [Gibson–Graham], 125 [Scott], 316 [McDowell]). This, in turn, reflects the fact that the repudiation by economic geography of its former positivistic phase was narrowly based on regional issues within the west, rather than being a response to the global movement of decolonization. The very term 'post-colonial' is commonly used by economic geographers for 'a body of work . . . which questions dominant notions of gender and work in order to include social categories such as race and ethnicity' (see Sheppard and Barnes, eds 2000: 61 [Oberhauser] and 331 [Sadler], and Barnes *et al.*, eds 2004: 389 [Schoenberger]).[11] A consequence of this depletion of the concept of colonialism within the economic geography literature is that the subject is forced out to the margins of the discipline, where it shares the ground with women's issues, racism, the environment and other issues, which, despite the best efforts of all concerned, inevitably assume the character of denizens of a theoretical fringe.

In terms of the academic division of labour as it currently exists, the heterodox or critical currents within development economics would seem to provide the most immediately suitable terrain from which to broaden the critique of neoclassical economics to the international level. Development economics has a heritage of debate on the 'developmental state' (Fine 2001: 136–38), long experience in confronting 'counter-revolution' in its own field (Toye [1987] 1993) and links with heterodox currents within economics itself. But if there is one lesson that has now emerged from placing the debate on geography in the context of the history of the social sciences in the past half-century, it is that the shifting ground of disciplinary and inter-disciplinary traditions and debates provides a poor basis on which to found a genuinely alternative approach to development issues. Rather than attempting further 'new' or 'new neo' initiatives on this terrain, what is needed is a more general response which, regardless of inter-disciplinary boundaries, can reintroduce a focus on the political economy of colonialism, in such a way as to conceptualize its history, legacy, and continuation in its neocolonialist and current revanchist phases. The obstacles to accomplishing this task will now be reviewed by way of conclusion.

Conclusions

This survey has shown that any attempt to construct an alternative or radical approach to the geography of development in the world today faces two major obstacles. On the one hand, there stands the unreconstructed market fundamentalism that underlies the orthodoxy's geographical turn, even in its ostensibly post-neoliberal forms. On the other hand, there stands the apparently irremediable absorption of the sub-discipline of economic geography in the assessment and reassessment of theoretical and methodological issues, at the expense of a focus on the struggle for development in the form in which it takes place in practice outside the academic sphere.

It has been seen how Krugman's attempt to reformulate development issues on 'new' neoclassical lines inevitably results in neoliberal policy assumptions seeping back in through the micro-foundations.[12] The same commitment to a market-oriented policy framework is, of course, present in far more explicit form in the work of Sachs, yet without theoretical rationalization in microeconomic terms, nor even any particular interest in economic theory at all, appealing as he does, instead, to populist interventions such as those of Landes and Diamond.

As for the geographical critique of these initiatives, it has minutely explored every aspect of the epistemological gap that separates Krugman's 'new economic geography' from the work of those who study 'real places', while at the same time ignoring the work of Sachs due to the lack of theoretical sophistication in its mode of presentation, and the consequent lack of opportunity it provides for theoretical and epistemological debate. What now remains to be done is to ensure that the selective and overly theoretical nature of this critique does not divert attention from the wider implication of the geographical turn in mainstream economics, which is that it effectively denies the role of colonialism in generating the global inequality of today (explicitly so in Sachs 2000: 42). This denial effectively contributes theoretical and ideological endorsement for policies that threaten to roll back former advances towards a more equitable post-colonial world order. This situation cries out for a critical response from within the social sciences, yet such a response is continually being limited, constrained and fragmented by the heavy hand of disciplinary and sub-disciplinary history, which constantly deflects the focus of attention away from the fundamental issues of the political economy of colonialism and its historical legacy.

Notes

1 Even today the idea of forming 'alliances' with that heterodoxy remains controversial within economic geography. See Amin and Thrift (2000) and the debate in ensuing issues of the journal *Antipode*.

2 These 'tricks' are principally those comprised within the Dixit–Stiglitz model of monopolistic competition, in a spatially adapted form that incorporates Samuelson's 'iceberg' model of transport costs. See Fujita, Krugman and Venables 1999: 3, Chapter 4.

3 For critical commentary on this concept by economic geographers, see Martin and Sunley (1998: 220), Martin (1999: 71, 78), and Sheppard and Barnes, eds (2000: 188–89, 191 [Chapter by Sunley] and 203–04 [Chapter by Rigby]). The 'new geography of global income inequality' proposed by Firebaugh (2003) is predicated on acceptance of the proposition that such convergence is an empirically verified fact.

4 He justifies this 'reticence' regarding policy by pointing to the fate of a previous initiative, the 'new trade theory', which was, he argues, 'hijacked' by advocates of strategic trade policy. Krugman (1994: Chapter 10–11), and Fujita, Krugman and Venables (1999: 348–49).

5 Sachs and Warner (2001). See also Sachs and Warner (1995), whose conclusions are contested in Rodrik, ed. (2003: Chapter by Hausman). Sachs and Warner (1999) is more open to the 'big push' argument that 'resource booms can be important catalysts

for development'. Sachs (2000: 41f.), in a volume co-edited by Huntington (who sees world history as a 'clash of civilizations'), appears to add the further exception that, in the case of Muslim countries, there may be adverse influences from within the sphere of 'culture' that can over-ride geographical factors.

[6] It is interesting that in this connection Temin (1998: 407–08, 414) compares Diamond's mode of analysis to that of endogenous growth theory in economics.

[7] This critique had already been anticipated at a less technical level by Barratt Brown (1999: 48–49).

[8] They describe their work as a 'marriage' of the approach of Marxist historians with that of Douglass North (on the latter, see the Chapter titled 'Pioneers of Economic History' by Milonakis in this volume). Their conclusions, however, differ from those of North himself, who traces the roots of the divergence in growth rates back to the period of the Roman empire, rather than to early modern times. See Acemoglu, Johnson and Robinson (2002b: 6).

[9] See Krugman (1995: Chapter 3), where he makes it clear that he regards the theories in question as not worthy of even the most cursory investigation. For critical responses, see Martin (1999: 82) and Boddy (1999: 817). For an apparently unique example of a careful review of the geographical critique by a mainstream economist, see Overman (2003).

[10] Commenting on the failure of Washington's former promises that liberalization of trade and privatization would lead to economic growth in Latin America, Krugman has written: 'I, too, bought into much though not all of the Washington Consensus, but now it's time . . . to take my beliefs to market. And my confidence that we've been giving good advice is way down.' *New York Times*, 9 August 2002, cited in Peet *et al.* (2003: 216).

[11] For an extensive critique of this standpoint, see Peet with Hartwick (1999), and also Peet *et al.* (2003: 223), though even here the peripheral state is excluded from the proposed 'democratic alliance of social movements', as it is also from the 'global communities world-wide' discussed by Glasmeier and Conroy in Peck and Yeung, eds (2003).

[12] The semi-clandestine existence of these assumptions in Krugman's theory suits the needs of neoliberalism at the present stage. For, the 'rollback' phase of the 1980s has now given way to a less 'destructive' and more proactive phase of re-casting the state along neoliberal lines. See Peck and Yeung, eds (2003: Chapter by Tickell and Peck).

References

Acemoglu, Daron (2003), 'Root Causes: A Historical Approach to Assessing the Role of Institutions in Economic Development', *Finance and Development*, 40 (2): 27–30.

Acemoglu, Daron, Simon Johnson and James A. Robinson (2001), 'The Colonial Origins of Comparative Development: An Empirical Investigation', *American Economic Review*, 91 (5): 1369–401.

—— (2002a), 'Reversal of Fortune: Geography and Institutions in the Making of the Modern World Income Distribution', *Quarterly Journal of Economics*, 117 (4): 1231–94.

—— (2002b), 'The Rise of Europe: Atlantic Trade, Institutional Change, and Economic Growth', NBER Working Paper 9378, National Bureau of Economic Research, Cambridge, Massachusetts.

Amin, Ash and Nigel Thrift (2000), 'What Kind of Economic Theory for What Kind of Economic Geography?', *Antipode*, 32 (1): 4–9.

Barnes, Trevor J. (2003), 'The Place of Locational Analysis: A Selective and Interpretive History', *Progress in Human Geography*, 27 (1): 69–95.

Barnes, Trevor J., Jamie A. Peck, Eric Sheppard and Adam Tickell, eds (2004), *Reading Economic Geography* (Oxford: Blackwell).

Barratt Brown, Michael (1999), 'Imperialism Revisited', in Ronald H. Chilcote, ed., *The Political Economy of Imperialism: Critical Approaches* (Boston: Kluwer Academic Publishers): 41–63.

Bloom, David E. and Jeffrey D. Sachs (1998), 'Geography, Demography and Economic Growth in Africa', *Brookings Papers on Economic Activity 1998*, (2): 207–95.

Boddy, Martin (1999), 'Geographical Economics and Urban Competitiveness: A Critique', Urban Studies, 36: 811–42.

Bryson, John, Nick Henry, David Keeble and Ron Martin, eds (1999), The Economic Geography Reader: Producing and Consuming Global Capitalism (Chichester: John Wiley).

Clark, Gordon L. (1998), 'Stylized Facts and Close Dialogue: Methodology in Economic Geography', Annals of the Association of American Geographers, 88 (1): 73–87.

Clark, Gordon L., Maryann P. Feldman and Meric S. Gertler, eds (2000), The Oxford Handbook of Economic Geography (Oxford: Oxford University Press).

David, Paul A. (1999), 'Krugman's Economic Geography of Development: NEGs, POGs, and Naked Models in Space', International Regional Science Review, 22 (2): 162–72; paper for World Bank Annual Conference on Development Economics 1998.

Diamond, Jared (1997), Guns, Germs and Steel: A Short History of Everybody for the Last 13,000 years (London: Jonathan Cape).

Dymski, Gary A. (1996), 'On Krugman's Model of Economic Geography', Geoforum, 27 (4): 439–52.

Fetter, Bruce S. (2002), 'History and Health Science: Medical Advances across the Disciplines', Journal of Interdisciplinary History, 32 (3): 423–42.

Fine, Ben (2001), Social Capital versus Social Theory: Political Economy and Social Science at the Turn of the Millennium (London: Routledge).

Firebaugh, Glenn (2003), The New Geography of Global Income Inequality (Cambridge, Massachusetts: Harvard University Press).

Fujita, Masahisa, Paul R. Krugman and Anthony J. Venables (1999), The Spatial Economy: Cities, Regions and International Trade (Cambridge, Massachusetts: MIT Press).

Gallup, John L., Jeffrey D. Sachs and Andrew Mellinger (1999), 'Geography and Economic Development', International Regional Science Review, 22 (2): 179–232.

Herrnstein, Richard J. and Charles Murray (1994), The Bell Curve: Intelligence and Class Structure in American life (New York: The Free Press).

Hoare, Anthony G. (1992), 'Review of Krugman (1991)', Regional Studies, 26 (7): 679.

Isserman, Andrew M. (1996), 'It's Obvious, It's Wrong, and Anyway, They Said it Years Ago, Paul Krugman on Large Cities', International Regional Science Review, 19 (1/2): 37–48.

Jian, Tianlun, Jeffrey D. Sachs and Andrew M. Warner (1996), 'Trends in Regional Inequality in China', China Economic Review, 7 (1): 1–22.

Krugman, Paul R. (1991), Geography and Trade (Cambridge, Massachusetts: MIT Press).

——— (1994), Peddling Prosperity: Economic Sense and Nonsense in the Age of Diminished Expectations (New York: W.W. Norton).

——— (1995), Development, Geography and Economic Theory (Cambridge, Massachusetts: MIT Press).

——— (1996), The Self-Organizing Economy (Cambridge, Massachusetts: MIT Press).

——— (1998), 'What's New about the New Economic Geography?', Oxford Review of Economic Policy, 14 (2): 7–17.

——— (1999), 'The Role of Geography in Development', International Regional Science Review, 22 (2): 142–61.

——— (2000), 'Where in the World is the "New Economic Geography"?', in Clark, Feldman and Gertler, eds, The Oxford Handbook of Economic Geography, 49–60.

Landes, David S. (1998), The Wealth and Poverty of Nations: Why Some Are so Rich and Some so Poor (London: Little, Brown and Co.).

Lee, Rodger and Jane Wills, eds (1997), Geographies of Economies (London: Edward Arnold).

Machado Ruiz, Ricardo (2001), 'The Spatial Economy: High-Tech Glossary or New Regional Economics?', Nova Economia, 11 (1): 9–36.

Martin, Ron (1999), 'The New "Geographical Turn" in Economics: Some Critical Reflections', Cambridge Journal of Economics, 23: 65–91.

Martin, Ron and Peter Sunley (1996), 'Paul Krugman's Geographical Economics and its Implications for Regional Development Theory: A Critical Assessment', Economic Geography, 72 (3): 259–92.

——— (1998), 'Slow Convergence? The New Endogenous Growth Theory and Regional Development', Economic Geography, 74 (3): 201–27.

Meardon, Stephen J. (2002), 'On the New Economic Geography and the Progress of Geographical Economics', in Stephan Boehm *et al.*, eds, *Is There Progress in Economics? Knowledge, Truth and the History of Economic Thought* (Cheltenham: Edward Elgar): 217–39.

Mellinger, Andrew, Jeffrey D. Sachs and John Gallup (2000), 'Geography and Economic Development', in Clark, Feldman and Gertler, eds, *The Oxford Handbook of Economic Geography*: 169–94.

Olsen, Joshua (2002), 'On the Units of Geographical Economics', *Geoforum*, 33: 153–64.

Overman, Henry G. (2003), 'Can We Learn Anything from Economic Geography Proper?', Centre for Economic Performance, Discussion Paper 586, London School of Economics and Political Science, London.

Peck, Jamie A. and Henry W.C. Yeung, eds (2003), *Remaking the Global Economy: Economic–Geographical Perspectives* (London: Sage Publications).

Peet, Richard *et al.* (2003), *Unholy Trinity: The IMF, World Bank and WTO* (London: Zed Books).

Peet, Richard and Elaine Hartwick (1999), *Theories of Development* (New York and London: Guilford Press).

Pomeranz, Kenneth (2000), *The Great Divergence: China, Europe, and the Making of the Modern World Economy* (Princeton: Princeton University Press).

Rappaport, Jordan and Jeffrey D. Sachs (2003), 'The United States as a Coastal Nation', *Journal of Economic Growth*, 8 (1): 5–46.

Rodrik, Dani, ed. (2003), *In Search of Prosperity: Analytic Narratives on Economic Growth* (Princeton: Princeton University Press).

Rodrik, Dani and Arvind Subramanian (2003), 'The Primacy of Institutions, and What this Does and Does Not Mean', *Finance and Development*, 40 (2): 31–34.

Sachs, Jeffrey D. (1999). 'Twentieth-Century Political Economy: A Brief History of Global Capitalism', *Oxford Review of Economic Policy*: 115 (4): 90–101.

—— (2000), 'Notes on a New Sociology of Economic Development', in Lawrence E. Harrison and Samuel P. Huntington, eds, *Culture Matters: How Values Shape Human Progress* (New York: Basic Books): 29–43.

—— (2001), 'Tropical Under-Development', NBER Working Paper 8119, February, National Bureau of Economic Research, Cambridge, Massachusetts.

—— (2003a), 'Institutions Don't Rule: Direct Effects of Geography on Per Capita Income', NBER Working Paper 9490, February, National Bureau of Economic Research, Cambridge, Massachusetts.

—— (2003b), 'Institutions Matter, But Not for Everything', *Finance and Development*, 40 (2): 38–41.

Sachs, Jeffrey D. and John W. McArthur (2001), 'Institutions and Geography: Comment on Acemoglu, Johnson and Robinson', NBER Working Paper 8114, February, National Bureau of Economic Research, Cambridge, Massachusetts.

Sachs, Jeffrey D. and Andrew M. Warner (1995a), 'Economic Convergence and Economic Policies', NBER Working Paper 5039, National Bureau of Economic Research, Cambridge, Massachusetts.

—— (1995b), 'Natural Resource Abundance and Economic Growth', NBER Working Paper 5398, December, National Bureau of Economic Research, Cambridge, Massachusetts.

—— (1999), 'The Big Push: Natural Resource Booms and Growth', *Journal of Development Economics*, 59 (1): 43–76.

—— (2001), 'The Curse of Natural Resources', *European Economic Review*, 45: 827–38.

Schmutzler, Armin (1999), 'The New Economic Geography', *Journal of Economic Surveys*, 13 (4): 355–79.

Sheppard, Eric (2000), 'Geography or Economics? Conceptions of Space, Time, Interdependence, and Agency', in Clark, Feldman and Gertler, eds, *The Oxford Handbook of Economic Geography*: 99–119.

Sheppard, Eric and Trevor Barnes, eds (2000), *A Companion to Economic Geography* (Oxford: Blackwell).

Smith, Adam ([1776] 1976), *An Inquiry into the Nature and Causes of the Wealth of Nations*, edited by Roy H. Campbell, Alexander S. Skinner and William B. Todd (Oxford: Oxford University Press).

Temin, Peter (1998), 'Evolutionary History: A Review Essay', *Journal of Interdisciplinary History*, 28 (3): 405–15.

Thrift, Nigel (2000), 'Pandora's Box? Cultural Geographies of Economies', in Clark, Feldman and Gertler, eds, *The Oxford Handbook of Economic Geography*: 689–704.

Toye, John ([1987] 1993), *Dilemmas of Development: Reflections on the Counter-Revolution in Development Economics*, second edition (Oxford: Blackwell).

Venables, Anthony J. (1998), 'The Assessment: Trade and Location', *Oxford Review of Economic Policy*, 14 (2): 1–6.

World Bank (1998), *Annual World Bank Conference on Development Economics*, edited by Boris Pleskovic and Joseph E. Stiglitz (Washington: World Bank).

Yeung, Henry W.C. (2002), 'The Limits to Globalization Theory: A Geographical Perspective on Global Economic Change', *Economic Geography*, 78 (3): 285–305.

Pioneers of Economic History

Dimitris Milonakis

Economic history and development have always been intimately related. The issues of development and growth have been the overwhelming preoccupation of economic history from its inception right to the present. As Goldin (1995: 207) puts it, 'in economic history the questions typically concern how whole economies have developed, why some grew while others did not, and what the consequences of economic growth have been. In this way, economic history is very much related to development economics.'

Indeed, the twin issues of growth and development seem to be the joining thread that unites such diverse figures as Gustav Schmoller, the leader of the German historical school, William Ashley, the leading member of the so-called English historical school and first president of the Economic History Society, W.W. Rostow, author of *The Stages of Economic Growth*, and the 1993 Nobel economics laureates, Robert Fogel, the leading cliometrician, and Douglass North, a founder of both cliometrics and the new institutionalist school in economics. Economic growth, however, in its modern meaning of the term, is mostly an economists' concept, normally defined in quantitative terms as a rise in per capita income over a period of time. Economic development, on the other hand, is a much broader concept encompassing all aspects of societal transformation from industrialization to 'modernization'.[1]

For many economic historians, especially since World War II, interest in historical aspects of development arose as a result of the problems facing less developed countries (Rostow 1957: 512). By studying the historical experience of industrialization, many lessons could be learnt by the less developed countries (Mathias 1970: 376). For Coats (1966: 332):

> Historians can shed light on the problems of the present by disclosing the secrets of the past, and as most of the underdeveloped countries are in a pre-industrial stage of development, and anxious to have an industrial revolution of their own, an added stimulus has been given to the study of the first 'classic' industrial revolution which occurred in eighteenth century England.

Broader issues related to development have always been high on the agenda of most economic historians, such as the causes and consequences of the industrial revolution, the character and sequence of the stages of economic growth, the role of religion, of institutions, of the market and of class conflict in the rise of capitalism, and the role of entrepreneurship and innovation in the developmental process. On the other hand, the past has provided a terrain on which to examine hypotheses about the role of agriculture, trade, income distribution, institutional change, etc., in development (Feeny 1995: 91). Other issues related to development and explored by economic historians include the level of employment, the standard of living, the organization of markets, etc. (Goodrich 1960: 536; Supple 1960: 550).

The aim of this chapter is to trace the evolution of economic history through the work of some of its pioneers, with emphasis on those economic historians whose work is of direct relevance to development. This is done by noting the emergence, with the marginalist revolution, of economic history and economics as separate disciplines. The initial thrust of economic history as primarily empirical in content is shown to be a consequence of reaction to the results of the *Methodenstreit*, a major debate in Germany over how economic science should be conducted. The subsequent history of economic history is marked by the unevenly paced re-introduction of economic theory, with the neoclassical to the fore in the form of cliometrics. The result has been to leave a nagging historical (guilty) conscience that is reflected in attempts either to refine economic theory to be more rounded in its historical content (in the 'newer' economic history), or to append the historical by appeal to institutions or ideology as with Douglass North. Neither of these is satisfactory, and the travails of economic history demonstrate that both it development require a historically rooted political economy to chart a course between being too abstract and universal, and too concrete and specific.

Political Economy and History

Long before the emergence of a distinctive economic history as such, growth and development had been central issues in political economy, especially in its classical version. Classical political economy – through its main representatives, Smith, Ricardo, Malthus and Mill – showed great concern for the nature and causes of the wealth of nations and its distribution to different fractions of society (classes). A similar concern ('to reveal the economic laws of motion of modern society') was also a prime objective of Karl Marx.

These writers were interested in long-term economic development and focused attention on the evolution of the economic system as a whole, on economic aggregates. Growth and change in the economy over time was their major concern. Such a macro-dynamic view of the economy opened the potential for history to become a valuable and integral part of economic analysis. The opportunity was taken up by most classical economists, with Ricardo a notable exception.

The marginalist revolution of the 1870s, and the subsequent emergence of neoclassical economics, brought about a rupture in the history of economic thought. The focus shifted away from dynamic processes of growth and distribution at the macro level, to static equilibrium analysis of price determination at the micro level. Methodological holism gave way to methodological individualism, accompanied by a change in the subject matter of economic science – from investigation of the causes and distribution of wealth to interrogation of the economic behaviour of individuals, especially the principle of (utility) maximization.

The concept of marginal utility proved instrumental in narrowing the scope of economic investigation to the study of price determination by focusing on market relations, treated in isolation from their social and historical context. This was reflected terminologically in the change from political economy to economics, not least in the title of the classic *magnum opus* of the new neoclassical economics authored by Alfred Marshall, *Principles of Economics* and not of *Political Economy*. With the far from token excision of the 'political', the social and the historical were also excised.

These developments are closely linked to a *second great divide* in economic thought, the schism between inductive and deductive methods. *Deduction* is an abstract scientific method based on *a priori* reasoning and the rules of logic, and, as such, can purport to be entirely devoid of historical specificity. *Induction*, by contrast, refers to the method of moving from the specific to the general, from empirical observation to general laws, by identifying characteristics of a specific phenomenon or situation and transposing them to other contexts. With induction, historical investigation occupies centrestage. The marginalists made exclusive use of the deductive method, whereas the German historical school was drawn to induction and sought to transform political economy into a branch of historical research.

The clash of methods, reflecting differences over the relationship between economics and history, came to a head in the famous *Methodenstreit*. Its chief protagonists in the 1880s were Gustav Schmoller and the Austrian marginalist, Carl Menger. Menger reacted to the historicists' inductivist claims by reasserting the legitimacy of the abstract deductive method in economic inquiry, with the individual as the basic unit of analysis (Menger [1883] 1985: 56). Whatever the merits of the two sides in principle, the aftermath of the *Methodenstreit* in practice proved to be instrumental in legitimizing the exclusive use of the abstract deductive method by mainstream economics, at the expense of the inductive/historical method.

The move from political economy to economics heralded the separation of the latter from the other social sciences. The anti-social and anti-historicist reductionism of the marginalist revolution gave economic science a rationale for developing independently of other social disciplines (Deane 1978: 75). Consequently, the birth of economic history as a separate discipline with a particular content can be attributed to other parallel developments. First was the emergence of sociology as the source of *social* theory, to occupy the space vacated in moving from political economy to economics. Second was the failure of the historical school to establish itself as an alternative school of economic thought, vacating space for the new field of economic history to emerge as primarily focused on empirical investigation (equally absent from the new economic theory).

During the inter-war period, there were dissenting voices seeking to keep the relationship between economics and sociology and (economic) history alive. In contradistinction to both Jevons' and Menger's separatist proposals, Max Weber, Joseph Alois Schumpeter and the American institutionalists (Veblen, Commons, Ayres) were dedicated to retaining the broader scope of economics. The American institutionalists did so by asserting 'the primacy of the problem of the organization and control of the economic system, that is, its structure of power' (Samuels 1987: 865). By focusing their attention on social change and on the role of institutions in the functioning of the economy, old institutionalists brought to the fore the social and historical nature of economic processes.

Weber's and Schumpeter's efforts revolved around Weber's concept of *Sozialökonomik*, a platform for integrating economic theory with economic history and economic sociology. According to Schumpeter (1954: Chapter 2), economic science consists of four basic fields: economic history, statistics, economic theory and economic sociology. Of these four fields, he identified economic history as 'by far the most important one', not least because it combines economic with non-economic or 'institutional' facts, and, as such, 'it affords the best method for understanding how . . . the various social sciences *should* be related to one another' (ibid.: 13). Economic sociology, on the other hand, represents 'a sort of generalized or typified or stylized economic history' (ibid.: 20). Schumpeter tried to implement his version of *Sozialökonomik*, both in his *Theory of Economic Development* and in *Business Cycles*, through a qualitative analysis of structural change, combining economic theory with economic history and statistics. Despite their best efforts, however, the separation of economics from sociology and history was complete by World War II (Swedberg 1991).

Early Pioneers of Economic History

The roots of economic history are generally considered to reach back to the Scottish historical school. This school includes David Hume, Sir James Steuart, Adam Ferguson, William Robertson, John Millar and Adam Smith, and it 'provided the first British signpost of the economic past as an essential element in the understanding of human society' (Coleman 1987: 5). Two basic ideas of the school were: first, that 'the process of social change exhibits certain uniformities and regularities and the great task is to explain these, in terms of the *laws* which lie behind social development'; and, second, that 'development should be regarded as proceeding through four normally consecutive stages, each based on a particular "mode of subsistence" – hunting, pasturage, agriculture, and commerce' (Meek 1971: 9–10).

The stages of growth view of history is a prime example of what Dugald Stewart (1794) called 'theoretical' or 'conjectural' history, or what is also called 'philosophical' history, as opposed to the 'orthodox' narrative type of history

(Skinner 1975: 154). Narrative history normally supplies the material on which the 'philosophical' type is based, while the latter refers to the 'Newtonian' type of history, based on certain basic principles or assumptions (ibid.: 169, 170). The latter type of history is especially apparent in Book III of Smith's *Wealth of Nations*, 'Of the Natural Progress of Opulence', where he tackles the question of the origins of the 'present establishments' in Europe through 'the natural course of things', in the form of the four-stage schema of the process of historical evolution. This historical part of Smith's work also relies on the proposition that social change depends on economic development.

Smith's stages theory anticipates Marx's *materialist conception of history* (or *historical materialism*) and its associated concept of modes of production. This is presented in a summary form in Marx's ([1859] 1970: 20–21) well-known passage in the Preface to his *Contribution to the Critique of Political Economy*:

> In the social production of their existence, men inevitably enter into definite relations, which are independent of their will, namely relations of production appropriate to a given stage in the development of their material forces of production. The totality of these relations of production constitutes the economic structure, the real foundation, on which arises a legal and political superstructure and to which correspond definite forms of social consciousness. The mode of production of material life conditions the general process of social, political and intellectual life. . . . At a certain stage of development, the material productive forces of society come into conflict with the existing relations of production or – this merely expresses the same thing in legal terms – with the property relations within the framework of which they operated hitherto. From forms of development of the productive forces those relations turn into their fetters. Then begins an era of social revolution. The change in the economic foundation leads sooner or later to the transformation of the whole immense superstructure.

This passage is as rich as it is controversial. Here, it suffices to suggest that it represents a sketch of Marx's version of 'philosophical' or 'conjectural' history. The dialectical, social, historicist and dynamic nature of Marx's approach to history is apparent. The passage represents the application of Marx's dialectical mode of reasoning to the whole historical trajectory, rather than to any mode of production in particular.[2] It enables Marx to identify and isolate what he thinks are the basic explanatory variables in the course of historical evolution. This is done in a holistic and materialist fashion through the identification of the 'economic structure' or 'mode of production of material life' as the basic unit of analysis.

With the emergence of the German historical school, there is a move away from attempts to build a 'philosophical' or 'theoretical' type of history, toward a more narrative type. This is a necessary corollary of the school embracing an inductivist and empiricist approach to analysing social and historical phenomena. Empirical generalizations and regularities come to the fore at the expense of the theoretical. Even so, following in the footsteps of the Scottish historical school, the German historicists also sought a periodization of history into stages of evolution. But, contrary to Smith and Marx, the historical school found no common criteria to differentiate the various stages. They lacked a unifying theoretical principle such as Smith's 'mode of subsistence' or Marx's 'mode of production'.

From within the ranks of the German historical school, Schmoller offered the most advanced stages approach to history through the application of his historical–ethical method to the problem of institutions and evolution, forming a 'stage history of institutions'. His periodization of European history into village economy, city economy, territorial economy and national economy is structured around the form that the organization of regional community takes, in order to control economic life and serve the public interest. It is a history of the institutions of community and is complemented by the evolutionary transformation of the state. Thus, Schmoller identifies the main role of the modern nation-state in the application of mercantilist policies, which are contemporaneous with the transition from the territorial economy to the national economy. It parallels the transition from the local to the absolutist state.

Schmoller's concerns are related to the socio-economic conditions prevalent in Germany in the nineteenth century. Compared to both England and France, Germany was an underdeveloped country both politically and economically, and in the process of forming a nation out of disunity and needing to forge international competitiveness (Betz 1988: 413–14). Thus the German historical school sought to form the nation and drag it into the modern world. Further, members of the younger historical school, in particular, who wrote in a period when the national and social questions were acute,[3] were staunch supporters of an active programme of social reform. In addition to the institution of the regional community, Schmoller also distinguishes the social systems of the family and the 'commercial firm', which are based on different organizational principles and involve different institutional arrangements. In short, the German historicist's approach to history has a strong empirical grounding and, especially in Schmoller's work, an equally strong institutionalist flavour (Koot 1987: 103, 36; Shionoya 2001: 10–15; Giouras 1992: 114–31).

According to Schumpeter, Schmoller's research programme is a 'prototype of economic sociology' and he praises him (together with Marx) for providing what he called 'unitary' or 'universal social science' (Schumpeter 1954: 441; Shionoya 1995: 67). Schumpeter is significant because of his own adherence to a dynamic theory of capitalist development based on the continuous process of innovation inherent in the system. His main focus of attention was the technological and institutional change that takes place through the process of *creative destruction* 'that incessantly revolutionizes the economic structure *from within*, incessantly destroying the old one, incessantly creating the new one' (Schumpeter 1987: 83). This continuous innovative process, which materializes through long waves of economic activity, is the result of the initiatives of the producer–entrepreneur (Schumpeter 1961: 65). 'But innovation is historical by nature, and can be understood only as a historical process' (Freeman and Louçã 2001: 63). Hence Schumpeter's (1939: 220) plea for a 'reasoned (conceptually clarified) history . . . of the economic process in all its aspects and bearings.' Schumpeter (1987: 44) praised Marx as being 'the first economist of top rank to see and to teach systematically how economic theory may be turned into historical analysis and how the historical narrative may be turned into *histoire raisonnée*'.

Sombart was one of the last political economists to attempt such a reasoned history of capitalism. Although he 'successfully stood on the shoulders of Schmoller, at least with one leg, the other one [was] supported by Marx', without, however, making use of any of his concepts (Betz 1993: 332). At a time when history was mostly empirical, Sombart was strongly in favour of combining theory with history. 'No theory – no history!' he says. 'Theory is the prerequisite to any scientific writing of history' (Sombart 1929: 3). His concept of the 'economic system' became the vehicle for such a combination. He defined it as 'the mode of providing for material wants', very close to Marx's notion of a 'mode of production', although Sombart added that this was 'animated by a definite spirit' or *geist* (ibid.: 13–14; Betz 1993: 347). On this basis, he offered a periodization of the capitalist economic system into early, full or high and late capitalism (Sombart 1929: 16; Hodgson 2001: 130).

The Emergence of Economic History as a Separate Discipline

The 'attempt to discover . . . the laws of social development – that is to say, generalizations as to the stages through which the economic life of society has actually moved', has also been posed by Ashley (quoted in Koot 1980: 108) and the British historicists in general, as the chief task facing historical economics.[4] Following in Schmoller's footsteps, Ashley's and Toynbee's view is that economic history cannot just be a history of wages and prices. Instead, they opt for a social history of the stages of economic development in the form of the genesis, development and decline of institutions, and their influence on social and economic arrangements. Theirs was a history of institutional development and change (Koot 1987: 87, 113).

What the English historical school targets, in effect, is the economic and social history of institutions in the service of social reform.[5] Indeed, social reform, through increased government intervention in the economy, is their *raison d'être*. They too stand for a more historical and inductive form of economic science geared towards practical purposes. If the 'social question' is the prime policy target of the younger German historical school, the social consequences of the industrial revolution became the leitmotif of their Anglo–Irish counterparts, following Toynbee's lead. Indeed, the focus on the 'cataclysmic' and 'pessimistic' interpretation of the social consequences of the industrial revolution, which took the form of higher prices and drops in the standard of living of the working class, cyclical crisis of overproduction, increased polarization, etc., is Toynbee's most

original contribution, continuing to exert a lasting influence on succeeding generations of economic historians (Koot 1987: 48–53, 84–89, 116–21, 150–55;
Coleman 1987: 57–62).

However, it was Cunningham's *The Growth of English Trade and Commerce* (written in 1882) that became the *locus classicus* of the writings of the
English historical school, as well as the foundation stone of economic history as
a discipline. Indeed, 'both critics and supporters of William Cunningham agreed
that the archdeacon's volumes on English economic history laid the foundation
of the discipline in England as an academic field of study' (Koot 1987: 135).
Cunningham was also instrumental in the emergence of economic history as a
discipline in other respects. With his adoption of an ultra-empiricist stance, where
facts are supposed to speak for themselves, the distance between historical economics and economic theory became even more pronounced. The reconciliatory
stance of both Schmoller in the *Methodenstreit* and Ashley subsequently, and
their plea for a combination of the historical method with abstract theory, was
abandoned, and an even more hostile approach to economic theorizing was
adopted. Cunningham's continuous academic and personal battles with the founder
of the neoclassical school, Alfred Marshall, played a major part.

Within British academia, Cunningham's empiricism marginalized him
and the historical school in general. 'Gradually pushed aside in academic argument, several members of the British historical school made their way into the
discipline of economic history, embraced empiricism, and abandoned economic
theory to the theorists' (Hodgson 2001: 111, Chapter 8). Marshall reinforced the
process through his wide influence and recognition. Although his stance on the
'British *Methodenstreit*', between him and Cunningham, was generally concilia-
tory, his inclination veered firmly on the side of abstract theory. His *magnus
opus*, *The Principles*, is a telling testimony. He opposed pure deductivism as well
as extreme empiricism, and urged a combination of both methods (Hodgson
2001: Chapter 8).

The British historical economists played the leading role in the birth of
economic history as a new discipline in Britain. Their role was particularly
pronounced during what Harte (1971: xii) calls the 'take off' era of economic
history between 1882 and 1904, which was followed by the years of 'the drive to
maturity' (1904–27)[6] and, afterwards, 'the age of mass consumption'. Ashley's
academic trajectory, in particular, was symbolic of this process. If Cunningham's
book became the *locus classicus* of British historical economics, Ashley is appropriately designated as the most prominent member of the 'school'. As Price (quoted
in Coleman 1987: 45) puts it, Cunningham and Ashley 'created Economic
History for English students'. Although Ashley started off in the 1880s as a staunch
supporter of the primacy of having 'a broad historical understanding of society's
evolution' over the universal truths of abstract deductive theory, by 1893 he had
already 'repudiated the goal of replacing all deductive theory with historical
economics . . . [and] called for the establishment of economic history as a
separate and respected academic discipline that provided conclusions as to the

"character and sequence of the stages of economic development"' (Koot 1987: 108, 112–13, Chapter 5; Koot 1980: 188–92; Ashley 1893: 7; Coleman 1987: 44–45).

The first decades of the twentieth century witnessed the first steps in the emergence in Britain of economic history paper, as opposed to historical economics. The last members of the English historical school, who presided over the transformation of historical economics into economic history, were Cunningham, Foxwell and Ashley. The historical economists, having lost out in the debate over method, were confined to the study of economic history. Having failed to make the historical the object of *economic* inquiry, they saw their own research programme being transformed into a branch of historical research. Historical economics thus gave way to a new discipline: economic history. Ashley (1927: 1), in the first issue of *The Economic History Review*, defined economic history as 'the history of actual human practice with respect to the material basis of life. The visible happenings with regard . . . to "the production, distribution, and consumption of wealth" form our wide enough field.'

The first steps of economic history proper bore all the birthmarks of its long gestation. Both the historical trend in economics and the muted British *Methodenstreit* left their imprints on the writings of the first generation of economic historians and gave rise to two opposing traditions in economic history. Coleman (1987: Chapter 5) aptly describes these as the 'reformist' and the 'neutralist' traditions. Tawney and the Hammonds are the main representatives of the reformists, adopting the legacy of the historical economists. Bequeathed to them were an empiricist and institutionalist orientation, coupled with a general hostility towards economic theory, a concern for the (negative) social consequences of the industrial revolution and advocacy of social reform (ibid.: 64–65).

Whether in the form of the mixture of 'religious theory' (such as Christian ethics) with the 'growth of individualism' and 'the triumph of economic interests', as in Tawney's *Religion and the Rise of Capitalism*, or in the comprehensive account of the effects of the industrial revolution on the standard of living of the working people, as in Hammonds' *The Town Labourer*, the first 'reformist' economic historians wrote, first and foremost, descriptive social history, based primarily on qualitative sources. In the writings of Tawney, but also of Unwin, economic history took a markedly sociological turn (Tawney 1932: 104; Court 1970: 142).

A social history emerged, set in a wider philosophical framework (Harte 1971: xxviii), and informed by categories such as class and industrialization that were far from methodologically and theoretically 'neutral'. According to Tawney (1932: 102–03), 'economic historians . . . cannot . . . understand historical changes in the distribution of wealth without a study of the corresponding changes in the institution of property, the class-structure of society, and the polity of states'. But, despite exerting temporary influence, the general trend was for economic history to become empiricist in content and, as such, to be divorced from theory, especially economic theory. 'The massive work that typified so much about the subject at this stage was J.H. Clapham's three volumes on the *Economic History of Modern Britain*, the first of which appeared in 1926' (Harte 1971: xxvi).

From Clapham to Rostow and Beyond

Clapham was, for many, including Tawney (1932: 95), the *doyen* of English economic history. He was a founder of the 'neutralist' trend, a tradition continued by Ashton. Being a student of Marshall, he was to initiate a wholly new tradition in economic history. In direct contradistinction to Toynbee's and the Hammonds' 'catastrophic' interpretation of the industrial revolution, one basic attribute of Clapham's work was his insistence on a balanced or 'neutralist' interpretation of the social consequences of the industrial revolution. Clapham was 'a severe critic of some social historians, notably Mr and Mrs Hammond, because he thought they were demonstrably wrong in their facts' (Court 1970: 148). But the chief characteristic of this tradition was its quantitative style and sources, coupled with limited use of economic theory. As Clapham (quoted in Coleman 1987: 77–78) puts it, 'every economic historian should have acquired . . . the habit of asking in relation to any institution, policy, group or movement the questions: how large? how long? how often? how representative?'.

Despite his intentions, Clapham's use of economic theory remained implicit, and mostly took the form of the general assumptions of Marshallian neoclassical theory. This reflected his dissatisfaction with the lack of historical applicability of the economic theory prevalent in his time, rather than any general aversion towards theory. He made this plain in his vehement attack on economists' abstract tools – as expressed by Marshall, but especially Pigou – as 'empty economic boxes'. Despite his intentions, Clapham's history remained empiricist if quantitative, although the questions he asked were mostly economic. 'He wanted to know what the disposable resources of the nation were; what changes occurred from time to time; how resources were organized; how the markets worked and what incomes for private persons and for the State came of all this' (Court 1970: 145; see also Coleman 1987: 77–87; Koot 1987: Chapter 9).

Ashton was more responsible for having 'made economic history the economists' history' by extending Clapham's quantitative type of history and making more explicit use of Marshallian economics (Coleman 1987: 82). In his inaugural lecture, appropriately entitled, 'The Relation of Economic History to Economic Theory', Ashton ([1945] 1971: 170–71) described the (economic) historian's tasks and relation shift to economic theory as follows:

> Understanding of the processes which it is the business of economic historians to trace through the centuries does not come by the light of nature. The data do not wear their hearts on their sleeves: it is only by selecting and grouping them that they can be made to yield a meaning. But . . . as soon as the historian begins to select his facts from the myriads available to him he becomes a theorist of sorts. . . . The economic historian, like the fisherman, needs a net, to help to separate those fish that may be marketable from those that may well be left in

the sea. . . . The men who make the special nets for the craft are the economists.

For Ashton, although until World War I, economic theory was cold, abstract and static, rendering it irrelevant to the problems of change over time, developments since the war changed this. He refers to 'a closer intimacy between economists and historians'. Yet, this depends not on theory but a switch of emphasis from theoretical to empirical research: 'economists became increasingly less theoretical and more statistical in their approach' (Ashton [1945] 1971: 171). Ashton, like Clapham, promoted a statistical and quantitative turn in both economics and history, rather than changing economic theory in doing so.

Into the post-war era, the two most influential figures are W.W. Rostow and Simon Kuznets. Their influence extends beyond economic history to development economics and, in the case of Kuznets, applied economics more generally. Renewal of interest among economists in problems of long-term economic growth and development stimulated study of its determinants, technical change and the distribution of income, in part through application of abstract theoretical models (Eichengreen 1994: 67). The comparative performance of the US and Soviet economies also received increasing attention, as did problems of long-run development in developing countries. Studies of comparative economic growth, past and present, were increasingly funded (Coats 1980: 201–02). In this environment Rostow wrote his two classics, *The Process of Economic Growth* (1953) and *The Stages of Economic Growth* (1960).

Rostow's (1960: 2) focus of attention was on the process of long-term economic growth and development. His aim was to provide 'an alternative to Karl Marx's theory of modern history'. Granted this and his interest in long-term growth, it is not surprising that he should turn his attention to other earlier dynamic theories, such as those of Schumpeter and classical political economy (Rostow 1953: Chapter 4). In his *Stages*, Rostow (1960: 2) identified five stages of growth through which, more or less, all societies pass: the traditional society, the stage of preconditions for take-off, the take-off stage, the drive to maturity and the age of mass consumption.

Of these, the take-off stage, Rostow's term for the industrial revolution, is the most important. During this stage, the economy enters into self-sustained growth. 'These stages', according to Rostow (1960: 12–13), 'are not merely descriptive . . . [but] have an analytical bone-structure, rooted in a dynamic theory of production.' He tried to identify in each stage what he called 'the leading sector', providing the engine that propelled the growth process forward. Although his theory was built on the British experience, Rostow thought he was building a general theory of stages through which most societies would pass. In this theory, he tried to integrate all non-economic factors, such as politics, social structure and culture, having a direct bearing upon growth (Rostow 1957: 521). Rostow's stages theory was debated throughout the 1960s.

Gerschenkron's (1962) aversion to general theories of economic development and to the notion of 'prerequisites' of modern growth is captured by his concept of 'relative backwardness' as applied to Russia. To the (Marxian or Rostowian) notion that industrialization 'must proceed . . . through certain more or less discrete stages', Gerschenkron (Ibid.: 7, 31) reacted by arguing that 'in several important respects the development of a backward country may, by the very virtue of its backwardness, tend to differ fundamentally from that of an advanced country'. Rostow's notion of a 'leading sector' was also contested by the early cliometric literature (Fogel 1964; see below). Rostow is highly symbolic of a liaison between old and new economic history. As an old type of historian, he was 'one of the leaders in applying economics to history' (McCloskey 1978: 18; Landes 1978: 3), a decisive characteristic of the coming cliometric revolution. He was also a participant in the 1957 conference (see below), widely understood to have inaugurated that revolution (North 1997: 5).

Also present in that conference was Simon Kuznets who, although considered a development economist, played some part in preparing the ground for new economic history. His most important contribution was in developing new quantitative and statistical procedures for national income accounting. Kuznets was the offspring of another new development of the inter-war and immediate post-war period, the emergence of applied economics as a separate field of study. In America, the National Bureau of Economic Research (NBER), co-founded by the institutionalist Wesley Mitchell, played a leading role in this. Indeed, Mitchell has been described as the initiator of 'the most prestigious empirical tradition of American economics' (Coats 1980: 187).

Between them, Mitchell and Kuznets, together with other researchers of the NBER, were responsible for the production of a mountain of statistical series in empirical studies of the development of the American economy. While Mitchell focused on the study of business cycles, Kuznets' pioneering national income accounting pushed statistical estimates back to 1869 (Coats 1980: 187; Fogel 1965: 95). Many of the participants in the cliometric revolution were students of Kuznets (Lamoreaux 1998: 64), with Fogel, Nobel prize winner, the leading representative.

Measuring History: The Cliometric Revolution

Following the publication of Samuelson's *Foundations of Economic Analysis* (1947) and the increasing mathematization of economics, the split between economics and history widened. The formalization of economics, signifying the triumph and widespread adoption of the deductive method, attained its climax, both conceptually and technically, in the mathematical proof by Arrow and Debreu (1954) of the existence of general equilibrium in a Walrasian framework.

At the same time, a new process was set in motion as far as the relationship between economics and other social sciences is concerned, what has been described as 'economics imperialism'.[7] This was partly made possible through the adoption by neoclassical economics of Lionel Robbins' (1935: 16) definition of economics as 'the science which studies human behaviour as a relationship between ends and scarce means which have alternative uses'. In this way, economics was transformed from the science of the economy to a science of choice (Hodgson 2001: 93, 82–83). Hence, (neoclassical) economics, at least in principle, became a science without a subject matter (Becker 1976: 3).

This was to have a huge impact on developments in economics, especially in its relations with other social sciences. Ultimately, it has given rise to a reversal of the trend initiated by the marginalist revolution: economics began to expand its domain through the colonization of other social sciences and of other areas of economics previously thought to be outside its domain. One of the first fields of study to be colonized by neoclassical economics was economic history.

Starting in the late 1950s and early 1960s, a group of researchers, mostly trained as economists, vigorously applied (neoclassical) economic theory and quantitative techniques to the study of the past. These early studies had an avalanche effect and gave rise to a movement, soon to be known as 'new economic history' or cliometrics. It rapidly dominated the study of economic history in America.[8] 'A revolution is taking place in economic history in the United States', one of the protagonists of the new economic history was already proclaiming in 1963 (North 1963: 128). This movement sought to make the study of economic history more rigorous by making it more analytical and quantitative (North 1965: 86).

The historic event that heralded the emergence of 'new economic history' was the September 1957 Conference on Research in Income and Wealth held in Williamstown, Massachusetts. Two papers presented by Conrad and Meyer, one on methodology and the other on the economics of slavery, provided a pseudo-manifesto for the cliometrics movement (Conrad and Meyer 1957, 1958; Coats 1980: 187). On methodology, Conrad and Meyer (1957: 541) made a plea for 'a more scientific approach to the study of economic history'. Any such endeavour, according to them, involves two basic elements. First is the use of theory in historical investigation in an attempt to identify causal relationships. Second is the use of formal quantitative analysis.

The verdict of participants in the conference was not unanimous. For Rostow (1957: 515, 519), although theory is essential in analysing the economic past, the kind of economic theory most useful for such a project is not to be found in the 'Newtonian section' of economic science as exemplified in Marshallian static equilibrium analysis, but in the 'biological strands in their heritage embedded in the *Wealth of Nations*, evoked in our time by Mitchell's leadership and by Schumpeter's fruitful suggestions'. It is interesting that all economic theorists who participated at the conference 'were doubtful of the value of theory in work on economic history', while most participants were concerned with the problems of quantification in history (Kuznets 1957: 548, 550).

Notwithstanding the concerns of these participants, there was no stopping those supporting the use of theory and quantitative analysis. The spark of the conference had ignited the cliometrics revolution. Old-style economic historians were either shoved aside or else withdrew into 'a kind of internal exile within the profession' (Landes 1978: 5) to pave the way for newcomers coming chiefly from the economics profession. Use of (neoclassical) theory and quantitative techniques (in conjunction with use of the counterfactual method) became the pillars on which cliometrics was consolidated.

Old economic history, mostly practised by historians and not economists, had laid emphasis on narrative, based on archival research and mostly using qualitative sources. As seen, theirs was mostly an institutional type of history. New economic historians differed. Every effort was made to put an end to the implicit, vague, incomplete and internally inconsistent 'models of the traditional historians', who used social theory in an informal way and rarely bothered to 'test the applicability of the theories to the particular historical situations on which they are imposed' (Fogel 1983: 26, 31–32). Instead, they offered more models in attempting to identify causal relationships, advocating quantitative statements, shifting attention to statistical sources and emphasizing the use of econometric techniques (Field 1995: 3).

Two topics stand out as principal areas of research: the effects of railroads on American economic growth in the nineteenth century, and the profitability of slavery. Typical cliometrics in its first phase was Fogel's *Railroads and American Economic Growth* (1964), while the later milestone was Fogel's and Engerman's *Time on the Cross* (1974). Fogel's study is a prime example of the counterfactual method. Old-type economic historians, among them Rostow (1960), had argued that railroads were indispensable for the 'take-off' into sustained growth of the American economy. One implication is that in the absence of railroads, American economic growth would have been much lower. So, Fogel opted to test this counterfactual. He did so by calculating the savings (additions to national income) that accrue because of the use of a lower cost transportation system (railroads) relative to other more expensive means (for example, canals). His findings indicated that although the social savings of railroads were higher, they were not high enough (US GNP would have only been 5 per cent lower in 1890) to make railroads indispensable to American economic growth.

Fogel's study was challenged, mostly coming from the ranks of what North (1977: 199) called 'the Harvard wing'. Dissent, sometimes running deep, was voiced from the beginnings of the cliometrics revolution. One area of concern was the use of counterfactuals – what Redlich (1970: 91) called 'as if', quasi or fictitious history, which 'is not really history at all'. Cliometricians were also regarded with suspicion for almost total reliance on received economic theory, excessive bias in favour of quantitative data at the expense of more qualitative sources, and the problems associated with quantification in history.

Criticism came from two quarters – from the older tradition of economic historians (Redlich 1965; 1970), and from other economic historians, including some practitioners of cliometrics (*inter alia*, North 1965, 1974; David, 1969; see also Sutch 1982: 28), who had started questioning their own practices. Early on, North (1965: 90) made no secret of his dissatisfaction with the practices of cliometricians by declaring that 'the results have been generally disappointing'. Following in the tradition of Clapham and Rostow, in later writings, North started questioning the very usefulness of neoclassical economics in analysing the past (North 1974: 2):

> Neoclassical economic theory has two major shortcomings for the economic historian. One, it was not designed to explain long-run economic change; and two, even within the context of the question it was designed to answer, it provides quite limited answers since it is immediately relevant to a world of perfect markets.

Next to the inadequacies of neoclassical theory lies exclusive reliance on quantitative sources and the problems associated with quantitative data. Historical data are mostly qualitative in character. For Landes (1978: 6–7):

> many, if not most of the important questions that we have to deal with do not lend themselves . . . to quantitative treatment. Sometimes the numerical data are lacking. There are whole areas of history where we probably will never have the numbers we need. Sometimes we have numbers but they do not tell us enough.

By the end of the 1970s, cliometrics as a revolution had run its course. Field (1995: 1) pronounced that 'the Cliometrics revolution is dead', echoing McCloskey (1978: 203). The final episode marking 'the beginning of the end of cliometrics as an intellectual movement promising a revolution in methods and results' was the publication of Fogel and Engerman's *Time on the Cross* in 1974 (Field 1995: 5). Burdened by the inadequacies of its underlying theory and the narrowness of the field of application of its mathematical techniques, coupled with the problems of quantification, new economic history could not sustain its forward momentum (Lamoreaux 1998: 59). It established far more than a significant niche for itself within history, but only at the expense of forcing other historians (including those examining economic issues) on to separate fields such as social and business history.

From New to Newer Economic History
The growing dissatisfaction with the limitations of neoclassical theory to deal adequately with the problems of history has led many economic historians to search for alternative theoretical frameworks as their main frame of reference. In this endeavour, more recent developments within mainstream economics have played a vital role. Particularly important is the emergence of new information economics and new institutional economics associated with appeal to market imperfections, transaction costs and game-theoretic approaches.

More broadly, these developments have promoted a new phase of economics imperialism (Fine 2003: 106), the application of which to economic history has given rise to what has been termed the *newer economic history* (ibid.; Fine and Milonakis 2003: 550), with its main practitioners being Lamoreaux, Temin, Greif, etc. The work of Douglass North, although part of this general trend, will be treated separately since he has diverged in important ways from his fellow travellers.

These endeavours share in common a belief that institutions play a vital role in historical evolution and, as such, need theoretically to be addressed explicitly. Neoclassical theory, with its reliance on perfect markets and the *absence* of institutions, can hardly assist. The result is that institutions, such as the firm, are treated as a 'black box' (Lamoreaux *et al.* 1997: 62; Temin 1991: 7). The newer approach can address the issue of institutions, politics, etc., on the basis of the existence of market imperfections. Institutions are explained as the result of responses of individuals to market imperfections. But these are amenable to formal modelling by means of the new information-theoretic or game-theoretic economics, with its emphasis on market imperfections. Not only can the 'black box' of the firm be opened, but intra-firm relations as well as the economy as a whole can be subject to close analytical scrutiny (Temin 1991: 2, 315; Lamoreaux *et al.* 1999: 10; Fine 2003: 108).

Another prominent feature of the newer economic history has been their concern for 'time and context' (Lamoreaux and Raff 1995: 5; Lamoreaux *et al.* 1999: 9). As Fine (2003: 110) puts it,

> aware of its reliance upon formal mathematical models with claims of universal applicability, the new approach is sensitive to the charge from historians of neglect of what it terms 'time and context'. However, the new theory presents itself as free from, or less vulnerable to, such charges because it deploys game theory in which history matters and for which outcomes and future strategies depend upon paths taken from or around multiple equilibria in the past.

So, use of game theory and the notion of path dependence are the ways in which history is brought back in.

Notwithstanding market imperfections, institutions, etc., the newer approach shares much more in common with the new economic history. It relaxes the assumption of perfect information but much else remains intact, including methodological individualism, the assumption of rationality, the use of abstract models, etc. As Bates *et al.* (1998: 3) put it, 'when we refer to theory, we refer to rational choice and, most often, to the theory of games'. But what unites the newer approach with that of its predecessors is its positivistic outlook: 'Rendering explanations explicit enables us to put them at risk. Do their assumptions correspond to what is known? Do their conclusions follow from their premises? How well do they stand up by comparison with other explanations?' (ibid. 1998: 14).

Paul David represents a special case within newer economic history and, as such, deserves special attention. What earned him a place in the economic historians' hall of fame was the notion of path dependence. As David (1986: 30) puts it, 'a *path dependent* sequence of economic changes is one in which important influences upon the eventual outcome can be exerted by temporally remote events, including happenings dominated by chance elements rather than systematic forces'. He derived this notion by generalizing from one specific case study based on the history of the QWERTY keyboard (ibid.). Once QWERTY was in place, he argues, there were '*technical interrelatedness, economies of scale*, and *quasi-irreversibility* of investment' (ibid.: 41), which caused QWERTY 'to become "locked in" as the dominant keyboard arrangement'. Provided the QWERTY story describes an 'essentially *historical* dynamic process' and there are 'many more QWERTY worlds lying out there in the past' (ibid.: 47), path dependence becomes the vehicle through which David brings history back in. However, in addition to bringing history back in through an otherwise ahistorical framework, such as that of the newer economic history, this also represents only one aspect, and a very thin one at that, of what is essentially a very rich and multifaceted process.

The Economic History of Douglass North

North's intellectual trajectory has been spectacular, passing through four phases.[9] The first is as a founder of cliometrics. From the late 1960s, North became a pioneer of the new institutional economics by introducing institutions and institutional change into economic history (North 1974, for example). In the 1980s, North (1981 and 1990) expanded his theoretical terrain to include the role of the state and ideology. All these elements are incorporated into the theoretical framework of *Structure and Change in Economic History* (1981), the *locus classicus* of his historical writings and point of reference in what follows. In the last, continuing phase, his attention shifts to cognitive science in attempting to explore further the way changes in ideology promote social change (North 1994: 362). This involves an exploration of the process through which human learning takes place.

North's central task in his post-cliometric phase has been to account for economic change and to find possible explanations for the diverse economic performances experienced in different parts of the world at different points in time. However, according to North, no existing theory provided an adequate framework for analysing the dynamics of change in economic history. Neoclassical theory, however, does have some virtue relative to its competitors (for North, old institutionalism and Marxism) in that it focuses on scarcity, competition and the individual as the basic unit of analysis (North 1997: 6). But its strengths are complemented by weaknesses in its static and timeless nature, and in being unable to explain the presence of large-group behaviour, especially in view of the potential for free-riding (North 1981: 11). Thus, the neoclassical world cannot fill out history by itself, and the extent to which it does prevail depends on non-market elements. Initially, North recognized that dealing with the deficiencies of neoclassical economics requires analytical 'retooling' (North 1997: 5).

The first port of call in this respect is the work of Coase (1937, 1960). The common ground, according to North (1995: 19), between new institutional economics and neoclassical economic theory, is that the former also 'begins with the scarcity hence competition postulate; it views economics as a theory of choice subject to constraints; it employs price theory as an essential part of the analysis of institutions; and it sees changes in relative prices as a major force inducing change in institutions'. Notwithstanding these common starting points, the new institutional approach also modifies and extends neoclassical theory by adding institutions as a critical constraint. The key concept lying behind his theory of institutions is that of transaction costs arising out of the incomplete, asymmetrically held and, hence, costly nature of information (ibid.: 18). As he puts it, 'when it is costly to transact, institutions matter'. They assume central importance in the explanation of differential performance (North 1990: 3–4, 1995: 23).

Institutions and institutional change then become the primary focus of North's writings. At the same time, North also feels the need to tackle three more theoretical problems: first, the sources of institutional change; second, the persistence of inefficient institutional arrangements; and third, the riddle of the free-rider problem associated with the rationality assumption. He adopts three basic building blocks: first, 'a theory of property rights that describes the individual and group incentives'; second, 'a theory of the state, since it is the state that specifies and enforces property rights'; and third, 'a theory of ideology that explains how different perceptions of reality affect the reaction of individuals to the changing "objective situation"' (North 1981: 7–8).

Thus, in accounting for the unprecedented growth of western economies in the modern era, North singles out the establishment of 'well-specified and well-enforced property rights' (North 1989: 1320) as the single most important institution. However, in contrast to earlier work (North and Thomas 1973), efficient property rights are no longer seen as the only possible outcome. Inefficient property rights can also prevail. However, their existence and persistence needs explanation, and the state offers a solution for North. In his hands, the state is treated as a Hobbesian institution standing above society (Hodgson 1988: 154). What is more, instead of being seen as a collectivity, the state is presented as if it were a profit-maximizing individual subject to constraints. Inefficient property rights in this framework arise, first, as a result of the state's dichotomy of interests (maximization of ruler's own revenue and of society's welfare); and, second, as a result of the constraints imposed upon its actions from potential rulers and from the transaction costs of collecting taxes (North 1981: Chapter 3).

With inefficient property rights explained by resort to the state, North deploys ideology to solve the issue of altruistic behaviour and what he calls 'the deviations from the individualistic rational calculus of neoclassical theory' (North 1981: 12). In broad terms, the state and ideology, between them, have the free-floating, universal power to explain more or less anything that happens and, correspondingly, figure prominently in North's analysis. Even so, the most pervasive element remains his use of neoclassical tools and analytical methods, including methodological individualism, rational choice and comparative statics. This is evident in almost every aspect of his theoretical excursion. Even when he departs from the neoclassical framework through the introduction of institutions and ideology, he does so in a complementary way, in order to make up for some deficiency in its underlying framework. As such, these concepts cannot but remain residual to the neoclassical framework.

Marxism and the Origins of Capitalism

If the 'neutralist' tradition was continued mostly through the work of Ashton, Postan and others after World War II, the 'reformist' tradition was kept alive mostly through the work of Marxist historians (Coleman 1987: 101–15). Their attention shifts from the individual to structural factors in the search for explanatory power to account for economic and social change. The issue of the transition from feudalism to capitalism has proved to be a fertile terrain for Marxists to test their analytical tools. There have been two main rounds in this debate: the famous Dobb–Sweezy debate (Hilton, ed. 1978) and the Brenner debate (Aston and Philpin 1985). The main dividing line among Marxists is between those who argue for an external force (trade) as the cause of the development and dissolution of feudalism (Sweezy 1978), and those who look for the agent of change in the internal class structure of the feudal mode of production (Dobb 1963; Hilton 1984; Brenner 1976).

The latter group of authors firmly asserted the role of class conflict as 'the determining factor in the movement of feudal society' (Hilton 1984: 88), and 'the key to the problem of long-term economic development and of the transition from feudalism to capitalism' (Brenner 1976: 12). For Sweezy (1978: 35), on the other hand, given the static nature of feudalism and its 'very strong bias in favour of maintaining given methods and relations of production', this system had no internal source of change. Following Pirenne, Sweezy resorted to the impact of the development of inter-regional trade, which acted as a battering ram, to explain the crisis and eventual demise of feudalism.

According to Brenner (1976: 30, 33), Wallerstein's (1974) position that 'a trade-induced world division of labour will give rise to an international structure of unequally powerful nation-states . . . [which] determines an accelerated process of accumulation in certain regions (the core), while enforcing a cycle of backwardness in others (the periphery)', has to be understood 'as a direct outgrowth of the arguments put forward by Paul Sweezy'. He calls this approach neo-Smithian Marxism, because it displaces class relations from the centre of the analysis of economic development and underdevelopment, in favour of a Smithian-type emphasis on the extent of the market and the international division of labour as the root cause of both development and underdevelopment (Brenner 1976: 27).

Conclusion

That use of theory is an indispensable part of a historian's work is hardly disputed nowadays. Since facts do not speak for themselves, it is very difficult, if not impossible, for any historian to avoid using some sort of theoretical framework, at least implicitly. Use of theory is mandatory once the historian tries to answer the question 'why'. Because, as Redlich (1970: 87) rightly argues, 'no answer to the question "why" is possible without recourse to theory or philosophy'.

What is in dispute is the type of history most suitable for the (economic) historian. This is directly related to the nature of and subject matter of economic history. According to Coats (1966: 332), 'economic historians have always regarded the study of long term economic change as an integral part of their work, if not its *raison d'être*'. If the process of change is the core subject matter of economic history, static and timeless theories, such as mainstream economic theory, are of limited use. What is needed is a dynamic theory, which can account for changes in history as internally generated processes. The analysis has to transcend the level of the individual to reach the social and structural factors affecting development.

This again is made mandatory by the nature of the subject matter of economic history, which 'can be viewed as the history of economic development' (Field 1995: 28). Economic historians are normally interested in broader aspects of the developmental process from a historical perspective. As such, economic historians are 'forced to become general theorists of whole societies' (Rostow 1957: 522–23). So, a strictly economic, let alone strictly quantitative, history will not do. What is needed is a dynamic economic and social history, taking into account the multifaceted and multidimensional nature of processes of change in history. As Dobb ([1946] 1963: 32) put it:

> It seems abundantly clear that the leading questions concerning economic development . . . cannot be answered at all unless one goes outside the bounds of that limited traditional type of economic analysis in which realism is so ruthlessly sacrificed to generality, and unless the existing frontier between what is fashionable to label as 'economic factors' and as 'social factors' is abolished.

This is to appeal for a reasoned history, one that would combine economic and social aspects of the development process in a dynamic and evolutionary way in order to account for change in history. Such a history would have much more to offer in understanding the problems facing less-developed countries today.

This chapter draws on Fine and Milonakis (2005a) and (2005b).

Notes

[1] Not everybody agrees with this conceptual distinction between growth and development. For many growth theorists and development economists, mostly of neoclassical persuasion, these two concepts are used interchangeably to denote simply increases in per capita income. For a conceptual clarification and the different usages of the two, see Brinkman (1995).

[2] The dialectical mode of reasoning, which Marx inherits from Hegel, refers to the method through which 'the whole world, natural, historical, intellectual, is represented as a process, that is, in constant motion, change, transformation, development; and the attempt is made to trace out the internal connection that makes a continuous whole of all this movement and development' (Engels 1968: 408).

[3] The 'social question' refers to the social problems created by the rapid changes taking place in the capitalist societies of the nineteenth century associated with rapid urbanization and industrialization. These problems include the housing problem, the phenomenon of mass poverty and the labour question (Giouras 1992: 128–31).

4 The following draws on Koot's (1987, 1980) excellent reviews of the English historical school.
5 As Hodgson (2001: 66) argues, the label 'English' for the school is a misnomer, since
  many of its members were Irish (Ingram, Leslie) or Scottish (Cunningham).
6 'The climax of this phase of the subject's development, its drive to maturity, came in
  1926 with the founding of the Economic History Society and the publication in 1927
  of the first number of the *Economic History Review*' (Harte 1971: xxvii).
7 See, *inter alia*, Lazear (2000), Fine (1997).
8 There exist a number of surveys of the history of cliometrics. For generally favourable
  surveys of the achievements of cliometrics see, *inter alia*, Landes (1978), McCloskey
  (1978), Sutch (1982), Atack and Passell (1994), Field (1995a and b), Lamoreaux
  (1998), and Freeman and Louçã (2001: Chapter 2) offer more critical accounts of the
  achievements and failures of the cliometrics revolution from different perspectives.
9 This section draws on Fine and Milonakis (2003). See also Milonakis and Fine (2004).
  For concise summaries of the evolution of North's thought, see Sutch (1982) and
  North (1997).

References

Arrow, Kenneth and Gerald Debreu (1954), 'Existence of Equilibrium for a Competitive Economy',
    Econometrica, 23: 265–90.
Ashley, William J. (1927), 'The Place of Economic History in University Studies', *The Economic
    History Review*, 1 (1): 1–11.
——— ([1893] 1971), 'On the Study of Economic History', inaugural lecture; reprinted in
    Harte, ed., *The Study of Economic History*: 1–17.
Aston, T.H. and C.H.E. Philpin, eds (1976), *The Brenner Debate: Agrarian Class Structure and
    Economic Development in Pre-Industrial Europe* (Cambridge: Cambridge University
    Press).
Atack, Jeremy and Peter Passell (1994), *The New Economic View of American History from
    Colonial Times to 1940*, second edition (New York: W.W. Norton).
Ashton, T.S. ([1945] 1971), 'The Relation of Economic History to Economic Theory', inaugural
    lecture; reprinted in Harte, ed., *The Study of Economic History*: 161–79.
Bates, Robert H. *et al.* (1998), *Analytic Narratives* (New Jersey: Princeton University Press).
Becker, Gary (1976), *The Economic Approach to Human Behavior* (Chicago: University of
    Chicago Press).
Betz, H.K. (1988), 'How Does the German Historical School Fit?', *History of Political Economy*,
    20 (3): 409–30.
——— (1993), 'From Schmoller to Sombart', *History of Economic Ideas*, 1 (3): 331–56.
Brenner, Robert (1976), 'Agrarian Class Structure and Economic Development in Pre-Industrial
    Europe', *Past and Present*, 70; reprinted in Aston and Philpin, eds, *The Brenner
    Debate*: 10–63.
——— (1977), 'The Origins of Capitalist Development: A Critique of Neo-Smithian Marxism',
    New Left Review, 104: 25–95.
Brinkman, Richard (1995), 'Economic Growth versus Economic Development: Towards a Con-
    ceptual Clarification', *Journal of Economic Issues*, 29 (4): 1171–88.
Coase, Ronald (1937), 'The Nature of the Firm', *Economica*, 4 (4): 386–405.
——— (1960), 'The Problem of Social Cost', *Journal of Law and Economics*, 3 (1): 1–44.
Coats, A.W. ([1966] 1971), 'Economic Growth and Social Historian's Dilemma', inaugural
    lecture; reprinted in Harte, ed., *Study of Economic History*: 329–48.
——— (1980), 'The Historical Context of the "New" Economic History', *Journal of European
    Economic History*, 9 (1): 185–207.
Coleman, D.C. (1987), *History and the Economic Past: An Account of the Rise and Decline of
    Economic History in Britain* (Oxford: Clarendon Press).
Conrad, Alfred and John Meyer (1957), 'Economic Theory, Statistical Inference and Economic
    History', *Journal of Economic History*, 17 (4): 524–44.
——— (1958), 'The Economics of Slavery in Antebellum South', *Journal of Political Economy*,
    66: 95–130.

Court, W.H.B. (1970), *Scarcity and Choice in History* (London: Edward Arnold).

David, Paul (1969), 'Transport Innovation and Economic Growth: Professor Fogel On and Off the Rails', *Economic History Review*, 22 (3): 506–25.

—— (1986), 'Understanding the Economics of QWERTY: The Necessity of History', in W.N. Parker, ed., *Economic History and the Modern Economist* (Oxford: Basil Blackwell): 30–49.

Deane, P. (1978), *The Evolution of Economic Ideas* (Cambridge: Cambridge University Press).

Dobb, Maurice ([1946] 1963), *Studies in the Development of Capitalism* (London: Routledge and Kegan Paul).

Eichengreen, Barry (1994), 'The Contributions of Robert W. Fogel to Economics and Economic History', *Scandinavian Journal of Economics*, 96 (2): 167–79.

Engels, Frederic ([1886] 1968), *Ludwig Feuerbach and the End of Classical German Philosophy*, in Karl Marx and Frederick Engels, *Selected Works* (London: Lawrence and Wishart).

Feeny, David (1995), 'The Exploration of Economic Change: The Contribution of Economic History', in Field, ed., *The Future of Economics*: 91–119.

Field, Alexander J., ed. (1995), *The Future of Economics* (New Brunswick: Transaction Publishers).

——, ed. (1995b), 'The Future of Economic History', in Field, ed. *The Future of Economics*: 1–41.

Fine, Ben (1997), 'The New Revolution in Economics', *Capital and Class*, 61: 143–48.

—— (2003), 'From the Newer Economic History to Institutions and Development?', *Institutions and Economic Development*, 1 (1): 105–36.

Fine, Ben and Dimitris Milonakis (2003), 'From Principle of Pricing to Pricing of Principle: Rationality and Irrationality in the Economic History of Douglass North', *Comparative Studies in Society and History*, 45 (3): 120–44.

—— (2005a), *Economic Theory and History: From Classical Political Economy to Economics Imperialism* (London: Routledge).

—— (2005b), *Reinventing the Past: Method and Theory in the Evolution of Economic History* (London: Routledge).

Fogel, Robert W. (1964), *Railroads and American Economic Growth: Essays in Econometric History* (Baltimore: Johns Hopkins University Press).

—— (1965), 'The Reunification of Economic History with Economic Theory', *American Economic Review*, 55 (2): 92–98.

—— (1983), '"Scientific" History and Traditional History', in Robert W. Fogel and G.R. Elton, *Which Road to the Past?: Two Views of History* (New Haven: Yale University Press).

—— (1997), 'Douglass C. North and Economic Theory', in G.N. Dvorak and J.V.C. Nye, eds, *The Frontiers of New Institutional Economics* (San Diego: Academic Press).

Fogel, Robert W. and S.L. Engerman (1974), *Time on the Cross: The Economics of American Negro Slavery* (Boston: Little Brown).

Freeman, Chris and Francisco Louçã (2001), *As Time Goes By: From the Industrial Revolutions to the Information Revolution* (Oxford: Oxford University Press).

Gerschenkron, Alexander (1962), *Economic Backwardness in Historical Perspective* (Cambridge, Massachusetts: Harvard University Press).

Giouras, Thanasis (1992), 'Gustav Schmoller: Historism and Critique', *Axiologika*, 4: 96–131 (in Greek).

Goldin, Claudia (1995), 'Cliometrics and the Nobel', *Journal of Economic Perspectives*, 9 (2): 191–208.

Goodrich, Carter (1960), 'Economic History: One Field or Two?', *Journal of Economic History*, 20 (4): 531–47.

Harte, N.B. (1971), 'Introduction: The Making of Economic History', in Harte, ed., *The Study of Economic History*: 11–34.

Harte, N.B., ed. (1971), *The Study of Economic History: Collected Inaugural Lectures, 1893–1970* (London: Frank Cass).

Hilton, Rodney (1984), 'Feudalism in Europe: Problems for Historical Materialists', *New Left Review*, 147: 84–93.

Hilton, Rodney, ed. (1978), *The Transition from Feudalism to Capitalism* (London: Verso).

Hodgson, Geoffrey M. (1988), *Economics and Institutions* (Cambridge: Polity Press).

—— (2001), *How Economics Forgot History: The Problem of Historical Specificity in Social Science* (London: Routledge).

Koot, Gerald M. (1980), 'English Historical Economics and the Emergence of Economic History in England', *History of Political Economy*, 12: 174–205.

—— (1987), *English Historical Economics, 1870–1926: The Rise of Economic History and Neomercantilism* (Cambridge and New York: Cambridge University Press).

Kuznets, Simon (1957), 'Summary of Discussion and Postscript', *Journal of Economic History*, 17 (4): 545–53.

Lamoreaux, Naomi R. (1998), 'Economic History and the Cliometric Revolution', in Anthony Molho and Gordon S. Wood, eds, *Imagined Histories: American Historians Interpret the Past* (Princeton: Princeton University Press).

Lamoreaux, Naomi R. and Daniel M.G. Raff (1995), 'Introduction: History and Theory in Search of One Another', in Lamoreaux and Raff, eds, *Coordination and Information: Historical Perspectives on the Organization of Enterprise* (Chicago: Chicago University Press).

Lamoreaux, Naomi R. *et al.* (1997), 'New Economic Approaches to the Study of Business History', *Business and Economic History*, 26 (1): 57–79.

Lamoreaux, Naomi R., Daniel M.G. Raff and Peter Temin (1999), 'Introduction', in Naomi R. Lamoreaux, Daniel M.G. Raff and Peter Temin, eds, *Learning by Doing: In Markets, Firms, and Countries* (Chicago: Chicago University Press).

Landes, David (1978), 'On Avoiding the Babel', *The Journal of Economic History*, 38 (1): 3–12.

Lazear, Edward P. (2000), 'Economic Imperialism', *Quarterly Journal of Economics*, 115 (1): 99–146.

Marx, Karl ([1859] 1970), *A Contribution to the Critique of Political Economy* (London: Lawrence and Wishart).

Mathias, Peter (1970), 'Living with the Neighbours: The Role of Economic History', inaugural lecture; reprinted in Harte, ed., *The Study of Economic History*: 369–83.

McCloskey, Donald (1978), 'The Achievements of the Cliometrics School', *The Journal of Economic History*, 38 (1): 13–28.

Meek, Ronald (1971), 'Smith, Turgot, and the "Four Stages" Theory', *History of Political Economy*, 3 (1): 9–27.

Menger, Carl ([1883] 1985), *Investigations into the Method of the Social Sciences with Special Reference to Economics* (New York: Lawrence H. White).

Milonakis, Dimitris and Ben Fine (2004), 'Douglass North's Remaking of Economic History: A Critique', processed.

North, Douglass C. (1963). 'Quantitative Research in American Economic History', *American Economic Review*, 53 (1): 128–9.

—— (1965), 'The State of Economic History', *American Economic Review*, 55 (2): 86–91.

—— (1974), 'Beyond the New Economic History', *The Journal of Economic History*, 34 (1): 1–7.

—— (1977), 'The New Economic History after Twenty Years', *American Behavioral Scientist*, 21.

—— (1981), *Structure and Change in Economic History* (Norton: New York).

—— (1989), 'Institutions and Economic Growth: An Historical Introduction', *World Development*, 17 (9): 1319–32.

—— (1990), *Institutions, Institutional Change and Economic Performance* (Cambridge: Cambridge University Press).

—— (1994), 'Economic Performance through Time', *American Economic Review*, 84 (1): 359–68.

—— (1995), 'The New Institutional Economics and Third World Development', in John Harriss, Janet Hunter and Colin M. Lewis, eds, *The New Institutional Economics and Third World Development* (London: Routledge).

—— (1997), 'Prologue', in G.N. Dvorak and J.V.C. Nye, eds, *The Frontiers of New Institutional Economics* (San Diego: Academic Press).

North, Douglass C. and Robert P. Thomas (1973), *The Rise of the Western World: A New Economic History* (Cambridge: Cambridge University Press).

Redlich, Fritz (1965), 'New and Traditional Approaches to Economic History and Their Interdependence', *Journal of Economic History*, 25 (4): 480–95.

—— (1970), 'Potentialities and Pitfalls in Economic History', in R.L. Andreano, ed., *The New Economic History: New Papers on Methodology* (New York: John Wiley and Sons): 85–99.

Robbins, Lionel (1935), *An Essay on the Nature and Significance of Economic Science*, second edition (London: Macmillan).

Rostow, Walt W. ([1953] 1960), *The Process of Economic Growth* (Oxford: Clarendon Press).

—— (1957), 'The Interrelation of Theory and Economic History', *Journal of Economic History*, 17 (4): 509–23.

—— (1960), *The Stages of Economic Growth: A Non-Communist Manifesto* (Cambridge: Cambridge University Press); third revised edition, 1990.

Samuels, Warren J. (1987), 'Institutional Economics', in John Eatwell, Murray Milgate and Peter Newman, eds, *The New Palgrave: A Dictionary of Economics* (London: Macmillan).

Samuelson, Paul (1947), *Foundations of Economic Analysis* (Cambridge: Harvard University Press).

Schumpeter, Joseph ([1934] 1961), *The Theory of Economic Development*, translated by Redvers Opie (New York: Oxford University Press).

—— (1939), *Business Cycles: A Theoretical, Historical and Statistical Analysis of the Capitalist Process*, 2 volumes (New York: McGraw Hill).

—— ([1943] 1987), *Capitalism, Socialism and Democracy* (London: Unwin).

—— (1954), *History of Economic Analysis* (London: Routledge).

Shionoya, Yuichi (2001), 'Rational Reconstruction of the German Historical School: An Overview', in Yuichi Shionoya, ed., *The German Historical School* (London: Routledge).

—— (1995), 'A Methodological Appraisal of Schmoller's Research Program', in Peter Koslowski, ed., *The Theory of Ethical Economy in the Historical School* (Heidelberg: Springer-Verlag).

Skinner, Andrew S. (1975), 'Adam Smith: An Economic Interpretation of History', in Andrew S. Skinner and Thomas Wilson, eds, *Essays on Adam Smith* (Oxford: Clarendon Press).

Smith, Adam ([1776] 1976), *An Inquiry Into the Nature and Causes of the Wealth of Nations*, Volume 1 (Indianapolis: Liberty Classics).

Sombart, Werner (1929), 'Economic Theory and Economic History', *The Economic History Review*, II (1): 1–19.

Supple, B.E. (1960), 'Economic History and Economic Growth', *Journal of Economic History*, 20 (4): 548–56.

Sutch, Richard (1982), 'Douglass North and the New Economic History', in Roger L. Ransom, Richard Sutch and Gary M. Walton, eds, *Explorations in the New Economic History: Essays in Honor of Douglass C. North* (London and New York: Academic Press): 13–38.

Swedberg, Richard (1991), 'Introduction: The Man and His Work', in Joseph Schumpeter, *The Economics and Sociology of Capitalism*, edited by Richard Swedberg (Princeton: Princeton University Press): 3–98.

Sweezy, Paul (1978), 'A Critique', in Rodney Hilton, ed., *The Transition from Feudalism to Capitalism* (London: Verso): 33–56.

Tawney, R.H. (1932), 'The Study of Economic History', inaugural lecture; reprinted in Harte, ed., *The Study of Economic History*: 87–107.

Temin, Peter (1991), 'Introduction', in Peter Temin, ed., *Inside the Business Enterprise: Historical Perspectives on the Use of Information* (Chicago: Chicago University Press).

Wallerstein, Immanuel (1974), *The Origins of the Modern World System* (New York: Academic Press).

Index